ROMANTICISM AND THE QUESTION OF THE STRANGER

ROMANTICISM AND THE QUESTION OF THE STRANGER

DAVID SIMPSON

THE UNIVERSITY OF CHICAGO PRESS
CHICAGO AND LONDON

DAVID SIMPSON is the G. B. Needham Distinguished Professor of English at the University of California, Davis, and the author of *9/11: The Culture of Commemoration*, also published by the University of Chicago Press.

The University of Chicago Press, Chicago 60637
The University of Chicago Press, Ltd., London

Printed in the United States of America

22 21 20 19 18 17 16 15 14 13 1 2 3 4 5

ISBN-13: 978-0-226-92235-5 (cloth)
ISBN-13: 978-0-226-92236-2 (e-book)
ISBN-10: 0-226-92235-9 (cloth)
ISBN-10: 0-226-92236-7 (e-book)

The University of Chicago Press gratefully acknowledges the generous support of the University of California, Davis, toward the publication of this book.

Library of Congress Cataloging-in-Publication Data

Simpson, David, 1951–
Romanticism and the question of the stranger/ David Simpson.
pages. cm.
Includes bibliographical references and index.
ISBN 978-0-226-92235-5 (cloth : alk. paper)—
ISBN 0-226-92235-9 (cloth : alk. paper)—ISBN 978-0-226-92236-2 (ebook)—
ISBN 0-226-92236-7 (ebook) 1. Romanticism. 2. Other (Philosophy) in literature. 3. English literature—History and criticism. I. Title.
PR447.S58 2013
820.9'145—dc23

2012019393

♾ This paper meets the requirements of ANSI/NISO Z39.48–1992 (Permanence of Paper).

FOR ROGER MALBERT

CONTENTS

Acknowledgments *ix*

Introduction: After 9/11: The Ubiquity of Others *1*

1. Theorizing Strangers: A Very Long Romanticism *16*
2. Hearth and Home: Coleridge, De Quincey, Austen *54*
3. Friends and Enemies in Walter Scott's Crusader Novels *82*
4. Small Print and Wide Horizons *109*
5. Strange Words: The Call to Translation *144*
6. Hands across the Ocean: Slavery and Sociability *179*
7. Strange Women *209*

Bibliography *249*

Index *267*

ACKNOWLEDGMENTS

An early version of part of chapter three was published as "'Which is the merchant here, and which the Jew?': Friends and Enemies in Walter Scott's Crusader Novels," in *Studies in Romanticism* 47, no. 4 (Winter 2008): 437–52. It is reprinted here with the permission of the Trustees of Boston University. Otherwise, what follows is previously unpublished work. Various audiences have listened to parts of it over the last few years, and I am grateful to those who invited me to present lectures and seminars and to those who helped me with their questions and their suggestions for further reading. So I thank my hosts at the University of Chicago (Bob von Hallberg), University of California, Berkeley, twice (Mark Allison and Ian Duncan), Rice University (Alex Regier), University of York (Harriet Guest, John Barrell), University of Cape Town (John Higgins), Stellenbosch University (Louise Green), Brigham Young University (Nick Mason), Edinburgh University (Susan Manning) the University of Western Ontario (Matthew Rowlinson), and my colleagues at the University of California, Davis. Among others who have answered my questions and inspired me with ideas and responses are Wendy Belcher, James Chandler, David Clark, Ian Duncan, Alysia Garrison, Kevis Goodman, Nigel Leask, Kari Lokke, Roger Malbert, Tom Mitchell, Tim Morton, Michael Oruch, Padma Rangarajan, Brenda Schildgen, Richard Strier, and Margaret Tudeau-Clayton, whom I also thank. Two readers for the press also offered valuable and constructive advice. Margaret Ferguson, once again, has been a constant source of almost everything—most recently a thorough vetting of my final draft.

I am profoundly grateful for a fellowship from the American Council of Learned Societies (2010–11), which enabled me to devote a full year to reading and writing.

I would have thanked my editor, Alan Thomas, long ago had he not told me that the press discourages such gestures. However, since I noticed that he was thanked by another of his authors in a recent Chicago book, I trust I too may thank him now for his support, insight, and advice over many years and several books.

1790s: that all deities reside in the human breast. So too do all monsters. This, of course, does not prevent both taking on critical or even catastrophic historical and empirical life.

Modern thought has been much concerned with theorizing the stranger. Freud's relatively short essay on the uncanny, like his even shorter one on fetishism, does not take up much space in the collected works, but it has become foundational for a whole range of disciplines engaged in the study of culture. Its central examples are etymological and literary, and the literature is significantly romantic. Social anthropology, sociology, economics, political science, psychoanalysis, philosophy, and literary studies have all engaged in depth with the descriptive model suggested by Freud's paradigm, though in doing so they have often been consigned to the margins of their own disciplines. (That fetishism itself, in its bizarre forms of displacement, can tend toward the uncanny, and that the uncanny can possess the imagination so completely as to take on fetish characteristics, suggests a confluence whose implications I cannot here pursue). The uncanny is one incarnation of the stranger—and an important one—but strangeness and the stranger are not the preoccupations of Freud alone. There are many other examples, some of which will be revisited at various points in this book, and which should certainly be remembered even when they are not explicitly revisited. Among them is the work of Carl Schmitt on friends and enemies and on sovereignty and states of exception (related to the friend-enemy distinction since the designated enemy is often the occasion for states of exception), written in the 1920s and 1930s but recently recovered as crucial for understanding late-twentieth-century predicaments. There is the etymological history of "hospitality" proposed by Benveniste and critical to Derrida and others, which enunciates the common linguistic positing and synthesis of host and guest, hospitality and enmity, welcome and unwelcome stranger. Then there is Derrida's own repeated insistence on the consequences of philosophy's attempt to exclude from its proper operations strange, or "improper," meanings and on the ubiquity of acts of translation that are unrecognized as such but which threaten the tidy borders between what is familiar and what is strange. Consider also Levinas's effort to outwit the border discipline of ontology by positing the self as always and *a priori* in a state of substitution in and for the other, a hostage, an entity already including the stranger and bearing responsibility for all strangers, in a moment beyond and before all sentiments about alienation and reconciliation. Before this there is Husserl, whom Levinas translated into French in 1931, seeking to prove by phenomenological reduction the inherence of the strange-foreign (*fremde*) in the self. More recently there is Ricoeur's effort, in *Oneself as Another*, to expand upon the migrant status of the word "I" as the basis of an impersonal and other-including model for moral thinking, making the stranger less strange by describing the strangeness of the self to itself. Rodolphe Gasché has described a tradition running from Husserl to Derrida (via Heidegger and Patočka) in which the idea of Europe, and of the Greek precursor through which that idea expresses itself, is founded on a reckoning with "what is other than Europe," a move toward the other that disturbs the "homeliness" of all worlds, including the European.[3] Europe, in other words, knows itself only in and through its strangers. Most recently, Judith Butler has argued that "liberal norms presupposing an ontology of discrete identity" will not help in understanding a modern subjectivity ineluctably constituted by global pressures and dependencies—in other words, by strangers.[4]

The critical and philosophical preoccupations I have just described were (and are) of course emanations of and addresses to a larger history marked by the often violent and involuntary movements of peoples and individuals. Tony Judt's magisterial *Postwar* records in encyclopedic detail the human displacements that followed the destruction of Europe's homelands and life-worlds, along with the unstable cycle of welcome and rejection that marked immigration policy through the 1950s and 1960s and on into the years when the European Union was "opening" itself to inhabitants of the Mediterranean and the former eastern bloc. Writing in the aftermath of 1989, Habermas reminds us that nation-state formation itself was at first "a fairly abstract form of solidarity among strangers," a placing together of factions that would otherwise have incentives to see themselves as different. So the Scots, Welsh, and Northern Irish have become, incrementally if unevenly, British.[5] Modernity itself, for Habermas, may be described as an evolving recognition of more and more strangers having the same rights as oneself, first within the nation and then beyond it into the sphere of cosmopolitan consciousness. Seyla Benhabib specifies a "disaggregation of citizenship" as the current phase of this process and sees therein a possible model for an eventual transformation of informal cosmopolitan norms (as human rights often are) into legislative fixity.[6] Along with such positive projections, there

3. Rodolphe Gasché, *Europe, or the Infinite Task: A Study of a Philosophical Concept* (Stanford, CA: Stanford University Press, 2009), 27.

4. Judith Butler, *Frames of War: When Is Life Grievable?* (London: Verso, 2010), 31.

5. Jürgen Habermas, *The Divided West*, ed. and trans. Ciaran Cronin (Cambridge, MA: Polity, 2007), 63.

6. Seyla Benhabib, *Another Cosmopolitanism* (Oxford: Oxford University Press, 2006), 45–46.

is of course a countervoice: the restrictions upon mobility, and especially on immigration, enacted or threatened by those who feel or see fit to cast themselves as vulnerable to the incursions of strangers.[7]

The enthusiasm for global flows—of capital, of information, of the world's human elites and their desired consumer products—is thus commonly overshadowed by an unease with or outright rejection of other possible known, unknown and "unknown unknown" strangers: the poor, the undesirable, the stateless, the potential terrorists, or the welfare dependents. In between the two extremes, there are, for example, illegal workers who are necessary to developed economies but who are disavowed and exploited by them, human traffickers of women and children for sexual and indentured or slave labor, and traffickers of goods that are deemed good by some but bad by others, such as illegal drugs. Some strangers are welcome, others not; the latter must be walled off, a phenomenon neatly encapsulated in the title of Wendy Brown's 2010 book *Walled States*. Walls, like fortresses, may at first glance look like protective shelter for those living within or behind them, but they also encourage the imagining of a state of siege, a threat from the outside that may or may not be serious. They can further enable the creation of closed spaces within which unpublicized acts can be carried out: the torture chamber, the internment camp. In the gothic novel, the castle is typically transformed from a defensive structure to a place of incarceration.

In Timothy Morton's *The Ecological Thought*, responding to a significant current pressure to acknowledge the nonhuman in and as the human and proposing the equivalence of all such selves in an expanded range of significant selfhoods, the "strange stranger" is everything and everywhere. "Far from gradually erasing strangeness, intimacy heightens it"; "environments are made up of strange strangers."[8] This very contemporary conviction can be seen to take form in the romantic period and in its various articulations of the uncanny: the doppelgänger, the automaton, the monster, the ghostliness of ordinary people (like Wordsworth's drowned man, leech gatherer, and discharged soldier).[9] This is, I think, something different and more pervasive than what is made of related and emergent motifs in, for example,

7. For a passionate but clear-headed assessment of this case, see Michael Dummett, *On Immigration and Refugees* (London: Routledge, 2001).

8. Morton, *The Ecological Thought*, 41, 51.

9. In *Romanticism, Nationalism and the Revolt against Theory* (Chicago: University of Chicago Press, 1993) I argued that theory itself has occupied the role of the stranger ever since Edmund Burke and Arthur Young declared its origins to be French.

the early years of the eighteenth century. To be sure, Margaret Jacobs may well have overestimated the complacency of an early modern cosmopolitanism emerging from the proliferation of informal associational networks, such as clubs, Masonic lodges, and scientific and commercial exchanges, all enabling an open reception of "foreigners at home and abroad."[10] For a qualifying view, one might turn to Felicity Nussbaum's *The Limits of the Human,* which offers an account of the darker side of a world in which cosmopolitan subcultures were hardly hegemonic, a world fascinated and repelled by exotic and grotesque—often racialized and gendered—figures. Nevertheless, it is hard to argue that a pervasive or obsessive awareness of the uncanny characterizes early-eighteenth-century images of the stranger in the way that I argue that it does by about 1800. The Earl of Shaftesbury, writing in 1710, was very aware of a popular rage for reading about barbarian customs and pagan countries, purveyed by authors who lead us from "monstrous brutes" to "yet more monstrous men."[11] He found this tendency threatening enough, but he did not see it as beyond the disciplinary functions of common sense and good taste. Such faith in the power of polite sociability did not by any means disappear with romanticism; it remained apparent in various idealist schemes like the Pantisocracy that Coleridge and Southey hoped to establish along the banks of the Susquehanna River. But it seems increasingly out of place and out of time, a utopian gesture that is more and more hemmed in by the complexities of dealing with truly strange strangers.

Take *Robinson Crusoe.* Defoe's 1719 novel is foundational in literary history for a whole range of issues involving the subaltern other, the environment, and the uncanny. Crusoe's discovery of the single footprint in the sand after eighteen years of living with only his animals and a pet parrot is one of the most memorable moments in the history of English-language literature. But to come upon this incident in the text of the novel is to be surprised at how little of the uncanny, of truly strange strangeness, Defoe attaches to it. Through all of Crusoe's initially terrified meditations on its origins—the devil, savages, his own foot—what is most bizarre, that there is one print where two or more would be expected, is something he reflects on not at all. The novel offers an array of narratives and narrative motifs: the

10. Margaret C. Jacobs, *Strangers Nowhere in the World: The Rise of Cosmopolitanism in Early Modern Europe* (Philadelphia: University of Pennsylvania Press, 2006), 5.

11. Anthony Ashley Cooper, 3rd Earl of Shaftesbury, *Characteristics of Men, Manners, Opinions, Times,* ed. Lawrence E. Klein (Cambridge: Cambridge University Press, 2001), 155. See Felicity A. Nussbaum, *The Limits of the Human: Fictions of Anomaly, Race and Gender in the Long Eighteenth Century* (Cambridge: Cambridge University Press, 2003), 3–5.

prodigal son, the puritan self-help manual, the drama of sin and/or repentance, salvation or abandonment by God, the sociability-solitude dilemma, and so on. It is full of incidents in which Crusoe sees or imagines omens and portents, signs of favor or punishment, and incentives to labor or relax. After the footprint, he expends massive energies on homeland security, building stockades and fortifications and storing food for emergency survival needs. But its startling singularity, the thing that cannot be explained, does not preoccupy him. Perhaps he lives in a world where supernatural signs are taken for granted or open to so many explanations that it is not worth dwelling upon any one of them. Whatever the reason, habit and prudence take over and the story moves toward becoming an encounter narrative; the residual strangeness of the footprint barely registers in the longer term. *Robinson Crusoe* is not a gothic novel, just as Shaftesbury could not have imagined *Frankenstein*. The undecidable or "uneconomizable" does not finally matter; it does not govern the narrative as it increasingly does by the end of the century.[12]

Shaftesbury's critique of the "barbarization" of British culture, however, does catch on to the pressure of desire, of *xenophilia*—a term that has never quite made it into common parlance despite the long history of what it denotes, which seems to be inextricably implicated in an erotic imagination as well as in a capacity for sheer curiosity. The familiar adage that good fences make good neighbors is only one voice in Robert Frost's poem "Mending Wall"; the other says that there is something that does *not* love a wall. The unfamiliar or unknown produces a desire to know that is not inevitably productive of panic or rejection, but that can sustain imagination and longing, and an obsessiveness that can be either positive or negative or both. Accepting the coexistence of fear and desire (and indeed fear of desire) means that reckoning with the stranger "in theory" very soon produces a sense that one cannot be either welcoming or rejecting without risking some degree of self-harm, and that a whole range of possibilities opens up between the extremes of unconditional hospitality (Derrida's term) and absolute aversion. Thinking upon the stranger can thus produce an awareness of thought itself as a moving event, a process of adjustment or dialogue, and not a preservation of boundaries and given definitions. When this movement stops there is violence, and then the discussion turns to the legitimacy of that same violence, that is, to states of exception and who decides them.

12. The term is David L. Clark's; see "Bereft: Derrida's Memory and the Spirit of Friendship," *South Atlantic Quarterly* 106.2 (2007): 296.

Romanticism itself revisits the long history of the stranger apparent in the Bible and in the classics: Hegel on Antigone, Rousseau on the Levite of Ephraim, Cugoano on the biblical discussion of slavery. That history is so long, indeed, that it appears coeval with culture itself; there seems to be no point at which some or other version of the dialectic of hostility and hospitality, friendship and enmity, desire and abjection, cannot be traced. The question of the stranger seems to remain with us and to be always still before us. But its details and consequences differ through place and time, and the age of romanticism witnessed a distinct ramping up of the depth and scope of the stranger syndrome, one that has given us many of the terms in which we commonly still address it. The matter of hospitality was, as I have said, placed under exceptional stress by the politics and rhetoric of terror and revolution, national and international, disseminated after 1789. Other circumstances contributed to the emergence of the stranger syndrome as a matter of urgent concern. The revolutionary and Napoleonic diasporas were not on the scale of 1914–45, but they were unprecedented in their time; never before had so many troops been on the move across Europe; never before had so many civilians been so involved in the constitution, dissolution, and reconstitution of nation-states, whether as citizen soldiers or civic participants. Before 1789, the movement of enslaved Africans across the Atlantic effected a major demographic shift: an estimated 6.1 million slaves were transported during the eighteenth century, though many died en route or soon after arriving. The abolitionists and emancipationists who became unignorable by the late eighteenth century proposed the radical equivalence of such abject bodies with those of their white masters in a sweeping assertion of potential substitutability. With the burgeoning of a global empire, administrative, criminal, and civilian populations followed the soldiers and sailors: to India, Canada, Australasia, and (at the end of the eighteenth century) southern Africa. Strange commodities were moving around too: tea, muslin, opium, and sugar among the most famous and historically decisive, but also such things as chinaware, pineapples, and exotic flowers and trees. In the slave trade, people *were* commodities. What was acquired for consumption or out of mere curiosity could also bring disease and contamination. Everything could turn into its opposite: one could be corrupted by sugar. Currency took on unfamiliar and untraceable identities; the development of commodity form made value an inscrutable entity, while money became more and more visibly unstable with the massive increase in the wartime national debt and by the much-deplored spread of "paper money." The economy could not manage without it, but it was widely (if not always rightly) perceived as transforming the real into the virtual, so that the coin of the realm itself passed over into the realm of the uncanny. Even plant life, as Alan Bewell has shown, was seen as evincing a process of change and transformation, and the importation of huge numbers of exotic species generated its own debate about unwanted immigrants.[13] The language formation apposite to understanding this condition, as Timothy Morton shows in *The Poetics of Spice* (2000), is not that of proper and distinct meanings but that of the *pharmakon*, the healing power that may poison, the poison that is the cure, the coincidence of opposites that cannot be untangled by philosophy—but which, Derrida tells us, philosophy is always compelled to simplify as the condition of its very existence.

With romanticism, the question of the stranger becomes more charged with anxious significance than it had been before, and the complexity of its figurations can seem to proliferate indefinitely in a process of cross-referencing that appears relentlessly accumulative. If one were to try to posit absolute causes and effects, all of the above and no doubt other factors would have to be considered. The power of the stranger syndrome, I suggest, lies in its capacity to reduplicate and intensify disparate references and allusions within a rhetorical-historical complex whose exact determinations (the war, the economy, the transnational experience) seem manifold: in literature at least, their representations often coexist without being resolved into clear doctrinal or analytic formats. An example: Coleridge's "Frost at Midnight" makes a famous reference to a *stranger* (the italics, as we will see in chapter 2, are Coleridge's). The mention is part of a narrated event, but it is also a folkloric reference, in other words doubly a rhetoric. Because it is not shared by all English speakers, it is open to (intralinguistic) translation. We learn that it is a metaphor but also a performative, an uncanny premonition. It also appears in the form of a footnote, a stranger to the text, setting up a play between what must be read about and what was supposedly experienced. Even if there had been no event, even supposing that Coleridge made the whole thing up (as his unabashed citation of Cowper's *Task* suggests he could have), the language of the poem is suffused with intimations of political and personal events, beyond and around the narrated evening by the fire, that render it as historically resonant as any poem could be. Some

13. Alan Bewell, "Erasmus Darwin's Cosmopolitan Nature," *English Literary History* 76 (2009): 19–48. Bewell's *Romanticism and Colonial Disease* (Baltimore, MD: Johns Hopkins University Press, 1999) is an indispensable study of the fear of the epidemic dispersal of illness that came with global empire.

of these render the stranger a familiar figure, others suffuse it with anxiety and threat. Coleridge's *stranger* brings with it an etymology and thus a history which it also projects into the future world of those readers who can still tap into that history (this means us). At the same time, it resides within and alongside certain other histories or events which are no longer current to most of us (for example whether or not to become a salaried Unitarian minister or to accept a legacy). The poem about the stranger is both strange and familiar. Some of it belongs to the past, some of it is very much at home—uncannily at home—in the present. It conjures up a stranger syndrome that articulates, in different but related ways, a profound concern of both romanticism and our contemporary moment.

Chapter 1, "Theorizing Strangers: A Very Long Romanticism," sets the 1790s debate about strangers within the necessarily selective but, I hope, exemplary contexts of classical, biblical, and later writings about responding to the challenges of alien persons (the political stranger) and alien languages and figures of speech (the rhetoric of strangeness). In both of these sites there is a visible difficulty in controlling the play between the despised and the desired, between what is said to be necessary or beneficial and what is to be resisted at all costs. In the political sphere, the stranger is needed for the foundation and maintenance of the state, even as the state will inevitably place limits on its hospitality toward strangers. In the sphere of rhetoric, the appeal of figurative speech, its capacity to make new connections, its hospitality to strangers, is also what is threatening about it, its challenge to "proper" limits. The proper names that embody these discussions include, among others, Robespierre, Dionysus, Plato, Moses, Simmel, Shelley, Aristotle, Aquinas, Dryden, and Young.

Chapter 2, "Hearth and Home: Coleridge, De Quincey, Austen," takes but three steps from embers to opium, from winter woolens to midsummer muslins. Coleridge's "Frost at Midnight" introduces a stranger who is at once supernatural, theological, historical, and rhetorical. This stranger never comes, but another comes to De Quincey in the form of an itinerant Malay who also hovers between illusion and reality, natural and supernatural, self and other. He is also a figure of the opium that brings on De Quincey's wild oscillations between ecstasy and despair. The mundane environs of Jane Austen's novels do not allude to the opium trade (which is important also in chapters 3 and 6), but their attentions to the popular appeal of foreign fabrics suggests that the midland counties of England cannot after all be walled off from the wider world. Tea and sugar, common to De Quincey and Austen, are also staged as instances of the *pharmakon*, able to operate as both poison and cure on both the constitution of the body and that of the nation-state.

Chapter 3, "Friends and Enemies in Walter Scott's Crusader Novels," proposes the identity-in-difference of Othello and Shylock in Shakespeare's Venetian plays as both a prefiguring of and source for Scott's analysis of the three monotheisms at work in *Ivanhoe* and *The Talisman*. Conversion and translation experiences are not endorsed in these narratives, but Christianity, Islam and Judaism are nonetheless each situationally open to occupying the place of the others in an unstable cycle of friendship and enmity. Scott's refusal to represent a national project of converting strangers into familiars may be read as respect for the otherness of the other or as a negative judgment on the impermeable boundaries that only modern commercial society will be able to breach. It is less convincing to read it as an endorsement of exclusionary policies in the homeland. His decision to fictionalize this premodern historical moment is made even more vividly present for his own time by his invocation (in an 1834 footnote) of the global opium trade.

Chapter 4, "Small Print and Wide Horizons," addresses the formatting and typography of the stranger evident in romantic uses of the paratext (footnotes and marginalia). Owing to the prominence given to "plain" texts like Wordsworth and Coleridge's *Lyrical Ballads*, we have often forgotten how many annotated poems and novels there were in the romantic period; we have missed noticing one of the ways in which real or imagined alien information (bibliographic, ethnographic, metaphysical) was presented to readers of the early nineteenth century in ways that invited either subordination or absorption. Many of these poems are long, encyclopedic narratives set in exotic places; they stage both the desire for knowledge of the stranger and the discomforts that come with that knowledge. Here Robert Southey is the exemplary figure, but he is by no means alone. Among various examples, I pay closest attention to Southey's *Thalaba the Destroyer* and to Coleridge's "The Rime of the Ancient Mariner."

Chapter 5, "Strange Words: The Call to Translation," takes up the topic of translation, whose operations indeed underlie the entire argument of the book. The stranger always raises questions of translation. I discuss the new emphasis on "foreignization" (Lawrence Venuti's term) associated with Schleiermacher, which gives priority to providing an encounter with the strangeness of foreign languages rather than with rendering them as familiar as possible. This emphasis provides a benchmark for assessing British attitudes to translation as they appear in (among others) Moore, Shelley, translations of German philosophy, the glossing of Scots dialect poetry, and the staging of America as an Anglophone outlier still requiring some translational effort. With Hemans's poetry I suggest the emergence of a global poetic English which images a single language across a widely dispersed geographical sphere.

Predicaments of translation and conversion also govern the topics of my two final chapters. Chapter 6, "Hands Across the Ocean: Slavery and Sociability," begins with the tense hospitality experienced by shipwrecked sailors in the South Seas, and with the visit to Britain of two exotic strangers, Omai and Lee Boo. Once again, the global opium trade makes its appearance as the shadowy analog of human trafficking. Discussions of the Atlantic slave trade (e.g., by Cugoano and Equiano) belong within the stranger syndrome, because it is commonly described as the result of a betrayal of hospitality. The rhetoric of strangeness and the strangeness of rhetoric appear again as the command of the enslaver's language (and of mimicry) allows the enslaved stranger to protest this betrayal and expose the instability of relations between strangers and familiars, which appears again in Mungo Park's *Travels in the Interior Districts of Africa*, the record of an exploratory visit to Africa by a member of the commercial (and white) master class.

Chapter 7, "Strange Women," gives full attention to the dynamic of desire and abjection that characterizes so many responses to the stranger, especially apparent in the portrayal of strange women: Stedman's slave-wife Joanna, Owenson's and Burney's heroines, De Staël's Corinne, Rousseau's version of a biblical story about dismembering the body of a woman, and Hegel's Antigone, among others. The suffering body of the woman—above all, the foreign or exotic woman—is an exemplary site for representing the ambivalence and latent violence of attitudes to the stranger. This site is often portrayed (or may be read) critically, but it also appears with a regularity that suggests how difficult it may be to overcome. Its association with a condition widely understood as biological (the condition of being female) while also prone to revision as contingent and historical (the predicament of feminization) instances the difficulty as well as the necessity of thinking about alternative imaginings of the stranger who is also woman.

Taken together, these chapters add up to a core sample, open to further exposure and expansion, of the stranger syndrome in romanticism. While much has been written about, for example, women and slaves, these figures are here not so much discussed in themselves as positioned within a coherent pattern of address to the antinomic figure of the stranger and to the reciprocally ambivalent representation of guest-host and friend-enemy relations that compose its articulation, mostly in literature but also in philosophy and political thought. The stranger syndrome is also the translation syndrome and the conversion syndrome: strangers raise questions about what can be made familiar and what resists familiarization and what can or cannot be made over. So too do the massively "overdone" footnotes of so many romantic texts. The challenge of the other comes from many places and in many forms, more than ever before. This is a romanticism we still inhabit, though many would prefer to ignore it in order to believe in a homeland in which they can hide and a castle they can defend.

CHAPTER ONE

Theorizing Strangers: A Very Long Romanticism

THE STRANGER POLITICAL

William Wordsworth has only a small role in this book, but I shall (out of habit) briefly invoke him here, close to the beginning. He is enshrined in popular literary history as a Lake District homebody, but his writings reveal complex experiences of being a stranger. Cambridge, as he tells it in *The Prelude*, was his first major experience of not fitting in; afterward came London, where even next-door neighbors were "Strangers, and knowing not each other's names," followed by more remote residences and extended expeditions.[1] But if Cambridge and London caused him to reflect on his alienation, his first travels abroad made him feel very much at home. On his first trip to France in 1790 he and his fellow travelers found themselves "Guests welcome almost as the angels were/To Abraham of old" (6:403–4; in 1805 text, 206). An affirmative host-guest dialectic played out on his second trip in 1791, where he joins the "files of strangers" and bonds with Michel Beaupuy, while he (Beaupuy) was "still a stranger, and beloved as such" (9:281, 286; in 1805 text, 326). Strangers and foreigners well disposed toward the Revolution were received as friends, and Wordsworth felt himself among them. But things turned sour. In late 1792, Wordsworth wended his way back to England by way of Paris, had waking visions of the recent "September Massacres," and returned to a homeland that, at least temporarily, had been ruined for him because of its complicity in the violence from abroad that had, he thinks, brutalized France itself. His preference from then on would mostly be for places like Helvellyn Fair, where

1. Wordsworth, *The Prelude, 1799, 1805, 1850*, ed. Jonathan Wordsworth, M. H. Abrams, and Stephen Gill (New York: Norton, 1979), 232 (1805 text, 7:120).

there was "here and there a stranger interspersed" (8:9; in 1805 text, 268) in a place otherwise entirely populated by locals who knew and were used to each other.

There is much that *The Prelude* does not reveal about these French sojourns, most famously the love affair with Annette Vallon and the love child born from it, the complex guilt that followed his leaving her behind, the later efforts at compensation, and the difficulties of moving in circles that were increasingly defined as counterrevolutionary. Wordsworth felt at home partly because he was at home in Annette's bedroom, enraptured by desire for the stranger: romanticists know the story well. But *The Prelude* also tells us little about the legislative history that impinges on the poet's feelings of belonging and rejection. In early 1790, the French National Assembly approved a motion whereby all foreign property owners residing in France for five years would be naturalized. As late as August 1792, even after Austria and Prussia had invaded France, distinguished aliens who had made contributions to reason and the revolution were granted citizenship, among them Paine, Bentham, Wilberforce, Washington, Madison, and Schiller. Perhaps, as Bonnie Honig has suggested, the French felt a need for their new society to be validated by foreigners as the sign of its very integrity, rather as the republican United States of America did and still does.[2] But the mood was changing. By March and April of 1793, by which time Wordsworth was back in England, laws targeting foreigners were being energetically debated.[3] The cosmopolitan ideals of 1789 were still very much alive, but were under considerable pressure from internal conflicts (most visibly in La Vendée and Lyon) and from the ongoing war with the European monarchies. By December 1793, Robespierre was able to conjure up the specter of the foreigner to explain all that was wrong in the homeland and to excuse the resort to state terror as the only remedy:

> For some time foreigners have appeared the arbiters of public tranquillity. Money flowed or vanished at their will; when they wished it, the people found bread; mobs formed and dissipated outside bakers' doors at

2. Bonnie Honig, *Democracy and the Foreigner* (Princeton, NJ: Princeton University Press, 2001), 160.

3. For a brief account, see Julia Kristeva, *Strangers to Ourselves*, trans. Leon S. Roudiez (New York: Columbia University Press, 1991), 155–63. Kristeva draws heavily upon Albert Mathiez, *La révolution et les étrangers: cosmopolitisme et défense nationale* (Paris, 1918). A more recent and extensive history can be found in Sophie Wahnich, *L'impossible citoyen: l'étranger dans le discours de la révolution française* (Paris: Albin Michel, 1997).

> their signal. They surround us with their hired murderers and spies . . . They seem inaccessible to the blade of the law.[4]

France is "flooded" with these aliens, in the pay of foreign tyrants while waiting patiently to work their "sinister designs." They have gone unpunished; they must be punished.

Robespierre was, rhetorically, the Rumsfeld of his times, the exponent of the dangers of the unknown unknowns. Alongside the public face of the French government he projected that there was a "secret government" set up and maintained by foreign powers, with its own invisible committees, treasuries and agents.[5] As the public government falters, the secret one flourishes. Nothing can be assumed to be as it seems; "they" are everywhere, operating by inverse reciprocity: "Are you weak? They praise your prudence. Are you prudent? They accuse you of weakness; they call your courage temerity; your justice, cruelty. Treat them well, they conspire publicly; threaten them, and they conspire in the shadows, behind a mask of patriotism" (104). They operate, in other words, according to the logic of the *pharmakon*, superimposing antithetical senses and applications upon the approved ones "we" think we are using. Their patriotism is our treason, our justice is their cruelty. We can never know they are not there because they look and sound like us: "Yesterday they were murdering the defenders of liberty; today they are attending their funerals, and demanding divine honours for them, while awaiting the chance to slaughter their fellows" (104). This giddying confusion, this rapid shift between appearance and reality, makes it impossible to know who is on whose side. Robespierre must work hard to keep his terms up in the air lest his words allow for the inference that *they* are just like us, that they are us and we are them, all unknown unknowns both to others ands to ourselves.

The French language itself, with its single term *étranger* describing both foreigner and stranger, adds to the confusion and complexity of the rhetoric governing the definition of those who are "other" to the revolution. Sophie Wahnich gives a good account of how the *étranger* could be a French national, either someone from another part of France not known to the locals who adjudicated and applied all decisions about the status of strangers, or a person, local or not, (deemed) unsympathetic to the revolution and thus a "political" or "interior" stranger. The foreign stranger, meanwhile, though

4. Maximilien Robespierre, *Virtue and Terror*, trans. John Howe (London: Verso, 2007), 104.
5. Ibid., 103.

belonging to a different sovereign, could also be a political insider, a fellow revolutionary. A foreigner could be a man of the people when a French national was not.[6] These categories were debated back and forth in the early 1790s. Some départements even sent foreign representatives to the National Convention, though in December 1793 this was forbidden. Wahnich finds that only the political strangers were deemed to deserve the scaffold. Foreign strangers, while under pressure and suspicion, fared better. Cloots went to the guillotine as a political stranger rather than as a foreigner, though being a foreigner did not help his case. Many more French nationals shared that fate. Parisian sections were monitoring strangers from early 1792, but sympathetic foreigners were allowed to join the armies of the revolution. No one ever wore the sinister "hospitality armbands" briefly approved on paper by the Convention, and no one appears to have carried out the bloody decree that all British troops were enemies of the revolution and thus to be executed rather than taken prisoner.[7]

With Robespierre's fall the campaign against foreigners lost much of its steam. Mathiez suggests that the discursive bark was always worse than the executive bite, and that the debate was heavily motivated as much by party rivalries as by concerns for the security of the state. Given France's early open borders policy and universalist claims, which produced a sizeable and visible population of non-French citizens in public life and even in military service, foreigners were a predictable object of scrutiny and manipulation. Some did go to the guillotine, but not in proportionally greater numbers than did French citizens; others, like Tom Paine and Helen Maria Williams, went to prison but were later released. Mathiez makes a pointed contrast between the relatively short-lived and ineffectual xenophobia of the revolutionary period and the more systematic abuse of resident "enemies" in France in 1914; mistreatment of foreigners, he says, was part and parcel of the Terror, when so many French nationals perished, and largely diminished when it ended.[8] Even after the fall of the Girondins in March 1793, exceptions to punitive laws were argued for certain kinds of foreigners: those holding property, or married to French citizens, or otherwise of good republican credentials.[9] The language of hatred and suspicion was circulated widely, but it was not fully embodied in deeds.

6. Wahnich, *L'impossible citoyen*, 217–33.

7. Ibid., 23, 116, 237–41.

8. Mathiez, *La révolution et les étrangers*, 161, 181, 183.

9. Ibid., 133–45.

But the awareness of the stranger, internal and foreign, must have produced a state of anxiety among a population fighting foreign wars and transforming its own social and political culture, especially since a host could be punished for extending hospitality to or failing to report the wrong sort of guest.[10] Helen Maria Williams, who lived through much of the 1790s in France and published timely reports of her experiences in various installments from 1790 to 1796, observed that under Robespierre, the "faction d'étranger" became an "inexhaustible source for the fabrication of all indictments and bills for conspiracies."[11] From the very first days of the French Revolution, when many foreign liberals were wholly supportive of it, Williams reported herself aware of the degree of stage management that went into representing that revolution to itself, to its own participants. The festival celebrating the first anniversary of the fall of the Bastille was an elaborate piece of theater culminating in the sounding of the alarm bells:

> At this moment the audience appeared to breathe with difficulty; every heart seemed frozen with terror; till at length the bell ceased, the music changed its tone, and another recitative announced the entire defeat of the enemy; and the whole terminated, after a flourish of drums and trumpets, with a hymn of thanksgiving to the Supreme Being. (64)

Williams named this the sublime, which is, as the aestheticians remind us, only to be experienced as bearable or enjoyable when the actual source of threat is at a relatively safe distance. So too, perhaps, with the frisson attached to the word "terror," which the readers of the 1790s could encounter in the pages of gothic novels as well as in the speeches of the National Convention, or perhaps in the British newspapers that reported them.

A few years later, in the newly constituted United States, there was another effort to mobilize the nation against the threat of foreign exiles and immigrants, most visibly the French and the Irish. In June and July of 1798, Congress passed four acts collectively known as the Alien and Sedition Acts. Federalist newspapers were full of bloodcurdling "lock up your wives and daughters" rhetoric about the imminent atrocities to be committed by violent radicals on the unsuspecting inhabitants of the homeland, but very few prosecutions were pursued, and the Republican press appears

10. Wahnich, *L'impossible citoyen*, 116.

11. Helen Maria Williams, *Letters Written in France*, ed. Neil Fraistat and Susan S. Lanser (Peterborough ON: Broadview, 2001), 182. It was Williams who gave Wordsworth the story through which he (mis)represented to himself, in an unpublished draft of his autobiographical poem, the sexual component of his time in France; see 115–40.

throughout to have been well aware of the party politicking that was behind much of the controversy. Edward Livingston, in the *Aurora or General Advertiser* (July 2, 1798), argued that the Federalists sought to "excite a fervor against foreign aggression only to establish tyranny at home; . . . like the arch traitor, we cry *'Hail Columbia'* at the moment we are betraying her to destruction."[12] If the darker purpose of all this was indeed, as Miller suggests (47–48), to deprive the Republican party of its foreign-born voter pool, the attempt misfired badly. The Alien Act expired in 1800, and on becoming president, Thomas Jefferson pardoned all those still serving prison terms under the protocols of the Sedition Act (231). This was by no means the end of the manipulation of the rhetoric of xenophobia in American politics, but its overuse on this occasion does seem to have helped demolish the Federalists as a viable political party forever after.

Meanwhile, in Britain, the pamphlet war that followed the 1790 publication of Burke's *Reflections on the Revolution in France*, which was followed by yet more extreme rhetoric in Burke's later speeches and publications on French affairs, was also high on melodramatic xenophobia. Like his sworn enemy Robespierre, Burke was obsessed with the dangers of money circulating under the control of foreign agents, a problem he localized under the name of "old Jewry."[13] Burke's later writings made much of the legions of anonymous and secret revolutionaries at work in Masonic lodges and in the back rooms of public houses, but in 1790 he was more concerned with defending the uses of obscurity as a vehicle for the best elements of traditional culture: religion, chivalry, and polite sociability, whose implicit and unsystematic rituals were threatened by the new empire of light and reason. The British government began a formal system of surveillance in the winter of 1792, paying informers and assigning observers (sometimes incognito,

12. Cited in John C. Miller, *Crisis in Freedom: The Alien and Sedition Acts* (Boston: Little Brown, 1951), 54. On the other side, readers were warned that they would be "torn limb from gut" and witness the "violation and expiring agonies" of wives and daughters by "outlandish sans-culottes Frenchman" and "lusty Othellos" (freed slaves) (6).

13. This is, literally, the part of London in which the dissenters' meeting house was located, allowing Burke to speak of his opponents as "the gentlemen of Old Jewry"; see *Reflections on the Revolution in France*, ed. L. G. Mitchell (Oxford: Oxford University Press, 1999), 10, 16, 17 passim. But given that his major objection to the French model is its production of paper money and the misuse of public credit, it is no surprise to find Old Jewry conflated with Jews themselves, hence the odious reference to "Jew brokers contending with each other who could best remedy with fraudulent circulation and depreciated paper the wretchedness and ruin" brought about by the wrong sort of politics (48). From this point on, Burke lists the Jew among the enemies of the patriotic state (e.g., 49).

sometimes not) to keep track of radical activities.[14] Pitt's own "Reign of Terror," as Fox dramatically called it, produced the famous Gagging Acts, which were aimed at inhibiting public assemblies and open discussion of reform, and the radical cause was consistently the object of aggressive legislation throughout the decade, partly prompted by fears of a French invasion and by the experience of the Irish Rebellion. But the spectacle of the foreigner-stranger was inflected in Britain by the fact that most of those seeking asylum were French royalists and members of the better classes. Pitt's Alien Act, passed in 1793 (33 Geo. III.c.4), thus aimed not to keep foreigners out but to control the terms on which they might be welcomed. Masters of ships were told to report all foreign passengers arriving in Britain or face a fine of £10, while the passengers themselves were registered and made to report to the local justices of the peace. The brunt of Pitt's legislative animus was directed toward radical Britons rather than toward foreigners. Habeas corpus was suspended between 1794 and 1801, and there followed two acts of 1795 against treasonable practices and seditious meetings.[15] A network of government spies was developed with sufficient manpower to tail Wordsworth and Coleridge and (in later years) to chase Shelley across the Welsh countryside. The designated enemy of the state was not so much or not only the foreign stranger but the stranger within, all the more credible for being unseen and unpredictable. All strangers, not surprisingly, become a potential threat: both the easy aristocratic cosmopolitanism of the eighteenth-century elites and the purely rational universalism of the prerevolutionary radicals become harder to sustain, and the preoccupation with the other takes on a heightened political urgency even when it does not devolve into outright violence. Categories become confused: domestic and foreign, strange and familiar, friend and enemy, unremarkable and uncanny lose their usefulness in a world where any one of them can look like its other or turn into its other. The emphasis on the secret and invisible workings of the radicals began to dominate the conservative press, taking popular form in Robison's *Proofs of a Conspiracy* (1797) and Barruel's *Memoirs* (1798). Here again we enter into the rhetoric of the unknown unknowns, where the evidence for the existence of dangerous organizations is precisely that we cannot find any evidence: they operate so secretly that we don't know we don't know them. The primary (non)exhibit in this paranoid discourse was

14. Albert Goodwin, *The Friends of Liberty: The English Democratic Movement in the Age of the French Revolution* (London: Hutchinson, 1979), 238.

15. For an account of the two acts, see John Barrell, *Imagining the King's Death: Figurative Treason, Fantasies of Regicide, 1793–1796* (Oxford: Oxford University Press, 2000), 551–603.

the Illuminati, a German secret society deemed largely responsible for the French Revolution and said to continue to function in deep cover all over the civilized world. Robison wrote of the "total uncertainty and darkness that hangs over the whole of that mysterious Association," which "still subsists without being detected, and has spread into all the countries of Europe."[16] Robison's book was also read in the United States, where it played its part in the debate about the Alien Acts.[17] The most dangerous stranger is the one you cannot see or even know that he is there—which leads you to be sure that he is.

Of course, the question of the stranger long predates 1789. It was important in the two foundational traditions to which eighteenth-century thinkers most often referred: the classic-pagan and the Judeo-Christian. These traditions have both historical and paradigmatic importance; they are often invoked as authorities, and they display complex exemplary episodes involving strangers. One of the most prescient classical paradigms is embodied in the arrival of Dionysus (though he goes by many names) before the gates of Thebes in Euripides's *The Bacchae*, a play he wrote late in life while in exile that was performed posthumously in Athens around 406 BCE, at about the same time as another host-guest masterpiece, Sophocles's *Oedipus at Colonus*. Sophocles's play is in part a vindication of prudent behavior by hosts toward guests, local dwellers toward strangers. The stranger is dangerous but responsive to benevolence; treated well, he imparts secrets, which will, if respected, preserve the security of the city. But Pentheus, the ruler of Thebes when Dionysus arrives, gets it horribly wrong. He fails to imagine the possibilities inscribed in his own name (*penthos* means "grief") and seems deaf to the synthetic identity of host and guest as designated in the single word *xenos*, which describes them both, so that in his efforts to keep his visitor boxed into the category of foreigner and enemy he unwittingly describes and destroys himself. Dionysus appears to Pentheus as both a foreigner and a political stranger, as neither Greek nor suitable for residence in Greece. Both distinctions are inadequate: Dionysus has a Theban mother, and his values are those which the Greeks must learn to respect and domesticate. He is also divine. The more Pentheus rejects and seeks to punish the

16. John Robison, *Proofs of a Conspiracy Against all the Religions and Governments of Europe, carried on in the Secret Meetings of Free Masons, Illuminati and Reading Societies* (Edinburgh, 1797), 15–16. Margaret Jacobs, *Strangers Nowhere in the World* (Philadelphia: University of Pennsylvania Press, 2006), 114–21, points out the particular anxieties about the Irish lodges in the decade of the rebellion.

17. See David Brion Davis, ed. *The Fear of Conspiracy: Images of Un-American Subversion from the Revolution to the Present* (Ithaca, NY: Cornell University Press, 1979), 35–65.

disguised god, the more he is seduced into fascinated identification with him. The more he resists the strangeness of women, the more like them he becomes. The more single-mindedly he tries to apply the law of the tyrant, the closer he comes to his own eventual dismembering at the hands of his maddened mother. His paranoid commitment to the safety of the state as he sees it leads to the exile of his surviving kin from their homeland. Prudence and piety alike dictate a different policy: welcome the stranger in case he turns out to be a god after all. You cannot be sure that the stranger is not a god in disguise, and angry gods mean trouble.

The same scenario comes up again in Plato's *Sophist*, written after Euripides's play, probably sometime between about 390 and 360 BCE. At the start of the dialogue, Theodorus introduces Socrates to a stranger from Elea, who will do most of the talking, thus taking on the role usually allotted to Socrates himself. Socrates asks Theodorus (whose name means "gift of god") whether he might be bringing not just a stranger but a god (*theon*). He cites Homer's *Odyssey*, which describes the gods, and especially the god of strangers, keeping company with pious men in order to observe the behavior of others. This leads to a reflection on the difficulty of assigning proper identities (and indeed names) to true philosophers who "appear disguised in all sorts of shapes," seeming "to some to be of no worth and to others to be worth everything."[18] We might say (though Socrates does not) that these philosophers are then just like Dionysus, son of Zeus—and it is Zeus himself who is "the strangers' god"[19] and the protector of suppliants. Dionysus too is a shape-shifter, sometimes a man, sometimes a bull, always a god. But whereas Pentheus thinks he knows already what he sees and how to behave, Socrates is trying to sort out distinctions between sophists, statesmen and philosophers, to justify a separate name for each defined by separate characteristics. Whether the Eleatic stranger achieves or intends to achieve such finished categorical definitions is a matter of debate, as is the question of whether he is or is not an incarnation of Socrates himself or of the ideal Socratic or Platonic method. If the sophist hides in darkness and the philosopher in excess of light, how sure can we be of the difference, even if they *are* different?[20] How firm are any such binary distinctions? Is Socrates

18. Plato, *Theaetetus, Sophist*, trans. Harold North Fowler (Cambridge, MA: Harvard University Press, 2006), 267 (216c).

19. Homer, *The Odyssey*, trans. A. T. Murray (Cambridge, MA: Harvard University Press; London: W. Heinemann, 1976), 9:270–71.

20. Ibid., 403 (253e–254a).

himself a sophist? A stranger? A foreigner? What of those who, as reported by the Eleatic stranger in his next appearance in the *Statesman*:

> separate the Hellenic race from all the rest as one, and to all the other races, which are countless in number and have no relation in blood or language to one another, they give the single name "barbarian"; then, because of this single name, they think it is a single species.[21]

All distinctions have consequences. What of those who separate out the sophist from the philosopher? Are they also guilty of mistaking a single name for a single species? Is sophistry philosophy's bad conscience or errant sibling or itself the image of true philosophy?

We have to wonder what effect Plato's incorporation of the stranger into the dialogue has on the possibility of consensus. All dialogues are potentially unstable in their assumed attributions of authority, even when it seems self-evident that the author is heavily committed to one point of view over others, as is often the case with the Platonic dialogues. In the case of *Laws*, Plato's last work, there are three interlocutors: an Athenian, a Cretan, and a Spartan, each a stranger to the others. The dialogue is set in Crete and in this case it is the Athenian who is denominated as a "stranger" (*xenos*) while he addresses the other two as "strangers" in their turn.[22] Does the partiality of the last two for the customs and reputation of Athens amount to a rubber-stamping of the Athenian's perspective? Or is this pure dramatic irony, to be set against the recent, vivid misdemeanor of Athens itself in putting Socrates to death?[23] What is the relation of the Athenian stranger to the now-deceased Socrates, or to Plato as author? Friedländer makes much of the silence of Socrates in the *Sophist* and the *Statesman*; he is to be imagined as present but not contributing, a figure whose response is always going to excite a curiosity that can never be satisfied (3:245, 270, 299), preserving "a silence that both speaks and questions" (3:304). Socrates in this way chooses to make himself strange.

Socrates here is hard to pin down, known to be present but not commenting on the debate. Is he then to be imagined as the sophist hiding in

21. Plato, *Statesman, Philebus, Ion*, trans. Harold N. Fowler and W. R. M. Lamb (Cambridge, MA: Harvard University Press, 2001), 25 (262d).

22. Plato, *Laws*, trans. R. G. Bury (Cambridge, MA: Harvard University Press, 1961), 1:5 (624a).

23. This is the view of Paul Friedländer, *Plato: The Dialogues*, trans. Hans Meyerhoff (Princeton, NJ: Princeton University Press, 1969), 3:440.

the darkness or as the philosopher blinding us with too much light? The dialogue tends toward questioning the status of all participants, even those who do not participate. Everyone becomes a potential shape-shifter. Turning again to the opening of the *Sophist*, where Socrates asks if the Eleatic stranger might really be a god, we do not find an explicit mention of a disguise for the god, only for the philosopher.[24] But the reference to Homer *does* imply the gods changing shapes and disguising themselves.[25] In the *Republic*, Socrates cites this very passage in Homer as an instance of what the poets should not do; they should not tell us that gods change their form, that they make themselves appear as strangers from other lands. These passages in Homer, where gods appear as "wizards in shape-shifting," should not be taught to the young.[26] If gods really did not disguise themselves, then Pentheus would not have had a problem. In *Laws*, the Athenian stranger endorses the idea that offenses against or mistakes (*hamartemata*) involving strangers are more serious because more often associated with an avenging deity: "whoso, then, is possessed of but a particle of forethought will take the utmost care to go through life to the very end without committing any offence in respect of Strangers." The "gift of Dionysus" is now to be welcomed, says the Athenian.[27] Mistreating strangers is still dangerous even when they are not gods in disguise because of the commitment of the gods to their protection under the codes of hospitality. Even if we do edit Homer to remove the disguised gods, the message remains clear: beware of the stranger.

This much is reflected in the laws discussed, as applied both to the resident alien (*metoikos*) and to the stranger-foreigner who is to be welcomed. Men who are "divinely inspired" can exist anywhere and one should be open to their wisdom. Some constraints on entry and exit from the homeland are recommended as prudent but there must always be a measure of openness. One needs the experience of the foreign to both amend and confirm the quality of one's own laws and customs. The influence of the foreign thus becomes part of the system of checks and balances required in all states ruled by men and not by gods. One can see here that even in taming the stranger, in reducing the threat to manageable proportions and placing limits on an open-border policy of the sort that the inherited, archaic culture of hospitality would seem to endorse, the *Laws* maintains a clear

24. Plato, *Theaetetus, Sophist*, 267 (216c).

25. Homer, *Odyssey* 17:485.

26. Plato, *The Republic*, trans. Paul Shorey (Cambridge, MA: Harvard University Press, 2003), 381d–e (383a), 193, 197.

27. Plato, *Laws*, 1:333 (729e–730a), 1:155 (672a).

commitment to the benefits as well as the risks of receiving the stranger. To this end, the Athenian stranger makes distinctions between various categories of outsiders and sets out what rules are to govern the admission of each of them.[28] Less manageable, however, are the formal and interpretative disruptions enacted by the incursion of the stranger into the Platonic dialogue itself. There is a long history of debate about what the Eleatic and Athenian strangers stand for, about the attitude implied toward them by Plato, and about their relation to the other interlocutors and above all to the silent or absent Socrates. Both strangers cause interpretative confusion, and there has yet to be an undisputed resolution of that confusion.[29] Putting strangers into the mix heightens the conventional dialogic puzzles about irony and authority by adding in the pressures and possibilities that come with the host-guest relation and its inherited association with powerful and potentially punishing gods.

One should clearly not romanticize classical or Hellenistic Greece as the high point of a cosmopolitan universalism; Marie-France Baslez argues that pragmatic reciprocity rather than an evolving open democracy is at the heart of the Greek attitude to strangers and foreigners.[30] Yet scholars do suggest that the negative connotation of the term *barbaroi*, denoting those who did not speak some version of Greek, came relatively late, perhaps at the time of the Persian wars, and that the sophists in particular stood for a proto-universalist idea of humanity and were thus at odds with the Greek

28. Plato, *Laws* 2:507 (951b), 1:287 (713e), 2:503–15 (949e–953e).

29. There is, however, a perceptible move away from the "unitarian" position that finds a coherent Platonic position or single voice (a.k.a., Platonism) running through all the works. Catherine H. Zuckert, *Plato's Philosophers: The Coherence of the Dialogues* (Chicago: University of Chicago Press, 2009), gives a recent summary of the debates, finding a strong distinction between Socrates and the Eleatic stranger but proposing that Plato intends to expose the deficiencies of both (682–95); the Athenian stranger comes out more positively as a learner-traveler who is more prudent than Socrates, in that he excludes the young from the discussion (58–62, 827–35). Jacob Howland, *The Paradox of Political Philosophy: Socrates' Philosophic Trial* (Lanham, MD: Rowman and Littlefield, 1998), also argues that Socrates and the Eleatic stranger represent incompatible alternatives, with the stranger choosing to appear as a sophist in the service of dramatic irony (viii–ix, 169–83). Howland also registers the "richly ambiguous Homeric subtext" (169). Harvey Ronald Scodel, *Diaeresis and Myth in Plato's Statesman* (Göttingen: Vandenhoek & Ruprecht, 1987), remains "agnostic"(14) on where exactly to locate Plato himself in the play of characters, but is clear that the Eleatic stranger does not speak for him (166). Scodel also presents a very interesting case for the dramatic importance of the delayed vocative at the opening of *Statesman*: "In no other dialogue is the vocative delayed for so long" (20n2, 21).

30. Marie-Françoise Baslez, *L'étranger dans la Grèce antique* (Paris: Société d'Édition les Belles Lettres, 1984), 203. Euripides's *Iphigenia in Tauris* offers a dramatic example of how obedience to a god can suspend the norms of host-guest relations.

exceptionalism argued by (or suggested in) Plato.[31] Perhaps the Greeks never entirely shake off the fundamentally synthetic identity of host and guest, of the one who is at home and the stranger who appears at the door, that is carried in the term *xenos*, so tragically misunderstood by Pentheus.[32] It is also perhaps misunderstood by the ancient mariner who, we are told in the marginal gloss Coleridge added to the poem, "inhospitably killeth the pious bird of good omen" and thereby triggers the response of another avenging god.[33] The albatross is a wanderer, an airborne stranger in need of occasional rest and repose. But the ship whose mysteriously nonpurposive voyage may or may not finesse its likely function as a slave ship is hardly itself a home, committed as it is to its own form of seemingly pointless wandering. The mariner too stands in a line of uncouth strangers, one whose power to compel attention is more selective than Dionysus's and less productive of wholesale destruction, but equally irresistible and beyond reduction to merely moral or community standards. The mariner is like the sophist who comes as a stranger and captivates the locals with his story. For the sophist, as Plato presents him, is always a stranger, one who moves from city to city making a living as a professional intellectual. The other thing that always firmly differentiates the sophist from the ideal Socratic philosopher is that the sophist accepts money. The "darkness of non-being"[34] that hides the sophist from plain sight is then the place of the stranger and the site where money changes hands; if this stranger could be a god then he could be the wrong sort of god. Money works in dark places but not always for the good.

The primary set of associations adduced so far is then as follows: sophist, stranger, darkness, money and corruption (peddling things that are not real). Robespierre, we may recall, had identified foreigners as in control of the flow of money, and thereby the secret motivators of the state, and Burke

31. Ibid., 183–201; see also Edith Hall, *Inventing the Barbarian: Greek Self-Definition Through Tragedy* (Oxford: Clarendon, 1989), who notes Pericles's law of 451 BCE as newly restrictive toward foreigners (175). Tzvetan Todorov, *The Fear of Barbarians*, trans. Andrew Brown (Chicago: University of Chicago Press, 2010), 14–21, sees a conflation of neutral evaluations of *barbaroi* (those who speak languages other than Greek) with denigratory ones (those who are uncivilized), a conflation contested by, for example, Eratosthenes.

32. Baslez, *L'étranger dans la Grèce antique*, 18–19, describes the range of the term. See also Émile Benveniste, *Le vocabulaire des institutions indo-européennes* (Paris: Minuit, 1969), 1:94–95. My entire discussion so far and henceforth is of course inspired by Jacques Derrida, *Of Hospitality: Anne Dufourmontelle Invites Jacques Derrida to Respond*, trans. Rachel Bowlby (Stanford, CA: Stanford University Press, 2000).

33. Samuel Taylor Coleridge, *Poetical Works, Part 1* (Princeton, NJ: Princeton University Press, 2001), 1:379.

34. Plato, *Sophist*, 403 (254a).

made similar accusations about "old Jewry." But if the Jews are the most familiar and most horribly punished figures of a hegemonic conflation of money and strangers, they are not the first or the only ones. Georg Simmel describes a widespread association of the two that includes Armenians, Parsees, Moors (in Spain), and emancipated slaves in Rome and Athens.[35] Because he does not belong to the group, because he is always liable to be persecuted or banished, the stranger needs to keep his assets in the most transportable possible form. But as the money form becomes more and more universal, *all* persons become strangers to each other. Along with this, Simmel proposes, there appears a respect for the "new uncanny power of the mind" which is "neutral and heartless like money" (227) and also transportable—exactly the attribute of the sophist but also of the true philosopher who becomes harder and harder to distinguish from the sophist unless by way of the former's refusal to take money for his teaching. Free-floating intelligence is another form of portable property, not infrequently deemed a threat to throne and altar (one of the more recent instances was the case against "theory" in the 1970s and thereafter).The Athenian stranger who narrates most of the *Laws* and who counsels proper behavior toward strangers is suspicious of the function of money. In book 5, the hoarding of gold and silver is vetoed; only as much circulating coin as is needed for basic exchanges should be possessed by the citizen. This should be local coin of no value elsewhere.[36] Wealth should be as evenly distributed as possible in an internal economy that remains as close to subsistence as it can. Restraints on the coming and going of foreign money are important means to these ends. Athens, as a commercially oriented city state, could not afford the strict laws against foreigners (*xenelasia*) that Sparta, for instance, observed. But Plato's *Laws* is aware of the negative as well as the positive potential inherent in contact with alien figures.

So why then might we still welcome the stranger? Because the godlike attributes of the stranger are as likely to prove positive as negative. The best laws come from those who do not have an interest in their being applied preferentially, those who are truly disinterested. No one living in the homeland can be trusted to be without vested interest, so that the best laws come, in the absence of a just god, from strangers. Or is it that in democracies, where no one is supposed to stand above others, the image of the stranger as lawgiver must be invented and maintained in order for there

35. Georg Simmel, *The Philosophy of Money*, trans. Tom Bottomore and David Frisby (Boston: Routledge and Kegan Paul, 1978), 221–27.

36. Plato, *Laws*, 1:371 (742a).

to be any laws acceptable to anyone? The classical paradigm reappears in the eighteenth century: Bonnie Honig, who addresses this question at some length, finds in Rousseau's *Social Contract* a primary role for the outsider as the giver of the law, for the "violation of the national" by a stranger that is staged as the original moment in the foundation of the nation.[37] According to Rousseau:

> When Lycurgus gave his fatherland laws, he began by abdicating the Throne. It was the custom of most Greek cities to entrust the establishment of their laws to foreigners. The modern Republics of Italy often imitated this practice. The republic of Geneva did so too, with good results.[38]

Again, to say *l'étranger* in French is to say both foreigner and stranger, to rub together the known-unknown identity and the potential bearer of the uncanny. The stranger-foreigner comes from outside to make the laws and in so doing takes away the natural forces of the inhabitant "in order to give him forces that are foreign to him and that he cannot make use of without the help of others" (155). Even in the earliest phases of society differential talents and contingencies have already produced unequal rewards and initiated the formation of hierarchies. There is no common experience and no common code. The law produces a shared condition, but does so in the form of an imposition that is actually or potentially violent: it is the thing to which we are all subject. The common experience is an experience of disempowerment, the responsibility for which is best received when attributed to a stranger, and one whose remoteness allows for the cultivation of a charisma that makes the foundational conventions unassailable by mere citizens.

> This is what has always forced the fathers of nations to have recourse to the intervention of heaven and to honor the Gods with their own wisdom; so that the peoples, subjected to the laws of the State as to those of nature, and recognizing the same power in the formation of man and of the city, might obey with freedom and bear with docility the yoke of public felicity. (156)

37. Honig, *Democracy and the Foreigner*, 18.

38. Jean-Jacques Rousseau, *The Social Contract etc.*, ed. Roger D. Masters and Christopher Kelly (Hanover, NH: University Press of New England, 1994), 155.

The stranger, after all, might not have been a god, but it suits the rulers of the state to pretend that he was or to affirm him as the next best thing. Enlightenment rationalism, whose project is one of demystification, cannot be patient with this predicament. Painite reason, if and when fully disseminated, would produce a world in which all would be known for what it is, a world where there are finally no strangers. The invention of charismatic origins is associated with the sustenance of priesthood as a means for enslaving the people: "Thus men forgot that All deities reside in the human breast."[39] A world governed by cosmopolitan rationalism would not need this sleight of hand, nor reward it. Such was the world briefly imagined and indeed instituted in the early phases of the French Revolution, before it came under pressure from party politics and foreign wars.

The invention of charismatic origins associated with the ambivalent attributions of the stranger is deeply ingrained in the Western tradition. And it is clearly double edged, like the blade (*glaive*) of the law that Robespierre invoked as the agent of terror. The attribution of the origin of the law to a long-departed stranger does displace the responsibility for legal violence away from the homeland community who are only the executors of an imposed demand for justice, allowing then to operate with the appearance of disinterest. But it also establishes the stranger as a scapegoat, as the one who can be blamed when the law is felt to be over-severe or even unjust. All present and future strangers thus risk being classified as violent interlopers bearing with them new and unacceptable regulations. Dionysus brings to life all of these implications; Pentheus's tragedy is that he cannot understand or control the volatile paradoxes that make the new god seem good and bad at the same time. Dionysus does demand obedience to a new law whose imposition is destructive only when resisted, and he is intended by Pentheus for the role of scapegoat that Pentheus himself will suffer. The arriving stranger is not a challenge in himself; he is a challenge because he has no self—or he has so many selves that no one can be isolated into a figure of identity: Rameau's nephew. Dionysus records a victory for the stranger because he has the superior power that comes with being a son of Zeus. Human strangers run a greater risk of themselves suffering violence.

The Judeo-Christian scriptures are also heavily marked by assertions about the status of strangers, and strangers again mean more than one thing. Christian scriptures have played up love for the stranger (or neighbor as

39. *The Complete Poetry and Prose of William Blake*, ed. David V. Erdman, rev. ed. (Berkeley: University of California Press, 1982), 38.

stranger) as a major principle differentiating them from the Jewish law. Thus, St. Paul (as reported in the King James Bible) seems to propose an absolute openness to others as characteristic of the Christian faith: "There is neither Jew nor Greek, there is neither bond nor free, there is neither male nor female: for ye are all one in Christ Jesus" (Gal 3:28). Such apparent indifference to distinctions would cause all sorts of difficulties for the defenders of an eighteenth-century plantation slavery maintained by a Christian country and would be embraced by emancipationists and feminists alike, leading slaves to argue quite plausibly that being baptized entailed becoming free. The Old Testament provides an equally (if not more) contentious field for the classification of strangers, and never more dramatically than in the debate about Moses. The Moses of Exodus is born to a Jewish mother whose child is discovered by Pharaoh's daughter, whose compassion for strangers is such as to knowingly hire a Hebrew nurse (the birth mother) for a child she knows to be Hebrew. The royal Egyptian conspires in the survival of the slave-enemy child, who will become the receiver of the laws and the author of the Torah. Jewish law, in this story, is enabled by an enemy stranger and also by an alliance between women. But the Exodus story undergoes a massive revisionary reading by Freud, who suggests that the device of the baby in the bulrushes displaces a very different and, indeed, antithetical truth: that Moses himself was really an Egyptian and thus a prime example of a foreign stranger who gives the laws to others. The literature on this question is extensive and fascinating, and of course involves questions of enormous political urgency in the present. Suffice it to recall here Freud's proposal that the definitive signature of the Jewish law is to be located not in an originating ethnic coherence (or protonational territory) but in an adoption of (or by) the other, the foreigner, on behalf of a god who, he argues, only came later in connection with a second Moses. First came monotheism, an exporting and translation of the cult of the Egyptian priest Akhenaton, adherence to which sent the first (Egyptian) Moses into exile along with the Israelite slaves he set out to convert. This first Moses is murdered, scapegoated as both a foreigner and the giver of the law. Then came the second Moses and the (belated) privileging of the uncanny volcano god Yahweh as the centerpiece of Jewish theology.[40] It is the second Moses who is declared the founding father, whose existence is premised on the

40. See the excellent summary by Jacqueline Rose in Sigmund Freud, *Mass Psychology and Other Writings*, trans. J. A. Underwood (London: Penguin Group, 2004), xxiii–xxxix.

murder of the foreign father before him.[41] Murdering the stranger is inseparable from the founding of the law; its memorialization (as trauma), Freud says, haunts later constructions of Jewish "national" identity, which avows by the very energies of repression its otherness to itself.

Freud's argument takes life from the life-and-death arguments about Jewishness in Europe in the 1930s, and its currency in the present only serves to remind us of the relatively unanalyzed transformations of those crises that render so much about Middle-Eastern politics undiscussable or "beyond reason" to so many today. For our purposes, Freud's extraordinary claim that "it was the man Moses and he alone who created the Jews" stands as the ultimate example of the extraneous source of official origins and thereby threatens to eviscerate all claims to ethnic-territorial authenticity as a historical legacy.[42] Here, as Honig points out, the founding foreigner is not just mystified into a retroactively created myth figure but violently destroyed. What is uncovered by (psychohistorical) analysis is thus not just the anti-Enlightenment preservation of mystery but the primacy of the most violent xenophobia as a response to having welcomed (or been converted by) the stranger. Like Euripides, whose Pentheus (as we have seen) fails to suspect the origin and thus the future realization of his own name, *penthos*, as a world-destroying grief, Freud too begins with the name. Pointing out the inadequacy of the biblical explanation whereby the Hebrew *Moshe* means "he who was drawn out of the water," Freud turns to a more obvious derivation from the Egyptian *mose*, meaning child (168). No historians, he says, have noticed this; like Pentheus, they have been blind to the name, to what stares them in the face. And as in the *Bacchae*, something about this has the aura of a repression: "possibly the idea seemed too monstrous that Moses the man may have been something other than a Hebrew" (169). The name may not be not decisive but it is a leading clue, the unraveling of which will take up the body of Freud's book.

References to strangers are all over the Old Testament, as one would expect in stories about a small tribe in close contact with lots of other small tribes among whom similarities and differences are a matter of constant

41. On the topic of the murder and its politics, see Jacques Derrida, *Archive Fever: A Freudian Impression*, trans. Eric Prenowitz (Chicago: University of Chicago Press, 1996), esp. 63–81. See also Honig, *Democracy and the Foreigner*, 38–40; and Edward Said, *Freud and the Non-European* (London: Verso, 2004).

42. Freud, *Mass Psychology and Other Writings*, 270. It is also Moses who brings from Egypt the mark of the Jewish covenant: circumcision (186). Freud declares the Abrahamic covenant a corruption: Egypt alone was known to practice circumcision (187).

curiosity, competition, and anxiety. Hospitality to the other is proffered and refused, honored and breached, with often dizzying interpretative possibilities. Moses speaks volumes, if we read along with Freud, in claiming that he has been "a stranger in a strange land" (Ex 2:22). Deuteronomy and Leviticus are especially dense with references to strangers and aliens—sometimes confusing, if not contradictory. We are to love and sustain the stranger (Dt 10:19) but not marry off our dead brother's wife to one (Dt 25:5). But who is meant by "stranger," according to the King James Bible? A whole range of Hebrew terms reflecting complex distinctions between residents, household servants, visitors, foreigners who have or have not converted to Judaism, and so on appears to be compacted into this one English word. Robert Alter, for example, translates Exodus 2:22 as "A sojourner have I been in a foreign land," with "sojourner" being the Hebrew *ger*.[43] The King James translators provide an unforgettable poetic line, but it is imprecise. Alter also has "sojourner" at Deuteronomy 10:19, and "stranger" at 25:5. As best I can tell from an uninformed survey of the literature, there are at least four different terms that get translated as "stranger," including *towshab*, who is always a non-Israelite and is usually treated badly. Any attempt to understand exactly what the Old Testament is saying about the "stranger" would have to negotiate the philological details with some care; some of the same distinctions are carried over into the New Testament texts.

Once, indeed, in anticipation of a crucial New Testament rhetoric, we are bidden to love our neighbor as ourselves (Lv 19:18).[44] But who *is* the neighbor? Naomi Tadmor has argued that the Hebrew *re'a* carries a range of meanings: friend, companion, fellow, even he who is an enemy. This possible range of reference has occasioned a legacy of dispute about who the neighbor is; some restrict it not just to Jews but to observant Jews.[45] Tadmor suggests that the common New Testament translation of this word as "neighbor" followed a sifting of senses that began with the Septuagint and the Vulgate but intensified in English Bible translations between Wycliffe and King James. The effect is to play up the power of local communities and

43. Robert Alter, *The Five Books of Moses: A Translation with Commentary* (New York: Norton, 2004), 316.

44. This challenging demand is the subject of Slavoj Žižek, Eric L. Santner, and Kenneth Reinhard, *The Neighbor: Three Inquiries in Political Theology* (Chicago: University of Chicago Press, 2005).

45. See Žižek et al., *The Neighbor*, 4: "Judaism opens up a tradition in which an alien traumatic kernel forever persists in my neighbor; the neighbor remains an impenetrable, enigmatic presence that, far from serving my project of self-disciplining moderation and prudence, hystericizes me."

to inscribe parochialism where there had once been a more ambiguous categorization. There were still residual elements of a wider reference, for example in one seventeenth-century catechism which included in "the name of neighbour . . . also those whom we know not, yea, and our enemies."[46] But for the active Protestant tradition founded in the King James Bible, neighborliness implies a more restrictive group, and thus embodies an exclusive component in its very specification of virtue. To love the neighbor, if we can manage that, is likely to not love the stranger. In tension with any such localizing tendency, there is, however, in Christian scripture an exorbitant imperative which demands that the faithful remove themselves from father and mother (Mt 11:35) and follow Christ into strange places.

Both the classics and the Bible, in and despite translation, will reappear at various points in this account of romanticism and the question of the stranger. For now I would like to dwell a little further on Freud's extraordinary study of Moses, written "with the boldness of one who has nothing or not much to lose"—nothing, or not much, at the end of the decade of the 1930s: "we are living in particularly remarkable times." It is boldness indeed, this idea that "the only way to understand religious phenomena is by using the model of the neurotic symptoms of the individual."[47] And yet the model invites consideration when one is pondering the operations of monotheism, which, after all, is about one very big individual who is claimed as like no other. The proper name, says Derrida, is that which cannot be translated, being the "reference of a pure signifier to a single being" and thereby outside the language to which it appears to belong.[48] But Moses is identified with two monotheisms, the renegade-Egyptian and the Jewish. Accepting both, *Moshe* and *mose*, involves accepting the equivalence of the two and thus spells the end of monotheism. *Moshe* aspires toward the unique proper name, even though there could be more than one who was drawn out of the water. *Mose* (child) remains rooted in the generic; there is always more than one. *Moshe* seeks to impose untranslatability, seeks the erasure of *mose*. With this substitution comes the violence of a single value or identity that will not be modified or related to other things that might be like it; for there must be nothing like it if it is to remain proper. The "proper" proper name is the linguistic analog of both atomic subjectivity

46. Naomi Tadmor, *The Social Universe of the English Bible: Scripture, Society, and Culture in Early Modern England* (Cambridge: Cambridge University Press, 2010), 23–49, 40.

47. Freud, *Mass Psychology and Other Writing*, 217, 221.

48. See Derrida, "Des Tours de Babel," in *Acts of Religion*, ed. Gil Anidjar (New York and London: Routledge, 2002), 105, 109.

and theological monotheism; each says that I am I, there is no other, nothing is like me, I am not to be compared with any other or conceived as appearing to anyone as disguised, as other than myself. Zeus, Dionysus, and their peers were always ready to take on human or animal disguise when it suited them; the gods of monotheism prefer to remain unseen, invisible, because as soon as they take form then other forms, including our own, can be imagined in their place. The theological injunctions against graven images are not for nothing. The three major monotheistic religions find it hard to tolerate each other, because for each there can be no other, except as false gods who must be discredited or defeated. (Christianity is committed to a struggle between one and more than one which it tries to solve through the model of the Trinity). In responding to Yusef Yerushalmi's account of the relation between history and memory in the Jewish tradition, Derrida describes himself "trembling" before a sentence about the uniqueness of the Jews in relation to memory, the one that begins "only in Israel and nowhere else," because "as soon as there is the One, there is murder, wounding, traumatism."[49] This is no mere concept, but the engine of a dismal and ongoing history whose pertinence to the present is all too obvious.[50]

To summarize Freud's case: the stranger Moses brings a name that is general, so a substitute must be found to accord with the new protonational culture it purports to uphold. The general name is simply eradicated and a new proper name, now made untranslatable, put into its place. Monotheism is reinvented as if there had been no earlier adoption. One name supplants another as if it had no history: *mose* becomes *Moshe*. What disappears is the history of an otherness to oneself and one's own. Any subsequent arrival of a stranger is going to threaten this establishment, unless that stranger enacts absolute submission to the one god and one law of the land. Greek polytheism, even when it seemed to be trying to sort itself into a coherent metaphysics founded on the justice (rather than the arbitrary whims) of Zeus, preserved a rationale for the openness to strange gods, and thus to strangers who might be gods. Unless a state is to preserve absolutely closed borders (a recurrent political ideal starting with Sparta), the stranger will always appear or be about to appear, offering something unknowable in ad-

49. Derrida, *Archive Fever*, 76, 78.

50. See the crucial examination of the "Mosaic distinction" by Jan Assmann, *Moses the Egyptian: The Memory of Egypt in Western Monotheism* (Cambridge, MA: Harvard University Press, 1997); and *The Price of Monotheism*, trans. Robert Savage (Stanford, CA: Stanford University Press, 2010). Assmann's contention is that polytheist religions relish the translation of every god into other gods. Monotheism began as a counter-religion obsessed with the extinction of any and all rivals; its analog and vehicle was the book and the written law.

vance: a radically new law, a figure of uncontrollable desire and disruption, a god in disguise, or simply a weary traveler.[51] Among the most mundane and widespread forms of this encounter is perhaps the experience of trading. Simmel, we have seen, identified the stranger with the money form, and principally with the onset of foreign exchange. In his short essay "The Stranger" (*Der Fremde*; 1908), Simmel further explores the stranger in a Hegelian way as never completely strange because always dialectically implicated in an act of recognition that combines closeness and remoteness, at once being within and being outside both the individual and the group, and mimicking thereby the act in which every subject places itself before itself in order to become spirit, which is in turn nothing less than the origin of the instinct for art.[52] The formal position of the stranger is a "synthesis of nearness and remoteness" (145). He is the bearer of trade, which "alone makes possible unlimited combinations, and through it intelligence is constantly extended and applied in new areas" (144). The trader alone is not "confined by custom, piety, or precedent" (146). Like Dionysus he brings in what is new and unexpected, and therefore loathed or desired, or both.

We are far from having solved the questions generated by the global movement of goods and people and of the persons trading them; here too the pattern continues to be an unstable oscillation between impediment and permissiveness, protectionism and free circulation. A pressure to decide underpins one of the most famous projections of cosmopolitan doctrine made by one of Simmel's precursors, that found in the brief but massively influential third section of Kant's 1795 treatise *Toward Perpetual Peace*. Kant states that universal hospitality is a cosmopolitan right (*Weltbürgerrecht*) but that it is the *only* such right, and that it is further limited by the permission given to the host to turn away the visitor if he can do so without causing him ruinous or perhaps fatal harm (*Untergang*).[53] The right is only a right of visitation (*Besuchstrecht*), not that of the guest, per se (*Gastrecht*). That is, he does not have a right to become a member of the household but simply to reside on the common earth that we all share in as a species. The implication is that the visitor is owed mere space but not any of the

51. See Richard Kearney, *Strangers, Gods and Monsters: Interpreting Otherness* (London: Routledge, 2003), a fascinating survey by no means limited by its well-intentioned but preemptive post-9/11 ambition to "welcome strangers" while acknowledging "monsters" (11) and to discriminate between "enabling and disabling forms of alterity" (67). Dionysus notably does not figure here.

52. '"The Stranger,'" in Georg Simmel, *On Individuality and Social Forms*, ed. Donald N. Levine (Chicago and London: University of Chicago Press, 1971), 143–49.

53. Immanuel Kant, *Practical Philosophy*, ed. and trans. Mary J. Gregor (Cambridge: Cambridge University Press, 1996), 328–29.

attributes of culture or society that might make that space humanly appealing or sociable. Common access to uninhabitable spaces (seas and deserts) is what makes visiting possible, and so the visitor has the right to comparable space when he arrives in an inhabited place, but not to anything more. It seems that Kant is primarily addressing his fellow European citizens, who were operating more critically as visitors than as hosts. He is less exercised by how "we" receive others than by how we behave when we visit them. So we do not have the right to plunder and enslave, but merely to "*seek* commerce" (329), even with those who do not themselves recognize our right to hospitality. Only then can trade relations remain peaceful and form the basis of a possible cosmopolitan constitution (*Verfassung*).

Kant's argument is thus an argument against imperialism, slavery, and exploitation of the resources of others. It is a *cri de coeur* against the behavior of imperial powers, and as such it remains wholly pertinent to present times. But it comes with a crucial limitation. If the price of universality is the trimming down of hospitality to an absolute minimum, with nothing more than basic sustenance (such as to prevent critical harm) included in the welcome—which is not even a welcome—then we (Europeans) in our turn owe nothing more than this to those who visit us. This is not a host-guest relation, with its more or less elaborate rituals, but a species-right of the most pared-down kind. But it is not bare life: it is a crucial step beyond this, and in its assertion of the right to space and subsistence it makes possible other more sociable relations. It is thus the foundation for a commercial relationship. There is no guarantee that one will develop, nor could there be if the equality of all parties is to be preserved. It is even possible that hostility will supersede the visit.[54] But trade cannot be imposed, nor can residency be claimed; after the visit, one must move on without putting down roots. Kant's model works as a schema for refugees or immigrants only to the point that they are allowed the space to appear and therefore apply for asylum or residency. He who risks being harmed cannot be turned away, but Kant stops short of making the affirmative case that asylum should be granted, perhaps because his primary interest here is in making an argument against the plunderers rather than in favor of the sup-

54. Jacques Derrida, *On Cosmopolitanism and Forgiveness*, trans. Mark Dooley and Michael Hughes (London: Routledge, 2002), 20–23, is notably attentive to the role of hostility in Kant's paradigm.

pliants.[55] As it stands, it is most coherent as a theorization of the potential power of noncoercive trading relations.

And what of those whose trade is images in words?

THE STRANGER RHETORICAL

When God gives the law to Moses, his first commandment (Ex 20:3) is that there shall be no other gods but him; his second is the prohibition of graven images, one that occurs several times thereafter in the Old Testament. The demand is emphatic and relates not just to graven images but to "any likeness *of any thing*" in heaven or earth or under the water. Then Moses is told not to bow down and worship such images, as if they already exist or inevitably will exist—for his god is jealous and, like a Greek god, will visit revenge upon later generations even if they have not themselves committed the sin of idolatry. This imperative is central to the Hebraic tradition, and has been only partly and uneasily accommodated within Christianity, most visibly as a point of schism between Protestants and Catholics. As such it has sponsored its own bloody history. But what is a likeness, *any* likeness? A figurative painting or statue, of course. But what about abstract expressionism? What about language and poetry? Is a poetic image like a graven image, and if not, what sort of likeness does it propose? Is Moses forbidden from saying that man is like a wolf, or that man is a wolf? Is the Hebrew god going to revenge himself on the tribe of poets (and their descendants) who have made their mark by exploring simile and metaphor in this way, thereby confusing our sense of what is a proper meaning with what we call *figure*, itself a suspiciously idolatrous term?

The new and unexpected combinations that Simmel attributed to the trader, who expands our intelligence and revitalizes stale custom with infinite variety, are also the product of poetry. In Shelley's *Defense of Poetry*, to take but one exemplary case, this is exactly the function of poetry in general

55. This minimal definition of right has occasioned considerable debate. For example, Benhabib, *Another Cosmopolitanism*, 20–26, sees here the expression of a primary conflict between hospitality and sovereignty, one that we should work to resolve in the direction of the former in a process of what she calls "democratic iteration," so that informal mandates eventually become positive law. Responding (in the same volume), Jeremy Waldron prefers to read Kant as describing an informal network of proximate persons, neighbors perhaps, who build up alliances that have nothing to do with the state (88–94). At issue here is a disagreement about the relative importance of civil society and the state; at issue also is how one translates *Verfassung*, whether in the strong sense (constitution), or in some less demanding way (as condition, state of mind, and so on).

and of metaphor in particular. Shelley did not share Simmel's happy view of the positive effects of commercial culture; he locates the civilizing function in aesthetics rather than in economics, and above all in language. Imagination introduces us to "the similitudes of things" in being "vitally metaphorical; that is, it marks the before unapprehended relations of things" and "forever develops new and wonderful applications." Poetry "turns all things to loveliness" and "subdues to union, under its light yoke, all irreconcilable things."[56] It generates an ethics of love and an inexhaustible pleasure principle. There are no gods here—Shelley was an atheist—but otherwise this is very much in the spirit of the seventeenth- and eighteenth-century tradition Assmann calls "cosmotheism" (not polytheism), in which a person believes in "a veiled truth that shows and conceals itself in a thousand images that illuminate and complement, rather than logically exclude, one another."[57] Once again, this is a world in which all forms of strangeness are to be welcomed and made familiar, but never so familiar as to become merely conventional or incapable of surprise: this would be dead metaphor, requiring a new generation of poets to enliven and refigure the language. It is a world without borders. Metaphor cannot negate, it can only unite. A metaphor may be intended as unflattering (man is a wolf) but it is always an act of bringing two things together with no way to limit absolutely the terms of the comparison: wolves are not just threatening and dangerous to humans but devoted to their young and loyal to their kind. The extreme implication of metaphor is that there may be no things in themselves in the first place: everything can be decomposed into parts or attributes that can be compared to those of other things. For this reason metaphor has always been perceived by rhetoricians as threatening "proper" meanings, unless it is kept under restraint: the stranger must be watched lest he render everyone and everything strange in an orgy of catachresis.[58]

It is then no accident that Aristotle compares unfamiliar (including figurative) language to the stranger: people are admirers of what is unexpected and will respond positively to the strange-foreign (*xenen*). They respond favorably to an uncommon style (*lexis*) just as they are more interested in

56. *Shelley's Prose*, ed. David Lee Clark (New York: New Amsterdam Books, 1988), 277, 278, 281, 295.

57. Assmann, *The Price of Monotheism*, 43.

58. In *Cratylus* (389d ff.) Socrates thus connects the giver of names with the giver of laws (*nomothetos*), but later disturbs his own argument with some aporetic contradictions governing the origins and functions of naming (437ff.).

strangers than in their fellow citizens.[59] However, while this is fine enough in poetry, where the uncommon is expected and respected, it should be used minimally in other sorts of speech or writing. Metaphor is the primary way in which a "foreign air" (*xenikon*) can be given to language, but only if appropriately arranged according to propriety (*prepon*), for metaphor is always enigmatic.[60] In the *Poetics*, Aristotle says that poetry cannot just stick to the common, standard words (*to kurion*) although those are always the clearest. Metaphors and rare words are the most important techniques whereby poetry renders itself unfamiliar (*xenikon*), estranges itself. But no poem can consist only of these things. A poem made up only of metaphors would be a riddle (*ainigma*); one full of strange words (*glotton*) would be unintelligible (*barbarismos*). But metaphor above all is the mark of genius.[61]

The metaphor-stranger is the genius who will, then, always be welcomed as long as he knows his place and does not turn us into barbarians—that is, into non-Greek speakers, which is what the Greeks meant by the term.[62] But it is not just a matter of using metaphor for ornamenting discourse and making it more striking and appealing, giving it a veneer of the exotic. The "strange" (*allotriou*) term that is metaphor is also useful for filling gaps in the vocabulary of a language by creating analogies. Greek has no word for the scattering of light by the sun, so we have the expression "sowing the god-created fire"[63] to say what we otherwise cannot say. Metaphor is now filling an empty space, providing the equivalent of a proper sense that was not there in the first place. The two functions of metaphor are summarized by Quintilian, who places considerable emphasis on the way in which metaphor ensures that nothing goes without a name:

> A noun or a verb, then, is "transferred" from a place in which it is "proper" to a place in which either there is no "proper" word or the "transferred" term is better than the proper one. We do this either because it is necessary or because it expresses the meaning better or (as I said) because it is more decorative.[64]

59. Aristotle, *The "Art" of Rhetoric*, trans. J. H. Freese (Cambridge, MA: Harvard University Press, 1982), 351 (1404b).

60. Ibid., 355 (1405a), 359 (1405b).

61. Aristotle, *The Poetics*, trans. W. Hamilton Fyfe (Cambridge, MA: Harvard University Press, 1973), 85, 91.

62. But see note 31 in this chapter.

63. Aristotle, *Poetics*, 81, 83.

64. Quintilian, *The Orator's Education*, trans. Donald A. Russell (Cambridge, MA: Harvard University Press, 2001), 3:427–29 (bk. 8:6). Quintilian's *proprium*, like the Greek *kurios*, has the

Again, the problem of not having a word for everything is solved by metaphor, by *translatio*, as it is here called in Latin. Another way to do this is to import a foreign word to fill in the vacant slot (as Latin would take many charioteering terms from Gaulish). Metaphor and the foreign thus function together to make up for omissions in the "native" language. But here there is a third term between the necessary and the decorative: metaphor can express "the meaning better" (*significantius est*) than the terms we already have. Thus, a further problem of discrimination is introduced. We must imagine a way to decide how the merely "better" is not quite necessary nor purely ornamental but approved nonetheless. Another kind of stranger emerges here, one who does not fill an empty space but improves the sense of what is already there in some epistemological rather than additive fashion. This stranger makes what is already proper still more proper. The first two uses of metaphor correspond to Derrida's logic of the *supplément*, which describes both that which adds to (or ornaments) something already there (as in English and French) and that which also (or rather) fills a gap or substitutes for an absence (as in French). Quintilian's third use of metaphor, making the meaning better, sits somewhere between or outside the two. One could suppose that it makes a new meaning, since it does not merely ornament the old one; but then one would admit that something comparable was already there. Does the stranger displace the already enfranchised citizen or become his helpmate in the specification of more exact but still dependent meanings?

Latin could hardly at any point image itself as simply native in the first place, given its high proportion of contact-derived words and, above all, its dependence upon Greek. Quintilian indeed imagines the orator's education as happening in both Greek and Latin, preferring the Greek to "come first."[65] He is quite comfortable with using Greek words "where we have none of our own" (1:153; bk. 1.5), and his own text is peppered with words in the Greek alphabet. But category confusions still arise. Improper strange words (*barbarismi*, another Greek adoption) pose a problem in that they are hard to distinguish from figures (1:125; bk. 1.5). And the foreign or ethnic word (*gente*) is only one of three kinds of barbarism, the other two involving the use of insolent speech or the adding, subtracting, or relocation of letters

sense of something conventionally understood: the word is still a sign, not essentially related to what it denotes. Grammatological use of the term *proper* in English wanders between indicating something purely conventional and general (apt, appropriate, proper use) and something still conventional but tending toward single ownership (by a particular person, proper noun). The second sense is overlain by a sense of possession (property in the name).

65. Quintilian, *The Orator's Education* 1:103 (bk. 1.4).

or syllables. These last two classes of barbarism have nothing to do with the foreign; the barbaric is at this point very much *within* the homeland, apparent in the language of the native speaker even when he is not using foreign words. Quintilian seems comfortable in affirming that the foreign is not the only and indeed not even the primary source of barbarism; inappropriately introduced foreign words are likely to be a lot less common than insolent or incompetent speakers.

Quintilian follows Cicero, who made a career out of adapting Greek into Latin and claiming to give Latin its best words (*optimis verbis*) and coining appropriate new ones by analogy (*imitando*),[66] while at the same time having to make the case for the value of the native literature against those who believed that everything of value was already written in Greek. (Along the way, he gave us the beginnings of a theory of translation that has been invoked time and again in discussions of how to convey an adequate sense of a foreign language to one who does not speak it.) Cicero's comments on metaphor, also a source for Quintilian, offer an interesting simile explaining how metaphor began out of necessity, in transferring names to things that did not have them, but passed over into aesthetic popularity:

> For just as clothes were first invented to protect us against cold and afterwards began to be used for the sake of adornment and dignity as well, so the metaphorical employment of words was begun because of poverty, but was brought into the common use for the sake of entertainment.[67]

Cicero gives no clue that this process is not entirely carried out in an autonomous homeland, generating its own passage from subsistence to luxury. But it is hard not to recall here the image of the foreign trader, bringing exotic goods into the state in the first place because they are needed and thereafter because they appeal on the grounds of fashion. The metaphor, by analogy, first supports mere survival and then keeps going a luxury economy, with all the presumed and well-known problems associated with the flow of money to the outside. Too much metaphor produces obscurity and riddles (*aenigmata*)—themselves often built out of metaphors (131; bk. 3.xli.167)—just as a pervasive fashion for certain kinds of clothing makes it impossible, as various eighteenth-century commentators would

66. Cicero, *De Oratore*, bks. 1 and 2, trans. E. W. Sutton, H. Rackham (Cambridge, MA: Harvard University Press, 2001), 107 (1.xxxiv.155).

67. Cicero, *De Oratore*, bk. 3, trans. H. Rackham (Cambridge, MA: Harvard University Press, 1977), 123 (3.xxxviii.155).

complain, to tell the servants from the masters and mistresses. The foreigner metaphor is admitted out of need but rapidly goes viral and refigures need itself into an object of compulsive desire.

As with human strangers so with words: the potential violence of the new arrival must somehow be softened (*mollienda*) and controlled. One can, for instance, offer "a word of introduction."[68] Sometimes a metaphor should appear like a polite guest or suppliant, with a modest or bashful (*verecunda*) air, "so as to look as if it had entered a place that does not belong to it," seeking rather than assuming permission to reside. This is one way in which the threat of both strangers and metaphors can be mitigated, for Cicero admits exactly what Shelley celebrates, that nothing is out of bounds for metaphor, that "there is nothing in the world the name or designation of which cannot be used in connexion with other things" (127; 3.xl.161). Likeness is all, and everywhere, and we take pleasure in having it pointed out to us, much more so than in hearing words used "in their proper sense" (125; 3.xxxix.159). Like all pleasures, this one must be kept within limits. But we cannot do without pleasure (the bursting of limits), especially when it comes accompanied by necessity (the provision of new names where none existed).

Just as metaphor is often imaged as a stranger, so the theory of metaphor is constructed around the same positive-negative dynamic as that of the stranger-foreigner, desired and detested, needed but open to suspicion. In a period of developing nationalist sentiments like the eighteenth century, this instability in the representation of the stranger can seem particularly apparent and calls forth some artful adaptations. So, for Edward Young, the habit of original composition is a place of refuge from the busy world and an effective substitute for its pleasures. We do not need to engage with actual strangers to have the pleasing experience of novelty and surprise: "How independent of the world is he, who can daily find new acquaintances, that at once entertain, and improve him, in the little world, the minute but fruitful creation, of his own mind?"[69] But once published or circulated, others can enjoy these compositions that are not their own. To read the work of imitators is tedious, as if hearing twice-told tales, but

> our spirits rouze at an *Original*; that is a perfect stranger, and all throng to learn what news from a foreign land: And tho' it comes, like an *In-*

68. Ibid., 129 (3.xli.165).

69. Edward Young, "Conjectures on Original Composition," in *The Norton Anthology of Theory and Criticism*, ed. Vincent B. Leitch (New York: Norton, 2001), 428.

> *dian* prince, adorned with feathers only, having little of weight; yet of our attention it will rob the more solid, if not equally new: Thus every telescope is lifted at a new-discovered star; it makes a hundred astronomers in a moment, and denies equal notice to the sun. But if an *Original*, by being as excellent, as new, adds admiration to surprize, then we are at the writer's mercy; on the strong wing of his imagination, we are snatched from Britain to *Italy*, from climate to climate, from pleasure to pleasure; we have no home, no thought, of our own; till the magician drops his pen: And then falling down into ourselves, we awake to flat realities, lamenting the change, like the beggar who dreamt himself a prince. (429–30)

The imagination as stranger is here pictured as, like Dionysus, a conjurer or magician; even a fake product peddled by a wily exotic, all feathers and no weight, is enough to distract us. If the originality is able to convince us of its excellence we are on safer ground, but we must still experience disappointment in coming back home to flat realities, to a "proper" sense of words. Young suggests that we will happily ignore the sun for every new star, which may be real enough but of much less significance to our well-being. Being open to the original compositions of others risks either being deceived or being taken out of ourselves and returned to a self that now feels itself a beggar instead of a prince.

Is this then something we should desire or not? Is it safer for the writer in the "little world . . . of his own mind" than for the reader who must be carried beyond the boundaries of the self? Young bids the would-be creative writer to "contract full intimacy with the stranger within thee." A stranger wholly within is supposedly a safe bet, assuming some measure of self-control can be exercised. But any peace of mind one might derive from this is complicated by Young's reversion to the example of the Indian:

> [L]et thy genius rise (if a genius thou hast) as the sun from chaos; and if I should then say, like an *Indian*, *Worship it*, (though too bold) yet I should say little more than my second rule enjoins, (*viz.*) *Reverence thyself*.[70]

Too bold indeed. The conjunction of pagan sun worship with the Pythagorean "reverence thyself" (not quite the Socratic *gnothi seuton*, know thyself) conflicts more than trivially with the Judeo-Christian command to

70. Ibid., 436.

reverence god alone; and, in the double-edged way that figures work, it might even be taken to approve building altars to ourselves. The growths of one's own mind may indeed seem superior to "the richest import from abroad," but the imported pagan stranger is already planted and at home in the mind that comports itself in the manner of a sun-worshiper. The stranger who is being excluded, along with the alien religion he professes, is already there. The translation has been made and is no longer noticed.

The stranger who is there and not there obeys, once again, the logic of the supplement as Derrida has explained it. The *supplément* is either that which substitutes for an absence—fills a gap—or that which adds on to what is already there. Or it is both at once, or undecidably one or the other. Just as metaphor fills a need by transferring a name to an unnamed thing or ornaments language in a way that is semantically superfluous but aesthetically delightful and surprising, so the stranger-foreigner brings us what we need and do not have or/but also tempts us to embrace things we do not need but only wish to add to what we already have. And because, to recall Cicero's words, "there is nothing in the world the name or designation of which cannot be used in connexion with other things,"[71] there is need for restraint, which in classical theory mostly took the form of allowing metaphors in poetry that were not welcome in descriptive prose or forensic oratory. But Young is writing critical prose *about* poetry, not the thing itself. The borders are permeable; the Indian, in being likened to genius, is within the homeland of the mind and the discourse of the nation-state that would prefer to think of him as elsewhere.

That nation-state is a Christian state, for which wild Indians belong at a distance. But the Christian god also chose to show himself as a stranger in the form of a deliberate use of figurative language. Early Christian philosophers found themselves faced with a puzzle: the scriptures are full of difficult metaphors and obscure figures, but they are the words of God, a god who is supposed (some say) to make himself available to all. So why might this god choose to generate enigmas and obscurities? Many Christians could not be comfortable with the idea that interpretation was a test to sort out the sheep from the goats, leaving their god's word open only to those with special skills or a divine inspiration. Augustine takes up the question and finds that it pays to know something about tropes in reading the scriptures, because "when the sense is absurd if it is taken verbally (*ad proprietatem verborum*), it is to be inquired whether or not what is said is expressed in this or that trope which we do not know; and in this way many hidden

71. Cicero, *De Oratore*, bk. 3, 127 (3.xl.161).

things are discovered."[72] The figurative is thus a way to introduce the unknown, perhaps even the unknown unknown. It is a form of economy because "things are perceived more readily through similitudes" and a source of pleasure because "what is sought with difficulty is discovered with more pleasure" (38; bk. 2, vi). God uses difficult expressions "to conquer pride by work and to combat disdain in our minds" (37; bk. 2, vi) but also, it seems, rewards that work with an onset of pleasure. Only those who are teachers need worry over this; Augustine allows that faith, hope, and charity can sustain a good life for ordinary people even without the scriptures (32; bk. 1, xxxix). What the learned will discover is the variety of ways in which truths can be imparted, including how the scriptures incorporate everything of value from the pagan traditions and then add what is distinctly their own (78; bk. 2, xlii). Some pagan material, when it has been appointed by providence to accord with the true faith that is to come, can itself be a source of pleasure, a "treasure" which can be used in "teaching the gospel" when "converted" (*in usum convertenda*) to Christian uses (75; bk. 2, xl). Conversion, one might say, is open to what is already converting.

How does the teacher of Christian doctrine decide what is true and what not, what is figurative and what literal? Anything in the scriptures that does not literally "pertain to virtuous behavior" must be taken to be figurative and wrestled around to fit in with the principles of the faith.[73] Christ's feet could never be "anointed with precious ointment by the woman in the manner of lecherous and dissolute men whose banquets we despise," so the good odor imparted by Mary Magdalene must be understood as emblematic of good fame (90; bk. 3, xii). Augustine's distinction between *res* and *signum*, the thing and the sign, admits that a word may be either thing or sign according to its context. By *res* he means not the "thing in itself" prior to signification but a simple sign that denotes only one thing, without inviting reference to metaphorical or allegorical senses (8; bk. 1, ii). *Signum* (as he uses the term) is a complex sign signifying something as really something else; so a "sign" points us to a thing which is itself a sign of something else. The "thing" is a sign that takes us to one thing and no further: it is a "literal" (*propria*) sign. What he calls a sign (*signum*) is "figurative" (*translata*) (43; bk. 2, x). The distinction is between single and multiple (literal and figurative) significations. Deciding which is which may seem relatively

72. Augustine, *On Christian Doctrine*, trans. D. W. Robertson (Indianapolis: Bobbs-Merrill, 1958), 104 (bk. 3, xxix). See also and especially the elaborate discussion in Aquinas, *Summa Theologicae*, Qu. 1 art. ix.

73. Ibid., 88 (bk. 3, x).

simple in ordinary exchanges. If I am building a fence and I ask you to hand me the hammer it is unlikely that I am suggesting I am about to take up arms against Scotland; "pass me the wood" does not normally invite serious reflection on the crucifixion. But when the context is unclear the possibilities are manifold. The scriptures contain many passages where it is hard to decide between things and signs. Effort is required, inspired by piety (99; bk. 3, xxiv). The more ingeniously this is applied, the more difficult it becomes to assume or achieve consensus, and the more the interpreter's piety can seem like madness, divine or other.

Piety is what motivates us to be sure that something cannot possibly be taken literally if it does not accord with the core of Christian doctrine. A deceptive metaphor, then, would be a sort of test for the learned and something to be interpreted for the layperson. Being bidden to eat the flesh and drink the blood of Christ is not an invitation to cannibalism.[74] In Augustine's Christian paradigm, the metaphor does not come as a stranger to threaten the citadel of the homeland, because we are, as fallen humans looking for redemption, *all* strangers in a strange land, emphatically not at home in this world in the first place.[75] Scripture and its obscure expressions are but a means to get us out of and beyond the world, which we should use to good purpose but never enjoy only for itself. To do so would be to choose to linger in a world that is not our true "native country" (*patria*).[76] Thus, both clear and pleasurable *and* difficult and obscure metaphors have in common an existence in a world that is not the truest or ultimate world, and in this sense they are all distractions and temptations to veer off the spiritual track. At the same time, it could be that the successful deciphering of obscure figures might be a way of publicizing, by virtue of the pleasure in difficulty itself, the truths of the faith, and perhaps of intensifying our desire to experience for ourselves the truths we have worked so hard to articulate. God may become less of a stranger as we become familiar with the intricacies of the language he has chosen to employ. If so, he would tend toward a god of love rather than one of discipline and terror.

A god of love? Perhaps, but principally so for those who are already believers or who bow to the logic of conversion. Monotheism (even in its Trin-

74. Ibid., 93 (bk. 3, xvi).

75. For an important argument about the constitutive relation between exile and metaphor (each involving a passage from a "proper" to an alien place), and for Augustine's sense of *all* language (even that of the scriptures) as figurative because exiled from the one true god, see Margaret Ferguson, "Augustine's Region of Unlikeness: The Crossing of Exile and Language," in *Innovations of Antiquity*, ed. Ralph Hexter and Daniel Selden (London: Routledge, 1992), 69–94.

76. Augustine, *Confessions*, 10 (bk. 1, iv).

itarian form) requires that the ultimate solution to every obscurity must tend to the same set of conclusions that absolutely exclude certain other conclusions. All figurative signs (*translata*) can be reduced back to a clear language by the believer whose effort is powered by a piety that preexists the puzzle itself and that is further reinforced by its solution. At the end there is no enigma. The god is what is beyond and outside metaphor; he is the foundational law to which all metaphor can be traced and from which it is generated. As the all-seeing; he knows in advance how the riddle will be solved and what its message will be. The god cannot himself be translated if he is to remain the originator of all translation, all naming and all law, all affirmations of how one thing is or is not like another and can or cannot be made to stand for something else.[77]

This god would also be the originator of language, the placeholder who solves the puzzle of how it could possibly have begun as something coming from nothing. The question of the origin of language was one of the great questions of the eighteenth century—one of the puzzles it chose to set itself. Among the reasons it was posed was that the assumption of a divine origin was no longer to be taken for granted. If not god, then what or how? How could the human species have nothing and then something if no one gave it to us from above or outside? How could we have language unless it were a gift from some or other stranger? Cadmus the Phoenician was an exemplary (and of course mythic) foreigner in that (according to Herodotus) he founded Thebes, introduced the prototype of the Greek alphabet, and caused warring soldiers to spring up from a dragon's teeth. Here we have the stranger as lawmaker-civilizer, as the giver of language, and as the begetter of violence all at once. Pentheus, had he remembered that his grandfather Cadmus and the founder of his city was once a stranger, might have done a better job in receiving his cousin Dionysus. If there is no clear curse on the house of Cadmus, the line of Cadmus is still punished through Pentheus. Is the bestowing of language associated with the stranger also to be understood as a transgression, or at least as a *pharmakon*, a gift that is also a poison? In the Socratic account of Theuth's offer of writing to the king of Egypt in *Phaedrus*, that is certainly the impression we have, perhaps irrefutably so after Derrida's powerful reading.[78] The king must control

77. These issues are explored in profound detail by Derrida, especially in "White Mythology: Metaphor in the Text of Philosophy," in *Margins of Philosophy*, trans. Alan Bass (Chicago: University of Chicago Press, 1982), 207–71; and in "Plato's Pharmacy," in *Dissemination*, trans. Barbara Johnson (Chicago: University of Chicago Press, 1981), 61–171.

78. See Derrida, "Plato's Pharmacy."

writing; the king cannot control writing. It is offered him from outside by a god who threatens to let loose a world of infinite signification and dispute.

With the onset of monotheism, all of this has to come from the one god. Absent the god, humans are on their own. Earthly strangers may bring us all sorts of things we need or merely desire, including foreign words, but who or what produced language? Did some independent subculture invent it, exporting it to others, or did it evolve from the efforts of a single genius faced with the overwhelming variety of nature, one who thereby became a stranger-lawgiver to his own kind? Some theorists imagine a moment in which nothing became something, while others are concerned with how a primitive language which is already in place and constitutive of human nature itself develops into something more complex and capacious. Is there a protolanguage only needing certain kinds of stimulation to generate new forms, or does everything have to be already in place in order for even the simplest spoken-written item to make any kind of sense? Is language a creature of sense or reason or is it some happy marriage of the two? Is reason itself sense-based? Does speech originate in self-interest, as persuasion, or in sociability, in the desire to communicate with others? What came first, verbs or nouns? Literal or figurative expressions?

Interest in these questions has waxed and waned at various points in the histories of philosophy and linguistics, but they were of obsessive concern to many eighteenth-century scholars and philosophers.[79] Not infrequently, metaphor and figure were at the heart of their inquiries. Shelley regarded poetry as "connate with the origin of man" and metaphor as the core activity of poetries.[80] Sensation and its organization into meaningful similitudes, presumably by way of language, occur at the same time. There is no point in this account where nothing becomes something, when not-language becomes language. Acts of mind and feeling are involved in even the most basic of human perceptions and expressions. In early human civilization, poetry and metaphor are everywhere—"every author is necessarily a poet"—because all the relationships between things in language have yet to be established, and in this sense the poets are also "the institutors of laws and the founders of civil society" (279). The metaphor is thus not a stranger;

79. See James H. Stam, *Inquiries into the Origin of Languages: The Fate of a Question* (New York: Harper & Row, 1976); Murray Cohen, *Sensible Words: Linguistic Practice in England, 1640–1785* (Baltimore, MD: Johns Hopkins University Press, 1977); Hans Aarsleff, *The Study of Language in England, 1780–1860* (Minneapolis: University of Minnesota Press, 1983); and Stephen K. Land, *From Signs to Propositions: The Concept of Form in Eighteenth-Century Semantic Theory* (London: Longman, 1974).

80. *Shelley's Prose*, 277.

or if it is, then the existence of the stranger is coterminous with the experience of subjectivity itself, before the self has become a citadel. But the new meanings generated by metaphoric activity through time are unpredictable and surprising and thus always embedded in a cycle of estrangement, domestication as dead metaphor, and re-estrangement. The health of a culture in this way depends upon its being continually made a stranger to itself, and the source of that estrangement can come from anywhere: "a single word even may be a spark of inextinguishable thought" (281).

Rousseau, at least in one of his formulations, went further, proposing that figurative meanings came before proper ones. The obvious *hysteron proteron* here, which Rousseau admits—if figures involve comparing two existing terms, how can figures come first?—is resolved by supposing that it is the internal human passion that is transposed and imposed, forming one half of the metaphorized pairing.[81] It is not about comparing two things already defined outside in the world but of relating subjective emotions to a single object. My acute fear of the other man as an enemy produces the idea that he is a giant; subsequent familiarization then reduces him to the status of a mere man like me. The "stranger-ness" of the figuration is in this way generated from within the perceiver: my fear plus other person equals giant, conjoining an aspect of the self with something in the world. Early human history produces more of these encounters than civilized life, so it is the primitive phase of language that is most replete with metaphors.[82] Rousseau's example suggests that in this hypothetical early stage of human society there are more strangers than familiars, resulting in a high incidence of figurative terms. The encounter with the stranger produces the figure as a first response; only as the other ceases to be a stranger does the "proper" sense (the giant is a mere man) emerge. Poetry comes before prose, imagination before reason, because of the primal experience of fear of the stranger. Sociability only accrues with the loss of fear, at which point the desire to

81. Jean-Jacques Rousseau, *Essay on the Origins of Language and Writings Related to Music*, trans. John T. Scott (Hanover, NH: University Press of New England, 1998), 293.

82. This argument should be set against the much more skeptical address to the matter of origins in the *Discourse on the Origins of Inequality*, trans. Judith Bush et al. (Hanover, NH: University Press of New England, 1992), 29–33, 45–47. See also Stam, *Inquiries into the Origin of Languages*, 80–93. Rousseau's oscillation between aporetic and assertoric analyses of the origin of language is central to Derrida's groundbreaking *Of Grammatology*, trans. Gayatri Chakravroty Spivak, corr. ed. (Baltimore, MD: Johns Hopkins University Press, 1997). There is a crucial discussion of the metaphor of the giant on 270–80; and another by Paul de Man in *Allegories of Reading: Figural Language in Rousseau, Nietzsche, Rilke, and Proust* (New Haven, CT: Yale University Press. 1979), 146–59. Both point out that the coining of the term *giant* is at once false (to the object) but proper and literal to the perceiver's state of mind (fear). For a historical survey of the arguments about metaphor and original passion, see Land, *From Signs to Propositions*, 50–74.

communicate kicks in. Rousseau has already said as much in an earlier statement that must now be understood as coming after what has not yet been said: "As soon as one man was recognized by another as a sentient, thinking Being and similar to himself, the desire or the need to communicate his feelings and thoughts to him made him seek the means for doing so."[83] The key point is that such recognition is *not* primary; it comes only after the fear has given way to comfort, when I can afford to see another man as similar to myself, which is also when the "proper" proper noun can come into being. Choosing between desire and need here is a secondary concern, not the originating motive for language. At this point the stranger is no longer threatening; he has become the person next door, and we can find a common name for ourselves and call it proper. But buried within the social contract is a primal moment of radical fear in which every still-unfamiliar person or thing has a name of its own, and a metaphor at that—a metaphor that has not yet been displaced into the world as the comparison between two things outside the self but retains half of the conjunction inside the speaker's mind. When we reinvent the stranger as the lawgiver or god, we forget, either out of uncritical habit or as a cunning device to intimidate our fellow citizens, Blake's affirmation that all deities reside in the human breast. But at this point the original stranger has been reintroduced in his primary form as the vehicle of the uncanny and the potential dispenser of fear and trembling, which may or may not be embedded in a notion of justice.

To summarize: the stranger may be a god, a friend, an enemy, or a friend *and* an enemy; he may appear in the form of money or in the guise of a merchant, a sophist, a lawgiver, or perhaps a philosopher; he is an agent of translation and of the resistance to it, an inciter and an object of conversion; he is called metaphor (*translatio*) and is also the source of metaphor. And since half of that source is, according to Rousseau, the fear within the self, then the stranger is also within us, habitually constrained by custom from erupting into crisis but always waiting to emerge again. The stranger is me and is outside me trying to get in. The stranger is a principle of risk to the self and in the self: "the subject is a hostage."[84] Again, "the welcoming *hôte* who considers himself the owner of the place, is in truth a *hôte* received in his own home" (41). The coincidence, in French, of *hôte* as meaning both host and guest (like the Greek *xenos*) assists Derrida in articulating the in-

83. Rousseau, *Essay on the Origins of Language and Writings Related to Music*, 289–90.

84. Jacques Derrida, *Adieu to Emmanuel Levinas*, trans. Pascale-Anne Brault and Michael Naas (Stanford, CA: Stanford University Press, 199), 57 (citing Levinas).

timate risk of seeking to differentiate, to assert one sense at the expense of the other, to claim power as the host, as Pentheus did, without taking the position of the guest. We are about to see that the stranger is also a promised or threatened arrival who can be conjured out of the embers of a dying hearth in a remote corner of rural England.

CHAPTER TWO

Hearth and Home: Coleridge, De Quincey, Austen

THE FLUTTERING STRANGER

The stranger does not come. The narrator of Coleridge's "Frost at Midnight" sits before a dying fire and meditates upon the near-absolute silence and stillness that marks the midnight hour of a winter's night. It is so still that even the flame in the fire fails to "quiver," but there is a "film," something less than a flame, which "flutters" on the grate, and which, in a footnote included in the first three printings of the poem (through 1812), references a popular belief that such phenomena, "called *strangers*," were supposed to "portend the arrival of some absent friend." Turning again later in the poem to this "fluttering *stranger*," he remembers seeing it when he was a schoolboy, and then fantasizing all through the following day that his lessons might be interrupted by a much-desired visitor:

> . . . and still my heart leaped up,
> For still I hoped to see the *stranger's* face,
> Townsman, or aunt, or sister more beloved,
> My play-mate when we both were clothed alike![1]

Through the first six printings of the poem (through 1829) all of these references to the stranger are italicized and they are every bit as striking as italics are supposed to be. For the stranger, it seems, is not strange but familiar, imagined as a friend whose presence is desired. The folkloric conflation of

1. Coleridge, *Poetical Works, Part 1*, 1:454–55 (original emphasis). The texts of the successive printings from which I quote can be reconstructed from Mays's editorial apparatus, included at 2:569–73.

stranger and friend explained in the footnote is repeated in the main text and again subjected to italics, as if asking for further attention. Reasonably so. How can a stranger be a friend, and why would a friend be called a stranger?

The conjunction of apparent opposites prefigures, almost precisely, Freud's interpretation of the uncanny: that what is *unheimlich* is also at the same time *heimlich*, belonging to the home or familiar within it. It prefigures also Derrida's interest in the Greek *xenos* and the French *hôte* as designating either host or guest or both at once, so that those who appear to differ—one at home and the other coming to the house and requesting hospitality—are bound together etymologically as codependent and perhaps even interchangeable: every host is a guest in the making, every stranger a familiar. The *Oxford English Dictionary* records a still-current sense of "stranger" as "one who has stopped visiting," someone who is familiar but has not been seen lately. American English speakers still say "don't be a stranger" in just this sense. *Stranger* and *foreigner* (another meaning of the Greek *xenos*) are historically unstable words. A hundred or so years ago one could still announce a decision to "go abroad" and mean nothing more than to leave the house for a walk through public space; now it would suggest getting on a plane, passport in hand. In sixteenth-century London, a "foreigner" could be either a person from another country or simply a person from outside the city who did not intend to take up residence there, while foreigners in the modern sense were called aliens or strangers.[2]

Strangers and foreigners, it seems, are as unstable etymologically as they are in the fantasies and phobias they generate. Coleridge appears to entertain no idea that the visitor might be other than familiar and beloved, whether as the nurturing adult aunt or the sister who causes him to remember happier times before the experience of sexual difference (and before the production of children like the one whose future life this same poem appears to celebrate). One could surmise that "Frost at Midnight" thus projects the happy illusion of a totally familiar and safe world in which everything that is to come is already known in advance; or one might speculate that it

2. See Jean E. Howard, *Theater of a City: The Places of London Comedy, 1598–1642* (Philadelphia: University of Pennsylvania Press, 2007), 8, 223n2. For a rich and detailed account of the stranger syndrome as it worked in Shakespeare's time, and for an updated bibliography of other work on this topic, see Margaret Tudeau-Clayton, "'This Is the Strangers' Case': The Utopic Dissonance of Shakespeare's Contribution to *Sir Thomas More*," in *Shakespeare Survey* (forthcoming). Tudeau-Clayton notes that Shakespeare himself would have come to London at first as a foreigner-stranger, proposing also a more extended usage of *stranger* as describing those estranged from their living on the land by enclosure—thus internal to the nation-state.

embodies a hyperbolic defensiveness against the possibility of a truly strange stranger, someone unknown and perhaps unknowable, someone who would present the excitement and the terror of an uncontainable arrival. The location of this dilemma in the narrator's past, without reference to what did or did not transpire, makes the past live on into the present and may even make the present of the poem seem empty. We do not know whether anyone came through the schoolroom door, nor who they were if they did. Nor do we know what the imagined prospects for a visiting stranger might be for the melancholy man now sitting in front of his fire at midnight. The silence suggests that no one came, and that no one will come this time either. The frost seems to have stilled all motion. Uncertainty about what one is to others, about whether there any friends to be expected, about the predictability of time passing from one moment to another, from solitude to sociability or not, is consonant with the odd, concluding imagery—in a poem that Coleridge insisted (in 1817) was not political—wherein a "secret ministry" changes the state of water drops and "hangs them up in silent icicles," a not-so-comforting sign of what can happen if one leaves the house for a public space where, in the mid-1790s, government ministries encouraged the stringing up of those deemed threatening to the national interest.

Coleridge's most important fire-watching precursor was certainly ambivalent enough about the great outdoors looming beyond the domestic hearth. William Cowper gave Coleridge the poetic formula for the fluttering stranger, or rather, Coleridge took it. As the far more famous of the two poets at the time, Cowper might well have treated Coleridge's borrowing as citational homage rather than as plagiarism: *The Task* was a widely read favorite, and no one could have failed to spot the resurrection of a section of book 4 in the text of Coleridge's poem.[3] Cowper's narrative, which has recently begun to attract the close critical attention and intellectual respect it deserves, is much too complicated on the matter of friends and enemies, strangers and familiars, for me to try to summarize here.[4] Let us just say that it both welcomes and deplores the news arriving from all over

3. On the topic of citation, to which I shall return, see Alexander Regier, *Fracture and Fragmentation in British Romanticism* (Cambridge: Cambridge University Press, 2010), 141–64. Regier shows that citation sets up a play between "fragmenting force and organic memory" and registers "both the loss of Language and language's coming into being through destruction and fragmentation" (156, 160). One of Regier's citations most pertinent to the poem under discussion comes from De Quincey, who writes that "quotations always express a mind not fully possessed by its subject" (156).

4. See, e.g., Julie Ellison, "News, Blues, and Cowper's Busy World," *Modern Language Quarterly* 62.3 (2001): 219–37; Kevis Goodman, *Georgic Modernity and British Romanticism: Poetry and the Mediation of History* (Cambridge: Cambridge University Press, 2004); Mary Favret, *War*

the world; exults over and undermines its own safe distance from the violent warmongering going on in the cause of national policy and security; celebrates the rustic life while deploring the existence of rural thugs and thieves; and enjoys the pleasures of the poet's domestic retreat even as it registers the punishing power of raging winter weather upon the lives of others. It is, in other words, bound up in antitheses. Notably, the "stranger's near approach" that "superstition" predicts in the "sooty films that play upon the bars" is, like Coleridge's, unfulfilled: no one comes.[5] But Cowper is yet more alone. There is no sleeping infant whose gentle breathing breaks the silence, and no remembering of any past stranger as potentially a friend or relative. The thoughts inspired by the dwindling fire are almost self-accusatory, those of lethargy and vacancy, until a stern admonition (in Cowper's words) "restores me to myself" (l. 307). The wake-up call comes from "the freezing blast / That sweeps the bolted shutter" (l. 303–4), in other words, the threat that what is outside might come inside, that the domestic idyll might be vulnerable. The poet goes back and forth between feeling safe and happy and feeling insecure, as his jeremiads against commerce, military life and lower-class malingering contribute to a growing sense that no place, even one at the heart of the homeland, is to be assumed inviolate. Cowper writes in the wake of global war—before the epic postrevolutionary conflict with France but in the aftermath of the American war for independence—when one could not assume that one's loved ones were sure to return or that any stranger who might show up in their place would be a benevolent rather than a threatening figure. The discharged and often disabled veterans of the various foreign campaigns who roamed the countryside were ambiguous figures indeed, as Wordsworth would record in a famous episode of *The Prelude*. And if they carried with them tropical diseases, they could infect the very air we breathe without our knowing it.[6]

How do you keep out such airborne infections? Perhaps in the same way that you keep out bad weather, by shutting tight all the doors and windows. But Coleridge's poem, unlike his or Cowper's cottage, is leaky, and permeable; it can be staged variously in terms of history and historicism, psychosexuality, anthropology, theology, and ontology, each in and through the others. In appending itself to Cowper, in hanging itself up upon a section of *The Task*, it produces itself as both companionable and parasitic form. But

---

at a Distance: Romanticism and the Making of Modern Wartime (Princeton, NJ: Princeton University Press, 2010).

5. *The Poems of William Cowper*, ed. John D. Baird and Charles Ryskamp (Oxford: Clarendon, 1995), 2:194 (*Task*, book 4, 292–95).

6. See Bewell, *Romanticism and Colonial Disease.*

fire-watching is a tradition larger than both, with a wide range of associations. In the cold northern winters, keeping the fire going through the night was once a task of some importance to survival and minimal well-being. In the middle of the night a fire is as much as we can have of the sun, the source of life. Fire-watching can be a primary religious activity and figures as such in, for example, Moore's *Lalla Rookh*, where its devotees have existed since long before the modern monotheisms that seek to exterminate them. It has been associated with sexual desire and with the funeral pyre, and thus, in another coming together of opposites, with living and dying.[7]

In folklore traditions fires generate omens, and fire-watching at midnight invites encounters with ghosts and spirits. The specification of the midnight hour is Coleridge's own (it is not in Cowper), and Francis Grose tells us that this is "the usual time at which ghosts make their appearance," and that if, "during the time of an apparition, there is a lighted candle in the room, it will burn extremely blue."[8] Coleridge's fire generates a "thin blue flame" that "quivers not," as if awaiting an uncanny arrival. Ghosts must be spoken to before they speak, but when they speak must not be interrupted; and according to Grose they are not willing or able to divulge "the secrets of their prison house" (13). Coleridge proved quite willing and able to give us details of his impounding in a lime-tree bower; but ghosts keep their secrets, as do the ministries of "Frost at Midnight." One version of the fire folklore recorded by Grose describes a "flake of soot hanging at the bars of the grate" as denoting "the visit of a stranger from that part of the country nearest the object" (68). Here we have a nearby stranger and another scene of hanging.[9] Hazlitt, writing years later in *The Spirit of the Age* (1825) and echoing both Cowper and Coleridge, makes Charles Lamb something of a ghost figure, one who is most engaged by "what verges on the borders

7. See Gaston Bachelard, *The Psychoanalysis of Fire*, trans. Alan C. M. Ross (Boston: Beacon Press, 1968).

8. Francis Grose, *A Provincial Glossary, with a Collection of Local Proverbs and Popular Superstitions* (London, 1787), 9–10. The conjunction of a midnight meditation next to a sleeping child occurs in Wollstonecraft's *Letters Written in Sweden* (1796), although here there is no fire, and the landscape is still visible (it being midsummer). Coleridge leaves implicit the speculations about solitude and society that Wollstonecraft makes explicit. See *The Works of Mary Wollstonecraft*, ed. Janet Todd and Marilyn Butler (New York: New York University Press, 1989), 6:248–49; and the discussion in Harriet Guest, *Small Change: Women, Learning, Patriotism, 1750–1810* (Chicago: University of Chicago Press, 2000), 309.

9. The *Oxford English Dictionary* (2nd ed., s.v. "stranger") notes other instances of portentous objects being identified with the coming of strangers, and thus *called* strangers: guttering candles, moths, floating tea leaves. Blue flames could also be corpse-lights, leading us to a grave, or vaguer indications of a spirit in the room. Blake surely conjures up a range of possibilities in the "vapour" and "wand'ring light" of his little boy lost and found poems in *Songs of Innocence.*

of oblivion" and who "evades the present" and "mocks the future," so that "a page of his writing recalls to our fancy the *stranger* on the grate" (again the italics) "fluttering in its dusky tenuity, with its idle superstition and hospitable welcome." Lamb, like Coleridge, is one who inclines toward the "retirement of his own mind" where "the film of the past hovers forever before him."[10]

Lamb is also the "gentle-hearted Charles" of "This Lime-Tree Bower My Prison," written earlier but not yet published, who will leave Coleridge alone in his garden bower in order to savor the pleasures of a walk. And Lamb it was who wrote a poem titled "To Charles Lloyd, An Unexpected Visitor," published in 1797 along with others by Coleridge and Lloyd himself and beginning thus:

Alone, obscure, without a friend
A cheerless, solitary thing,
Why seeks my Lloyd the stranger out?
What off'ring can the stranger bring?[11]

So it seems that strangers were very much on the minds of the Nether Stowey circle in the last years of the century. Lamb is another lonely heart waiting for a visit, but it is *he* who is the stranger: "Why seeks my Lloyd the stranger out?" Lloyd the unexpected visitor seems to become the host, and Lamb the host is the stranger he seeks out. Or is it the other way round, with Lloyd instead of Lamb here being cast as the solitary thing in need of an offering? Each can change places with the other, the host with the guest and the strange with the domestic. Lamb seems to be both at home and a stranger on the move, *bringing* an offering, an odd enough attribution to make us think that the stranger in the third line is not after all the stranger in the fourth line. The poem somewhat resolves this later on, but only somewhat. Its syntax hangs for a time suspended. Lamb and Lloyd are each strangers to the other, one at home and one visiting. Each is host and guest (*xenos*) to the other. Lamb's "estranged ears" are actually at home,

10. *The Complete Works of William Hazlitt*, ed. P. P. Howe (New York: AMS Press, 1967), 11:180, 179. Leigh Hunt's essay of 1812, "A Day by the Fire," also cites Cowper but makes no mention of strangers, offering instead a rhapsody on the pleasures of low-burning fires, happy sociability, and the more benign elements of folklore and fairytale associated with fire-watching. See *A Day by the Fire; and Other Papers, hitherto Uncollected* (Boston: Roberts Brothers, 1870), 13–41.

11. *Poems by S. T. Coleridge; Second Edition, to which are now added Poems by Charles Lamb and Charles Lloyd* (Bristol, UK: J. Cottle and Messrs. Robinsons, 1797), 238.

and Lloyd is arriving, but "cheerless, friendless solitude" will be his future fate (239).

Yet at least briefly Lamb is lucky: someone comes, the fluttering film turns to welcome flesh and blood. Not so Coleridge, nor indeed Cowper, who invents for himself a nonthreatening visitor in the form of a personification of evening whom he gratefully acknowledges as the bringer of both peace and poetic production: "Composure is thy gift."[12] Cowper's "parlour twilight" (l. 278) is another moment out of time, between day and night, just dark enough that the fire sends shadows to the ceiling, "Dancing uncouthly to the quiv'ring flame" (l. 276) while the poet sees "strange visages express'd / In the red cinders, while with poring eye / I gazed, myself creating what I saw" (l. 288–90). Cowper's "sooty films" stage another scene of hanging as they "play upon the bars / Pendulous, and foreboding in the view / Of superstition prophesying still / Though still deceived, some stranger's near approach" (l. 292–95). Cowper's stranger remains strange—not familiar—and does not come. Yet, the stranger is always about to come, still promised even as still deceiving. Superstition is disavowed and preserved at the same time. He is hard on his own "indolent vacuity of thought" (l. 297) but also forgiving of it: what man has not felt this? Coleridge too cites a "most believing superstitious wish" in his poem's first three printings[13] and spectralizes himself as an "idling Spirit" (l. 20) whose improprieties—making "a toy of thought"—he justifies retrospectively in the figure of the dreaming schoolboy, "presageful" (l. 25) not least because not yet wise.

What, then, are Cowper's "strange visages" and why the ambivalence about superstition? Neither of the poets enters into the realm of faerie, with its pagan hobgoblins and spooks. The folkloric ambience has disappeared for them and there is nothing to replace it. Coleridge also refuses to embrace the vocabulary of the Gothic, although he constantly seems on the point of doing so: we await the shrieks and knockings of the spirit world, but they do not come.[14] The Enlightenment project of demystification has (almost)

12. "The Task," 4:260. *The Poems of William Cowper*, 2:193.

13. Coleridge, *Poetical Works, Part 1*, 2:571.

14. See Anne Williams, *Art of Darkness: A Poetics of Gothic* (Chicago: University of Chicago Press, 1995), 202–7, for a very suggestive reading of the poem as written within a "female gothic" subgenre. I should at this point at least briefly explain why I have not in this book devoted any space to the Gothic novel: partly because its place in the stranger-syndrome is obvious and comprehensive, and partly because it has been well-described by others in just this way. Among many pertinent studies, I mention just three. Marshall Brown's *The Gothic Text* (Stanford, CA: Stanford University Press, 2005), argues in detail for the importance of the defamiliarization of the mind; E. J. Clery, *The Rise of Supernatural Fiction, 1762–1800* (Cambridge: Cambridge University Press, 1995), is eloquent on the marketing of strangeness as well as on the strangeness of the market;

done its work, but leaves only an empty space that can be reoccupied by all sorts of strange figures. Mere self-mythologizing is not a trustworthy solution. Coleridge is uncomfortable with seeing himself in and making his own sense of the inanimate shapes and forms of a dying fire. In contrast, the unitarian or pantheist God who teaches "Himself in all, and all things in himself" (l. 62) enacts a permitted self-projection, one that is at the core of Christian doctrine. The merely mortal spirit (though spirit still) is not so privileged but is judged to be making a "toy of Thought" (l. 23). This is the voice of the stern preceptor Coleridge who took issue with Wordsworth's poem about the daffodils, pointing out that a proper bliss of solitude would have to involve not the self-pleasuring recollection of a patch of flowers in the wind but "the images and virtuous actions of a whole well-spent life."[15] Wordsworth's infamous bliss of solitude was an onanistic gratification—shamelessly so (from being lonely as a cloud he moves to lying alone upon a couch, like the aroused female novel reader of numerous popular prints). Coleridge has the fruits of an achieved sexual relationship lying beside him in the form of his sleeping babe. But he is not in bed with his wife; he is sitting up by the fire at midnight, and his fondest memory is of a time when sexual difference had not yet marked the point of no return, when he and his sister still dressed alike. (She, remember, was the last example given of the hoped-for familiar stranger).

By now one might surmise that the stranger has taken the form of the child, an uncanny incarnation whereby two secretly then suddenly become three, in a complete change of state. So it is that Coleridge almost passes out of and beyond life, becomes himself suspended or imagines himself not breathing, becomes a ghost, in a place where the fluttering film is the *sole* "unquiet thing" (l. 16) where the child's breathing fills up the silence like a metronome and where the "interspersed vacancies" (l. 46) of composition itself seem to be enacted outside time. If Coleridge has left the world of the living, at least for the wrinkle in time that is the midnight moment, has he then been abandoned by God (as Cowper feared he too might be), whose benefits will accrue only to the child who has just arrived, who will learn "far other lore" (l. 50) and perhaps far other *law*, not just the folk beliefs and unstressful pleasures of nature but a less exacting regulation of the law of God that consigns the fallen adult to its prison in the cottage and to the

---

and Cannon Schmitt, *Alien Nation: Nineteenth-Century Gothic Fictions and English Nationality* (Philadelphia: University of Pennsylvania Press, 1997), shows how England's imaging of otherness made it other to itself.

15. Samuel Taylor Coleridge, *Biographia Literaria*, ed. James Engell and W. Jackson Bate (Princeton, NJ: Princeton University Press, 1983), 2:136.

laws of man that threaten him with capital punishment? Folklore, remember, is not fully approved; it is the production of idling spirits and perhaps outright superstition. Is the child going to recover a good-faith relation to popular belief in a new world purged of such critical judgments? Or, if the lore really is the law, if lore and law will become one, dissolving distinctions of class and education, will that law arrive as the gift of a stranger, in the manner described by Rousseau and intimated by Plato before him?

What is it to live under the law that we have? In remembering himself "pent 'mid cloisters dim" (l. 52) Coleridge is remembering not only Milton and his own situation in the already-written lime-tree bower poem; he is casting himself as a prisoner gazing through the bars of his cell and seeing only "sky and stars" (l. 53). Like a prisoner, he has his fellow "inmates" (l. 4). It seems his life has been one constant imprisonment, for at school he also "gazed upon the bars" (l. 25) hoping it was visiting day. It is a life of loneliness and near-solitary confinement; only his baby son can be imagined as enjoying a better world. The isolation is existential and domestic: a hastily made marriage and a habitually unsettled mind. But the prison imagery surely derives also from the poem's historical predicament and from the implicit politics that would pressure him to insist, overemphatically in 1817, that this poem, despite the hangings and the secret ministries, is *not* political. There are various ways to read these images of frost formation. Reading for analogs of aesthetic creation, we might categorize the conversion of water to ice as the incarnation of artwork itself as effecting a magical change of state, giving form to what was formless. Something of this is adumbrated in the lines that Coleridge published as the conclusion to the 1798 printing (and there only), in which he anticipates his child waking in the morning and responding to the "novelty" of ice and frost, in response to which he will "shout / And stretch and flutter from thy mother's arms / As thou would'st fly for very eagerness."[16] Coleridge claimed that he removed these lines because he wanted to preserve the "rondo" of cyclical form; but their removal also weakens any endorsement of nature as a figure of the artist, as well as getting rid of any sense that there is an imminent moment of present mutual delight and thus a solution to the experience of loneliness and alienation that the poem otherwise transcribes. (Notice also, however, that in being seen as a *fluttering* form the child is associated with the film on the grate, the piece of soot, and the "fluttering stranger" whom the soot portends). Or perhaps the ministry is a religious one, a sign of a supernatural overseer of natural life who comes secretly in the night and is gone by dawn,

16. Coleridge, *Poetical Works, Part 1*, 2:572

missed by the watchman but evident in or to be inferred from what remains behind? Then we might wonder what sort of ministering is involved. Unitarian, we suppose, with all things coming together as one in a landscape transformed by winter.

In "Fears in Solitude" the owlet is an analog of atheism, flying at noon and unable to see the sun.[17] Here its significance is not so grossly summed up. Why an owlet, not an owl? If this is a young owl (and not just a small owl) has it not yet learned to hunt, so that it is crying out for sustenance to be supplied by a parent bird, rendering it thereby a companion spirit to the human infant sleeping inside? Does its loud contrast with the otherwise prevailing silence indicate either an unmarked threat or none at all? Is it a reminder that nature red in tooth and claw still goes about its business, indifferent to human thoughts and dealing out death just as surely as do man-made laws? If so, then we are not living in a world where all creatures embrace a single spirit of benevolence, sharing instead a darker spirit that makes space for warfare, violence and predation. Questions about the just order of the world and god's place in it might well have been on Coleridge's mind at the time this poem was written. Writing to Josiah Wedgwood early in January 1798, he explained why he had hitherto rejected a career in the ministry: "it makes one's livelihood hang upon the profession of *particular opinions*."[18] One could not, in other words, remain suspended. But then it would still be a livelihood, and perhaps better than nothing. He had the offer of a position as a Unitarian minister in Shrewsbury, and though he feared "to go among *strangers*" (1:367; original emphasis), he was inclined to take it. He turned down the bequest that the Wedgwood brothers had offered him and left Stowey for Shrewsbury and the ministry, only to change his mind within the week, resign the position, and gratefully accept an annuity of £150 for life, without conditions, from the Wedgwoods. Not surprisingly, this change of heart and mind seems to have occasioned some discomfort. He professed in a letter to Isaac Wood that "active zeal for Unitarian Christianity, not indolence or indifference, has been the motive for my declining a local and stated settlement as a preacher of it" (1:377). But in the middle of February, he wrote to Cottle that he intended to become assistant minister to the Bridgewater congregation "without any salary" (1:387).

God's ministry, then, was very much on the poet's mind in the winter of 1798. What of the political ministry that had been, throughout the 1790s,

17. Ibid., 1:472.

18. *The Collected Letters of Samuel Taylor Coleridge*, ed. Earl Leslie Griggs (Oxford: Clarendon, 1956–71), 1:365 (original emphasis).

so eager to hang up dissidents and reduce them to silence? According to Hazlitt, who met Coleridge during that brief salaried ministry in Shrewsbury, the sermon "was upon peace and war," upon the separation of church and state, and upon the cruel inhumanity of warfare.[19] Being a minister seems not to have involved quitting political commentary. Cowper saw in the silent onset of winter snow a radical transformation: "To-morrow brings a change, a total change!" The snow "assimilates all objects,"[20] and earth is grateful not only for the covering that keeps out the worst of the cold but for the disappearing of class and species distinctions that seems to promise something like democracy at last, an imagining perhaps the more appealing before 1789 and the subsequent demonization of all such aspirations by the antirevolutionary lobby. Coleridge, of course, had been identified as a revolutionary in the making and had been secretly observed during the summer of 1797 by a man from the ministry, the man who (Coleridge's story goes) had heard the word *Spinoza* and reported to his masters on the whereabouts of a certain spy Nozy.[21] A man who was eavesdropping, indeed, and whose "eve-drops" may impinge upon those that "fall" in line 70 of the poem, along with the tears of the mother of our species lamenting her sins and thus saturating Coleridge's poem both politically and theologically.[22] Secrecy, of course, is in the eye of the beholder who claims not to be able to behold; so secrecy on the part of government was justified as a response to the secret plottings of radicals like John Frost (not quite Jack Frost, but almost) who was in Paris in 1792 and who was tried for seditious words in 1793.[23] The year 1794 had seen the creation of the Secret Committee of the Commons to combat the oppositional secrecy of the radicals, and another followed for the House of Lords. By 1797, according to Albert Goodwin, the nadir of the British democratic movement had been reached, and in the next two years radicalism went fully underground, becoming as secret as it could.[24] Pitt's Gagging Acts of 1795 against certain kinds of public speech made a "strange and extreme silentness" seem a necessary tactic for those at odds with government. Strange, because unnatural, even as associated with the silence of

19. *Complete Works of William Hazlitt*, 7:128.

20. *The Poems of William Cowper*, 2:195.

21. But see the more prosaic account in Kenneth R. Johnston, *The Hidden Wordsworth: Poet, Lover, Rebel, Spy* (New York: Norton, 1998), 525–28.

22. Another topic here invites us: the prince of deathly strangers picks on Eve, while Adam draws the luckier straw and gets to welcome the "heavenly stranger" Raphael (*Paradise Lost*, 5:316).

23. See Barrell, *Imagining the King's Death*,100.

24. Albert Goodwin, *The Friends of Liberty*, 514.

the stranger; extreme, because more than just silent—a secret or yet more silent silence, which earns the unusual word *silentness*.

Coleridge's secret architect of changes of state could have been someone like radical John Thelwall, whose visit the previous summer had contributed to the bad publicity generated by the poetical bohemians in the West Country. In March 1798, Coleridge wrote the famous letter to his brother George in which he claimed to have given up on politics and to have snapped his "squeaking baby-trumpet of Sedition."[25] But just six months earlier, he wrote warmly to Thelwall, whose own poetry was (as J. C. C. Mays has noted[26]), everywhere imitated or absorbed into (or even cited in) "Frost at Midnight." For Thelwall, too, had written poems to his children meditating on his own state of homelessness and exile and hoping for better things for them. He too celebrated and regretted the hospitality of friends and lamented his entrance into a world of strangers. And when he wrote of gazing through his own "grated dungeon" with "straining eye" for the approach of his visiting wife, the prison was a real one.[27] Coleridge's prison may seem imaginary to us but could have seemed real enough to him, whether as present feeling or future prospect. His fireside might have seemed a place of safety, a retreat of the sort that Cowper found protective when he was not all too aware of its vulnerability; but it could hardly keep him from either the threats of invasion that were sounding over the "silent hills" of "Fears in Solitude" (silence here is an index of nasty noises on the way)[28] or indeed from the midnight knock at the door that might perform notice of arrest, detention, and trial. Putting together the historicism and the hauntology, we can imagine strangers that would not be friends but bad spirits, figments of the imagination all too likely to turn real.[29] Perhaps this is why Coleridge no longer felt able to wish for the arrival of a stranger in the present, preferring to remember a time when he could do so in a state of hopeful anticipation.

Let us return to that footnote to line 15, explaining the folklore about the fluttering stranger, which was left out of the later printings of the poem. The italics call attention to the word *stranger*, but the footnote takes us halfway outside the poem and stands itself as a sort of stranger, at a distance

25. *The Collected Letters of Samuel Taylor Coleridge*, 1:397.

26. Coleridge, *Poetical Works, Part 1*, 1:452.

27. John Thelwall, *Poems Chiefly Written in Retirement* (Hereford, 1801), 144.

28. Coleridge, *Poetical Works, Part 1*, 1:471.

29. Thus, Peter Melville, *Romantic Hospitality and the Resistance to Accommodation* (Waterloo, ON: Wilfrid Laurier University Press, 2007), finds the scene "more like a home invasion than a . . . welcome of the other" (125).

from the rest of the text.[30] When it disappears in the later printings, so too does the typographic stranger. The "rondo" that turns the end of the poem (after 1798) upon its beginning also secretes the poem (that is, makes it secret) from the outside world, enfolding it in cyclic form. The loss of the footnote is also the loss of any supposition of a community of those who believe in folklore, in the relation between the soot and the stranger-friend. When it disappears, the poet is more alone than he was, and the theological and/or political drama becomes more central. The aesthetic polish provided by cyclic form (intimated also in the poem's repetitive diction) encloses the poem as an artifact while at the same time distancing its narrator from access to human exchange: he ends by talking to his own beginning. In contrast, the diffusive form of Cowper's *Task* is impossible to hold steady in the mind, as one lyric moment tumbles into another and reflects backward and forward upon all other moments in the poem. Thus, reading out from Cowper's fireside scene, one can construe a whole associational narrative that echoes and mirrors its topics and produces a series of attitudes, often contradictory, between which we need not and cannot choose. Following such a trail is like unraveling and constructing the disseminative logic of a dream, although every moment has a history, a politics, and an existential charge. Coleridge's poem turns back upon itself instead of turning outward, but provides no end; its form is like a snake "coiled with its tale round its head," as he wrote in the copy owned by Sir George Beaumont.[31] The cyclic form encloses the poem but does not explain it; it substitutes repetition for resolution, and in the repetition we enact our own experience of waiting for the stranger who never comes.[32]

The mechanisms of repetition are obvious enough, but they are worth listing if only to demonstrate the obsessive artfulness of their devising: "Came loud—and hark, again! Loud as before" (this in line 3, already a repeating); "'Tis calm indeed! so calm" (l. 8); "Sea, hill, and wood, . . . Sea, and hill, and wood" (l. 10–11); "that film, which fluttered on the grate / Still flutters" (l. 15–16); "But O! how oft/How oft . . . /. . . and as oft" (l. 23–26); "Lulled me to sleep, and sleep prolonged my dreams!" (l. 35); "and still my heart leaped up, / For still I hoped" (l. 40–41); "Dear Babe, that sleepest . . .

30. See Jan Plug, "The Rhetoric of Secrecy: Figures of the Self in 'Frost at Midnight,'" in *Coleridge's Visionary Languages: Essays in Honour of J.B. Beer*, ed. Tim Fulford and Morton D. Paley (Cambridge: D. S. Brewer, 1993), 27–39.

31. Coleridge, *Poetical Works, Part 1*, 1:456.

32. One thinks of the *rime* (frost) of the ancient mariner, which also repeats itself endlessly as it possesses an ever increasing circle of passing strangers, and rhymes them into mesmeric inertia, freezing the blood.

My babe so beautiful" (l. 44, 48); "far other lore / And in far other scenes" (l. 50–51); "By lakes and sandy shores, beneath the crags . . . / . . . both lakes and shores / And mountain crags" (l. 55–58). Others still can be detected. The strong chiasmus at line 62: "Himself in all, and all things in himself" is a licensed repetition, since god himself, the ultimate teacher, is allowed to replicate his own identity upon the face of the material world. The more dispersed chiasmus that marks lines 1 and 72 ("The Frost performs its secret ministry. . . . the secret ministry of frost") and which holds within it the whole poem except the last two lines introducing (and enacting) the image of hanging, is the product of the poet's artistry. That artistry also encompasses a heavy use of exclamation marks (twelve by my count), which disrupts the quietness of the midnight hour with the signatures of urgent address and importunate vocalization.

The imaged repetition of vocalic effort asks questions of the repetition of words and phrases already noted. What is repetition? Does it soothe its hearers by the invocation of known sounds and senses, as in a lullaby designed to put a child peacefully to sleep? Or does it alert us to a certain lack of conviction in the speaker, whereby he has to say things over and over in order to convince himself that they are true or believable? Most readers would find the repetition to be a symptom of enjoyment rather than trauma. Kierkegaard proposes a distinction between repetition and recollection whereby the first is a source of pleasure and the second an index of unhappiness, because it marks the awareness that something has been lost.[33] Coleridge's poem is full of repetition, but at its center there is a powerful instance of recollection as he remembers a time when, as a schoolboy, he was able to look forward to the arrival of the stranger who is not strange. Does the repetition perhaps work to keep the recollection under control, to hold in the emphatic present a tendency to dwell upon a vanished past that would, if allowed to develop, lead to deep nostalgia or to explicit grief? The insistence on that presentness, with its strong effect of the real, seems to keep at bay the Freudian interpretation of compulsive repetition, such as that which overcomes the pleasure principle and signals an unresolvable syndrome. For it is a case here of the present repeating the present and not a long-lost past. The turn back to the "Dear Babe" at line 44 is a turn away from nostalgia toward a future for the sleeping child. But *only* the child has a future. The speaker evinces no such hope, and the lack of it takes form as the absence of any desire for the coming of the stranger, that which he once

33. Søren Kierkegaard, *Repetition: An Essay in Experimental Psychology*, trans. Walter Lowrie (New York: Harper and Row, 1964), 33.

felt but feels no longer, for several reasons: theological disapproval of superstition, sex-gender discomfort, fear of arrest, and imprisonment.

Verbal repetition, then, may function like cyclic form itself as a technique of restraint that keeps the body of the poem in an enduring present, one that functions even within the recollected experiences that govern lines 23 through 43. For while Cowper's poem has no boundaries, Coleridge's poem is *all* boundary. And yet, it is itself parasitical upon *The Task*, boldly (for this is not plagiarism) attaching itself to a famous scene in book 4 and itself operating like a long footnote, like a stranger who comes after the event, picking out the fire, the stranger, the vacancy, and the frost and infusing it with an afterlife. What does it mean that this apparently most intimate of experiences is reported through a literary precursor? Is there a certain security in hanging one's poem (and perhaps one's experience) upon the rhetoric of a much-loved masterpiece? In purely intrinsic and formal terms, Coleridge's poem stands out of time, timely and timeless at once, like a ghost appearing at midnight. Like the change of state from water to ice or from life in the womb to life outside, it occupies a zero-point between one day and another, a point that clock time cannot identify or record without subdividing itself again and again. The poem seems as if sequestered from the spirit of the age and the threats of its times, when no one is safe abroad and when the domestic space is sensed as a prison, so that there is no place to go. The poet sits by a fire but no one comes, and he recalls a former life in which he sat by another fire, and still no one came. The "stern preceptor" (l. 37) will be replaced by a "universal Teacher" (l. 63), but not for him. Can anyone comfortably come and go under such conditions? Only perhaps the fellow poet William Cowper, whose familiarity mitigates the loneliness of an event otherwise reported as fearful and on the edge of pain.

If there is a world elsewhere, it will be for the sleeping child. For the narrator, there seems to be no life at all. Once he hoped for the arrival of strangers, but he now appears not to be able to do so. So he is deprived of those he might well not want to see—a double deprivation, not just experiential but spiritual, not wanting what once was wanted. The risk that the present stranger might prove not to be a friend seems high. The predicament of remembered desire for and current fear of the stranger ties the poem into a knot. No anticipated proper name has replaced the "townsman, or aunt, or sister more beloved" (l. 42) whose advent he looked forward to when a lonely schoolboy. The role of stranger is open, but the inhabitants of the cottage might be well advised to keep the door locked. Let us now look at another romantic writer who does hear a knock at the door, and who does receive a stranger.

THE STRANGER COMES: AN ORIENTAL GENTLEMAN

To move from Nether Stowey to the Lake District, as Coleridge himself did, would seem to involve exchanging one remote rural location for another perhaps yet more remote. But the Lake District had its surprises, among them the discharged soldier who popped out of the hedge on a moonlit summer night, surprising the young student-poet Wordsworth out of his complacency and leaving him with thoughts whose depths he could not fathom and yet could not forget. But Wordsworth's uncanny soldier may not be the strangest of lakeland visitations; that honor may well go to the Malay traveler who knocks upon Thomas De Quincey's door in 1816, or who is at least described as so doing in *Confessions of An English Opium Eater*, and who is given, in a moment that seems perfectly to combine hostility and hospitality, a very large piece of opium. De Quincey was what we might now call a drug addict. To the modern reader living in a culture that has criminalized most drug-taking, eating opium in Dove Cottage, Grasmere, probably looks pretty exotic already, so that the appearance in 1816 of an unexpected Malay at the front door might seem either par for the course or itself part of a drug-induced hallucination. It certainly partakes of the uncanny—the *unheimlich*—very much as Freud explains it. The sense of the uncanny turns on the intuition that what is strange and unfamiliar is felt at the same time to be deeply familiar, the secret (*heimlich*) that is suddenly revealed and recognized as belonging to the home it appears at first to be intruding upon. Coleridge's poem teeters on the edge of the uncanny and does indeed fear the publication or suspected existence of secrets, but nothing happens. De Quincey does receive a visit from the stranger whom he takes to be his uncanny companionate spirit or double, not only as a fellow opium eater. To this degree, De Quincey reveals his own Orientalization, a condition he also deeply resists, as we shall see.

The uncanny also comes with an empirical history, just as it does in "Frost at Midnight." Possession and use of opiates was not illegal in De Quincey's time—indeed, it was common in the bohemian classes—and the traveling Malay is credible enough as a symptom of the demobilization of the British navy after 1815, or of the transfer of a merchant seaman from one port to another (perhaps nearby Whitehaven). Opium alone was responsible for about a third of the entire wealth of British India, where it had been imposed as a profitable monoculture by the East India Company, whose need for an expanded market would eventually lead to the so-called Opium Wars with China. There will be much more to say about this later. Rural Grasmere, in other words, because of what is in De Quincey's pocket, is embedded within a global drug trade whose living analog is the itinerant Malay.

The man speaks no English, and De Quincey no Malay. So he addresses the stranger in classical Greek, gets an unintelligible response in a language he assumes to be Malay, and watches his visitor lie down upon the floor for an hour to rest, which is what he was presumably asking for. All of this takes place in front of the rather nervous servants. The whole episode does seriocomic duty as an anecdote of British class politics, a display of De Quincey's uninhibited racism, and an episode of linguistic irony and ambiguous sociability. It is also a host-and-guest event in which host and guest seem radically different but are one in what De Quincey assumes (correctly) is their mutual habit of opium-taking. Does each of the interlocutors agree to pretend to understand one another in order to impress the servants, or to ease the tension, or to get what he wants (a display of competence for the host, a place to rest for the guest)? The apparent agreement to pretend to understand allows this strangest of strangers to enter into a minimal social relation with a host whose narrative has already vilified him as a figure of monstrous Orientalism and to rest his tired body. What could it have been like for an exotically dressed stranger, turban and all, to make his way through the more remote regions of a country of whose language he has absolutely no understanding? How could he even find his way, presuming he had a destination at all? *Confessions* tells us a good deal about what the Malay meant to De Quincey; but what could the Malay himself possibly have made of his experience? How had he avoided picking up at least a smattering of pidgin or a seaborne special diction that would have made it possible for him to function within a ship's discipline? Was he part of a crew that did not speak *any* version of English? De Quincey cannot even be sure that he is a seaman; that is just his best guess. Was he a real figure at all?

The social exchange is sealed with a parting gift, one that is also a poison: a drug that oscillates between killing and curing, a *pharmakon*. De Quincey gives him a large piece of opium on the assumption that he would be used to it (don't all Orientals take opium?) and that it might ease the pains of travel. He then declares his astonishment and concern when the Malay eats the whole piece, breaking it into three and swallowing the lot: "the quantity was enough to kill three dragoons and their horses."[34] To have forced him to vomit out the opium, says De Quincey, would have violated "the laws of hospitality, by having him seized and drenched with an emetic,

34. Thomas De Quincey, *Confessions of an English Opium Eater*, ed. Alethea Hayter (Harmondsworth, UK: Penguin, 1975), 91.

and thus frightening him into a notion that we were going to sacrifice him to some English idol" (91–92), so he bids him farewell and hopes for the best, but thereby (as he can hardly expect us not to realize) also presumably violates another component of the law of hospitality in failing to take precautions against his possible death. To avoid a temporary offense against politeness and face-to-face embarrassment at an action he cannot explain, he risks a more absolute offense but one that he would not have to witness or be associated with.

As we have seen, Kant's presentation of the obligations of hospitality in *Toward Perpetual Peace* gives a clear account of what the stranger in foreign lands should (in the best of all worlds) expect. He cannot claim the right to be a guest but does deserve the right to visit.[35] This is exactly what De Quincey affords him. The visitor can be turned away, Kant opines, but only if it does not lead to his critical harm. Here, in an ironic twist, it is the permission to visit itself that risks the destruction of the stranger, who stands to be destroyed by hospitality, by a gift that is a poison. But, no dead Malay being reported in the next few days, the relieved host declares the episode to be evidence of the extraordinary tolerance of the Oriental (though this is qualified by a footnote) for a drug that is for most others to be enjoyed only with restrictions. Either he is not dead or reports of his death have not been circulated. No more is heard about the real Malay—if indeed he was real—but a threatening, turbaned figure haunts De Quincey's dreams for the rest of his life, seeming or promising to "run a-muck"[36] and cause terrible destruction. De Quincey has got away with being (or knowing he is, or being seen to be) responsible for a stranger's death, but the stranger, meanwhile, has taken up residence within.

It is, then, a complex hospitality that De Quincey offers his visitor: a welcome that provides much-needed rest only with the possibility of bringing on death. If he had read Kant's *Anthropology* by 1821, he might have sensed as apposite to his story Kant's invention (in a footnote) of a Turk who is imagined to be reporting on the negative components of the European national characters, partly as permission for Kant himself (in the main text) to come up with some of the more positive qualities.[37] Among the good things about Germans, Kant notes their cosmopolitanism and their being "more hospitable to foreigners than any other nation" (413). The English,

35. Kant, *Practical Philosophy*, 329.

36. De Quincey, *Confessions of an English Opium Eater*, 92.

37. Immanuel Kant, *Anthropology, History and Education*, ed. Günter Zöller and Robert B. Louden (Cambridge: Cambridge University Press, 2007), 408.

on the contrary, are notoriously inhospitable, regarding foreigners as less than human. The English are not sociable, preferring to eat alone rather than in company (410). This has consequences. De Quincey does not share in the dangerous opium feast and thus cannot indicate (speaking no Malay) the size of a safe dose. The Malay might have agreed with the Turk; he might have imagined that De Quincey was keen to get rid of him in both the short term and the long term.[38]

This is at odds with the official line. De Quincey begins his essay with the Terentian claim that nothing human is alien to him,[39] and affirms again that "at no time of my life have I been a person to hold myself polluted by the touch or approach of any creature that wore a human shape" (49–50). Such liberal pieties, however, do not sustain further narrative elaboration. His decorous face-to-face interactions with the Malay are followed by virulently racist dreams and reflections fully consonant with the imperialist violence of De Quincey's later support for the Opium Wars. There is no doubt that there is an attraction-repulsion dynamic at work which is to do with the ambivalent, *pharmakon* qualities of opium itself. Weakening the boundaries of selfhood is critical to De Quincey's artistic capabilities but also deeply threatening: "I was the idol; I was the priest; I was worshipped; I was sacrificed" (109).[40] Whatever empathy De Quincey might have felt toward his exotic guest—and this was always uneasy—disappears in the after-experiences in the memory, wherein the Malay becomes "a fearful enemy" (108). Fearful or fearsome? Both? Terror passes into "hatred and abomination" (109) as the entire eastern part of the globe is subsumed within an

38. For a fine reading of Kant's views on eating alone and in company, see Melville, *Romantic Hospitality*, 61–98. Melville's view of Kant's own discomfort with strangers is consonant also with David L. Clark's important study, "Kant's Aliens: The *Anthropology* and Its Others," *New Centennial Review* 1.2 (2001): 201–89. Clark makes a striking case for Kant's distrust of the "radically sincere" alien as one who cannot tolerate what for him is a necessary secrecy. On Kant and the other, see also Gayatri Chakravorty Spivak, *A Critique of Postcolonial Reason: Toward a History of the Vanishing Present* (Cambridge, MA: Harvard University Press, 1999).

39. De Quincey, *Confessions of an English Opium Eater*, 33.

40. A strong case for De Quincey's perverse attraction to the Orient he also despises, and for this dynamic as constitutive of his selfhood, is made by Sanjay Krishnan, *Reading the Global: Troubling Perspectives on Britain's Empire in Asia* (New York: Columbia University Press, 2007), 59–93. The important precursor for this argument, which factors in the circumstances of the author's life along with the larger historical determinations playing upon the expressive psyche, is John Barrell, *The Infection of Thomas De Quincey: The Psychopathology of Imperialism* (New Haven, CT: Yale University Press, 1991). Nigel Leask, *British Romantic Writers and the East: Anxieties of Empire* (Cambridge: Cambridge University Press, 1992), 170–228, explores the known antithetical effects of opium as an extended analog of the operations of the global capitalism of the times. For De Quincey on China, see also Schmitt, *Alien Nation*, 65–75.

extravagant racist denunciation. The rhetoric that associates opium with the creative imagination itself, in its "command, over pain," its provision of pleasure and energy, and its "mysterious" nature (136, 140, 206), cannot be domesticated into producing a simply positive cosmopolitan ethos. Like the image of the Malay in the author's mind, the imagination under the influence of opium is prone to "run a-muck" (92), to destroy affiliations with those very others who are required to produce the desired stimulus in the first place.[41]

The host is taken hostage by his guest, who only appears to leave the house but continues to haunt De Quincey's dreams and waking reveries. This is the pattern Derrida identifies in Oedipus's arrival at Colonnus, where Theseus falls under the compelling power of his unexpected (and physically repellent) visitor: "So it is indeed the master, the one who invites, the inviting host, who becomes the hostage—and who really always has been. And the guest, the invited hostage, becomes the one who invites the one who invites, the master of the host."[42] Derrida explores the pertinence of Benveniste's account of the etymological overlap of the enemy (*hostis*—also foreigner, stranger) with the host-guest (*hospes*), in a circle that includes *hostia*, the animal offered as sacrifice, the scapegoat.[43] Host-guest reciprocity is founded in the idea that each might change places with the other; so too might hospitality be supplanted by the hostility it is designed to discourage. De Quincey stages an uninhibited display of *hosti-pitality* (Derrida's coinage), as the uncouth stranger is admitted, over-welcomed, dismissed, and then discovered never to have left. If opium is De Quincey's route to creativity, then the internalization of the figure of the Malay is a disturbing version of Edward Young's already complex image of genius as a rising sun to be worshiped as if outside the self while still of the self; and De Quincey has indeed become a pagan idolater, "like an *Indian*," and one who fears what he also adores.[44]

The topic of opium leads De Quincey into a meditation upon happiness outside the world of drugs, and thence at once to a scene that recalls Cowper and Coleridge with uncanny exactness:

41. See Krishnan, *Reading the Global*, 77–84, for an important history of this term, which he suggests may itself have become critical just at the time when the British were introducing opium to the Malay peninsula; an instance, in other words, of blaming the victim.

42. Derrida, *Of Hospitality*, 123–25. We might recall the most famous romantic instance of this inversion: Hegel's master-slave dialectic.

43. Benveniste, *Le vocabulaire des institutions indo-européens*, 1:87–101.

44. Leitch, *The Norton Anthology of Theory and Criticism*, 436.

> I put up a petition annually, for as much snow, hail, frost, or storm, of one kind or another, as the skies can possibly afford us. Surely every body is aware of the divine pleasures which attend a winter fire-side: candles at four o'clock, warm hearth-rugs, tea, a fair tea-maker, shutters closed, curtains flowing in ample draperies on the floor, whilst the wind and rain are raging audibly without.[45]

Give me winter, he says, that I may enjoy to the maximum the experience of being protected and sequestered from the outside world, the world out of which strange strangers might come knocking on the door, but presumably won't do so as long as the weather is so bad that no one would be out of doors in the first place. If no one comes, no one can call for hospitality. How indeed would the fair tea-maker react to sharing the warm fire with a Malay opium eater who spoke no English? The close juxtaposition of this fantasy of intact domesticity with the just-told story of an actual knock at the door is surely not accidental. In the logic of artful representation it asks us to hold together extreme versions of the experience of being at home, so extreme that each reflects upon the other *as* other, and thus as a distorted mirror image of itself. Tea and crumpets with your opium, sir? This fireside is a very literary, almost tongue-in-cheek fireside; it is Leigh Hunt's sociable scene, and in its specification of a "winter evening" it cites once again, of course, the title of the fourth book of Cowper's *The Task*. It is narratively positioned as a follow-on from dreaming about the Malay and as a prelude to an account of the pains of opium (as if the pleasures have not already brought plenty of pain, as if pleasure and pain could be kept separate). Its very framing calls out its artificiality: "paint me, then, a room . . . paint me a good fire" (95), he says to the imaginary artist he rhetorically summons to his aid. Any such painting would be a still life, with the stranger always kept out of the picture, even if always about to arrive. The fraught scenario of outside-inside, host-guest anxieties apparent in Cowper's poem (and, less melodramatically, in Coleridge's) can here be kept at bay, but only by self-consciously resorting to the assistance of a painter who is very obviously not De Quincey, not the man who has opened his door to the Malay visitor and had nightmares ever since.

Moreover, the apparently intended contrast of this fireside scene with the world of opium is not quite as complete as it seems. His comfort in tea, "the favourite beverage of the intellectual,"[46] and thereby in the "fair

45. De Quincey, *Confessions of an English Opium Eater*, 93.
46. Ibid., 94.

tea-maker," are themselves massively dependent upon the world outside, upon global trade, and in particular upon China, which was the source of tea before the Indian plantations were cultivated in the 1830s. Tea, along with silk, was the principal cause of the balance of payments deficit that, in the view of capitalists and imperialists like De Quincey, required a war to force the Chinese to import "British" opium from India. As if to take us outside the sitting room and into the spheres of global trade and dominion, De Quincey specifically refers to the 1757 review by Samuel Johnson of Jonas Hanway's diatribe against tea-drinking. Hanway, Johnson reports, argued that this "modern luxury" was "injurious to the interest of our country."[47] Johnson professes himself an inveterate tea drinker—like De Quincey and Cowper, but unlike Coleridge, he "solaces the midnight" with the teapot—, but dutifully reports Hanway's case that tea offers but the "insipid entertainment" of a "barren superfluity," one that brings about a critical loss of revenue to China.[48] Hanway mentions a deficit of £150,000 annually flowing to the Chinese in the tea trade. It is hard not to suspect that in turning our attention to this review of 1757, De Quincey is artfully opening out the still-life painting of secure domesticity he is, with an equal knowingness, at the same time constructing. For tea, like opium, was perceived as embedded in the logic of the *pharmakon*. Markman Ellis notes that "medical writers vigorously contested its pharmacological status as anything from a remarkable panacea to a pernicious toxin."[49] Tea was a drug just like the opium it was so closely tied up with in the global economy; the shadow of opium looms by the fireside whose scene of domesticity seems set up to exclude it.

There is more. Where there is tea, there is sugar. And sugar, as the most important product of the Caribbean slave economy, was the object of a massive public-relations campaign by the abolitionists throughout the later eighteenth and early nineteenth centuries.[50] Cowper, whom we must assume took no sugar in his tea, was an active supporter of the abolitionists.

47. *The Works of Samuel Johnson*, ed. Arthur Murphy (London, 1824), 2:334.

48. Ibid., 2:334, 346–47. Cowper invokes "the loud-hissing urn" and the cups "that cheer but not inebriate" at the beginning of "The Winter Evening" (*The Poems of William Cowper*, 2:188).

49. Markman Ellis, ed., *Tea and the Tea-Table in Eighteenth-Century England* (London: Pickering and Chatto, 2010), 2:vii.

50. See, among others, Sidney Mintz, *Sweetness and Power: The Place of Sugar in Modern History* (New York: Viking, 1985); and Timothy Morton, *The Poetics of Spice: Romantic Consumerism and the Exotic* (Cambridge: Cambridge University Press, 2000), 171–206, which studies the "blood sugar topos" (180), whereby what gets put into a cup of tea is a distilled essence of human blood.

The crisis engendered by tea drinkers was, as the British saw it, already both medical and economic; the consumption of sugar was a yet more consequential habit. De Quincey does not admit to taking sugar in his tea, but in opening the analysis to tea itself he cannot prevent the question coming up. Tea with sugar seems to have been a common enough habit to prompt eighteenth-century silversmiths to build sugar compartments into tea caddies.[51] The "favourite beverage of the intellectual," as De Quincey called it,[52] was as habitually conjoined with sugar as it has been with sympathy. The sympathy did not always extend to those laboring as slaves on the West Indian sugar plantations.

COLONEL BRANDON'S WAISTCOAT

In the case of De Quincey, a gifted classicist and translator from the German and well-read enough to regret the absence of a copy of Adelung's *Mithridates* when he meets his Malay visitor, it is perhaps not so surprising that he cannot or will not keep the foreign element out of his rural English sitting room, and that he stages the domestic scene as perhaps deliberately ironic. But surely we can look to Jane Austen—who, along with Wordsworth, is the key romantic literary figure in the modern English heritage industry—to keep the doors shut and the windows bolted? Colonel Brandon, the admirable early-middle-aged male figure in *Sense and Sensibility*, has been in the East Indies. But this seems so unimportant to the plot of the novel that even a careful reader might miss it, making it more like what we now call a "factoid," something whose only interest is that it exists as contingent truth instead of not existing at all and thereby functions to make the novel sound real: he went to the Far East rather than, say, to Timbuktu. He went there, we are told, to recover from a romantic disappointment, and because people at this time really could make a good career in India. The information is convincing. But his time abroad seems to have left no marks on his character or demeanor. In Thackeray's *Vanity Fair* and in Conan Doyle's *The Sign of Four*, persons coming back from India are visibly affected by it: they dress like natives and adorn their living quarters with mementos of the Orient, even recreating self-sustaining microenvironments, making little Indias out of a room or turning an ordinary suburban house into a palace. Not so Colonel Brandon. Only Willoughby's sarcasm alerts us to the tales

51. According to James Walvin, *Fruits of Empire: Exotic Produce and British Taste, 1660–1800* (London: Macmillan, 1997), 129, taking sugar in tea was a confirmed habit before 1700.

52. De Quincey, *Confessions of an English Opium Eater*, 94.

he could have been telling: "Perhaps . . . his observations might have extended to the existence of nabobs, gold mohrs, and palanquins."[53] But they do not. For that, as we shall see, we have to go to Robert Southey's epics. Brandon is a homespun hero of the homeland. His dwelling is an English country house, and his sartorial preference is for a flannel waistcoat, for which he is at first mocked by the young woman who ends up becoming his wife. Perhaps the tropical climate has had its effect on Brandon, because early in the book he confesses to a "slight rheumatic feel in one of his shoulders" (40): hence the flannel waistcoat, the thick, protective covering of good old English wool that so well suits the climate—though not the fashions of the times. Or perhaps it is that same English climate that brings on the rheumatic symptoms after one reaches the ripe old age of thirty-five. One cannot know whether to blame the foreign or the domestic element for Brandon's ailments, which anyway largely exist in the minds of others. He is, in fact, most of the time the embodiment of robust, native energy, always on the move in carrying out his many good deeds. The frailest of the protagonists is actually the English rose, Marianne Dashwood, who is also the most sensitive to the negative associations of flannel waistcoats, all of which may tell us more about her than him. So far so good—English wool for a very English gentleman.

The historical timing of this novel is vague. It is set after the publication of Cowper's *The Task* (1785), which is quoted, and so it is either between the American and French revolutions or within the protracted conflict with revolutionary and Napoleonic France that continued more or less constantly between the early 1790s and the novel's publication in 1811. But the book was written by 1797, and so must certainly be situated among some significant events in the history of British India, most notably, the impeachment and acquittal of Warren Hastings, which occupied public attention from 1787 to 1795, in other words, for most of the time during which the novel might have been set. None of this impinges on Brandon's dialogue; he shows no interest in politics or geography, and neither do any of the other characters. And yet, after the reading of *Mansfield Park* by Edward Said (and the film version by Patricia Rozema) that brought out the significance of what was always hidden in plain sight—the source of the Bertram family's wealth in slave labor in the Caribbean—we have become more attuned to look out for the possible significance of the passing factoids in Jane Austen's stories.[54] In *Sense and Sensibility*, Mrs. Jennings offers "fine old Constantia

53. Jane Austen, *Sense and Sensibility*, ed. Ros Ballaster (London: Penguin Group, 2003), 52.
54. Edward Said, *Culture and Imperialism* (New York: Knopf, 1993), 80–97.

wine," which may or may not allude to Britain's gaining control of the Cape in 1795; and homebody Brandon has a sister in Avignon, a country with which Britain was quite likely at war, an implication strengthened by Mrs. John Dashwood's handing out gifts of needlework "made by some emigrant."[55]

Sense and Sensibility thus has no punctual historical location and yet is completely of its time. Elinor, according to Lucy Steele, at one point has on her "best spotted muslin,"[56] the highly fashionable unbleached white cotton that took its name perhaps from Mosul but more probably from Masulipatam and that was imported into England from India throughout the eighteenth century. Brandon may have slept through the Warren Hastings affair or declined to express an opinion, but India is carried on the back of his future sister-in-law, a follower of fashions designed to reveal as much as to conceal and to face down the harsher realities of the northern climate with a display of Oriental-classical eroticism and grace. We are not often asked to imagine Elinor as a modern woman looking to draw attention to her physical beauties, but here she is sporting the very latest slinky little garment. By the 1790s, this could as well have come from Lancashire as from India, but the associations of muslin with the exotic East—and with the same sort of balance of payments deficit generated by the tea trade—were well established in popular knowledge. Here is Elinor, the sensible one, the constant defender of Colonel Brandon's claim to sense and virtue, dressing up in spotted muslin.

Jane Austen's other early novel (though one of the last to be published), *Northanger Abbey*, also appears to offer a set-piece education into British common sense, redirecting an exoticizing imagination fed by gothic novels toward the predictable realities and expectations prevailing "in the midland counties of England."[57] And yet these secure midland counties are suffused with foreign elements. For sure, no Malays come knocking on the door. But General Tilney, the most prominent patriarch in the book, is a glutton for exotic consumer goods. His pineapples are the product of a lavish attempt to reproduce tropical benison in the land of grey skies, and the "Gothic" chest that the heroine imagines as containing murky family secrets has been imported from Japan. True, his breakfast set is English porcelain, "because he thought it right to encourage the manufacture of his country," and because

55. Austen, *Sense and Sensibility*, 187, 71, 238. Charlotte Smith's poem *The Emigrants*, dedicated to Cowper and describing the lives of those who fled the turmoil of the French Revolution, was published in 1793.

56. Austen, *Sense and Sensibility*, 258.

57. Jane Austen, *Northanger Abbey*, ed. Susan Fraiman (New York: Norton, 2004), 137.

"the tea was as well flavoured from the clay of Staffordshire, as from that of Dresden or Sêve" (120). But this piece of boastful patriotism is comically at odds with his otherwise indiscriminate appetite for luxury goods. And, of course, it is tea from China that is poured into English chinaware. Elsewhere in the novel, much French (and pseudo-French) is spoken by the fashionable set, despite French having become the language of the enemy.[58]

Above all, and more than any other Austen novel, *Northanger Abbey* is attentive to exotic textiles.[59] These were sensitive items, and had been since the 1699 legislation against the import of calicos (supposedly from Calicut), which was deemed threatening to the market for British woolens. The Calico Acts of 1699–1721, which first banned textiles imported from India and then placed restrictions on the sale of all cotton goods, were repealed in 1774, well before the novel was conceived, but the aggressive promotion of English woolens remained in the memory even after English factories began themselves to produce fashionable cottons in order to capture the domestic and eventually the export market.[60] Indeed, the volume of Indian textile imports peaked only in 1802, despite the history of increasing import duties designed throughout the late eighteenth century to maintain the dominance of the domestic muslin industry. The discussion between Henry Tilney and the ladies about the price of muslin does not indicate the source of the product, although by the end of the eighteenth century British-made cottons were a substantial part of the market. But the frequent references to textiles—Mechlin, jaconet, mull, sarcenet—bespeak foreign associations or origins in their very names. Tilney's intervention here marks him as either a satirist or a dandy, a feminized male or a mocker of feminization. Is 5 shillings a yard indeed a bargain price for his "true Indian muslin," as Henry claims? Mrs. Allen's dress cost "but nine shillings a yard,"[61] for we know not what material. Austen seems once again to be winking in the direction of a readership that might know more about the textile industry and

58. See Janet Sorensen, *The Grammar of Empire in Eighteenth-Century British Writing* (Cambridge: Cambridge University Press, 2000), 197–223, for a strong argument that Austen's language is ironized and even alienated in its commitment to "proper" English, making Austen an "ambivalent transcoder." Austen's dramatic breaches of the polite norms are described in Jill Heydt-Stevenson, *Austen's Unbecoming Conjunctions: Subversive Laughter, Embodied History* (New York: Palgrave-Macmillan, 2005).

59. Marilyn Gaull's edition of Austen's *Northanger Abbey* (New York: Pearson-Longman, 2005) gives detailed notes on the textiles mentioned in the novel.

60. See Chloe Wigston Smith, "'Callico Madams': Servants, Consumption, and the Calico Crisis," *Eighteenth-Century Life* 31.2 (2007): 29–55; and Beverly Lemire, *Fashion's Favourite: The Cotton Trade and the Consumer in Britain, 1660–1800* (Oxford: Oxford University Press, 1991), 12–42.

61. Austen, *Northanger Abbey*, ed. Susan Fraiman, 22.

foreign competition than her characters themselves either know or admit to.[62] At the very least she signals that these insulated midland counties of England are thoroughly open to the attractions of a busy commercial world, embracing in the form of luxuries those foreign elements that are denied intellectually and declared otherwise marginal to British culture. Colonel Brandon's waistcoat places him in a distinct sartorial as well as moral minority, and it is hard not to suspect that he is a little bit duller because of it. Austen's destructive and dangerous characters are commonly the strangers, the ones who come from outside the locality—Willoughby, the Crawfords, Wickham, Frank Churchill, and so on—but she is also prone to suggest the limitations of the traditionally embedded "roast beef of old England" set. The result is often the creation of a void which no single figure or set of values can occupy with a convincingly heroic identity. Caddish strangers and cloddish squires compete for the status of ideal male, but few escape without Austen's critical retractions. There are no out-and-out foreigners, to be sure—as there are, for instance, in Fanny Burney's novels—and the midland counties of England may be poorer without them. The foreigners that do invade the countryside are inanimate, virtual, or nonhuman ones: pineapples, muslins, and the characters in gothic novels.

One could go on—to recall, for instance, Wordsworth's acquisition of a "Turkey carpet." In the form of the commodity, the stranger has become thoroughly familiar, and foreign commodities that were once luxuries (tea, sugar, chocolate) were already assimilated as necessities among the lower echelons of society as well as among the middle and upper classes. Karl Marx, in the first book of *Capital*, restores some of the primal strangeness to commodities by giving them arms and legs and imagining them speaking to one another in transactions where no human agent is involved. Similar attributions can be found in the eighteenth century "thing" novels narrated by sofas, coins, or hackney coaches. These are only incipiently uncanny; they partake also of comic fairy tales. Far more uncanny are the things that do not speak but which have life nonetheless: modern commodities. Austen is content to record the pervasive at-homeness of things which come from far away while maintaining a relatively intact community of native persons. Those who knock on the door are almost always familiar. This combination of highly endogamous societies craving or enjoying an inex-

62. Between 1780 and 1800, the average price for British cottons was 3s to 5s per yard (Lemire, *Fashion's Favourite*, 113). But Lemire also gives figures claiming that in 1797, 80 percent of printed textiles cost less than 2s 6d per yard, and a full 50 percent were less than 1s 6d (95–95, 106). Perhaps some very expensive high-end items drove up the average. At least, if Indian muslin was more expensive and/or of better quality, Tilney would seem to have done very well here.

haustible range of consumer goods made by strangers from all over the earth prefigures a very modern fantasy held by some liberal-conservative spirits today: free trade in things accompanied by tight borders against persons. De Quincey, if we can trust him, represents an open-door policy where even the strangest of strangers may, and should, be received, but records also the traumatic consequences of coming close to those whose sameness-in-difference from oneself will subsist long after as the source of terrible nightmares and generate powerful and violent prejudices of the kind we now call racist. He suggests, indeed, that things can transform into persons, and persons into things. For Coleridge, on the other hand, the stranger does not come and is not desired, but he writes a poem in which the play between what is desired and feared for the future includes an anxiety about the stranger who might yet come. The onset of the human stranger remains open and unpredictable, gesturing toward an absolute hospitality that the poet does not feel comfortable extending. The ingested stranger that is opium, so important to both De Quincey and Coleridge, has already crossed the threshold after crossing the globe, though the size and significance of the opium trade is a secret well kept by many at the time and by more than a few of their latter-day historians and critics. And who would come in the form of the human stranger? It could be one of the Charleses (Lloyd or Lamb), but it could also be a government agent or even some modern Dionysus (like John Thelwall) who would push his commitment to hospitality to the limit and bring with him unavoidable dangers. Best to answer the door warmly wrapped in English flannel; best not to have to answer the door at all.

CHAPTER THREE

Friends and Enemies in Walter Scott's Crusader Novels

"WHICH IS THE MERCHANT HERE, AND WHICH THE JEW?"

Throughout most of the performance history of *The Merchant of Venice,* there would have been little or no motive to attend closely to this question Portia asks of the assembled Venetians. If the stage is crowded, with Shylock skulking somewhere in the background and Antonio indistinguishable from the other well-dressed Gentiles, then the question is merely instrumental: where are the litigants? Perhaps it works also to establish the legal propriety of what is about to happen: plaintiff and defendant are bidden to stand forth before their judge, rendering the assembly both formal and performative. But there would probably be only one Jew, so the incident might be played as a joke; for how is it possible that Portia could possibly not see the difference between the engaging albeit anxious young man on one side of the stage and the bearded, spooky old figure in the black cape and yarmulke on the other?

But Leslie Fiedler is right when he refers to the "common error which takes the 'Merchant' of the title to be Shylock" seeing it as "symptomatic of a whole syndrome of misconceptions about a play which few of us have ever really confronted."[1] Shylock is by law not allowed to be a true merchant, but without him and his coreligionists the merchants could not make their living; there would be no one to extend them credit and to take upon themselves (or have put upon them) the stigma of usury that Christians are supposed not to indulge in (though this was far from the case). The popular imagination that thinks of Shylock as the merchant of the title is certainly responding to the power of his presence on the stage and in the cultural

1. Leslie A. Fiedler, *The Stranger in Shakespeare* (New York: Stein and Day, 1972), 97.

imagination evident in productions of the play over the last two hundred years—since, indeed, the powerfully revisionary stagings of Edmund Kean in 1814, which removed him from the gallery of monsters and made him a figure of sympathetic understanding. But it also suggests an intuition about the interdependence of merchant and Jew reflected in a modern world where Jews have become merchants and Christians are more than happy to lend money. The distinction that the play proposes to uphold, on which its narrative depends, is not one that could be made fully credible even in its own time. The Tudor state, wherein there were officially no Jews, *did* in fact permit usury, but tried in a statute of 1571 to limit interest rates to 10 percent, everything beyond that being deemed excessive.[2] Excessive interest rates were figuratively associated with Jews, but Gentiles were prone to the habit; indeed, Shakespeare's own father was twice accused of demanding extortionate interest and was once fined for it. Shylock is moreover an *English* name, not a Jewish one, as Stephen Orgel has shown.[3] There is a lot of evidence, then, for having doubts about who is the merchant and who is the Jew.

The line that everyone remembers, the line that is often cited by people who have never even seen or read the play, is the one telling us (Portia again) that "the quality of mercy is not strained" (4.1.88). This *mercy* is the key word that purports to keep apart the old law, the Jewish law, heavy with an idea of inflexible justice, from the Christian doctrine of forgiveness. It is one of the keywords whereby Christians affirm that they are not Jews. It is not "strained" in the sense that it is not sorted or sifted, not restrained or limited, not portioned out in calculated measures as if it were the payment of an interest. It is also not "strained" in the sense that it is not pressured nor itself the cause of strain. It is effortless and life-giving like the gentle (Gentile) rain. But these happy associations also do not stand up to scrutiny. Portia is very much given to apportioning in specifying that famously exact pound of flesh. She is also, as Fiedler notes, the "focal center" of the play's staging of xenophobia, "the stranger-hater *par excellence*."[4] It takes a French Algerian Jew, a stranger several times removed, to see the trickery in this word *mercy*, touching on (and touching off) "the entire history between the Jew and the Christian, the entire history of economics (*merces*,

2. See James Shapiro, *Shakespeare and the Jews* (New York: Columbia University Press, 1996), 98–100, which is indispensable on the Shylock question. Shapiro further directs us to the work of Norman Jones.

3. Cited in Shakespeare *The Merchant of Venice*, ed. Leah S. Marcus (New York: Norton, 2006), 240.

4. Fiedler, *The Stranger in Shakespeare*, 101.

market, merchandise, *merci*, mercenary, wage, reward, literal or sublime) as a history of translation."[5] Is the Christian mercy also mercenary, also being marketed for some sort of profit? What is it to demand, as Portia does, that the Jew must be merciful? Is it to demand the conversion to Christianity—the Jew must be Christian—that ends the play, and which renders the supposedly unconstrained mercy a violently imposed contract? Or is it also to state, more or less as a fact, that the Jew must be mercenary, in order that the punitive logic of the plot can unfold according to the routines of Christian stereotypes: the Jew must be a "Jew"? Portia the stranger-hater (notice her scorn for suitors of other races even as she is polite to their faces) goes on to speak of the godlike act open to mere humans when "mercy seasons justice" (4.1.201). How, Derrida asks, can anything "season" another thing that is being proposed as its categorical opposite? Can chalk season cheese? Here indeed is another tricky word. "Season" obeys the logic of the *supplément*: it can be that which adds spice or taste to a dish, a different but compatible substance (making a happy *discordia concors*) or that which brings something to its own proper state of ripeness, and so a function of the original substance itself.[6] Do we then have here mercy plus justice, or an entity we could have to call (or think of) as "mercyjustice," something that is already what it will become, and which another now-lost sense of "season" as "impregnate, copulate," also moves toward? The stage is further darkened by Antonio's bizarre recognition of the stranger's rights as belonging to the "justice" of the state, because it allows free trade pursuant to its "trade and profit" (3.3.33–34). Justice is nothing more than obeying what trade and profit require as law: the mercy that seasons justice may indeed be, after all, *merces*.

Derrida puts it beautifully: "At the word go we are within the multiplicity of languages and the impurity of the limit."[7] Orgel notes that figure of the Jew would have been little known in Shakespeare's England: they had been banished in 1290 and would not return until Cromwell's era. The few who were in evidence were of Spanish or Portuguese origin and often associated with Jesuit plots. According to William Prynne, Catholic secret agents were indeed deemed to come "under the title, habit, and disguise of Jews," so the Jews were not Jews at all, but figures of figuration itself, that which

5. Jacques Derrida, "What is a 'Relevant' Translation?," trans. Lawrence Venuti, *Critical Inquiry* 27 (2001): 186.

6. Ibid., 195.

7. Ibid., 176.

is other than it seems.[8] Orgel supposes that "the association of Jews with usury in England was entirely conventional" (241). Jews were also invoked as figurative embodiments of radical Protestant sects (242) for whom Shakespeare famously had little affection. Dressed in sober black, Shylock might bear comparison to Shakespeare's Puritans, who also disapprove of music and merrymaking. The impurity of limits indeed: the Jew is us, and well deserves his English name. Beneath the permissive fiction that Shakespeare's audience was seeing, Venice on the stage, lies a very English gentleman, one who is both merchant and usurer.

In recent times, we have had more and more occasions to reflect on the similarity in difference that marks Shakespeare's apparent attempt to preserve intact a binary distinction between the Christian and the Jew, the friend and the enemy, the self and the other. In particular, the relation of posited difference that recent and contemporary global-political alliances in the West have sought to maintain between the Jew and the Arab, with the Christian interpellating itself as author and arbitrator of that difference (between democratic and terrorist/absolutist, friend and enemy, modern and primitive, civilized and barbaric) have been brilliantly investigated (in the spirit of Derrida) by Gil Anidjar, whose work I draw upon and who has resolutely insisted on Christianity's formative role in creating and exploiting notions of the Arab and the Jew as interchangeable instances of the enemy and therefore structurally identical and interchangeable in the imagination of the West.[9]

Walter Scott knew something of this syndrome. He might also have known something about the interdependence and arguable identity of Shylock and Antonio. In his 1790 edition of Shakespeare, Edmund Malone had noted an English translation of the seventeenth-century Italian historian Gregorio Leti's anecdote of the life of Pope Sixtus V, in which the pope himself played Portia's role as the judge, and where the threatened debtor was a Jew and the cruel creditor determined on full payment was a Christian.[10] In this version of the story the roles are reversed, and Antonio becomes the Shylock figure, implacable in his desire for the pound of flesh. There is no evidence that Shakespeare knew of this variant (whose first known publication came well after his death), or even that it was true, but it appealed to

8. Orgel, "Shylocks in Shakespeare's England," in Shakespeare, *The Merchant of Venice* (241) cites Shapiro, *Shakespeare and the Jews*, 27.

9. See Gil Anidjar, *The Jew, the Arab: A History of the Enemy* (Stanford, CA: Stanford University Press, 2003). Much of Derrida's well-known work on the complexities of hospitality addresses issues of friends and enemies.

10. There is a good account of the sources in Shapiro, *Shakespeare and the Jews*, 123–25.

Maria Edgeworth, who used it in her fascinating philosemitic novel *Harrington* (1817)—in other words, before *Ivanhoe* (1819) and Scott's later Crusader tales, *The Betrothed* and *The Talisman* (published together in 1825). The debate about the so-called Jew Bill of 1753 and the very public conversion of Lord George Gordon to Judaism, along with a few notorious criminal trials involving Jews, kept the issue of Jewishness very much alive in public and political circles before the French Revolution; thereafter, they were inevitably implicated in the "loyalty test" mentality that was directed at all persons who could be associated with foreign or alien interests.[11] For the most part, however, Jews were not specifically targeted (unlike the Freemasons and the supposed Illuminati) and somewhat sympathetic literary portraits of Jews were put abroad by Thomas Dibdin and Richard Cumberland, as well as by Byron in his *Hebrew Melodies*, the product of his cooperation with Isaac Nathan, who had first offered the job to Scott, who declined.[12] Scott was no avowed philosemite, but the popular success of *Ivanhoe* was significantly owing to its portrait of a complex romantic heroine in the Jewess Rebecca. Michael Ragussis has argued persuasively that both *Harrington* and *Ivanhoe* were careful and conscious responses to and rewrites of the plot of *The Merchant of Venice*, which had previously functioned in the literary tradition as the embodiment of conventional anti-Semitism.[13] As such, both authors were countering the conservative identification of Jews with revolution (virulently apparent, as we have seen, in Burke's *Reflections* in 1790) and, in Scott's case, undermining the myth of racial synthesis and inclusion (always under the rubric of Englishness) put about by the nationalist historians and to some degree in Scott's other novels, those which seem to anticipate and celebrate the happy union of England and Scotland after 1707.

Before we move on to Scott, let us recall that there are *three* peoples of the book, three monotheisms competing for spiritual and geographical

11. See David S. Katz, *The Jews in the History of England, 1485–1850* (Oxford: Clarendon, 1996), 240–322. For an account of the "Jew Bill" controversy, see Dana Rabin, "The Jew Bill of 1753: Masculinity, Virility, and the Nation," *Eighteenth-Century Studies* 39 (2006): 157–71. See also Todd M. Endelman, *The Jews of Georgian England, 1714–1830: Tradition and Change in a Liberal Society* (Philadelphia, PA: Jewish Publication Society of America, 1979).

12. Katz, *The Jews in the History of England*, 347; Endelman, *The Jews of Georgian England*, 274–78. For a more skeptical and (I find) convincing account of Cumberland, see Judith W. Page, *Imperfect Sympathies: Jews and Judaism in British Romantic Literature and Culture* (New York: Palgrave-Macmillan, 2004), 34–40.

13. Michael Ragussis, *Figures of Conversion: "The Jewish Question" and English National Identity* (Durham, NC: Duke University Press, 1995), 57–88, 89–126.

territory: Judaism, Islam, and Christianity. Anidjar shows us that the conflict is never simply binary, although it can seem so when any one of the three seeks to affirm itself as the absolute one—as all of them have done and still do—making the other two into a composite and flexible figure of error and exploitation, each open to contingent alliance and disavowal. In Christian eyes, the figure of Shylock affiliates and changes places with the figure of Othello, the Muslim convert to Christianity (or so it seems), who is estranged by Venice just as Shylock is estranged. Unlike Portia, Desdemona chooses marriage with the stranger, the "extravagant and wheeling stranger" who is as cosmopolitan as a Jew "of here and everywhere" (1.1.134–35) but who is allowed to serve the state because he is willing to lend them his military prowess.[14] If Shylock the Jew enacts trade, Othello the (lapsed?) Muslim protects it, while the Christians sit back and congratulate themselves on their purity. Like Pentheus, Desdemona carries her story in her name: *ill fated, wretched,* in Greek (but also, in English, demonic), and as with Agave there is no ultimate benefit for her in taking up with the friend-enemy of the state. Desire for the other, if that is what it is, is not here rewarded in the way that it seems to be in the happy elopement of Jessica and Lorenzo (where it is also enabled by desire for money, never fully distinct from love in *The Merchant of Venice*). Nor is it completely clear that the marriage of Othello and Desdemona is even consummated, given the pace of the plot and its nocturnal interruptions. (This accords with the fetishism of the handkerchief: Othello has avoided looking closely at his wife.) Othello's extraneous identity is further confirmed in the famous textual crux whereby he describes himself as throwing away a precious pearl, like the "base Iudean" or "base Indian" (5.2.345), depending on whether one follows the First Folio or the First Quarto. Both Jew (Judean, Judas) and Indian (North American or South Asian) are in Christian terms followers of false gods. The "circumcised dog" or "turbanned Turk" whom Othello smote in Aleppo (5.2.351, 353) is a figure of himself "turned Turk" (2.3.166). The circumcised Turk is also a figure of the Jew who is, as we have seen in *The Merchant of Venice*, a figure of everything.

14. William Shakespeare, *Othello*, ed. E. A. J. Honigman (London: Arden, 2001). On the pairing of Shylock and Othello, see Anidjar, *The Jew, The Arab*, 101–12; Fiedler, *The Stranger in Shakespeare*, 139–96; and Julia Reinhard Lupton, "*Othello* Circumcised: Shakespeare and the Pauline Discourse of Nations," *Representations* 57 (1997): 73–89. According to Nussbaum, the Othello-Desdemona coupling was paradigmatic of eighteenth-century anxieties about interracial marriage: see Nussbaum, *The Limits of the Human*, e.g., 4–9, 206–8.

EUROPE AND ITS OTHERS; OR, SCOTT WITHOUT SCOTLAND

Scott wrote three novels set in the time of the Crusades: *Ivanhoe, The Betrothed*, and *The Talisman*. They do not belong among the positive modernization narratives of the Waverley novels because they are set in dim and distant times, long before any Whiggish justification of commercial and political union between England and Scotland could be argued to have become clearly emergent. They are also not set in Scotland and so are at something of a tangent from the task Scott so often set himself, that of creating a national history for a nation that is no longer a nation. *The Talisman* is indeed the story of a Scotsman in the service of the Christian princes among whom the English loom large, and Scots-English rivalries are at issue in its plot. Kenneth of Scotland's experiences by no means reflect well on the character or career of Richard Plantagenet, who had also been far from heroic in *Ivanhoe*.[15] And it is fair to say that the modern culture of civility, with its commitment to the nonviolent or minimally violent resolution of social conflict, is endorsed by way of the negative in Scott's critical portrayal of the chivalric violence of the Middle Ages. The final marriage contract between Edith Plantagenet and Sir Kenneth (who turns out to be the heir to the Scottish throne) does function as a one-off prefiguring of eventual union five hundred years later. But the period of the Crusades is itself dark and brutal, and too many transitions and interruptions would have to be explained in order to defend a gradualist model of steady-state development; the emergent benefits of commerce and integration do not really become a convincing theme for historical fiction until much later, or at least Scott chooses not to discover them in the twelfth century. The crusader novels are full of what one critic has called "carnivalesque heteroglossia," which appears as a variety of dictions, interests, and identities that are never reconciled within a permitted space or an enduring historical formation.[16] Diversity, as we now call it, is not gathered up within any emerging sociopolitical unit (e.g., a nation-state) that can be imagined as containing or incorporating its

15. For a fine reading of *The Talisman* as an analysis of variously successful subaltern responses (including the Scottish) to English dominance, see Caroline McCracken-Flesher, *Possible Scotlands: Walter Scott and the Story of Tomorrow* (Oxford: Oxford University Press, 2005), 118–27. Judith Wilt, *Secret Leaves: The Novels of Walter Scott* (Chicago: University of Chicago Press, 1985), 178–84, also argues that the deserts of Palestine sustain displaced debates about the British political landscape.

16. Tara Ghoshal Wallace, "Competing Discourses in *Ivanhoe*," in *Scott in Carnival*, ed. J. H. Alexander and David Hewitt (Aberdeen: Association for Scottish Literary Studies, 1993), 304.

components into a peaceable kingdom. Instead, it persists in the form of discordant ethnic fragments unincorporated either into politically tolerant entities or into the more spontaneous harmonies of an evolving civil society. Saxon and Norman, English and Scottish factions may hint at the mutual accommodation to come later in history, but even these are rudely and inefficiently sketched; the Jew and the Arab figure much more intransigently as incarnations of the other who is in the first instance (which we must soon complicate) also the enemy.

Perhaps we overdo the evolutionary optimism of even the mainstream Scottish tales. Ian Duncan has argued against any complacent endorsement of enlightenment or Whig historicism even in the Waverley novels, finding there (for instance, in *Rob Roy*) the model of a modernity that has by no means exorcised its primitive precursors in the production of an integral British nation-state, but which rather consists of "a global network of uneven, heterogeneous times and spaces, lashed together by commerce and military force, the dynamism of which is generated by the jagged economic and social differences of the local parts."[17] This is much more obviously the case for the period of the Crusades, which had in fact been subjected to negative historical judgments long before Scott took up the topic. For David Hume, the Crusades were "the most signal and most durable monument of human folly that has yet appeared in any age or nation" carried out largely by the riff-raff of Europe, whose entry into Jerusalem produced a bloody massacre of women and children, as well as combatants.[18] Herder, who endorsed the civilizing effects of trade and commerce in a peaceful world, described the Crusades as "nothing more than a mad enterprise, which cost Europe some millions of men; and reconveyed to it in the survivors, for the most part, a loose, daring, debauched, and ignorant rabble."[19] Greed rather than religious zeal was the motivator of these expeditions, and the new nobility that was created out of the turmoil was both violent and ambitious. The army led by Peter the Hermit began its operations with a massacre of

17. Ian Duncan, "Primitive Inventions: *Rob Roy*, Nation, and World System," *Eighteenth-Century Fiction* 15, no. 1 (Fall 2002), 81–102, 100.

18. David Hume, *The History of England* (London: T. Cadell, 1789), 1:292, 311.

19. Johann Gottfried von Herder, *Reflections on the Philosophy of the History of Mankind*, trans. T. O. Churchill (1800), ed. Frank E. Manuel (Chicago and London: University of Chicago Press, 1968), 357. For a good beginning account of the debate about the Crusades in the early nineteenth century, see James Watt, "Scott, the Scottish Enlightenment, and Romantic Orientalism," in *Scotland and the Borders of Romanticism*, ed. Leith Davis, Ian Duncan, Janet Sorensen (Cambridge: Cambridge University Press, 2004), 94–112. Much of Watt's reading of *The Talisman* accords with and anticipates my own.

Jews in the Rhineland,[20] slaughtering them as if to practice for the task of slaughtering Turks and Arabs. Scott does not much approve of Richard the Lionheart either in *Ivanhoe* or in *The Talisman*, but he is still portrayed there as better than he was, for it was in his reign that some of the worst persecutions of the English Jews took place. According to Hume, Richard's coronation was accompanied by brutal anti-Jewish riots across all of England, including the spectacular forced suicide of "five hundred of that nation" at York,[21] the home of Isaac in *Ivanhoe*. Richard too, it seems, was as comfortable exploiting and punishing Jews as doing battle with Saracens. In this respect he did not much differ from his predecessor Henry II or his successor King John. The punitive treatment of English Jews ended in 1290 only when they were expelled by Edward I. So much for "merry England," as Scott habitually calls it, tongue in cheek.

The Saracen is figured as the foreign enemy abroad, but his companion is the Jew, the enemy inside the nation, who stands for a general enemy of the homeland, a shape-shifter who can appear in different guises. The convertibility of the figure of the Jew into a range of versions of the enemy other is registered two years before *Ivanhoe* in Edgeworth's *Harrington*, where the hero's mother cries out "Jew, Turk, or *Mussulman*, let me hear no more about him," and where the anti-Catholic, anti-French mob active in the Gordon riots turns also on the Jews merely because of an unfortunate rhyme:

> without any conceivable reason, suddenly a cry was raised against the Jews: unfortunately, Jews rhymed to shoes: these words were hitched into a rhyme, and the cry was "*No Jews, no wooden shoes!*" Thus without any natural, civil, religious, moral, or political connexion, the poor Jews came in remainder to the ancient anti-Gallican antipathy felt by the English feet and English fancies against the French wooden shoes.[22]

The Jew, whatever he might be in himself, is a general figure of the enemy, as such assimilable to any of the variously scorned national or racial (and sometimes gendered) others: the French, the Catholics (and hence also the

20. Herder, *Reflections on the Philosophy of the History of Mankind*, 374.

21. Hume, *The History of England*, 2: 3–4.

22. *Tales and Novels by Maria Edgeworth* (London: Baldwin and Cradock, 1833), 17:103–4, 215. Endelman (*The Jews of Georgian England*, 46–47) makes no mention of Anti-Jewish violence during the Gordon Riots. On the relation of Scott and Edgeworth to each other and to Shakespeare, see Silvia Mergenthal, "The Shadow of Shylock: Scott's *Ivanhoe* and Edgeworth's *Harrington*," in Alexander and Hewitt, *Scott in Carnival*, 320–31.

Irish), the Turks, the Arabs. Like the ready money with which he is so often associated, he can change hands and take on new forms, shift shape and place while always remaining somehow himself, always available and always disavowed.

There seems to be no clear evidence for any meditated or sustained ill-treatment of Jews during the Gordon Riots of 1780, although foreigners and at least two foreign embassies were attacked by the mob. Anti-French sentiments were strong; since Britain was in the middle of the American Revolutionary War, France was allied with the colonists, and Lord George Gordon was leading a Protestant revolt against any lightening of the restrictions placed on Catholics. Gordon's public identity as an avenging Puritan might even have pushed him toward philo-Semitism, and indeed, he made a spectacular conversion to Judaism in 1787, living as a Jew for the rest of his life.[23] Edgeworth's favorable image of the Jew in *Harrington* is partly driven by a conscious desire to make up for a negative portrayal in *Castle Rackrent* fifteen years earlier and is very much in tune with the liberal movement building toward the mid-nineteenth-century emancipation of both Catholics and Jews. Scott arguably goes even further in his sympathy for the oppressed Jews and also examines some of the more complex racialized stereotypes that could credibly be associated with the English Middle Ages. In *Ivanhoe,* the most prominent attribute of the Jewish heroine Rebecca is her ability to heal the sick, producing near-magical cures for seemingly incurable afflictions. But Scott consistently has a hard time offering a critique of anti-Semitism without claiming (albeit in a smaller voice) that there are aspects of the Jewish character and culture that seem to invite it, and his account of the Jews' command of medical science is no exception. He admits that the attribution of "supernatural arts" is one lodged by superstitious Christians, but also identifies it as a myth exploited by the rabbis to increase their own influence. (Here he resembles Southey in his critique of the priestly orders.)

Rebecca's education as described in the novel, however, is completely rational and conventional; she was the diligent student of a gifted teacher, and her extraordinary talents came by ordinary means.[24] Nonetheless, it is these talents which almost cost her her life in being interpreted by Lucas de Beaumanoir—for his own priestly reasons—as magical, the work of a witch. Rebecca herself tries to disambiguate the always unstable function of the

23. See Katz, *History of the Jews in England,* 303–11.

24. Walter Scott, *Ivanhoe,* ed. Graham Tulloch (Edinburgh: Edinburgh University Press, 1998), 232.

pharmakon by insisting that her role is entirely curative: "Our nation, as you well know, can cure wounds, though we deal not in inflicting them" (236). In so claiming she is opposing a historically embedded tradition casting Jews as poisoners as well as healers, which proves much too powerful for her to overcome by mere good deeds. And indeed, she goes on to speak of her own family's possession of "secrets which have been handed down since the days of Solomon" (236) in ways that could only reintroduce the very aura of mystery that her secular-scientific education might otherwise refute. Where there are secrets, there is suspicion. Rebecca's control of the power of healing withholds information from public inspection and establishes her as the mistress of the *pharmakon*, one who embodies in the eyes of the other the potential for both cure and poison.[25] That it is also a career and a talent that might earn her the protection of those who otherwise despise her only adds to the complexity of Scott's narrative.

As with the Jew, so with the Arab. In *The Talisman*, Rebecca's role as healer, as controller of the drug, is played by Saladin in his disguise as Adonbec El Hakim. Scott, like Shakespeare, stages a conflation of Jew and Arab in the debate among Richard's courtiers about whether a heathen should be allowed to offer medical treatment to a Christian king. Says one:

> Again, Jews are infidels to Christianity, as well as Mahommedans. But there are few physicians in the camp excepting Jews, and such are employed without scandal or scruple. Therefore, Mahommedans may be used for their service in that capacity—*quod erat demonstrandum*.[26]

The Christian Bishop of Tyre is not convinced, protesting that the Saracens are "curious in the art of poisons" (3:193) and thus assimilating them to the negative stereotype of the Jew. In his disguise as Ilderim the warrior, Saladin responds to Sir Kenneth's amazement at his mastery of both healing and fighting:

25. I allude here again, of course, to Derrida's extraordinary essay "Plato's Pharmacy," in *Dissemination*, 61–171. Derrida reads the *Phaedrus* as unraveling the effort sustained by Socrates in the *Republic* and elsewhere to choose a preferred sense of *pharmakon*, either poison or cure, malady or remedy: an unraveling that extends to the historical institution of Platonism itself, whose supposedly intact binaries are the core of Western metaphysics.

26. Walter Scott, *Tales of the Crusaders* (Edinburgh: Constable, 1825), 3:192. This (first) edition contains both *The Betrothed* and *The Talisman*, each taking up two volumes. In *The Talisman*, Scott cites *Othello* when one of the barons asks for "ocular proof" (3:199) and almost cites *The Merchant* when Edith denies any interest in Saladin's "sun-burnt beauties" (4:170). There are also two references to Venice as a major creditor to the Crusade.

> I say to thee, Nazarene, that an accomplished cavalier should know how to dress his steed as well as how to ride him; how to forge his sword upon the stithy, as well as how to use it in battle; how to burnish his arms, as well as how to wear them; and, above all, how to cure wounds as well as how to inflict them. (4:202)

Saladin's last acts in the novel—his attempt to cure Conrade of Monserrat and his execution of the grand master of the Templars—represent his successful and judicious control of both harming and healing, which at this point is nothing less than control of the plot itself; without him there would have been no just conclusion. If he is not the stranger who invents the law, he is certainly the one who enacts it. His opposite number, Richard the Lionheart, is out of control, unaware of what is happening, and a much less efficient politician (albeit less destructive) than he was in *Ivanhoe,* where he showed himself prone to loutish drunkenness, pointless fighting, and adolescent chivalric fantasy as well as to occasionally helpful interventions. Indeed, when Saladin refuses Richard's offer to settle the fate of Palestine by single combat, political maturity is here embodied in the pagan rather than the Christian monarch, who has, moreover, been perfectly willing to condemn to death a loyal dependent for the sake of a mere flag.[27] Saladin has been throughout the perfect master of disguise and is the faultless controller of the disposition of healing and harming: hence, he is the *pharmakeus,* the master of the *pharmakon.*

The talisman itself, the wondrous elixir that heals both men and dogs, is passed on by him as a wedding present to Sir Kenneth and his bride, and thus from Palestine to Scotland and thence from medieval to modern times, but its powers are lessened in the passage:

> but though many cures were wrought by it in Europe, none equalled in success and celebrity those which the Soldan achieved. It is still in existence, having been bequeathed by the Earl of Huntingdon to a brave knight of Scotland, Sir Mungo of the Lee, in whose ancient and highly honoured family it is still preserved; and although charmed stones have been dismissed from the modern Pharmacopeia, its virtues are still applied to for stopping blood, and in cases of canine madness.[28]

27. Judith Wilt, *Secret Leaves,* argues that Saladin and not Richard is the embodiment of the "Christian chivalric ideal" (156).

28. Scott, *Tales of the Crusaders,* 4:363–64.

This is Scott's little joke, of course, reminding us that life is not much like literature, and that what works wonders in the pages of a historical novel does not fit so well into a story of local life in the present, especially one obliged to register the achievements of modern medical science. But it is more than that: it suggests that modern Scotland lacks not only the political crisis but the personal expertise and discretion that makes the talisman so much more efficacious and indeed world-historical in the hands of Saladin than in those of anyone else, and anyone coming after. In the days of primitive cures and folk medicines, any effective drug would have stood out for attention. But this one was deployed by a master who healed his enemies in the pursuit of a lasting peace by which he hoped to hang on to his territories. Its passage to western Europe is the opposite of the *translatio studii et imperii* that the British liked to invoke; it is a decline and not a summation. According to Hume, Saladin's cosmopolitan sympathies extended even beyond the grave: "By his last will he ordered charities to be distributed to the poor, without distinction of Jew, Christian, or Mahometan."[29] So too his healing powers extend to all human beings, as well as to dogs, which are, by his own law, deemed unclean.[30] This is a very different legacy from the one left by Richard the Lionheart, who contributed a lot more to popular folklore than he ever did to the well-being of his own or any other country. Saladin as dispenser of the drug-poison remains invulnerable to both the malign acts of his enemies in the story and the judgment of his narrator. His mastery of disguise makes him a Dionysus figure, but a Dionysus who does only good things for the right reasons. Unlike Rebecca's, his control of the *pharmakon* does not cause him to switch a letter and become a *pharmakos*, a scapegoat. Saladin is on his own turf, or at least a turf where he is very much at home; for all his diplomatic decorum and scrupulous hospitality he has no wish to visit the Christian homelands. Rebecca is only marginally tolerated in a country that needs her but does not want her. The talisman, when it moves north and west without its proper master, loses its power. Gifts (and implicitly commodities), it seems, cannot move neutrally across the face of the earth and have the same effect in different places. The imperfect translation of the talisman is a fantasy of precapitalist dwelling in

29. Hume, *The History of England*, 2:22.

30. *Tales of the Crusades*, 4:6. For an account of the largely positive portraits of Saladin in French, Spanish, and Italian medieval romance, see Americo Castro, "The Presence of the Sultan Saladin in the Romance Literatures," in *An Idea of History: Selected Essays of Americo Castro*, trans. Stephen Gilman and Edmund L. King (Columbus: Ohio State University Press, 1954), 241–69. Narcotics and magic figure commonly here.

place, a strike against the modern commodification of sugar, tea, and cotton that, Scott knew perfectly well, preserved their power all too well as they ruled the world of global trade in the early nineteenth century.

And what might this talisman be, that works such magic in the hands of its proper possessor, Saladin? In the revised edition of 1832, Scott provides a rare footnote toward the end of the novel, just as Sir Kenneth subsides into a healing narcotic slumber, to the effect that "some preparation of opium seems to be intimated."[31] If it is opium that "Allah hath sent on earth for a blessing, though man's weakness and wickedness have sometimes converted it into a curse,"[32] then the reported decline of its powers in modern Scotland, where it merely stops blood and mitigates canine madness, asks to be read in a rather complex spirit of irony. On the one hand, Scott seems to be saying that the Scots have a healthy contempt for opiates, that they are not addicted in the way that Coleridge and De Quincey were. In this same spirit, *Noctes Ambrosianae* published, in October 1823, a spoof of De Quincey's book in which the relation between opium intake and genius is debunked by Scottish common sense.[33] De Quincey's awed acknowledgment of the bottomless mystery of opium—"mysterious to the extent, at times, of apparent self-contradiction"—is here aggressively pooh-poohed.[34] But Scott is also making the absurd claim that such opiates have been "dismissed from the modern Pharmacopeia," knowing full well that they have not, that they are a ubiquitous staple of popular self-medication and occasionally of addiction.

Saladin too is mysterious to the point of "apparent self-contradiction," both in his mastery of disguise and variety of names—Sheerkohf, Ilderim, Adonbec el Hakim—and in the ways in which he calls up and conjures away any ocular proof of the exact physical nature of the talisman itself. Early mentions of his "drugs" focus on the difficulty of keeping apart killing and curing,[35] which Saladin himself emphasizes in stressing the vital importance of timing the action of the drug: "To awaken him now, is death or deprivation of reason" (3:176). The Christian bishop who approved

31. See the text of *The Talisman* published as volume 38 of the Magnum Opus edition (Edinburgh: Robert Cadell, 1829–32), 370. Scott worked on the revisions for the Crusader novels in March–April, 1831; see Jane Millgate, *Scott's Last Edition: A Study in Publishing History* (Edinburgh: Edinburgh University Press, 1987), 25, 70.

32. Scott, *Tales of the Crusaders*, 4:195.

33. For an account, see Margaret Russett, *De Quincey's Romanticism: Canonical Minority and the Forms of Transmission* (Cambridge: Cambridge University Press, 1997), 129–32.

34. De Quincey, *Confessions of an English Opium Eater*, 240.

35. Scott, *Tales of the Crusaders*, 3:165–169.

El Hakim's credentials as a healer also articulates a fear of Saracen talent "in the art of poisons" that can take weeks to act, and of the ability to infuse ordinary objects—cloth, leather, paper, and parchment—with fatal substances (3:193). It is not clear whether there is a single drug that Saladin dispenses over and over again in different forms, or whether he carries a diverse supply, only one of which is the talisman of the novel's title. He first applies to Sir Kenneth's servant "a sponge from a small silver box, dipt perhaps in some aromatic distillation," which works like smelling salts but whose exact identity is not specified (3:200). He then administers a "second cup" (we did not see the first) of a "most holy elixir" made with water and the contents of a "small silken bag . . . the contents of which the byestanders could not discover" (3:202). When he treats King Richard it is with the contents of a "small red purse" (3:231), also withheld from the sight of others and from us. Later on the power of what is called the "talisman" is attributed to "Divine Intelligences" apparent in the movements of the heavens and requiring its possessor to perform twelve cures a month. Here again it is a substance infused in water, but it is also called an "amulet" (4:75–76). When Sir Kenneth is sent into his blissful sleep later still in the story, he is given a "small portion of a dark-coloured fluid" (4:195).

On this last occasion El Hakim/Saladin is explicit about the *pharmakon* nature of the talisman (if that is what it is), and what he says sounds very like De Quincey's account of the antithetical properties of opium:

> "This," he said, "is one of those productions which Allah hath sent on earth for a blessing, though man's weakness and wickedness have sometimes converted it into a curse. It is powerful as the wine-cup of the Nazarene to drop the curtain on the sleepless eye, and to relieve the burthen of the overloaded bosom; but when applied to the purposes of indulgence and debauchery, it rends the nerves, destroys the strength, weakens the intellect, and undermines life. But fear not thou to use its virtues in the time of need, for the wise man warms him by the same firebrand with which the madman burneth the tent."[36]

Did Scott have opium in mind all along as the identity of the talisman, though it went unmentioned until a footnote toward the end of the second edition? The 1832 revised text came with a new preface, which, interestingly, discusses the interactive, dialectical relation between the Christian and pagan monarchs, with Richard showing "all the cruelty and violence

36. Ibid., 4:195.

of an Eastern sultan" while Saladin shows his expertise in the "deep policy and prudence of a European sovereign."[37] Extremes meet, solid identities dissolve, the strange becomes the familiar, rather as they do in the operations of the talisman. Scott's preface goes on to give an extended account of the folklore behind the last page of the novel, where the afterlife of the talisman in Scotland is described. Here he says that there is a specific "relic," also called a "pebble" and an "amulet" and now known as the "Lee-penny" (ix–x), which can be dipped in water for medicinal purposes, including the cure of persons bitten by mad dogs. There is an appendix to the preface in which an old tale of Richard as a cannibal, eating the heads of Saracens to make up for the short supply of pork, is reprinted. Is there here an implied parody of the consumption of exotic substances associated with opium eating (and De Quincey), coming as this does close on the heels of the anecdote about the fate of an exotic drug?

As with so many of Scott's editorial incursions, this is all rather undecidable, a sort of textual *pharmakon* in itself, a strange device for the production of estrangement. But in thus reducing the power of the talisman in modern Scotland, Scott seems to be wishing away the global opium trade that he must have known was critical to the wealth of British India and, by the end of the 1830s, was to bring about war with China (I shall have more to say about the opium trade in chapter 6; only a brief outline is called for here). Asia Minor was indeed the only commercial source of opium in the twelfth century, from whence it spread into India and perhaps China along with the expansion of Islam; but since 1757 opium had been the exclusive monopoly of the East India Company, which took over the China trade from the Portuguese in 1773, after which the rest, as they say, is history. Inability to manage the dosage afflicted not only such famous individual cases as those of Coleridge and De Quincey, but also the body of the British Empire as it sought to channel opium toward the abjected stranger by enforcing Chinese consumption and its own economic gain by military violence. Opium, when Scott was writing *The Talisman*, was no merely residual curiosity left over from times past but a critical component of the global-imperial economy. Sir Mungo of the Lees would then have been lucky to be able to more or less ignore it. Only Saladin shows himself able to maintain the rigorous personal discipline necessary to the successful administering of the talisman: "severe restrictions, painful observances, fasts, and penance."[38]

37. Scott, *The Talisman* (1832), vi.

38. Ibid., 4:75. Thus, Derrida reads Socrates in the *Timaeus* as counseling avoidance of the use of medicine altogether whenever possible; see *Dissemination*, 101.

Above all, the talisman is not a commodity but remains outside the sphere of commerce and profit, the very protocols of modern empire:

> "I sell not the wisdom with which Allah has endowed me," answered the Arabian physician; "and be it known to you, great Prince, that the divine medicine, of which you have partaken, would lose its effects in my unworthy hands, did I exchange it either for gold or diamonds." (3:269–70)

The positive application of the purely beneficial element of the *pharmakon* is then no longer possible in a nineteenth-century world governed entirely by the rage for profit; much better that it remain hidden away up in Scotland and applied only to low-level domestic ailments. Sir Mungo of the Lees, we must assume, either had no investments in the China trade or did not look too carefully at what his brokers were buying and selling. Comically enough, Scott himself embarked on the Magnum Opus edition largely to pay his debts, and the cheap editions it made available were intended to sell in as much bulk as possible.[39] That *The Talisman* might have been itself a talisman, a sort of literary opiate helping Scott regain his own commercial health, is knowingly suggested in the introduction to the first edition, which invents a meeting of a would-be joint stock company at which there is some discussion of the mechanical mass-production of novels.[40]

The end of the novel leaves us, in this way, uncomfortably back in the modern world, where satire produces the very conditions it is pretending to dismiss: a mass market for both books and opium. But even in the twelfth century, very few positive ambitions or performances are evident in the England that Scott describes in his Crusader novels. At the end of *Ivanhoe*, Rebecca and her father, Isaac, both of whom narrowly escaped being murdered, are on their way to Moorish Spain, "for less cruel are the cruelties of the Moors unto the race of Jacob, than the cruelties of the Nazarenes of England."[41] The agent of healing—here Jewish and, unlike Saladin, unable or unwilling to kill her enemies—goes into exile, seeking in the Islamic world a tolerance that is not available in Christian England. She still holds the secrets of the *pharmakon* but has become the scapegoat, the *pharmakos*. She and Saladin both refuse to share their medical secrets with those Saladin calls the "uncircumcised," as if to align himself with the Jew, as he

39. See Millgate, *Scott's Last Edition*, 2–10.

40. Scott, *Tales of the Crusaders*, 1:i–xxviii.

41. Scott, *Ivanhoe*, 336.

does again in invoking the myth of Moses (Moussa ben Amran).[42] Both of them share a refusal to eat pork. But Rebecca the Jew is alone in becoming a scapegoat, and in this respect she is very like Othello the Moor. He too is accused of dark magic in winning Desdemona's affections: "Damned as thou art, thou hast enchanted her," says Brabantio (1.2.82), a suspicion he repeats twice more. Lucas De Beaumanoir chooses to explain Rebecca's power over Sir Brian in just the same way. In one of the last dialogues of the novel Rebecca tells Rowena that "the people of England are a fierce race, quarreling ever with their neighbours or among themselves, and ready to plunge the sword into the bowels of each other. Such is no safe abode for the children of my people. . . . Not in a land of war and blood, surrounded by hostile neighbours, and distracted by internal factions, can Israel hope to rest during her wanderings."[43] This speech counters Rebecca's earlier avowal, in the first flush of romantic affection for Ivanhoe, of belonging where she is: "I am of England, Sir Knight, and speak the English tongue, although my dress and my lineage belong to another climate" (235). In pressuring Rebecca into exile, England is losing its most efficient agent of healing the wounds which its own violent culture inevitably creates. Rebecca's departure makes her healing powers an inverted image of Saladin's talisman: she is exiled and abjected though still willing and able to heal, while the talisman *is* imported but proves less efficacious in the rational north than it had been in its native place—and correspondingly less able to affect in a positive way the course of national and international politics.

The violence that dominates English life is both transnational and intranational, and its portrayal in *Ivanhoe* is unremittingly negative. Jews and Saxons alike are brutalized by the Normans—the novel contains some powerful scenes of the physical torture of both—and Saxons and Normans fight each other and compete in violence against Jews and Arabs. The romanticized culture of chivalry that figures so prominently in Western culture is pointedly undercut by Scott's verdict on the tournament at Ashby, the so-called "Gentle and Free Passage of Arms" that left behind it a pile of dead and wounded men, including one "smothered by the heat of his armour."[44] In *The Talisman*, Scott suggests that the culture of chivalry is a European invention[45]—implicitly denying the arguments of Herder, Warton, and others that it was in fact of Arabic origin and imported into Europe through

42. Scott, *Tales of the Crusaders*, 3:228, 4:80.

43. Scott, *Ivanhoe*, 399.

44. Ibid., 115.

45. Scott, *Tales of the Crusaders*, 3:19.

Spain—and that it has had a moderating influence on the primitive barbarism of the desert dwellers. But it is Saladin who is now the exemplary bearer of the chivalric ideal; the disciples seem to have improved upon the wisdom of their teachers. And in *Ivanhoe*'s portrayal of the chivalric code operating within the homeland there is little or nothing said about its benefits. The expense of horses, armor and the pageantry of public display is only met by coercive borrowing from the Jews, and the glitter of "merry England" is but a mask for the basest policies and practices.

The chosen exile of Rebecca and Isaac, a fictional foretaste of the historical banishment of English Jews in 1290, rebukes any claim England might have to a benign cosmopolitanism, a tolerance or welcoming of the other, an ability to entertain the enemy as a friend (as Saladin does in *The Talisman*). The three peoples of the book are all gathered briefly under the roof of Cedric of Rotherwood at the beginning of the novel and kept briefly from mutual violence by a Saxon culture of hospitality that is visibly part of a dying world; it is negated explicitly in the insulting treatment of Saxon guests by the Norman Prince John later in the book. Even Ivanhoe, who speaks Saxon, French, and Arabic and who is the novel's best image of the accommodationist new generation, is unable to imagine intimacy (let alone marriage) with a Jewess. Apart from the pacificist Rebecca, and to some degree her father, the transnational personalities in the novel are largely negative, so that the stubborn ethnic traditionalisms of the Saxons are balanced most visibly only by an unappealing, self-interested Norman cosmopolitanism typified by the cynical Sir Brian Bois-Guilbert and the ruthless Lucas de Beaumanoir. Sir Brian is a figure of rational enlightenment whose secularism and openness to the other is accompanied by a violent self-interest and a willingness to pursue his desires almost to the point of rape. He will join any nation or religion that lets him have his way. Beaumanoir is even less admirable, a repressed sadist in office who exemplifies the Christian conflation of the enemy other as both Jew and Arab, interchangably; he is, in Isaac's words, "a cruel destroyer of the Saracens, and a cruel tyrant to the Children of the Promise,"[46] one who holds "the murther of a Jew to be an offering of as sweet savour as the death of a Saracen" (303). He blames the corruption of his order on its openness to the cultures of its enemies: "they are charged with studying the accursed cabalistical secrets of the Jews, and the magic of the Paynim Saracens" (306). Jew and Arab are again joined together as agents of corruption, but the corruption (and Beaumanoir cannot see it as anything else) is unavoidable. The Templars cannot manage con-

46. Scott, *Ivanhoe*, 302.

tact with foreign culture except by self-barbarisation, creating the brutality they claim to discover. In both *The Talisman* and *Ivanhoe* the Templars are an embodiment of a subversive transnational faction owing no allegiance to anything beyond their own self-interest. Scott here makes of a medieval Christian subculture what many would later make of the Jesuits, the Freemasons and the Illuminati. When the Templars go into exile at the end of *Ivanhoe*, it is to the music of a "wild march, of an oriental character" (394). The black slaves standing ready to feed the fire that was to consume Rebecca, and the Saracen servants assisting Front-de-Boeuf in the torture by fire of Isaac, are both images of Orientalized brutality that claim as victims the similarly Orientalized Jews, who prove unable to register in the eyes of the English (Saxon or Norman) as anything other than threatening exotics. Even Robin Hood's outlaw band, which shares with the Jews a position of exclusion, is unable to respond to its fellow sufferers with anything much beyond outright and violent racism.

The Betrothed gives a similarly dark account of the chaos and confusion wrought upon the homeland by the Crusade, which De Lacy joins against his will and better judgment, leaving a power vacuum along the Welsh borders that was then filled with even more cruelty and corruption than existed there already.[47] Jews are only a peripheral presence in this novel, figuring incidentally along with the Lombards as opportunistic traders "despising danger when there was a chance of gain"; there is also a "learned Jewish leech" reported as giving an opinion on the fragile health of Damian de Lacy.[48] Here the role of the despised other is played by the Flemings, though when their property is pillaged they are explicitly compared to the Jews who suffered a similar fate:

> There have been tumults among the English rabble in more than one county, and their wrath is directed at those of our nation, as if we were Jews or heathens, and not better Christians and better men than themselves, They have, at York, Bristol, and elsewhere, sacked the houses of the Flemings, spoiled their goods, misused their families, and murdered themselves.—And why?—except that we have brought among them the skill and the industry which they possessed not; and because wealth,

47. The anarchy and confusion created in the homelands by the campaigns of kings and barons in Palestine on behalf of a dangerous transnational power, the papacy, is one of the themes that might allow us to read Scott as favoring by historical anticipation the coherently administered modern nation-state.

48. Scott, *Tales of the Crusaders*, 1:180, 318.

> which they would never else have seen in Britain, was the reward of our art and our toil. (2:191–92)

There finally is a place for the Flemings but it is a close call, and in this avowal of identity with the Jews, who also famously suffered massacre at York, Wilkin Flammock (the speaker here) pinpoints the hostility to any improvements or benefits that appear to be under the control and at the dispensation of the other, the foreigner. Flemish prudence and industry and Jewish healing and moneylending (this last necessary not only to the routine functions of the state and to the tax base but specifically to the wholesale financing of the Christian crusades) are similarly despised and feared despite (or perhaps because of) the positive things they contribute.[49] Jews and Flemings both work hard to preserve and make flourish the very nation-state that maintains the persecution of their own persons. The Flemings are eventually accepted, but for the Jews, there is no enduring tolerance.

In *Ivanhoe* and *The Talisman*, only one prospect for acceptance and integration is proposed and then denied: conversion. Rebecca is first offered this option by Bois-Guilbert, though not in any form that she might respect. While professing knowledge of and respect for "the Great Father who made both Jew and Gentile."[50] Rebecca is deeply committed to remaining a Jew and is able to resist also the less aggressive blandishments of Rowena, who once again offers her a safe life as a Christian: "I may not change the fate of my fathers like a garment unsuited to the climate in which I seek to dwell, and unhappy, lady, I will not be" (400). Her loyalty to her faith and her sense of its exclusive importance to her own identity are nonetheless figuratively breached by Scott when he casts her in the role of Christ healing the bedridden man (324), just as her trial before Beaumanoir deliberately recalls the appearance of Jesus before Pilate (who was rather less sure of himself than is Scott's fanatical grand master). The Jew here seems to be the best Christian. Rebecca is also more open to Ivanhoe's charms than he is to hers, making her not just a sentimental heroine but a figure of greater sympathetic capacity than he ever manages to become; she is able at once to feel the beginnings of love and also refrain from blaming him for the display of coldness that comes when he learns that she is Jewish, a coldness she herself never feels or shows (235–36). Her refusal of the offer of conversion is then all the more meaningful because of her emotional openness to the other, her

49. According to Endelman (*The Jews of Georgian England*, 13), at the end of the twelfth century, one-seventh of the state's revenue came from taxes and exactions on the Jews.

50. Scott, *Ivanhoe*, 237.

willingness to answer enmity with friendship, while remaining committed to her faith and identity.

The question of conversion is raised again in *The Talisman*, after Saladin proposes a marriage between himself and Edith Plantagenet. The political prudence of such an alliance begins to convince even the initially prejudiced King Richard that it might be worth encouraging, but Edith is resolute to the point of bigotry and will on no condition entertain the idea of marrying a pagan. Richard for a while thinks that there might be a possibility of converting Saladin to the Christian faith, but Saladin shows himself immoveable in the face of any such temptation, and it is he who utters the strongest denunciation of any conversion not achieved as the result of sincerely spiritual motivations: "Have I not told thee that Saladin desires no converts saving those whom the holy prophet shall dispose themselves to submit to his law? Violence and bribery are alike alien to his plan for extending the true faith."[51] The topic of conversion was very much in the air in the early nineteenth century. Sydney Owenson's (Lady Morgan's) *The Missionary* (1811), which will be discussed in chapter 7, tells the story of a Franciscan monk who sets out for India greatly confident of assisting the spread of Christianity only to learn both personally and professionally the powers of habit and tradition both in himself and in those he sets out to convert. Southey's *Madoc* (1805) and *Tale of Paraguay* (1825) explore the same topic. Edgeworth's *Harrington* finesses the problem of an apparently unresolvable romance between a Christian and a Jewess (with no conversion in sight) by pulling a rabbit out of a hat, revealing the heroine as a Protestant after all. Berenice's Jewish father indeed approves of Harrington's unwillingness to give up his Christian religion for the sake of his passion. In all of these cases, the pains and even tragedies of the effort at conversion are transcribed (as they are by Southey and Owenson) and the persistence in one's faith is approved even if it does not produce happiness. Scott similarly seems to endorse Rebecca's commitment to Judaism and Saladin's equally principled adherence to Islam. This leaves open only two outcomes: toleration within an inclusive and unprejudiced nation-state (the usual example at the time was the United States) or separate development in different places.[52] Richard's ignominious return from Palestine leaves Saladin in

51. Scott, *Tales of the Crusaders*, 4:204.

52. There is a very good account of Scott's understanding of the problems of acting on one's recognition of the rights of others in Harry E. Shaw, *Narrating Reality: Austen, Scott, Eliot* (Ithaca, NY: Cornell University Press, 1999), 168–217. Shaw argues that moments of passion undermine whatever habits of tolerance and respect have been built up between exemplary individuals of different nations or affiliations. Shylock's punishment, we recall, is forced conversion.

charge and can be read as a rebuke to acts of militant empire building and violent religious proselytism. For Saladin's state is the one within which genuine tolerance appears possible: there is no urge to convert the other into an image of the self. "Saladin desires no converts."[53] Richard's England is a much less wholesome environment, and offers little prospect of either ethnic unity or benign cosmopolitan tolerance. It cannot close its borders nor can it comfortably welcome strangers.

The Crusader novels can then be taken to register a possibility, need, or desire for the sort of open-mindedness to foreign elements that the historical record (and its depiction in the novels) could not support. By the time of their setting, Saxon, Norman, and Welsh had over a century to fashion a respectful coexistence but failed to do so, and there was no place for the Jews. Michael Ragussis has argued that *Ivanhoe* is a powerful critique of the besetting English zeal for conversion that was explicit in Sharon Turner's history of the Middle Ages and made empirically present to Scott's own generation in the form of evangelical societies aggressively seeking to convert the Jews.[54] He shrewdly notices that the novel opens in a place where Druid artifacts have been destroyed "probably by the zeal of some convert to Christianity,"[55] and that the story is full of variously comic and violent efforts at conversion, mostly directed at women: Rowena and Rebecca are pressured to change their affiliations and/or religions, and Ulrica (Urfried) succumbs to a similar coercion. Wamba and Gurth's opening conversation about the differences between Anglo-Saxon and Norman French words highlights translation as another attribute of the trope of conversion and spells out the influence of power and social class in governing the evolution of the language that would come to be called English. All of these observations lead Ragussis to decide that Scott is engaged in a sustained dismantling of the model that seems to govern some of his other novels, one celebrating the evolving accommodation of different identities subgroups within a unified nation-state.

This seems right. There is something deeply disturbing and uncontainable in the actual and incipient violence between and among the subgroups

53. Scott, *Tales of the Crusaders*, 4:204. The same claim has been made by Judaism, and the historical evidence is variable in both cases. But Christianity alone seems to have had *no* phase at which conversion was not its object.

54. Ragussis, *Figures of Conversion*, 89–126. See also Gauri Viswanathan, *Outside the Fold: Conversion, Modernity, and Belief* (Princeton, NJ: Princeton University Press, 1998), 2–43, for an account of the general tensions about conversions among and between Catholics, Protestants and Jews in the early nineteenth century. There is a more detailed summary in Endelman, *The Jews of Georgian England*, 71–85.

55. Scott, *Ivanhoe*, 18.

that appear in the Crusader novels. Ian Duncan has suggested that Scott is here (and elsewhere) representing "an oriental horizon of imperial conquest, which is the site of an uncanny or demonic figuration of cultural origins."[56] These figurations are often deadened or dismissed. The talisman is robbed of its uncanny powers with the passing of time and its movement through space, while Rebecca is sent back to the south. In neither case is a premodernized England able to explain, control, or deploy the conjunction of benefit and disturbance that marks the *unheimlich* in the *heimlich*, the strange in the familiar, the foreign in the domestic. Saladin's command of the powers of destruction and restoration (sword and talisman) for political and human good is not matched by the returning Richard; Rebecca's near-magical healing abilities are not assimilable or properly appreciated by a bigoted population of self-styled patriots who cannot distinguish the human from the purportedly demonic, and who must interpret good as somehow the signature of evil. In *Ivanhoe* there is a more or less conscious unanimity among the Saxons and Normans that Jews are out of place in the England they are trying to divide up between them. Yet both Sir Brian (in an extreme form that will destroy him) and Wilfred of Ivanhoe (in a milder form that marks him as a prototypical Englishman) undergo a desire for the other in the shape of the exotic Rebecca. In neither case is the desire allowed to approach fulfillment; nor does Saladin's interest in Edith get beyond its early appearance. In *The Talisman*, the Islamic other is left behind, forgotten, and (as the talisman itself) fictionally disempowered as a significant agent in the development of the homeland. In *The Betrothed*, the Flemings fare rather better, but it is a close call; and they are, after all, "racially" akin to their hosts.

The compound Jew-Arab/Arab-Jew identity functions as the limit case of the foreign, as well as that of exotic womanhood and queer, shapeshifting sexuality. Both of these novels are full of disguises. In *Ivanhoe*, Wilfred, Richard, Robin of Loxley, and Gurth all hide their identities, and in *The Talisman* Saladin himself is a near-magical shape-shifter, although Sir Kenneth also plays the role of a Nubian, hard to maintain for a commonsense Scotsman but driven by duty. Saladin does not quite dress as a woman, but it would not have been beyond his talents, and in some ways he is more thoroughly feminized (in the eyes of others) than the pious and inflexible Edith. He certainly appeals to a strong urge for homosocial and perhaps homoerotic companionship in both Richard and Sir Kenneth, who get to

56. Ian Duncan, "Scott's Romance of the Empire: The *Tales of the Crusaders*," in Alexander and Hewitt, *Scott in Carnival*, 370.

teeter on the edge of playing the Pentheus figure without having to take the tragic plunge. Saladin replicates Dionysus in his ability to be both terrible and gentle[57] according to the behavior and desserts of others; the master of opium and the god of wine share a function as deciders of positive and negative outcomes from ambivalent substances. Saladin's godlike dimension works only for the good; it also has about it a touch of Socrates, as he guides his bewildered Crusader friends to a knowledge of the complexity of human relations.[58] When he teasingly reveals himself to Sir Kenneth it is by posing a riddle about what proper term he might be named by. Requesting admission to Sir Kenneth's tent, he disavows successively the roles of master, physician, and friend: "But if I come not as a master? . . . Neither come I now as a physician . . . Yet once again . . . supposing I come not as a friend?" Finally he "reveals" himself: "I come, then, . . . as your ancient foe; but a fair and generous one."[59] The devil himself, the ancient foe, is here included in the benign catchment of the shape-shifter, more generous than those willing to ravage the health and well-being of millions of people (domestic and foreign) by maintaining the nineteenth-century opium trade.

The respective fortunes of Saladin and Rebecca, who have so much in common as figures of the *pharmakeus*, make for an instructive contrast. Saladin, though originally a stranger to Syria—he was a Seljuk Kurd from Tikrit (in modern Iraq)—is very much at home in the deserts of Palestine, and always in control. He is the host who teases his enemies into becoming his friends. He is also a man, and one who does not hesitate to wield the power of death when the need arises.[60] Rebecca is a woman and a despised interloper not even accorded the status of a guest worth properly receiving. She is from the first out of place, and her treatment is a reflection of her absolute vulnerability to the same kinds of persons who will receive much-needed lessons in basic civility from Saladin. Saladin is too powerful ever to suffer as a scapegoat (*pharmakos*), which is the fate that befalls

57. Euripides, *The Bacchae*, translated Arthur S. Way (Cambridge, MA: Harvard University Press; London: W. Heinemann, 1962), 860–61.

58. Derrida reads the *Meno* as evidence of Socrates's incarnation as a worker of magic in *Dissemination* (118); and the *Phaedrus* for its playful invocation of Socrates as (like) a foreigner (70–71).

59. Scott, *Tales of the Crusaders*, 4:201, 202. Where Saladin "stands" is further complicated by his habit of referring to his Christian enemies collectively as belonging to "Frangistan." This term (as *Frankistan*), according to the *Oxford English Dictionary* (2nd ed.), could either include or exclude the Ottoman Empire, depending upon which particular alliance was being projected.

60. Herder, *Reflections on the Philosophy of the History of Mankind*, attributes the West's knowledge of both gunpowder and rag paper to the Arabs: the power to destroy and the power to educate. They also introduced "spiritous liquors" as "medicines" which have since "spread themselves as poisons" (396).

Rebecca when both the desire she arouses and her healing talents are ascribed to witchcraft. But the gruff and brutal Christians in Richard's desert camp are not so different from the Norman barons on the home front, many of whom are indeed returned crusaders; they just have fewer opportunities to be cruel. Let us recall those words of Portia about the "quality of mercy" that were produced to belittle Shylock's moral status while talking up the superiority of Christian doctrine. In *Ivanhoe,* the Saxon lady Rowena forgives the Norman De Bracy who has set his heart on her, and forgives him "as a Christian." Wamba the fool says that this means "that she does not forgive him at all."[61]

It will not have passed unnoticed that the world I have been describing is very like our own. The modernization narrative of the Waverley novels is at best historically specific to one reading of the period from about 1600 to 1800, a two-hundred-year span in which one could defend (though not everyone has defended) the idea of a Whig history, but only (if at all) with the admission that this is a long way from an uncontested paradigm. How fully Scott ever embraced this model is now—and because of now—more open to question than before. Perhaps he really did intuit the collapse or failed emergence of peaceful cosmopolitanism, as he could well have done given the global politics of his time. Certainly his insistence on the integrity of the refusal to convert, along with his refusal to suggest that tolerance of radical difference is attainable, makes the Crusader novels apt indicators of a condition of antagonism that is, then as now, typified by the conflation of Arab and Jew as the figure of the enemy of the West. What the Crusader novels also suggest is something that we are not currently much in the habit of imagining: that the exclusion of the most foreign of foreign elements entails a critical loss of curative power for the West. They imply that what most threatens the self-image of the Christian nation-states is also that which offers them almost magical capacities for physical and political regeneration under the conditions of friendship. Lavishing as they do so much creative attention and affection on the charismatic figures of Rebecca and Saladin, the Jew and the Arab, the mistress and master of the *pharmakon,* these novels perform a memorial function in the realm of fiction that is similarly antagonistic to the West's prevailing figment of the other who is the enemy, but who is also the desired erotic object or ego ideal and thus the figure of romance itself. Scott reminds us not only that in subscribing to a gesture of radical "othering" we are possibly missing out on the benefits of welcoming the stranger, the person who knows just the right dose

61. Scott, *Ivanhoe,* 275.

of the drugs we most need, but also that the current twenty-first-century obsession with the enemy as Arab is just a hair's breadth away from, indeed may be deeply at one with, a hostility toward the Jew. Hospitality, as Derrida has shown us over and over, is a concept whose time is yet to come, and may never come. It is also a risk: one never knows what or who is to come. Scott's Crusader novels, despite their nod toward a potential coming reconciliation of Saxon and Norman, are masterful portrayals of the refusal of hospitality, and they offer a very gloomy account of the consequences of that refusal. As such they are inevitably novels for our time.

CHAPTER FOUR

Small Print and Wide Horizons

STRANGERS ON THE PAGE

Recall that in "Frost at Midnight" the figure of the stranger is, in the early printings of the poem, explained in a footnote, made familiar as an attribute of folklore even as it typographically estranged by being set aside from the main text. Its meaning is thereby "called out," to use publisher's parlance, and rendered more exact, while at the same time the main text is implicitly found wanting, in need of further explication. Something more needs to be said, but it appears in small print, as if not fully belonging to the poem, and yet somehow pertinent. There is no poem "in itself," the beloved object of the New Critical tradition, until Coleridge removes the footnote in the later printings. Coleridge's footnote does not much distract us, though it does reflect back upon the poem by making the narrator seem less alone, part of a folk community. In the second edition of *The Talisman*, as we have just seen, Scott's simple annotation—"Some preparation of opium seems to be intimated"[1]—is somewhat more explosive. Its coyly casual rhetoric, seeming to demand only the most minimal attention as a sort of aside, opens the novel to a global-historical-economic narrative that could hardly be imagined if Saladin's healing elixir were *not* an opiate. Following one brief incursion of the typesetter's hand, the whole modern opium trade comes pouring onto the pages of the novel.

What happens when fiction and poetry invite us to turn to a footnote, an endnote, a marginal gloss? Not the least of the challenges posed by the appearance of T. S. Eliot's *The Waste Land* in 1922 was its inclusion of footnotes. How is one to read them? Are they part of "the poem" or just

1. Scott, *The Talisman* (1832), 370.

addenda, items one might opt to consult but not essential to an understanding of the verse? Eliot does not help much in suggesting that his own notes are but pale reflections of the sources he is drawing upon, so that if we really want to unscramble the poem's "difficulties" then further reading is required, especially in Jessie L. Weston's *From Ritual to Romance* and in Frazer's *The Golden Bough*.[2] The notes, in other words, do not resolve or clinch the meanings of the poem but simply send us on to other references behind them; and if some of these in turn contain footnotes of their own then the process risks becoming inexhaustible. To enter into reading the extended poem is then to give up on any prospect of exiting with any assurance of adequate meaning. One must commit to reading, in prospect, all the books ever written: strangers all the way down.

Eliot is certainly anxious to get something across. He seems not to trust his reader to recognize citations from Shakespeare or the Old Testament, let alone the more obviously obscure items from Wagner, Ovid, Hesse or Baudelaire. Along the way that reader might or might not care to know that the North American hermit thrush has been described by the ornithological experts as sounding much as Eliot transcribes it, and that Tiresias (in case we are struggling) is really "the most important personage"[3] in the poem's narrative. The notes, then, are something of a miscellany, a bit of this and a bit of that, sometimes precise and sometimes not. The message seems to be that we can take them or leave them, but that if we leave them then we are not quite serious or intellectually curious enough. To a generation of readers who grew up with Tennyson, Swinburne, and Browning, or even Keats and Wordsworth, this must have been something of a shock. If the notes are intended to put us fully in the know, then there are nowhere near enough of them. Are they instead there to remind us of how much we don't know, standing in as the tips of all sorts of icebergs afloat on the strange seas of the world's cultures, past and present? Eliot, like Arnold before him, had a habit of accusing poets he did not like (Tennyson and the romantics among them) of a failure of knowledge. What knowledge or ignorance is imparted or implied by his own poem and its notes?

One hundred and twenty-one years earlier, in 1801, Robert Southey published the first edition of his *Thalaba the Destroyer* in two small octavo volumes. One would have a fair chance, opening either at random, of coming upon a few lines of poetry floating above a sea of small print, for Southey's poem is full of footnotes. He claims to have wanted them gathered at the

2. T. S. Eliot, *The Complete Poems and Plays of T. S. Eliot* (London: Faber and Faber, 1969), 76.

3. Ibid., 78.

end of the poem, as endnotes, so as not to interfere with the flow of the verse, and in later editions this indeed came about.[4] But in this first edition, for whatever reason, Messrs Biggs and Cottle of Bristol and/or Longman and Rees of Paternoster Row produced the book with the notes at the bottom of the page. Not uncommonly, there are only two or three lines of verse set at the top of the page with the rest given over to the notes. But Southey's reader would have been less shocked than Eliot's at what the book performed, though some of them certainly complained about the density of references. The reader of 1801 could have looked back to Southey's own 1796 *Joan of Arc* (whose second edition in 1798 came out with even more footnotes than the first), to Sir William Jones's translations from the Persian and Sanskrit, to annotated novels like Fielding's *Tom Jones* and Beckford's *Vathek*, and beyond that to the poems of Thomas Gray and to the satires of Pope and Swift, among other things. If that same reader had lived another twenty years or so then he or she would have seen a whole array of annotated poems and novels come onto the market. Many of them, like Scott's, were best sellers. The first three decades of the nineteenth century saw the heyday of a genre that has almost disappeared: annotated poetry and fiction. Perhaps most remote of all from the modern mainstream sensibility is the encyclopedic long poem, something between epic and romance, taking as its topic some real or fanciful episode in history or fiction, whether local and national or set in some far-flung corner of the remoter world, and requiring for its proper assimilation an army of footnotes. Scott, Shelley, Moore, and Southey, among others, wrote such poems.

There is no ready and easy name for this genre. We would need a Henry Fielding to lend us a form of words. Let us call it, for now (and just this once), the geopolitical encyclopedic epic-romance in English verse. It has been more or less forgotten by canonical literary history, but it was itself a late emanation of a debate that took form a hundred or so years before Southey, that between the so-called ancients and moderns, where what was at stake was nothing less than the matter of what we can know about other cultures or about our own culture's pasts, and how we might best go about finding out. Recourse to notes is the symptom of an uncertainty or anxiety about the remote, the foreign, the unfamiliar or the strange. Notes may expand our horizons into uncontainable archives or perform closure by providing a seemingly incontrovertible source or fact. But when the gesture of closure

4. There is some doubt about what he really wanted: see Dahlia Porter, "Formal Relocations: The Method of Southey's *Thalaba the Destroyer* (1801)," *European Romantic Review* 20 (2009): 677.

becomes too emphatic it can generate further doubt. Perhaps it is only now, in the light of a professional responsiveness to questions of globalism, diversity and postcoloniality, and under pressure from a history now commonly perceived as one of racism and imperialism, that we might be driven to speculate about the significance of Robert Southey's footnotes.

What *is* a footnote? Above all, and quite mechanically, it is a demand or an invitation to lift our eyes off the page, to disturb the contemplative spell that good poetry weaves around us as we read, and to look outside a main text (though not of course *hors-texte*) for significant information. It is, in a very simple physiological way that involves the movements of the body and the persistence or failure of the attention span, a technique of estrangement even as it can promise to render something more familiar and more assured in its pedigree or provenance. It sends us *elsewhere* without really settling in advance what we will find when we go there. It threatens the uncanny even as it may actually deliver nothing more alarming than a title and a page number. There is no way to know whether its content will prove ironic, as Gibbon's notes famously do; or satiric of the whole genre of scholarship itself, as Pope's usually are; or irrelevant, nothing more than a defensive display of authority; or simply false, the citation of a nonexistent source invoked in a spirit of parody or sheer fraud. There is also no way to know whether the next footnote in a given text will be of the same sort as its predecessor. It can be the briefest of references or the longest of digressions; it can even be a thing unto itself and generate its own footnotes. But it is always, as Gérard Genette writes, "a break in the enunciative regime" which subsists on "a very undefined fringe between text and paratext."[5] As such, it is a stranger who may or may not be welcome, depending upon what it has to say, how long it takes to say it, and where it leads us and leaves us; upon whether it confirms us in what we know or challenges us with new and difficult acknowledgments; upon whether it returns us safely to ourselves or abandons us on some unknown frontier, in a land of strangers.[6]

5. Gérard Genette, *Paratexts: Thresholds of Interpretation*, trans. Jane E. Lewin (Cambridge: Cambridge University Press, 1997), 328, 332. The French title, *Seuils*, more fully captures the author's placing of his inquiry in the context of the host-guest syndrome: at the threshold. See also Shari Benstock, "At the Margin of Discourse: Footnotes in the Fictional Text," *Publications of the Modern Language Association* 98 (1983): 204–25. Benstock, analyzing Fielding, Sterne, and Joyce, finds that such footnotes embody a "genuine ambivalence" (204), pointing inside and outside the text at the same time.

6. Thus, Shari Benstock: "to read a footnote is to be reminded of the inherent multitextuality of all texts" ("At the Margin of Discourse," 220n2).

We have not always had the footnote among us, though it seems to have been very much in the typographic picture by about 1700.[7] It relates to but is not the same as the marginal gloss which preceded it historically and which famously lives on in the second version of Coleridge's poem about the ancient mariner. One might speculate that it became popular for technological, rhetorical, or ideological reasons, or any combination thereof. Perhaps footnotes were less expensive to set than glosses, as Lawrence Lipking suggests; perhaps they were felt to be useful in curbing a tendency to mental or bodily enthusiasm, which was a common concern about the increased popularity of reading.[8] There are no absolute distinctions between footnotes and marginal glosses, headnotes, endnotes, and appendices, all of which are open to various uses. Southey's footnotes stage an encounter between English and foreign poetry, history, and culture and open questions about the relations between imagination and fact, and among poetry and ethnography and history. Southey does not give much away in calling *Thalaba the Destroyer* the "*Arabesque* ornament of an Arabian tale" that he proposes to hand over to his public with "something like the accident of feeling."[9] The poem goes undiscussed in Edward Said's *Orientalism*, and indeed in his subsequent *Culture and Imperialism*, but for obvious reasons it has recently interested romanticists who have been alerted by Said's work and its aftermath to the implications of Orientalism around 1800, when competition between Britain and France in the Middle and Far East suggested an inevitably political dimension to aesthetic representations.

7. The fullest account is Anthony Grafton, *The Footnote: A Curious History* (Cambridge, MA: Harvard University Press, 1997). Much of the theoretical, formal, and historical interest in notes and margins that appeared in the1970s and since surely derives from Derrida's textual experiments, most obviously in *Glas* and in *Margins of Philosophy.* The whole assumption of a hierarchy marking off text from paratext is unsettled by Derrida, as it was, I would argue, by others in the eighteenth and early nineteenth centuries. See also J. Hillis Miller, "The Critic as Host," in *Deconstruction and Criticism*, ed. Harold Bloom et al. (New York: Seabury Press, 1979), 217–53. Miller explores the dialectical host-parasite syndrome as typifying the relation of literature to criticism (and thus of text to context or paratext), "each feeding on the other and feeding it, destroying and being destroyed by it" (249).

8. Lawrence Lipking, "The Marginal Gloss," *Critical Inquiry* 3 (1977): 622. On the debates about reading and the stimulation of the passions, see (among others) Adrian Johns, *The Nature of the Book: Print and Knowledge in the Making* (Chicago: University of Chicago Press, 1998), 380–443. See also Richard Kroll, "Mise-en-Page, Biblical Criticism, and Inference During the Restoration," *Studies in Eighteenth-Century Culture* 16 (1986): 3–40. Kroll shows that the polyglot Bible editions employed very complex arrays of text-paratext conjunctions.

9. Robert Southey, *Thalaba the Destroyer* (London: Longman and Rees, 1801), 1:vii, ix.

Southey's politics at this stage of his career are not easy to decipher; they seem muddled or indecisive, not fully those of the youthful radical he is thought to have been but not yet those of the complacent Tory he is believed to have later become. And indeed, the very first footnote to the poem presents a dramatic instance of what I will call *impacted reading*: it stops us in our tracks before we have even settled into them and throws open the entire question of interpretive relations between English poets and Islamic stories, overpowering the lyrical sweep of the verse (over which Southey took a good deal of trouble and in which he was very successful) by the seemingly dry apparatus of small print. But the substance is far from dry, so little so that the subtext threatens to overwhelm and digest the main text. Zeinab responds with pious resignation to the loss of her husband and all but one of her children, invoking God's will—"He gave, he takes away."[10] The appended note cites a line from the Book of Job which says almost word for word the same thing: "The Lord gave, and the Lord taketh away." Southey then offers a further note on his note, a remarkable opener for the first footnote of a very long and densely footnoted poem:

> I have placed a scripture phrase in the mouth of a Mohammedan; but it is a saying of Job, and there can be no impropriety in making a modern Arab speak like an ancient one. Resignation is particularly inculcated by Mohammed, and of all of his precepts it is that which his followers have best observed: it is even the vice of the East. It had been easy to have made Zeinab speak from the Koran, if the tame language of the Koran could be remembered by the few who have toiled through its dull tautology. I thought it better to express a feeling of religion in that language with which our religious ideas are connected. (1:3–4n).

This is quite an opener, and makes things very hard for the reader who just wants to get back to the verse and carry on reading for the plot or for the gratifications of poetic form and diction.

Let us address some of the issues raised by this first footnote, one that seems to be in violent rebellion against its relegation to small print at the bottom of the page. How "modern" is Southey's story, and in what ways do "ancient" Arabs differ from "modern" ones? If his inspiration is Robert Heron's 1792 translation of a sequel to the *Arabian Nights*, then he is responding to a "French faux-Arabian collection" and enacting an imitation

10. Ibid., 1:3.

of an imitation.[11] No exact historical setting is established for the events of the poem except by way of this note. Why would an ancient and a modern Arab *not* use the same phrase, and why might an impropriety even be suspected? Is Southey supposing that an Arab living before the time of Mohammed might have had easier recourse to the Judeo-Christian scriptures, but that a common tradition survives? If Southey here intends some allusion to the dispute between ancients and moderns, how are we to read it? What would ancient or modern Arabs know of the story of Job, and how would this information (if we were given it, which we are not) impact upon poetic license? Does Southey perhaps mean to allude to the primordial unity among the peoples of the book (as Derrida calls them): the Jews, Muslims, and Christians whose faiths are generated from the same texts and who interpret the same mythical figures in different ways? Jews go unmentioned here, but Job is an Old Testament text, and what is more emblematic of resignation than the response of Abraham when God demands the sacrifice of Isaac? Christians too are supposed to demonstrate resignation to God's will, and Southey's reference more or less converts Zeinab into a good Christian (he would later find himself very interested in questions of conversion). If Islam (or "the East" in general) has "almost" turned resignation into a vice, at what point did this happen, and is Southey proposing to maintain the integrity of an earlier, premodern phase in which it was still a virtue? Or is Zeinab wrong, in his eyes, to accept so passively the loss of her husband at the hands of a tyrant by invoking the fiction of a God who demands abjection? This would be the radical Southey, here replicating the argument of, for instance, Volney's *Ruins of Empire*, which suggests that political tyranny precedes and brings about religious doctrine, which is then no more than a piece of ideological consolation for earthly and therefore disputable oppressions.[12] The critique of Islam would then also tell against the Christian ethic of resignation, and against all faiths similarly disposed. But any hint of radical universalism on Southey's part is qualified by his splenetic condemnation of the particular dullness of the Koran, which of course he knew only in Sale's translation. Do we have to get rid of formalized and corrupted written doctrines to get at the universalism? Southey does promptly invoke a level at which "our religious ideas are connected." Who is meant

11. Here I cite Tim Fulford's introduction to his edition of the poem in *Robert Southey: Poetical Works 1793–1810*, ed. Lynda Pratt (London: Pickering and Chatto, 2004), 3:x.

12. Constantin Volney, *Volney's Ruins; or Meditations on the Revolutions of Empires* (New York: Dickens and Sickels, 1828), 54.

by this "our"? Is it just those of us in the Christian West who have a better chance of making some sense of the feelings of a Muslim protagonist if she is represented as using the diction of the Bible? Or is the sentence to be read as referring to the synthetic mythology that holds together (connects) all three of the major monotheisms, all of the peoples of the book?

Southey's note is clearly not flattering to the religion of Mohammed, but it holds back from the outright condemnation and demystification he could have found in George Sale's English translation of its sacred book, which deemed Mohammed (despite his virtues) an impostor and the Koran itself "so manifest a forgery." Sale is a zealous Protestant eager to correct the open-mindedness of previous translators, especially those Catholics who were in the business of defending their own "idolatry and other superstitions."[13] But even he feels compelled to acknowledge that Islam accepts the Hebrew Pentateuch and Psalms and the Christian Gospels as God's primitive and imperfect revelations superseded by the true doctrines imparted to Mohammed himself.[14] Thus there is indeed a Mohammedan version of the Job story, which he transcribes in a long footnote.[15] Southey's poem cites passages from Job twice more in later footnotes and on at least one occasion the purely Islamic "resignation" of another character, the old man Moath, is presented as a persuasive virtue.[16] So the description of resignation in the first footnote as "even the vice of the east" may not after all be a dismissal of resignation itself, which appears in the poem embodied in two distinctly sympathetic characters.

These speculations have perhaps served to suggest the complexities of this first footnote, but they have certainly not resolved them. Of the twenty-one footnotes in the first book of the first edition of *Thalaba*, only two are simple references or identifications. Three describe exotic trees

13. George Sale, *The Koran; commonly called the Alcoran of Mohammed* (London, 1734), i–iv. Another of Southey's precursors in the genre of the annotational sublime, Pierre Bayle, whose footnotes far exceed Southey's own in their length and multiplicity, pronounced Mohammed a complete scoundrel driven entirely by lust and successful only because he disguised his epilepsy as a sign of divine inspiration: see *An Historical and Critical Dictionary by Monsieur Bayle* (London, 1710), 2092–112.

14. Sale, *The Koran*, 2. Mohammed Sharafuddin, *Islam and Romantic Orientalism: Literary Encounters with the Orient* (London and New York: Tauris, 1994), xxix–xxx, 49–50, finds Sale to be generally less negative about Islam than his preface suggests, while Southey, who used him as a source, is deemed to approve of eastern resignation (93–98). Sharafuddin finds a "scholarly seriousness" in Southey's treatment of Islam (87) and makes a strong case for his belief in a universalist theology founded in individual resistance to tyranny, proposing Thalaba as a "Christo-Islamic hero" (74).

15. Sale, *The Koran*, 271.

16. Southey, *Thalaba the Destroyer*, 1:136, 141, 2:93.

(ebony, palm, mimosa), and four identify analogies or prototypes and perhaps sources for Southey's verse in foreign languages (French, Spanish, the Old Testament in English, and a passage in Purchas referring to "the Rabbis"). Five notes cite corroborative descriptive details from ethnographic and travel literature. So far, simple enough. But some notes fall into more than one category. Six notes launch out into substantial stories within the story, and at these points the prose definitely overmatches the poetry—the small print takes over. Four notes (at a conservative count) engage in or arouse substantial interpretive controversies and open out into new topics, like the first footnote I have been describing, which offers us more than one way to resolve the issues it raises. One note may well be pure satire. And there are three further reference notes within the notes themselves. One stranger begets another, and another. Impacted reading takes the form of indefinite dissemination.[17]

Southey presents us with a miscellany, an unpredictable sequence of different sorts of notes inviting very different levels of attention and distraction. The second note to book 1 is less controversial, although in citing a French poet as precursor it confesses the sheer literariness of Southey's performance: poetry in English references more poetry in French. The third note opens once again the question of how West meets East, as it passes from the extended citation of a source to deriding the "waste of ornament and labour" that typifies "all the works of the Orientalists."[18] Southey, or his annotating persona, launches into a diatribe against the aesthetic of abstraction that eschews "representations of life and manners" in favor of curves and lines "absurd to the eye" because "conveying no idea whatsoever." Is it possible that with even minimal research into the traditions of the Arab world, Southey could have failed to register the predominantly antifigurative conventions of Islamic art, not so very different indeed from radical Puritan and Hebraic injunctions against graven images, and thereby, once again, conjoined in a synthetic theological foundation with the two other monotheisms? (The long fifth footnote beginning at 1:15 notably records the prophet Houd as upbraiding idolatry from *within* the Arabic tradition.) This third footnote matches the first one's contempt for the Koran with a dismissal of the habit

17. In a similar spirit Javed Majeed, *Ungoverned Imaginings: James Mill's "The History of British India" and Orientalism* (Oxford: Clarendon, 1992), 56, suggests that Southey makes deliberate use of divergent landscapes to hint "at the way in which cultures in some sense actually constitute each other, and inhabit each other's centres in the process of defining their 'Others' and so themselves." Cultures have no simple originals (62–64).

18. Southey, *Thalaba the Destroyer*, 1:9n. Southey oddly denotes the primary authors of the tradition, not its Western interpreters, as "orientalists."

among "our *barbarian* scholars" of comparing Ferdusi with Homer, which would be like "transmuting lead into gold." The allusion to Joseph Champion, a follower of Sir William Jones, implies that the barbarians are within the homeland, barbarians themselves as much as scholars *of* barbarians.[19] The note goes on to claim that the "genius" of the Arabian Tales is accessible to us only because "they have lost their metaphorical rubbish in passing through the filter of a French translation." The translation has thus improved upon the original, allowing what is good in it to shine forth unencumbered by cultural clutter and spurious ornamentation.

A translation that improves upon the original: this is fighting talk. What then is the status of Southey's own verse, *ornamenting* as it does, and with considerable labor, an Arabian tale which he probably well knew to be already itself an imitation, and which as such would have had little enough originality? Is it too offered as an improvement by virtue of being rendered into good English diction and meter? This mostly abusive footnote is appended to a line describing the "studding azure tablatures" of the airy palace Zeinab sees before her, part of a "prodigious pile" that outdoes anything built anywhere else "For Idol, or for Tyrant."[20] This is a palace of art, the "Paradise of Irem" (1:15) shown only to God's chosen (as the note tells us) but shown as an emblem of vanity, and the subject of a long story told by Aswad, the sole survivor of a divine punishment who lives on only because of a kind deed done to a camel. The wild oscillations of mood and tempo between notes and verse text are almost impossible to follow; or, if one follows them, then any prospect of a coherent, progressive narrative that can be held in the memory seems to disappear as surely as the palace itself does at the end of book 1. There is a particularly striking disjunction when the verse describes Aswad saving the camel's life. Two lines that one might otherwise pass over describe the camel recognizing her rescuer:

> She knew me as I passed,
> She stared me in the face (1:29)

Southey notes (this is the tenth footnote, though they are not numbered) that the second of these lines is taken from "one of the most beautiful passages of our old Ballads, so full of beauty." He then transcribes, he claims from imperfect memory, five stanzas from a poem called "Old Poulter's Mare" which he probably wrote himself, which reads like a parody of Words-

19. See Fulford's note in *Robert Southey: Poetical Works 1793–1810*, 3:332.
20. Southey, *Thalaba the Destroyer*, 1:8.

worth or Coleridge (perhaps specifically of Coleridge's "To a Young Ass"), and which either abandons the story before it ends or chooses to end on a note of utter bathos.

Is *this* ballad an instance of the superiority of the Western literary tradition over the ornamental dross of the Orient? While there is in it nothing of the arabesque, it is quite devoid of "metaphorical rubbish" only because it has no metaphor at all. It reads best as a satire upon the dominant style of *Lyrical Ballads* by a mischievous editor-narrator. Reading it as a spoof has the effect of dignifying the verse which it annotates: it makes Southey's main story, which is full of highly worked figures and complex meters, look good. But then it looks good by taking over Oriental material at the expense of what is now becoming fashionable in England: Wordsworthian plain speaking. Jeffrey's notorious review of *Thalaba* took Southey's poem as an occasion to attack the emergent Lake School for its commitment to the language of ordinary men; but nothing here *except* the poulter's mare smacks of an everyday encounter or of ordinary language. The impression (and confession) is rather of high artifice, of a story worked over by imitation and translation that, while getting rid of some of the "metaphorical rubbish" of an Eastern tale that in fact has no simple original, still leaves behind elaborate enough metaphors to look very different from the language of ordinary men even in a state of vivid sensation. Moreover, Aswad's act of mercy toward the camel has a particular dignity for a British reader who might well have in mind a recent memory of the Ancient Mariner's impulsive killing of the albatross (and who could look forward to Saladin's willingness in Scott's *The Talisman* to spend his precious elixir on curing a dog against the persuasions of his own cultural orthodoxies).[21] So perhaps the import of "Old Poulter's Mare," while it comes in doggerel, is not just satirical. We seem indeed to have reached a point where there is "no there there" unless it is the space and place made by Robert Southey himself, through whom all of these disparate and dispersed raw materials take shape and form as an airy palace of poetic art. The pastiche has taken over the place of the original; the East meets the West in a confluence of derivative forms and terms that work together only as sheer artifice, as mesmeric poetry.

But the magic, I am arguing, is weighed down and perhaps even submerged by footnotes. Some of them are critical and demystificatory, exposing the absurdities of superstition in all its forms, whether Muslim or Christian. One goes so far as to quote Richard Pococke's opinion that the

21. For an account of the new affectionate attitude to animals, see Keith Thomas, *Man and the Natural World: Changing Attitudes in England, 1500–1800* (London: Allen Lane, 1983).

Arabs "are great levellers"[22] and thus useful analogs of the radical spirit among Southey's contemporaries. Others remind us again of the foundational mythology shared by the three major monotheisms, suggesting that the object of Southey's interest is no one nation or religion but the entire apparatus of mythological or religious thinking: "I must remind my readers that an allusion to the Old Testament is no ways improper in a Mohammedan" (1:118n). To stand outside these mythologies is to stand outside culture itself and to suggest—even in the act of critique—the equivalence of each to the others. This was, we recall, arguably one implication of the poem's very first footnote. If Islamic beliefs are not finally distinguishable from Christian ones, then all of them have common roots and any of them is open to properly pious or purely superstitious application. No one culture has a monopoly either on tyranny or on piety. The Koran (in translation) may be to Southey a boring book, but it is not so clear whether the holy scriptures preferred in the West (themselves in translation for all but a few scholars) might not also look inadequate to others outside the fold. If the "filter of a French translation" has purified the ornamental excesses of the Arabian tales, allowing their "genius" to shine through (1:10n), what would one say of the origins and transmission of the Judeo-Christian Bible?

In sum, it must seem that there is no single purpose to Southey's use of footnotes. He comes across as variously antiquarian, polemicist, and satirist. He can look like an ethnographer of the exotic other or a critic of its absurdities. His literary analogs suggest a primary affiliation between East and West in their uses of stories and images, and the existence of common narrative and doctrinal features implies a unitary theological and perhaps ethical foundation to the different religions.[23] The play between text and subtext, large print and small print, as well as among the various kinds of notes themselves, sets up an unstable vehicle for a reading that is always impacted. This is especially the case in the first edition, where Southey's compositors and/or publishers decided in favor of footnotes over endnotes. Whatever Southey really wanted, the choice between the two options instances the dispersal of control and of subjectivity itself that accrues most obviously when text and subtext are in play and are open to technical manipulation by agents who are not conventionally thought of as authors.[24]

22. Southey, *Thalaba the Destroyer*, 1:90n.

23. For a brief introduction to this important tradition of inquiry, see Nigel Leask, "Mythology," in *An Oxford Companion to the Romantic Age: British Culture, 1776–1832*, ed. Iain McCalman (Oxford: Oxford University Press, 1999), 338–45.

24. For an account of the traditional independence of compositors in the setting of texts, see Johns, *The Nature of the Book*, 85–90.

Even when Southey may have had his way in the later editions of *Thalaba* and succeeded in separating the verse and the notes, the mere knowledge of their presence, the more haunting for being unseen, is enough to unsettle anyone who is concerned about carrying out a careful and respectful reading. If we ignore the notes altogether, we project ourselves as lazy or incurious readers; if we turn to them several at a time, we lose the thread of the story they are supporting; if we read them one at a time, as they occur, the disruption is even more radical. The array of verse and small print, however it is organized, presents a constant challenge to a reader's self-identification: am I a scholar, an aesthete, or a mere antiquarian, and what does the poet want me to be? The second (1809) and third (1814) editions place the notes at the end of each of the twelve books of the poem but do not indicate in the verse narrative exactly when we are to turn to them. The diligent reader must thus operate in a state of constant distraction, wondering if and when to look at the notes. (These later editions also interpose two new footnotes keyed to the first three stanzas of the poem.) Such challenges were felt at the time. An early reviewer of the first edition protested that the notes were "as nonsensical as the text itself," and obviously imported to bulk up the book and raise the price of purchase; another shrewdly surmised that the notes were not so much illustrations of the poem but the very "materials" for it, implying that there would be nothing there without them; and a third found the whole production "entirely composed of scraps."[25]

Is there a genre at work here, one we have forgotten, or is Southey his own man in fashioning this baffling array of text and paratext? Northrop Frye's description of Menippean satire comes close, involving as it does a "violent dislocation in the customary logic of narrative" along with a "display of erudition," but he characterizes it as a prose form given only to an "incidental" use of verse.[26] There are numerous poetic instances in the eighteenth century where indeed the play between verse and prose is itself an aesthetic strategy. But Southey's poem does not settle itself as raillery against either pedantic learning or his mistress the world. The range of sources and variety of attitudes contained in the footnotes do not add up to a single purpose or set of clearly coherent attitudes. What does consistently

25. *Robert Southey: The Critical Heritage*, ed. Lionel Madden (London: Routledge and Kegan Paul, 1972), 64, 65, 83.

26. Northrop Frye, *Anatomy of Criticism: Four Essays* (New York: Athenaeum, 1967), 309–11. Howard D. Weinbrot, *Menippean Satire Reconsidered: From Antiquity to the Eighteenth Century* (Baltimore, MD: Johns Hopkins University Press, 2005), sees it as a moralizing genre addressed to a failing world, as it often was in the hands of Pope and Swift, who of course made ample use of footnotes.

feature is a curiosity about the Arabian Orient, in both text and subtext, as a poetically imagined place and as an occasion for critical and ethnographic digressions. Southey's major precursor here was almost certainly William Beckford's *Vathek*, a novel whose own history of publication instantiates many of the pros and cons that late-eighteenth-century authors and readers felt about the footnote.[27] Beckford wrote his novel in French and published it first in Lausanne in 1786 with only 4 footnotes.[28] The manuscript was handed over to Samuel Henley for translation and publication in English, but when it appeared (under a different title) in 1786, it came along with 121 pages of notes, all produced by Henley himself from an impressive roster of historical, literary, and ethnographic sources. Beckford too seems to have been a serious scholar of Oriental culture and history, taking the trouble to study Arabic in hopes of making his own translations. His own 1787 Paris edition includes some but by no means all of Henley's notes (some 23 pages), and these were retained and even expanded in later editions. But Henley's translated and heavily annotated edition remained the only English version of the novel until 1816, and it was thus the one best known to the romantic poets and their readers. The story line of *Vathek* thus came to them heavily laden with small print.

The plot and elaboration of Beckford's Oriental gothic tale is even more fanciful than Southey's *Thalaba*, but it has a readily apparent moral, being the story of a faithless caliph who rebels against the conventions of orthodox Islam and is at the end punished accordingly. Along the way, he leads a brutal and darkly erotic life in the service of the infernal powers, the details of which are wildly implausible and fully embedded in the world of fable: an adults-only version of the *Arabian Nights*. Since the story is not rendered in poetic form but in often ungainly prose, it might have been hard for readers to have been swept away by its style; one might surmise that *Vathek* took itself less seriously than did *Thalaba* as a model of polite taste. But Henley's notes are something else. The great majority of both the notes and the notes within notes (of which there are a good many) are motivated by a profound literary-historical curiosity. Far from dismissing the Orient as the site of tyranny and superstition, Henley projects it as the source of a series of vivid

27. Southey himself made the comparison (see *Robert Southey: Poetical Works 1793–1810*, 3:viii). He also confessed his debt to Landor's *Gebir* (1798), the second edition of which (1803) was published with new annotations that seem to suggest the reciprocal influence of poems like Southey's own.

28. For an account of the publishing history, upon which I here rely, see William Beckford, *Vathek, with the Episodes of Vathek*, ed. Kenneth W. Graham (Peterborough, ON: Broadview, 2001), 378–80.

poetic images that percolate through the classical and Renaissance masterpieces of the West. Homer, Aeschylus, and the Hebrew scriptures share a common fund of images with the Arabic poets, and various borrowings back and forth are suggested. Milton, in taking over images from the Greeks, tapped into the same repository, and Shakespeare is said to adopt figures of Oriental origin.[29] A long note to a note conjectures, for example, that the banyan tree might have been the origin of European Gothic architecture (256f). The impression given is of a single culture and a single image-bank available to writers in biblical, classical, Islamic, and Christian traditions, the elucidation of which is the main function of Henley's endnotes.

The notes to *Thalaba* are, as we have seen, much less unitary in their effect. If anything, Henley's literary scholarship serves to dignify Beckford's rather flimsy narrative with an ethnographic and aesthetic complexity that the tale alone hardly provides. There are few moments in the story where an unassisted reader would be likely to bring to mind the likes of Homer, Virgil, Milton, and Shakespeare. But if the Vathek fable might not in itself be placed on the list of the world's great books, it does at least, after Henley's efforts, share with them a continuous tradition: it evolves from the same poetic roots as they do. Southey's poem flaunts its command of artifice in a verse that might seem charismatic enough to subsume all questions of origins and analogs, but in the small print he shows himself unable or unwilling to suppress the various and often discordant attitudes generated by his sources. The form of Southey's poem is thus more conducive than Beckford's novel to staging the sheer otherness of his Oriental world. Even as his footnotes hint at a collective culture, they also dispute it; their manifold sources, records and reports cannot be reduced to a single narrative that accords with and sustains the poetic line. Formal and aesthetic closure are impeded by a series of punctuations, asides and analogs whose effect is inevitably one of distraction. Because each note is independent of its neighbors, their sequence generates nothing of the suspenseful flow of good prose, although some of the notes are themselves miniature fables. To read *Thalaba* is to experience impacted reading from start to finish and thereby to risk becoming a stranger to oneself.

Some of the same effects can be traced in the text-note relationship of *The Curse of Kehama* (1810), Southey's second Oriental epic. The poem is set in India, and once again the apparent authorial-editorial voice is outspoken in its contempt for the "monstruous fables" of a "false religion,"

29. William Beckford, *An Arabian Tale, from an Unpublished Manuscript, with Notes Critical and Explanatory* (London: J. Johnson, 1786), 217, 220, 228, 236, 282, 285–86.

which, in order to appear pleasing or interesting, must be processed through the filters of a classically inspired European style.[30] At the same time there is a distinct residue of the universalist libertarianism of the early Southey. The poem's protagonists stand up against a cruel tyranny in the faith that "nature is never false," that "the virtuous heart, and resolute will are free" (149–50), that love conquers all, that "every God is still the good Man's friend" (100), and that courage and suffering on earth will be rewarded by a spiritual and erotic paradise thereafter. Like *Thalaba*, this poem opens by staging an explicit (and even more melodramatic) encounter between East and West, as it conjures up a horrifying scene of suttee. There is absolute clarity in the verse narrative that the woman is a victim, and that the husband for whom she dies was completely unworthy. Such is also the tenor of most of the notes, which are here collected at the end of the book. But some among them record instances of willing sacrifice; others offer ethnographic and cultural rationalizations of the practice of widow-burning; and in producing one British writer, Colonel Wilks, as an apologist for suttee, Southey inevitably records the substance of a debate on this issue even as he himself vigorously takes the other side (195). Signaling that debate as he does, Southey conjures up an extended late-eighteenth-century conflict over the British presence in India, a complex and perhaps inexhaustible topic, and one well beyond what can be shaped into charismatic verse. Southey the poet seems unable to pass over an opportunity to raise questions about the scope and sufficiency of poetry itself, and once again he does it in his notes.[31]

This pattern holds for the rest of his career. Between *Thalaba* and *Kehama*, Southey published *Madoc* (1805), one of his most worked-on poems, and one again accompanied by an army of endnotes, in this case deriving from Welsh national traditions and sources and from historical and ethnographic accounts of the Aztecs. Thereafter he would preserve the same format in *Roderick* (1814), which appends long untranslated sources and poems in Spanish, Portuguese, and Latin and takes the odd step of continuing the story of the versified events in a long prose appendix, so that both

30. *Robert Southey: Poetical Works 1793–1810*, 4:3.

31. For wise and witty account of the poem, see Balachandra Rajan, "Monstrous Mythologies: Southey and *The Curse of Kehama*," *European Romantic Review* 9 (1998): 201–16. Rajan finds that the poem embodies a tension between imperialism and humanist universalism, ideological rigidity and literary fascination. Southey cannot quite bring himself to slay the monster. On literary interest in suttee (sati), see Felicity A. Nussbaum, *Torrid Zones: Maternity, Sexuality and Empire in Eighteenth-Century English Narratives* (Baltimore, MD: Johns Hopkins University Press, 1995), 183–88. Shelley also loved the poem while distrusting its author; see John Drew, *India and the Romantic Imagination* (Delhi: Oxford University Press, 1987), 235–40.

are necessary for full narrative resolution: you have to turn to the notes to finish the story.[32] And Southey was in the historical mainstream in his predisposition for footnotes and endnotes. Landor's *Gebir* first appeared in 1798 as an unadorned poem in seven short books. By the second edition of 1803, each of those books came prefaced with a prose argument (in the style of the reissued first edition of *Paradise Lost*) upheld by a series of complex footnotes variously explaining the plot (which, indeed, was often not easy to follow), which supplied antiquarian and philological information and elucidated a number of obscure, over-compressed locutions in the verse text. *Gebir*'s strangeness could only have been further enhanced by Landor's publishing it in Latin (in which he had himself begun its composition) as well as in English. Campbell's popular "Gertrude of Wyoming" (1809) came with lengthy historical and ethnographic endnotes (again revised and expanded in later editions) embedding in an encyclopedic format its tale of an "Indian" massacre and the historically complex Anglo-French contributions to the tragedy. Charlotte Smith's *The Emigrants* (1793) appeared with historical and literary footnotes, and her later poem *Beachy Head* (1807) contained notes detailing the flora and fauna of the south coast of England, as well as its geographical features and archaeological remains. Then there was Walter Scott, whose *Minstrelsy of the Scottish Border* (1802–1803) was heavily annotated with historical and contextual information, in the manner of *Ossian* and of Percy's *Reliques*, and whose huge corpus of poetry and prose, from the *Lay of the Last Minstrel* (1805) up through the revised versions of the "Waverley" novels, was encumbered or adorned with notes wherein good faith and authenticity are sprinkled among comic or pseudo-antiquarian items in bewildering sequences of small print.[33] So too Edgeworth's *Castle Rackrent* (1800) and Owenson's *The Wild Irish Girl* (1806) make use of elaborate notes aiming to educate the metropolitan readership about the language and culture of the Celtic periphery.

HOSTING THE PAST: ANCIENT FRIENDS AND MODERN STRANGERS

Having reminded ourselves of just how many annotated poems and novels were published in the eighteenth and early nineteenth centuries—and there

32. Robert Southey, *Roderick, The Last of the Goths* (London: Longman, Hurst, Rees, Orme and Brown, 1814), cviii–cxxxv.

33. For recent account of Scott's footnotes and their effects on modern editors, see Bianca Tredennick, "'A Labor of Death and a Labor against Death': Scott's Cenotaphic Paratexts," *European Romantic Review* 21 (2010): 49–64.

are many more I have not mentioned—we might reasonably think that the sparse, free-standing verse lines of *Lyrical Ballads* were the exception rather than the rule, and that the long-accepted romantic canon that is based on them is quite unrepresentative of at least the format of much of the poetry of the period, which was heavily invested in footnotes and endnotes.[34] So powerful has the unadorned lyrical model become that we tend to forget that other canonical writers like Byron and Shelley also wrote annotated poetry—in Byron's case, extensively so. The modest and apparently modern layout of the 1798 *Lyrical Ballads* emphatically projected its authors as believing that good writing did not need the encumbrances of context and explanation for its effective transmission through time and across space. Their claim (largely Wordsworth's) for a stripped-down diction that might withstand the changes wrought by place and time inscribes them within what had once been a very well-known debate between the "ancients" and the "moderns," which for my purposes here might be described as a debate about strangers, about who and what is always familiar, can be made familiar, or must remain forever alien. Broadly speaking, the ancients took the line that great writing can represent and express some enduring core of human nature or experience that will survive transmission through the ages, and that that is what matters most about it. The moderns, conversely, were what we might now call cultural and historical relativists, believing not only that human nature differs significantly in different times and places but also that we cannot know the terms of such differences without considerable scholarly effort and expertise. For a modern, to understand Homer means to learn Greek and study ancient civilizations; you can't just pick up Pope's translation.

This debate has not gone away; it just takes different forms and goes by different names. It appears, for instance, whenever readers protest against the idea of novels and poems that come with footnotes. Wordsworth's wide and empty margins proclaim him an ancient even though the word is never mentioned. Does that make Southey a modern? One reviewer of his epic poem *Roderick* (1814) seems to have thought so: "Our Shakespeares and Miltons never thought it necessary to ballast their poetry with a mass of

34. The first edition of *Lyrical Ballads* (1798) is almost polemically void of annotation; Wordsworth's declared antipathy to prefatory apologetics, which he included in the very preface he *did* write for the second edition, is as well-known as Coleridge's tendency in the other direction. There are only five footnotes in the whole volume (two of them in the "Tintern Abbey" poem), along with one "argument" and one headnote. The long endnote to "The Thorn" appeared first in 1800, as did the substantial prose preface to the expanded second edition.

prose, and perhaps felt secure that, if they found the text, posterity would not fail to find the commentary."[35] William Temple, one of the founding fathers of the "ancient" lobby in English, argued in 1690 that great poetry is both independent of rules and conventions and able to communicate its essential meanings without the interposition of critical and historical pedantry:

> Whoever does not affect and move the same present Passions in you that he represents in others, and at other times raise Images about you, as a Conjurer is said to do Spirits, Transport you to the Places and to the Persons he describes, cannot be judged to be a Poet, though his Measures are never so just, his Feet never so smooth, or his Sounds never so sweet.[36]

Homer is always Homer, and essentially the same Homer, wherever he is met. Temple's case against pedantry is a case against professionalization and against the division of labor itself, and thus offers the would-be modern poet the pastiche-aristocratic role of a freely ranging spirit responsible only to himself and committed to the unconstrained expression of "Spirit and Grace, which are ever Native, and never learnt."[37] So it was no accident that so many of those who were or wanted to be poets cast their votes for the ancients. Temple himself was none too sanguine about the prospects for great poetry in the modern world, which he saw as too dependent upon epigram and satire (too Menippean and miscellaneous) to be likely to produce the best that can be known and thought. He thus opens up a space in his own argument for speculation about whether any modern reader, given a climate of opinion and habit that is as he describes it both historical and distinctly national—he notes the influence of England's changeable weather (75–76)—can manage to apprehend anything of Homer in his own terms, while still suggesting that the best of the ancients is the best we can hope to have, and what is most likely to transcend its moment of first production.

The most divisive issue separating eighteenth-century ancients and moderns had been philology, which was at the time no mere dry-as-dust

35. *Robert Southey: The Critical Heritage*, 188.

36. *Sir William Temple's Essays on Ancient and Modern Learning and On Poetry*, ed. J. E. Spingarn (Oxford: Clarendon, 1909), 55. Remarkably, a similar figure reappears in Derrida: "A masterpiece always moves, by definition, in the manner of a ghost." See *Specters of Marx: The State of the Debt, the Work of Mourning, and the New International*, trans. Peggy Kamuf (New York: Routledge, 1994), 18.

37. *Sir William Temple's Essays*, 54.

obsession with etymologies and derivations: it expressed real anxieties among the educated classes about what it meant to be at such great historical distance from Homer and Virgil, whose works were still held to be at the heart of a humane education. Philology, as Joseph Levine puts it, meant "techniques of recovery—techniques made necessary by the lapse of more than a thousand years."[38] Words changed in form and meaning because of the passing of time and the transformations in their contexts and applications to such a degree that no simple continuity of meaning could ever be assumed, especially when there was scant evidence of any "original" text to begin with. Temple had the misfortune to cite as evidence of an ancient "Original"[39] *The Epistles of Phalaris*, supposing them the work of the sixth-century BCE Sicilian tyrant of that name. This text was already suspect as a forgery, and on the evidence of style and reference, Richard Bentley, the archdeacon of the modern faction, showed conclusively (for all whose minds were open) that the letters were indeed late Greek forgeries of the sort associated with sophist practices; far from embodying the spirit and grace of Temple's true ancients, they were, Bentley wrote, entirely "without life or spirit."[40] Christ Church, Oxford, was the headquarters of the ancients, from whence Charles Boyle answered Bentley and earned widespread approval among wits and gentlemen. The case for the moderns was in the hands of the Cambridge-based Bentley and a prodigy of modern learning called William Wotton.

This dispute is one of the formative moments in the development of literary scholarship and criticism, and it has been reinvented over and over again in the history of higher education and in various articulations of the academy's relation to the nonprofessional man or woman of letters. Since the most gifted writers of the period, Swift and Pope, took the side of the ancients, a casual or exclusively canonical inspection of the record produces an inevitably one-sided verdict on the case. Swift's *Battle of the Books* ends with Bentley and Wotton slain together by the single blow of a well-placed spear wielded by Boyle, but not before it has set out a definition of the "malignant Deity, call'd *Criticism*" that has displaced both wit and true knowledge by the worship of dullness, pedantry, and (most tellingly) "*Ill*

38. Joseph M. Levine, *The Battle of the Books: History and Literature in the Augustan Age* (Ithaca, NY: Cornell University Press, 1991), 45. Here and throughout the discussion of Bentley, Pope, and Swift, I have drawn heavily upon Levine's excellent study.

39. Temple, *Sir William Temple's Essays*, 35.

40. Cited in Levine, *The Battle of the Books*, 53.

Manners."[41] Swift has Scaliger upbraid Bentley with a grossness of character that matches his imputed physical identity as "the most deformed" (250) of all the moderns: "*All Arts of* civilizing *others, render thee* rude *and* untractable; *Courts* have taught thee ill Manners, *and* polite Conversation *has finished thee a* Pedant" (252). This association of learning with uncivil and antisocial behavior would persist in many eighteenth-century novels, plays, and poems, and for good reason: those who stood with the moderns were those who refused to take for granted the powers of natural intuition to produce reliable knowledge, and thus they necessarily called into question any form of social consensus that could not be justified by reason and analysis. They were not, in other words, clubbable, and they caused discomfort among those who were and who preferred to get along as they always had, without looking too deeply into things. The moderns, with their sense of the power of "the Circumstances of Time, Place and Person" (43) and their reluctance to endorse a naively foundational human nature, were felt to be dangerous to church and state. Indubitably they had no manners because they were pedants, suspicious of common sense and committed to close analysis of everything others took to be obvious.

The moderns, in other words, are alert to the arrival of strangers; they suppose a very broad category of persons who should be carefully examined before they can be recognized for what they really are. The ancients profess a more open, aristocratic sense of hospitality; anyone is welcome provided that his or her manners are recognized as familiar. Such strangers are not truly strange; they are already just like us. A centerpiece of the apparatus of a modern critic was annotation—footnotes, endnotes, and appendices. The critical apparatus is what points us to the need to work toward knowledge; to the need to know what we don't know and perhaps to discover what we don't know we don't know. Pope set about his translation of Homer knowing not very much Greek and was perfectly comfortable with the idea of presenting archaic Greek in English rhyming couplets (as Dryden had done with Virgil's Latin). This is fully consonant with the view of an ancient, because it implies that what is essential and natural about Homer can survive any amount of translation and transformation, whether formal or historical, and still remain "the thing." But the startling shift from unrhymed dactyllic hexameters in Greek to heroic couplets in modern English threatens to expose the sheer distance between then and now, here and there, and cannot fail to conjure up the debate about the relative merits of rhyme and blank

41. Jonathan Swift, *A Tale of a Tub*, ed. A. C. Guthkelch and D. Nichol Smith (Oxford: Clarendon, 1958), 240 (original emphasis).

verse in British literary circles, ongoing at the time of Pope's writing. This explains something of the zeal with which Pope introduces Homer as a force of nature and not of art, the possessor of a "poetical fire" that "burns every where clearly, and every where irresistibly," so that in despite of all critical tendencies "the reader is hurried out of himself by the force of the Poet's imagination," and is rendered a "hearer" rather than a "reader."[42] Homer is no stranger. His words are "living words" (xxiv) whose poetic force transcends any restrictions of philosophical or religious doctrine (xvi)—exactly the things that according to the moderns might make it hard or even impossible for us to understand the words at all. To say that Homer's similes are "like pictures" (xxxvii) is to suppose that they are as transparent to the mind as visual images are thought to be to the eye. But these comments come in a lengthy prefatory essay in which, far from simply pointing us to the beauties that await us (one function of the preface as anticipatory declamation) we are given very explicit directions about how to read—precisely, in other words, the thing that we are supposed not to need.[43] And indeed, Pope cannot here repress the confession that there are some limits to what we can understand or sympathize with, that some things—he calls them "defects"—"proceed from the nature of the times he lived in" (xxxviii). And that is the top of the modern slippery slope: where does one draw the line, and how? Pope comments as follows on the matter of diction:

> Perhaps the mixture of some *Graecisms* and old words after the manner of Milton, if done without too much affectation, might not have an ill effect in a version of this particular work, which most of any other seems to require a venerable antique cast. (li–lii)

The poem must, in other words, be made to look old, but what is used to achieve the antique cast is not the original Greek but Greek*isms* and bits of *Paradise Lost*. It becomes a construction that in itself belongs nowhere except in a poetic present whose need for the effect of the antique is driven not by historical curiosity but by aesthetic frisson. Even scriptural language may be used in moderation, on the grounds that Homer was as close to the "divine spirit" of his own times as any poet could have been (1–li) and therefore fits comfortably with the language of the Bible.

42. Alexander Pope, *The Iliad of Homer*, ed. Gilbert Wakefield (London: J. Johnson etc., 1806), 1: vii–ix, xxi.

43. Pope's long preface is in place from the first edition (1715).

One of Southey's footnotes to *Thalaba*, we recall, tells us that neither Ferdusi nor any other Oriental poet can bear comparison with Homer. But Pope's Homer is asking some of the same questions as arise in reading Southey's poem, which is not a translation of a single text but which does stage the whole issue of translation between cultures, and which also confesses its artificial qualities, its predilection for a venerable exotic cast. Pope's perhaps inadvertent admission that his Homer is really not Homer (just as Bentley said it wasn't) is corroborated by the fact that his edition is, after all, full of footnotes. The recourse to footnotes may well be a symptom of anxiety, one that Pope seeks to defuse in his preliminary note by complaining that all previous editors have ignored "the poetical beauties of the author" in order to comment on matters "philosophical, historical, geographical, allegorical, or in short any thing rather than critical and poetical."[44] But do we need notes to alert us to the ways in which Homer writes "as a poet" (5)? If "men of a right understanding generally see at once all that an author can reasonably mean" (4), and if the Homeric fire really does burn so brightly across the centuries as to survive translation, why bother with the notes? Is Pope sensitive to the needs of a readership that would have even less of the Greek than he had himself, and that would need some help? Is he shoring up his translation by laying claim to a poetic tact and intuition that marks him as different from the mere pedants, a true conduit of the divine fire and different enough from the rest of us that we will not see the high points without the footnotes? Or does he recognize that an unadorned text (Dryden's Virgil was almost this, appearing with only a few endnotes) could no longer expect to succeed in a marketplace where the reception of a classic requires the typographic display of small print as the imprimatur of gravity and properly qualified, scholarly attention? Levine suggests that many of Pope's notes are both borrowed and insufficient, gesturing toward the authority of reference while avoiding all of the most difficult cruxes, but still compelled to rely upon the pedantry he claimed to despise.[45] Swift's *Battle of the Books* had been able to get away with presenting the footnote as part and parcel of the pedantry he was satirizing. Pope tries for the same effect in *The Dunciad*, but in translating Homer he tends toward good faith, and perhaps even crosses the line, a modern in spite of his own desires. Moreover, more than a few readers of *The Dunciad* have found it difficult to be sure that the objects of the poet's invective do not overwhelm the verse

44. Pope, *The Iliad of Homer*, 4.

45. Levine, *The Battle of the Books*, 195. Levine's entire account of Pope and the ancient-modern debate (181–244) is invaluable.

that seems intended to put them in their place, according an unintended victory to the armies of small print against which ancient versification cannot after all hold the line.

After *The Iliad of Homer*, Pope tried his hand at editing Shakespeare, halfheartedly and to little acclaim. Bentley followed on with his own edition of Milton. What did it say that the two giants of the emerging national canon required some of the same packaging as did Homer? G. K. Hunter suggests that the habit of annotating Shakespeare was at once intended to establish him *as* a classic, worthy of the same attentions as the Greek and Roman texts, while at the same time recognizing that the production of a reliable text required editorial work in the modern mode.[46] The testy reviewer of Southey's *Roderick*, it will be remembered, would claim a hundred years later that Shakespeare and Milton "never thought it necessary to ballast their poetry with a mass of prose," being confident that "posterity" would find the commentary if they but provided the verse.[47] But Pope's ally Francis Atterbury apparently complained to him that he could not understand much of Shakespeare, whom he found as obscure as Aeschylus.[48] Among moderns, these difficulties could be attributed to the gothic barbarisms of Shakespeare's works, the rude products of an uncivilized time, a not-uncommon eighteenth-century view. Bentley did not find anything like this in Milton but justified his project on the conjectured existence of slips between dictation and printed book, which he thought might explain the poem's infelicities. Taken together the two cases suggest that the transmission of texts is vulnerable both to the rapid pace of historical change that (in this case) improves taste and simplifies language, and to the ever-present errors and distortions of putting any and all thoughts into print. In 1751, seven years after his death, Pope's own works would appear in an edition put together by his friend Warburton that reprinted all of the poet's own notes, often adverting to the classical originals he was imitating, along with the manuscript variations and corrections gathered by the editor. Even poetic fire, it seems, can burn unevenly.

We have gone some way back in time from Southey's *Thalaba*—far enough, I hope, to show that there was a lively and varied tradition in the purposive deployment of footnotes and endnotes for various effects: comic, seriocomic, antiquarian, philological, and ethnographic. Pope used the notes

46. G. K. Hunter, "The Social Function of Annotation," in *In Arden: Editing Shakespeare*, ed. Ann Thompson and Gordon McMullan (London: Thomson, 2003), 177–93.

47. *Robert Southey: The Critical Heritage*, 188.

48. Cited in Levine, *The Battle of the Books*, 226.

to *The Dunciad* for satirical purposes but was compelled to something more conventional in annotating his translation of Homer. Gibbon's notes are like the text above them, ironic and serious in turn.[49] Hume's *History* used them hardly at all and thus stood out against the antiquarian fashion for exhaustive documentation and dispersed authority, as if he carried the whole substance of the national narrative in his memory.[50] Southey's notes seem to draw upon the conventions observed by almost all of those who came before him, without ever settling into a single pattern or genre. They are therefore more than usually disruptive. The ethnographic focus does provide a common thread, one that would have been unusual in earlier annotated poems. But ethnographic conclusions are hard to find, or to hold on to. Nigel Leask has noted the discrepancy between Southey's text and annotation and the resulting disruption of absorption, while finding that the notes themselves embody a "totalizing project" inscribing the reader into a position of "epistemological power; nothing other than the commanding vision of imperialist objectivity."[51] For him, the footnote, even as it distracts from the verse text, becomes the vehicle of a unified intention to impose the enlightened Western worldview on primitive, Oriental material. This is I think to suppose too coherent a project, as Leask himself may inadvertently admit in noticing that the technical strategies of this panoramic mode of poetry (which he relates to the informational components of the commercial panoramas of the time) "compromise" the imperialist discourse they otherwise seem to publicize.[52] Claire Simmons also finds Southey's notes to be engaged in an effort at "cultural mastery" while admitting that the poem preserves an "ambivalence" about its entire engagement with the arabesque.[53]

49. See Grafton, *The Footnote*, 97–104. Grafton sees Pierre Bayle as Gibbon's model in this respect (190–200). For a fine, brief essay on the footnote in Gibbon and in general, see G. W. Bowersock, "The Art of the Footnote," *American Scholar* 53 (1983–84): 54–62.

50. See Rosemary Sweet, *Antiquaries: The Discovery of the Past in Eighteenth-Century Britain* (Hambledon, UK: Palgrave-Macmillan, 2004), 6.

51. Nigel Leask, "'Wandering through Eblis': Absorption and Containment in Romantic Exoticism," in *Romanticism and Colonialism: Writing and Empire, 1780–1830*, ed. Tim Fulford and Peter J. Kitson (Cambridge: Cambridge University Press, 1998), 168–69.

52. Ibid., 183.

53. Claire Simmons, "'Useful and Wasteful Both': Southey's *Thalaba the Destroyer* and the Function of Annotation in the Romantic Oriental Poem," *Genre* 27 (1994): 94, 102. See also Carol Bolton, *Writing the Empire: Robert Southey and Romantic Colonialism* (London: Pickering and Chatto, 2007), 174–206, which finds various tensions between verse and footnotes. Marilyn Butler remarks that the notes "could be kept for separate study or enjoyed when the reader was older" while admitting that "the best of the entries are as compelling as the best of the episodes." See her "Orientalism," in *The Romantic Period*, ed. David B. Pirie (London: Penguin Books, 1994), 413–14. Stuart Curran, *Poetic Form and British Romanticism* (Oxford: Oxford University Press,

Even if these notes were indeed open to being received as a uniform affirmation of the disciplinary power of an imperializing ethnography—which I do not think they are—one might still be enchanted by the masterful verse narrative, which exercises its appeal in despite of historical truth or falsehood, indeed perhaps appeals precisely because it beguiles away all such distinctions. *Thalaba* crucially enacts a geographical displacement; it is far more than a mere allegory of British concerns about revolution and tyranny transposed into an Oriental setting. It positions itself at a spatial distance from the homeland of its readers and represents strangeness as more a matter of place than of time: here it differs from earlier footnote fictions like *The Dunciad* or *Tale of a Tub*. We are to be awed by the physical, cultural and aesthetic features of the Arabian desert, which we are encouraged *not* to familiarize. In translation studies, as we will see in the next chapter, what Southey does is called *foreignizing*. The notes participate fully in this process by frequently taking over the page and claiming the typographic space as their own; what is supposed to be adjunct suddenly becomes primary. The reviewers noticed this. Francis Jeffrey, astute even when at his most negative, finds the poem to be composed of "scraps" of information, little else but "his commonplace book versified." The notes come first, the poem is patched together afterward; at least two other contemporary critics come to the same conclusion.[54] Paratext becomes text—scraps indeed, and items prone to scrapping with one another as they set loose, in free circulation, all of the forms of information that the book embodies. Where one reader might find an imperial project latent or explicit in the gathering up of up recondite sources from faraway places, another can (like me) find evidence for the footnote as a place of refuge from that very same ambition.

So, albeit writing about a later and mostly French romanticism, Lionel Gossman has argued that footnotes do not so much reduce the power of the other as preserve it from being fully conquered, giving it "sanctuary and protection from the appropriating energy of the historical narrative."[55] Adopting a Hegelian model of subject formation, Gossman exposes the threatened or actual loss of integrity that comes with all engagements with difference, whereby the subject that wants to dominate or reconstitute

1986), 134, finds *Thalaba* "essentially uncommitted to its own mythos." Dahlia Porter, "Formal Relocations," 675, also senses a disruptive poetics at work.

54. See *Robert Southey: The Critical Heritage*, 64, 65, 83–84.

55. Lionel Gossman, "History as Decipherment: Romantic Historiography and the Discovery of the Other," *New Literary History* 18 (1986): 25, 40–41.

itself must struggle with alien forms and materials. The footnote comes to life as an alternative form of life and contests the typographic space to which it is supposed to be a mere appendage. Fredric Jameson suggests—in a footnote placed in the middle of a sentence—that Adorno uses the footnote as "a small but autonomous *form*, with its own inner laws and conventions and its own determinate relationship to the larger form which governs it," a "momentary release" from the demands of the main text and thereby the repository of a fitfully existing "living thought."[56] Here there is an alternative life happening alongside the main text but separate from it. Taken together, these two formulations lead us to speculate about the text-subtext relation as *dialogic*, and as such, embodying an unstable and unpredictable interaction whose exposition cannot be known in advance. All dialogue has this potential, however scripted it might seem: even the patsy who chips in with a "yes, Socrates," every few lines can be imagined as winking at his audience or rolling his eyes. Southey's notes seem to me neither complacent judgment nor romantic exoticism; their proliferation of the forms and varieties of otherness make it hard to be sure what they are. In ranging across so many Western as well as Eastern and other cultures and literatures, they open up questions of time and space, of how past relates to present and how what is distant relates to the domestic. And every note, insofar as it is an extract from some longer source or analog, refers us to a textual "elsewhere," a whole that can never be completely apprehended because it too will generate footnotes of its own. The gap that the note presumes to fill is thus in fact an opening, an invitation to an infinitely regressing pursuit of sufficient knowledge.[57] The moderns—Bentley, Wotton, and their successors—had threatened to render us foreigners to ourselves in suggesting that we could no longer understand Shakespeare and Milton, never mind Homer. Every writer who shifts through space or survives the passing of time becomes a potential stranger. Among the means of transport, in all directions, is the footnote.

56. Fredric Jameson, *Marxism and Form: Twentieth-Century Dialectical Theories of Literature* (Princeton, NJ: Princeton University Press, 1974), 9. I thank Kevis Goodman for pointing me to this passage.

57. Lipking, "The Marginal Gloss," finds that glossing "demonstrates that the space surrounding print is not a vacuum but a plenum" (613); it is the historical precursor of the footnote, which he sees as coming into its own in the eighteenth century. Thus is the vacuum of empty space around the poem as conventionally printed filled in by the small print of an indefinitely expandable archive. Lipking notes that both gloss and footnote propose a commitment to "perpetual commentary" (625).

A WIDE, WIDE SEA OF PRINT

Unlike Henley's notes to *Vathek*, Southey's *Thalaba* and its notes do not observe the conventions of serious comparative literary history. They are not coherently ethnographic, they do not regale us with information about ruins and relics in the manner of the antiquarians, and they keep to a minimum the popular scientific mode detailing the particularities of flora and fauna in faraway places. They are occasionally polemical and judgmental, but not enough so to be received as a sustained jeremiad. If they are not always diligently objective, seeking to inform and educate in purely neutral terms, then neither are they coherently subjective, always the product of authorial whimsy. They remain informative but also digressive, and in their habit of drawing parallels between the great religions they tend toward the enlightenment doctrine of the one mythology without ever stating anything like a coherent universalist or anti-Christian position.[58] Southey's high-flown Oriental verse invention shackles itself, aided by its printers and compositors, to a series of digressions and interruptions so diverse as to be beyond summary or epitome. The net effect, I suggest, is to make the "other" radically unpredictable and, having arrived, always still to come.

Southey also refrains from suggesting that there is anything in the Arabian past that looks forward to modern European civilization. If the "primitive" characteristics of far flung places could be mined for information about the earlier stages of our own culture, as theorists of stadial history imply, then every instance of otherness becomes part of the cultural inheritance, however diluted it might have become with the passing of time. For Henley, Shakespeare, Homer, and Ferdisi really do share the stage in the history of the West. Models of progressive and subsumptive history, by virtue of their acceptance of the principle of change itself, were often balanced by an equivalent tendency toward regression or repetition. Such indeed was the message of Anna Barbauld's poem *Eighteen Hundred and Eleven*, which went so far as to envision future American visitors coming to inspect the ruins of London with the same emotions as govern British travelers to Egypt's Valley of the Kings. Thomas Moore's *Lalla Rookh* (1817) closely resembles Southey's poem in many ways and is surely modeled upon it. Moore uses both short footnotes and longer endnotes to get around the problem of over-

58. E. S. Shaffer's *"Kubla Khan" and "The Fall of Jerusalem": The Mythological School in Biblical Criticism and Secular Literature, 1770–1880* (Cambridge: Cambridge University Press, 1975) argues for the importance of the tradition of a "primitive spring of faith in one God for all mankind" (37), so that Islam could be considered a variant of Christianity, albeit perhaps a heresy (115).

loading the pages of the poem with small print. But Moore's notes do not produce the same impacted reading as do Southey's, because they do not open up arguments of their own or depart from the norm of being largely illustrative. They employ many of same sources as Southey used (D'Herbelot, Sale, and Jones, among others) but they are predominantly additive. They do not subvert the main text or radically unsettle the typographic hierarchy. Moore's Mokanna, the charismatically evil veiled prophet, moreover, is a clear allegory of Napoleon and a Satan stereotype, as well as an ambivalent figure of the prophet Mohammed, widely deemed in Christian culture to be an impostor.[59] Equally clear pointers to the colonized Irish are offered in the depiction of the Persian fire worshippers who unsuccessfully resist being conquered by the Arabs. Unlike Southey's *Thalaba*, *Lalla Rookh* consistently invites its readers to receive it as allegory, as a poem with a firm foot in the present. Moore's way of interrupting the absorption generated by his verse tale is to interpolate prose incursions by a disgruntled literary critic figure and religious bigot called Fadladeen, apparently an incarnation of the poet's friend Francis Jeffrey.[60] The spell of Orientalism is woven and unraveled at the same time. Unlike *Thalaba*, and perhaps because of these witty presentisms, *Lalla Rookh* was a best seller, into its ninth edition within a year.

A different sort of contrast with *Thalaba* is provided by Shelley's *Queen Mab*, also the work of a writer deeply inspired by Southey's poem even as he was disappointed in the politics and person of its author. Shelley seems not to have intended any aesthetically disturbing interaction between text and subtext; he used endnotes rather than footnotes and wrote to Hookham that he meant to avoid the stupidity of "a poem very didactic" even though the notes themselves were intended to compose a statement of his "principles." He might also have intended some subterfuge in resorting to small print: "The notes will be long philosophical & Anti Christian—this will be unnoticed in a Note."[61] But Shelley has his ways of calling out passages for particular attention. Neil Fraistat argues that he was a keen typesetter and probably the author of the eight "indicator" hands (previously used by Leigh

59. See Sharafuddin, *Islam and Romantic Orientalism*, 152–69. I may be overstating the contrast. Majeed, *Ungoverned Imaginings*, 101, points out that more than eighty sources are cited in the notes to Moore's poem.

60. See Curran, *Poetic Form*, 144.

61. *The Letters of Percy Bysshe Shelley*, ed. Frederick L. Jones (Oxford: Clarendon, 1964), 1:350, 361. For an argument that the notes are to be read as a continuous, independent narrative, see Timothy Morton, "The Notes to Queen Mab," in *The Unfamiliar Shelley*, ed. Timothy Webb and Alan Weinberg (Ashgate, UK: forthcoming).

Hunt to mark his own insertions into *The Examiner*) that feature in the right-hand margins of the endnotes. These hands point outward, away from the text, as if to signal an imperative to go forth into the world, to propagate Shelley's doctrines for a wider audience.[62] Shelley is thus at once subordinating the notes to the poetic line in order to signal an aesthetic priority while at the same time formatting the notes in a way that focuses attention on their independent value. The notes do not negate the verse, but they have a life of their own. Either can be a conduit to the other, though both can be appreciated separately. He is not seeking to replicate the ambition of Erasmus Darwin, whose heavily footnoted *Botanic Garden* had proposed to "enlist Imagination under the banner of Science; and to lead her votaries from the looser analogies, which dress out the imagery of poetry, to the stricter ones which form the ratiocination of philosophy."[63] Shelley wants instead to respect the claims of each without interference from the other.

Almost none of the major annotated poems—not even Darwin's popularized science—has featured prominently in the received canon of romantic poetry, even as that canon has been expanded to include all sorts of hitherto neglected texts.[64] But there is one exception: the revised version of "The Ancient Mariner" published in Coleridge's *Sibylline Leaves* (1817). As is well-known, this poem first appeared in the 1798 *Lyrical Ballads* as a gothic ballad written in Chattertonian old English under the title of "The Rime of the Ancyent Marinere." Some of the archaisms disappeared in the second edition of 1800, but by 1817 the poem had been wholly made over with the addition of a marginal gloss in mock-seventeenth-century English purporting to explain the story told in the verse. Little need be said here on a topic about which so much has been written, but Coleridge's recourse to marginal glossing is striking in the context of what we can now recognize as a tradition of footnotes and endnotes in the long poems of the period. Jerome McGann, building upon the insights of E. S. Shaffer, offers a major interpretation of the poem as "an English national Scripture" assembling various pagan, Catholic and Protestant components into a text embodying the principle of ongoing interpretation through time and thus a demonstration of the hermeneutic method itself.[65] Reading the verse and its prose

62. Neil Fraistat, "The Material Shelley: Who Gets the Finger in *Queen Mab?*," *The Wordsworth Circle* 33 (2002): 33–36.

63. Erasmus Darwin, *The Botanic Garden*, 2nd ed. (London: J. Johnson, 1791), v.

64. The novel has fared rather better thanks to the recent renewal of interest in Scott, though many readers and critics still prefer the more lightly annotated editions.

65. Jerome J. McGann, *The Beauty of Inflections: Literary Investigations in Historical Method and Theory* (Oxford: Clarendon, 1988), 135–72, 160, 141, 153.

marginalia as the productions of two distinct personages, the poem becomes an exercise in both estrangement and synthesis; Coleridge becomes the exponent of a theological wholeness that parallels and echoes what some have found in Southey, a single evolutionary tradition of human spiritual experience that crosses national and denominational frontiers and holds together "original" texts and the subsequent commentaries upon them within a continuous, intersubjective sequence revealing more and more truth.

McGann's powerful reading undoubtedly explains an important constituent ambition for a kind of wholeness that fits well with much of Coleridge's work, published and unpublished. It might, however, seem a bit too comforting as a description either of the tradition of Bible interpretation or of the mentality of a poet for whom a sense of marginality was practically an existential condition. The role of annotation was something of a crux in the evolution of the English Bible. The Geneva Bible printed a text heavily adorned with cross-references and interpretive marginalia, thereby unsettling any intention its editors might have had toward the production of a plain text of the word of God. It makes for a highly impacted reading and requires real concentration on the part of the reader who wants to connect text with paratext. When read aloud in church, only the main text would have been sounded, but the marginalia were clearly felt to be a challenge and perhaps a threat by those who produced the King James Bible in 1611. The Reims-Douay Catholic Bible that answered Geneva had made notably heavy use of marginalia to combat the "false and vain glosses of Calvin and his followers," so that the first policy of the King James editors was to stipulate that no marginalia be added, unless "for the explanation of the Hebrew or Greek words which cannot, without some circumlocution, so briefly and fitly be expressed in the text."[66] This is not quite what happened, but the "Authorized" English Bible is nonetheless much less marked by annotations than its predecessors. A right rendering of the word of god would not unnaturally lead to the idea of a plain text, although any scholar involved in acts of translation would be likely to acquire a taste for complexity. Nor does a plain text in itself offer any assurance of accuracy: it has been estimated that between 1611 and the 1830s some twenty-four thousand variations found their way into the text.[67]

66. I draw here upon *The Cambridge History of the Bible: The West from the Reformation to the Present Day*, ed. S. L. Greenslade (Cambridge: Cambridge University Press, 1987), 162–68.

67. Johns, *The Nature of the Book*, 91. Johns suggests that heavy use of annotation could be associated with deceit, partly because it signaled the power and wealth of one printing house over another; see 424–27.

Although the revised "Ancient Mariner" is Coleridge's only heavily annotated poem, his publishing career is very much invested, both literally and figuratively, in marginalia. *Biographia Literaria* is famous for its obtrusively self-editorial apparatus, and many of the sources and analogs it produces are strangers in time and place, many speaking other languages. Jerome Christensen finds in it "a fragmentary, mobile, aggressively rhetorical mode of argument that reads like a series of marginalia on the texts of others," whereby texts become "pretexts for his notes."[68] It is never clear in this dialectic who is the host and who is the guest. Coleridge as marginalist, says Christensen, experiences "the contingency of living in a borrowed home . . . someone else's text" (109). As is well known, this predicament has involved him in accusations of rampant plagiarism, but it must be said that conscious playing off of center and periphery is central enough to romantic aesthetics in general, and in particular to Coleridge's dramatically allusive style, that some deliberation must be suspected. That is very much what is evident in the decision to *add* marginalia to a poem that did not at first have them. Readers have habitually experienced the disruption of trying to read the two texts in parallel, one in prose and the other in verse. Even though the one is roughly a paraphrase of the other, it is also a commentary, adding in items of information and interpretation that are not self-evident (and certainly not obvious) in the poetic lines. There are even some apparent contradictions. Lawrence Lipking reads the gloss as a symptom of a desire to relate part to whole, and to suggest that there *is* a whole to be apprehended if only we are diligent enough to pursue it: "above all, the author of the gloss knows that the world makes sense."[69] The replacement of the gloss by the footnote that Lipking notices as increasing throughout the eighteenth century might then suggest a loss of confidence in the availability of a whole and a recognition of the infinitely expansive and diffusive quality of encyclopedic knowledge: there can always be more. We can surmise that Coleridge's interest in anachronism in this poem extends also to its very form, as it resorts to an outmoded marginal gloss that signals at once the desirability of an emergent whole and its historical implausibility.

The gloss can be read as its own story, one that ends three stanzas before the end of the rest of the poem with the closing comforts of third person narration not afforded by the verse. Only in a single instance does the gloss take on the attributes of a footnote: toward the end of part 2, where we are

68. Jerome Christensen, *Coleridge's Blessed Machine of Language* (Ithaca, NY: Cornell University Press, 1981), 29, 104.

69. Lipking, "The Marginal Gloss," 616.

briefly directed to "the learned Jew, Josephus, and the Platonic Constantinopolitan, Michael Psellus."[70] This is the only point where we are sent off the page and outside the poem. Disconcerting as it is, then, Coleridge's gloss is considerably less distracting than Southey's footnotes, which produce a more obtrusively impacted reading. But in splitting the first- and third-person narratives while differentiating their styles, Coleridge at least suggests a potentially unbridgeable gulf between firsthand experience and another person's understanding of it. The charismatic (and mesmeric) effect of the mariner's tale thus presents its reader with the risk that having heard it he will, like the mariner, be unable to reestablish himself comfortably in ordinary life. The verse sequences of *Thalaba* are also charismatic enough in themselves, but they are reportage, and the footnotes punctuate the verse with continual bursts of rationality and polemic, so much so that if they are read diligently along with the verse they make poetic absorption impossible. Where Southey tells a story that is mostly seen as if from a distance, Coleridge wants to involve us (even as, after 1817, he also works to remove us) in the evolution and consequences of a critical act, a crime whose aftermath is not fully (if at all) appeased by the supposed repentance but which must go on and on being experienced.

There are no encounters with other human cultures in Coleridge's poem, which is stripped of precise geographical locators. But the notorious emptiness of the oceans through which the mariner sails—round one of the southern capes and back again, as if the point of his voyages is voyaging itself—does not fully disguise the degree to which the ship, with its living dead, asks to be read as a participant in the slave trade, the debate about which was unignorable in England at the time. The crime that goes on and on as it is repeated in the transference of affect from mariner to wedding guest (and thence out into the world) suggests that there has been no closure just as there are no innocents: the entire British economy was implicated in the profits from West Indian plantations. The neatly moralized conclusion to the gloss does not conclude the story told in verse. Coleridge thus has his own way of intimating the presence and power of the other in the drama of the poem. The most important stranger is a bird, welcomed but then abjected. There are no ethnographic notes (and here, for example, he could have readily tapped into the controversy generated after Cook's voyages about the physical stature of the Fuegians or the morals of the Pacific Islanders) and no specifications of flora or fauna (was it a black or white

70. Coleridge, *Poetical Works, Part 1*, 1:383. Mays reprints the 1834 text but the gloss was there from 1817.

albatross? Latin name?). Locational knowledge, which can either comfort or estrange, is altogether withheld. But the ocean, or the mariner's mind, is haunted by a ship of death and by dreadful living forms whose incidence bespeaks a terrible disjunction in the sphere of human history and of its moral relations. If we are fully captured by the glittering eye of the old seaman, we might almost wish for the relief that would be offered by a footnote, a chance to look away, to break the spell, to bury ourselves in the distractions of small print. Coleridge's verse, in other words, disturbs contemplative aesthetic norms in a different way from Southey's idiosyncratic poetic-prosaic encyclopedia, but it disturbs them nonetheless. "The Rime" interjects the ghost of an other we cannot invest with shape or form but which is insidiously familiar, while *Thalaba* destroys peace of mind by the sheer oversupply of information. Neither poem provides a comfortable place to stand from which to attempt to move the world; yet both insist that there is a world with which we are critically involved. To get to that point, both resort to paratexts as a way of making explicit the mechanics and responsibilities of reading; both face their readers with questions about whether and how to welcome strangers in their midst.

Like Coleridge's "The Rime of the Ancient Mariner," *Thalaba* raises questions of trust and credibility, authenticity and forgery. Southey does so explicitly in revealing the degree to which he has "improved" upon his exotic sources, while the Gothic conventions of Coleridge's poem tap into a tradition identified from the first with fake documents and a dubious or false supernatural. Both poems thus embody some of the ambivalence Barbara Benedict describes in the eighteenth-century estimate of curiosity as on the one hand "always transgressive, always a sign of the rejection of the known as inadequate, incorrect, even uninteresting," and on the other hand all too prone to make a monster or a fool of the person tempted to pursue the strange and unfamiliar.[71] Readers of exotic travel narratives were always open to accusations of gullibility (being "gullivered"?), since they could not hope to verify for themselves most of the information being published. Figures of cultural authority like Samuel Johnson took upon themselves the task of distinguishing true from false, plausible from implausible. The Cock Lane ghost, the authorship of *Ossian*, and the real stature of the Patagonian "giants" were just some among a whole list of strange phenomena put before a curious public, often for money, and requiring decisions about truth or falsehood. Benedict suggests that novels like *Caleb Williams* and *The*

71. Barbara M. Benedict, *Curiosity: A History of Early Modern Inquiry* (Chicago: University of Chicago Press, 2001), 4.

Mysteries of Udolpho can be read as instances and analyses of the compulsion to curiosity; so too can *Vathek*, whose protagonist is driven by the search for various kinds of recondite and forbidden knowledge of which we may approve, or not, as the fancy takes us.[72] So too can Southey's *Thalaba*. How does one draw the line between what is to be believed and what is unbelievable? (And what does this entire culture of hermeneutic drama have to say about reading the Bible?). Nigel Leask has shown that James Bruce's classic account of his exploration of the Nile was widely received not as honest reporting but as a fraud or fantasy; and Margaret Russett has recently made the point that the entire romantic cult of authenticity was in fact constructed within a culture of fakes and forgeries and thus was arguably itself a reactive fiction.[73]

The hermeneutic instability of Southey's footnotes thus belongs within a more general syndrome of referential indeterminacy that we can see as also governing Walter Scott's use of small print and Coleridge's marginal glosses, among many other cases. Whatever we decide about the intention or function of particular footnotes, every footnote has the potential (if we read it at all) for interruption and change of direction, for impacting our reading again and again. *Thalaba* sends its reader in many different directions; and when the verse performance is so much the fabric of a dream, an inspired imitation of texts that are already copies, one might be forgiven for resorting to the notes for the consolations of sound knowledge. This would be a mistake. Once afloat on the sea of Southey's small print, we can never return to shore with any sense that the voyage is over. In this way, *Thalaba*, like "The Rime of the Ancient Mariner," disturbs our peace of mind and leaves us with a strong sense that the issues involved in engaging with strangers are not to be resolved easily if at all. The typographic aspiration to know and record everything that matters produces an annotational sublime threatening to locate the reading imagination as always outside and beyond itself—if not quite all alone on a wide, wide sea, then still grasping at the flotsam and jetsam of an indefinitely proliferating archive, in the face of which we can never know enough. We are thereby positioned to await forms of knowledge and figures from afar whose capacity for arousing desire or detestation cannot be known in advance. There will always be another footnote, likely bearing another stranger, and often in another language.

72. Ibid., 175–77.

73. Nigel Leask, *Curiosity and the Aesthetics of Travel Writing, 1740–1840: "From an Antique Land"* (Oxford: Oxford University Press, 2002), 54–101; Margaret Russett, *Fictions and Fakes: Forging Romantic Authenticity, 1760–1845* (Cambridge: Cambridge University Press, 2006).

CHAPTER FIVE

Strange Words: The Call to Translation

THE POSSIBLE IMPOSSIBLE

If we concur with Derrida that translation is "at the very threshold of all reading-writing" and that "at the word go we are within the multiplicity of languages and the impurity of the limit," how is it possible to set out a territory, let alone a mere chapter, to be occupied by the topic of translation, as if it did not already involve the whole of human experience in language, and even perhaps outside it, if there is any such place?[1] And yet, much writing and theorizing about translation, past and present, has found ways of setting limits and preserving boundaries, as if one could turn at will to the topic and then away from it. The history of rhetoric has maintained similar restrictions around the discussion of figurative language, and above all of metaphor, as if to enshrine in that very gesture a belief in a semantic and grammatological bedrock upon which figuration can (but need not) be supported and against which its propriety can be assessed. Metaphor is intricately coexistent with translation. One way Latin "translates" our word "metaphor" and the Greek *metaphora* is as *translatio*; one of the Greek verbs meaning "to translate" is *metapherein*. Archaic German (and Heidegger) use *Übertragung* to mean translation; and one way of saying "metaphor" (if not the most common) is *übertragener Ausdruck*. Metaphor, the identification or substitution of one thing as or for another, is a form of translation. Metaphor, like and as translation, makes the stranger familiar and the familiar strange. Within a concept of translation, everything comes together, everything happens at once; it is a concept ruled by the very stranger (the giver of law, the breaker of laws) it purports to address

1. Derrida, "What is a 'Relevant' Translation?," 175, 176.

and to familiarize. "Translation" itself cannot be translated as such—there is no as such. Barbara Cassin lists a range of Greek words for which we in English would say translation: *hellenizein, metapherein, metaphrazein, metagraphein, hermeneuein.* Then, in Latin, *vertere, convertere, exprimere, reddere, transferre, interpretari, imitari.*[2] In Heidegger's German it can all come down to stress: *ÜberSETZung or ÜBERsetzung.* The conflation of the one with the other, or the failure to apprehend the difference—in English we might have to say transLAtion and TRANSlation—results in nothing less than "the rootlessness of Western thinking."[3] TransLAtion is an abstraction, a false equivalent; and TRANSlation, as the passage of an experience from one to another, may be impossible.

The most famous romantic formulation of the task of translation, the one that all the theorists and historians of the topic have fastened upon, is Schleiermacher's, which has become famous for its simplicity. It seems to give us only two options: bringing the author to the reader (source language to target language, as we now say) or the reader to the author. Here is the famous sentence: "Either the translator leaves the author in peace as much as possible and moves the reader toward him; or he leaves the reader in peace as much as possible and moves the writer toward him."[4] That the personae are here cast as author (*Schriftsteller*) and reader (*Leser*) immediately presumes that the question involves delayed communication by way of writing, as if to imply that face-to-face interactions between speakers, whether of the same or different languages, are not also thoroughly conditioned by acts of translation (for a speaker of one's own language can raise all sorts of questions about what is "really" meant). Schleiermacher abides by the dominant understanding of translation many of us share, which is based on the lonely efforts of learned persons to turn the great books written in Greek or Aramaic or Sanskrit (and so forth) into a language we can understand. But the focus on writing arguably weakens the force of those ethical and consequential translation events experienced in real time and without the resources of scholarly support. The story of the *shibboleth* is a famous example. The Ephraimites who could not make the "sh" sound were put to death by the Gileadities, who could (Jgs 12:6). Perhaps the oddest thing

2. Barbara Cassin, ed., *Vocabulaire européen des philosophies: dictionnaire des intraduisibles* (Paris: Seuil, 2004), 1307.

3. Martin Heidegger, *Off the Beaten Track*, trans. Julian Young and Kenneth Haynes (Cambridge: Cambridge University Press, 2002), 6.

4. Friedrich Schleiermacher, "On the Different Methods of Translation," trans. Susan Bernofsky, in *The Translation Studies Reader*, ed. Lawrence Venuti, 2nd ed. (New York: Routledge, 2004), 49.

about this story is that the sound was construed as unheard ("say now Shibboleth; and he said Sibboleth") or unlearnable by near neighbors, among whom there seemed to be no bilingual speakers. It thereby preserves the myth that language marks the stranger, and that something crucial to one tongue cannot be reproduced by another. Every dialect speaker—in other words, every speaker—has experienced something like this.

In fact, at the beginning of his lecture, Schleiermacher carefully establishes that translation is everywhere and everything, happening between two native speakers of the same language and even in accounting for oneself to oneself. He purposely limits his discussion to writing, excluding the "interpreter" (*Dolmetscher*), who merely serves the short-term needs of businessmen and indeed all spoken, real-time transactions.[5] Even with these caveats, there is still a way to read his sentence that does not quite align with the binary neatness of its apparent logic. Both writer and reader are to be left "in peace as much as possible" (*lässt . . . möglichst in Ruhe*). Peace *as much as possible*: how much peace *is* possible? Are these two paths really "so very different from one another that one or the other must certainly be followed as strictly as possible" (again, *as possible*), or do they come down to much the same thing in the end, which is a place "at some point between the two" which, as Schleiermacher goes on to specify in a passage that has received less attention than it deserves, "will always be the position of the translator" (49)? The translator, on this finding, will not bring much peace; he will aim for one extreme that already affords only a certain amount of peace, but he will end up falling short and bringing, presumably, even less peace. The position he is always in will be the position of presenting the challenge of the stranger, the foreign tongue (*Fremde* in German does service as both stranger and foreigner). This is at the heart of the second major legacy that translation studies has taken from Schleiermacher's work: the importance of what has come to be called *foreignizing*.[6] This involves understanding the major task of the translator who operates under the preferred tactic of bringing the reader toward the author as that of handing over "a feeling of the foreign," or indeed, of the strange (*das Gefühl des fremden*), of what is extraterritorial (*ausländisches*) (53). Here the target language must be "bent to a foreign likeness" so that the native speaker is taken to a place that is not his own, but one that can be made his own with enough effort and good will. There are risks here, not just of offending good

5. Ibid., 43–44.

6. See Lawrence Venuti, *The Translator's Invisibility: A History of Translation*, 2nd ed. (London: Routledge, 2008), e.g., 15–16, 18, 20.

taste but of being seen to produce "mongrels" (*Blendlinge*), children who do not replicate their parents, "ungainly" and "alien" noises (53).

Schleiermacher hints at something more stressful and demanding than Paul Ricoeur's model of "linguistic hospitality . . . where the pleasure of dwelling in the other's language is balanced by the pleasure of receiving the foreign word at home, in one's own welcoming house."[7] For Ricoeur, this pleasure is consequent upon a mourning for the perfect translation we cannot have and thus devolves from a desire to make small amends for the curse of Babel. Ricoeur's welcoming subject is thus a universal one: it is mankind that here suffers and desires. Schleiermacher, on the other hand, is a historicist. Not all languages are in a position to respond positively to being foreignized. Those "confined within the narrow bounds of a classical style"[8]—a dig at the French, presumably—will not welcome the stranger. Only those "freer languages" with a tolerance for innovation can do so, those where the foreign is welcome and the rules of speech are flexible. It is no surprise that, in a lecture delivered in Berlin in the summer of 1813 at the height of the allied push against Napoleon, it was the German language that fulfilled this requirement. In seeking to set up German as a cosmopolitan alternative to French, and above all as a medium that might eventually bring together all the German-speaking political entities into a nation, Schleiermacher was a man of his times. This helps explain why he stopped short of the absolute cosmopolitanism that seems at this point to beckon. To tolerate and appreciate the foreign element in one's language is not to give up a primary loyalty to that one language, "just as to one nation." German (and a putative Germany) was driven to "translation *en masse*; there is no turning back, we must keep forging on."[9] The health of the language depends upon "extensive contact with the foreign": the stranger is indispensable to the health of the homeland. But what predictably emerged from this was not a Germany that was disseminated out into the world but a world that was absorbed into Germany:

> our people, because of its esteem for the foreign and its own mediating nature, may be destined to unite all the jewels of foreign science and art together with our own in our own language, forming, as it were, a great historical whole that will be preserved at the center and heart of Europe, so that now, with the help of our language, everyone will be able to

7. Paul Ricoeur, *On Translation*, trans. Eileen Brennan (New York: Routledge, 2004), 10.
8. Schleiermacher, "On the Different Methods of Translation," 54.
9. Ibid., 58, 62.

> enjoy all the beautiful things that the most different ages have given us as purely and perfectly as possible for one who is foreign to them. Indeed, this seems to be the true historical goal of translation as a whole, as it is now native to us. (62)

The non-German foreigner will be able to enjoy the best that has been known and thought in the world by learning German; to learn German is both to learn the principle of foreignization and to acquire its fruits. The imperative seems to generate an ethical demand to open the borders of the mind, but not everyone can do it. It is easier for the Germans than the French.

So the German speaker can have it both ways: he or she can fully receive the stranger without threatening the integrity of the German language, which works with the foreign, and completes itself through the foreign, without ceasing to be itself. Antoine Berman's important study of the German tradition upon which Schleiermacher draws—Herder, Goethe, and the Schlegels, among others—finds in Humboldt the critical moment at which this process must stop short if it is not to produce the stranger as a threat: the goal of translation is to make us feel the foreign (*Fremd*) but not the strangeness (*Fremdheit*).[10] This *Fremdheit* is disturbing: it is the foreign "in all its force . . . It may be the terror of difference, but also its marvel" (155). This is something like what it was to welcome Dionysus, to take the risk of what is unknown. There is no prospect of preserving the peace; or, one might say (reverting to Schleiermacher's terms), we have gone astray along the route from author to reader and found ourselves in an extraneous space where not much peace is possible. It is Hölderlin, in Berman's account, whose work lives in that space by way of a "sovereign and violent archaism" which does not shy away from violence as the inevitable accompaniment of revealing what is hidden (168, 171). Here, translation is a way of being possessed, as if by a new or alien god.

Schleiermacher wrote for a world in which, of course, there was no state called "Germany," and where a common German language could have been proposed either as the precursor of a political unity to come or as an alternative to and perhaps even a prohibition against state formation. It is easy to both imagine and defend a cosmopolitanism that depends only on learning or preserving a language, one that need not encounter problems of citizenship and of national borders. But he was still confident of the German language as occupying the "center and heart of Europe" in a sense that must

10. Antoine Berman, *The Experience of the Foreign: Culture and Translation in Romantic Germany*, trans. S. Heyvaert (Albany: State University of New York Press, 1992), 154.

seem at least territorial, if not fully national. The ghost of a politics and an emergent history thus loomed over the ideal of a group of language users whose tolerance for strangers was not yet constrained by modern nationality. He knew well that the French Republic had embraced highly restrictive policies (albeit only partially imposed) about its own dialects and regional languages; the political coherence of the state was seen to depend upon everyone speaking French (not Occitane, Breton, Gascon, and so on). The declared openness of German was thus a staged rebuke directed at the punitively centralizing theories of the Abbé Grégoire and others like him.[11] But even Schleiermacher, though he was less overtly statist (and anti-Semitic) than his contemporary Fichte, sought to avoid the creation of linguistic "mongrels."

Derrida took up an alternative instance of the paradigm of translation that he sees as constitutive of another German romanticism, one found in the work of Schelling and there wedded to a theology in which sameness and difference combine to insist on translation as both an obligation and a (mis)representation. As god needs man for his own revelation (to himself?), so man is at one with god even in his distance from him. This, in Derrida's terms, entails an obligation to translation, *devoir-traduire*, in all of the various senses of *devoir*: to be bound to, to be in debt for, to have a duty to, to take up a task.[12] Man is one with other men in the eyes and being of god (sameness) but yet different from them in his empirical life as an individual. The same logic of sameness in difference governs the institutions of human inquiry, for instance, poetry and philosophy: there can be no absolute distinction between the two of the sort that would put philosophy, for example, in the place of foundational knowledge, beyond translation or absolutely translatable. Philosophy, according to Derrida, cannot be a single language, any more than a culture can be a single culture.[13] What is translated is the same even as it is different, neither distinctions nor similarities are absolute.

11. Grégoire's address to the convention on the need to suppress the *patois* is reproduced in Renéé Balibar and Dominique Laporte, *Le Français national: politique et practiques de la langue nationale sous la Révolution française* (Paris: Hachette, 1974), 198–215. In 1782, the Berlin Academy ran a competition for essays explaining why French had become the "universal" language of Europe, though it surely had not, notwithstanding its currency among some national elites.

12. Jacques Derrida, *Eyes of the University: Right to Philosophy 2*, trans. Jan Plug et al. (Stanford, CA: Stanford University Press, 2004), 65.

13. See Jacques Derrida, *Negotiations: Interventions and Interviews, 1971–2001*, ed. and trans. Elizabeth Rottenberg (Stanford, CA: Stanford University Press, 2002): "Philosophy does not have just one memory . . . it has always been bastard, hybrid, grafted, multilinear, polyglot" (337).

Derrida, however, does not find Schelling to be experiencing a simple access of liberal right-mindedness in positing all difference as sameness, but as marking a choice of tendencies. His position can be taken as a liberal rebuke of Kant's commitment to the primacy of philosophy, but it has within it also the potential for absolute statism, a "totalizing . . . temptation whose consequences can reverse the liberal demand."[14] What is between the two is a state of constant vigilance, the elucidation of which David Clark understands to be Derrida's purpose in taking up Schelling in the first place. If the formation of culture and individuality (*Bildung*) involves the duty to translate, and if the work of translation accepts that nothing is either fully translatable or fully untranslatable, then every attempt to affirm or construct *Bildung* involves "a risk whose outcome cannot be determined in advance."[15] It is this that gives German romanticism, for Derrida, what Clark calls its "deterritorializing force" and its sense of the individual subject as always other to itself, or on the point of so becoming.

Did English speakers in the romantic period take this risk, putting themselves in the hands of strangers with no guarantee of a return to the selves they left behind? They had lived for centuries knowing the miscegenated nature of their language and even fought bitterly over the status of Norman-French and Latinate terms as compared with those of Anglo-Saxon origin, a struggle kept alive in the eighteenth century by Sharon Turner and others and taken up again by Noah Webster in his efforts to produce a politically correct American English based on the Saxon model. Scott's *Ivanhoe* opens with some acerbic reflections on the relative currencies of Anglo-Saxon and Norman-French words, which embody in their usages all the violent ethnic and economic differences of twelfth-century England. These were exactly the assumptions that the eighteenth-century Saxonists sought to keep alive and to deploy toward a new democracy. But Scott himself takes a sunny view of the subsequent history of the language. Saxons and Normans were obliged to create a *lingua franca* from which there "arose by degrees the structure of our present English language, in which the speeches of the victors and the vanquished have been so happily blended together; and which has since been so richly improved by importations from the classical languages, and from those spoken by the southern nations of Europe."[16] The events of the novel, however, offer no evidence of this happy outcome.

14. Ibid., 78.

15. David L. Clark, "Lost and Found in Translation: Romanticism and the Legacies of Jacques Derrida," *Studies in Romanticism* 46 (2007): 175.

16. Scott, *Ivanhoe*, 17.

Above all, as we have seen, England has no place for the book's most accomplished translator, whose talents in both languages and medicine allow others to proclaim her a witch: the Jewess Rebecca.

There is in British romanticism no equivalent to the great speculative and practical project of translation going on in German at the time. To find a comparable moment one would have to go back to Dryden, who was writing at a point in history when English was imagining itself for the first time as about to conquer the world. There is no British romantic theory of translation that significantly advances beyond Dryden. To be sure, there is a display of theory and an effort toward it: Alexander Tytler's anonymously published essay seeking to set out "the general principles of the art."[17] But Tytler endorses the old Lutheran position (which indeed goes back to Cicero) that Schleiermacher rejected: the best translations are those in which "the merit of the original work is so completely transfused into another language, as to be as distinctly apprehended, and as strongly felt, by a native of the country to which that language belongs, as it is by those who speak the language of the original work" (14). To this end considerable license is allowed: the translator can, for example, correct "what appears to be a careless or inaccurate expression of the original" (59) or engage in "happy amplification" (76). Thus, Pope is deemed to have improved on Homer (90), just as Southey thought the French translators had improved upon their Arabic sources. Tytler's idea that a "man of genius" can rise above his original by "substituting figure and metaphor to simple sentiment"(47) can be read as a powerful counterargument to any tendency toward foreignization. Here, the spirit of the original seems to be less important than its shelf appeal to the British reader: the translator must never "suffer his original to fall" (81). Since there is almost nothing in Tytler's book that represents an advance on the classical theorists of translation, what is most striking is the book itself. At four hundred pages, it suggests a market for a topic that had not previously existed. Its encyclopedic effort to survey all important existing translations (including translations of novels) and to establish principles for undertaking future ones suggests a need for a working guide to what has been done and a template for what is to come. In that prescription, the challenge of strangeness is deemed less desirable than the production of acceptable and pleasurable reading matter.

Few—even among romanticists—have cause to remember that Wordsworth, the poet widely considered the founding father of British romanticism, the author of *The Prelude* and coauthor of *Lyrical Ballads*, and the

17. [Alexander Fraser Tytler], *Essay on the Principles of Translation*, 2nd ed. (London, 1797), 10.

exponent of an intensely native style intended to displace those "sickly and stupid German Tragedies" from the literary marketplace, was in fact himself a translator.[18] Hardly any of this work was published, whereas Dryden's *Virgil* of 1697 was the culmination of a distinguished career in translation and the summation of a major effort at projecting the culture of Restoration England as the latest incarnation of *translatio studii et imperii*, the westward movement of classical culture and civilization from Greece to Rome and Rome to London (admittedly after a detour through Paris). Dryden's prefaces to his various translations established him as a major theorist of translation itself, and his Virgil made a good deal of money; Pope's Homer made even more. Wordsworth barely notices or admits to the habit, and the Homer translation published by William Cowper in the 1790s made a relatively small splash. The most formative and original translation of the times was Henry Cary's English version of Dante, which served to inspire poets and readers to a new experience of all things Italian. French and then German literature continued to make their way into the British literary marketplace, and Wordsworth and Coleridge went to Germany in part out of a sense that learning German would be a good career move as well as an intellectually profitable skill. But Coleridge's cosmopolitan spirit went mostly into philosophy and theology, while Byron wore his so lightly that it could never take on the ungainly appearance of a project. Blake, Austen, Clare, Keats, Crabbe: almost nothing. Shelley did quite a bit of translating but published almost none of it, and what is most often remembered is his negative view of the possibility of translating poetry. What had happened?

In fact there *was* a good deal of translation, though if one were to construct a canon of romantic translators there would be relatively little overlap with the familiar list of great writers that has come down to us: Southey and Hemans would appear as major figures, while Wordsworth might earn a footnote. It is partly the post-romantic canonization of the unadorned (but purified) native tongue that has persuaded us to ignore the kinds of translation that were occurring, and partly the relative scarcity of claims made by the translators themselves for the urgency and importance of their work. The mainstreaming of the native ballad tradition, largely by way of the Ossian phenomenon (itself marketed as a translation from the Gaelic), made it less likely that a man of the times would argue, as Dryden had done, the need for sustained attention to classical or foreign models as a way of contributing to the refinement of English. Cowper's case for a new English-

18. *The Prose Works of William Wordsworth*, ed. W. J. B. Owen and Jane Worthington Smyser (Oxford: Clarendon, 1974), 1:128.

language Homer was founded on the preeminence of Milton and the blank verse standard. Many British writers felt that they already had a national language and no longer felt the need to turn to Greece and Rome to make it better. If readers wanted the challenge of the unfamiliar they could turn to Burns, who was staged (though only thanks to the glossaries) as part of the British national consensus; at least his work inspired little or no discussion of translation. At the same time, and in reaction, there was a late-romantic revival of Hellenism and a new enthusiasm for teaching Greek, largely to supply those elements of the mind and heart that native culture was felt to be lacking.

Dryden had been more confident: "when I want at home, I must seek abroad." In describing how he does so he displaces the traditional images of grafting and rerooting in native soil by a very modern reference to imports and balance of payments:

> But what I bring from *Italy*, I spend in *England*: Here it remains, and here it circulates; for if the Coyn be good, it will pass from one Hand to another. I Trade both with the Living and the Dead, for the enrichment of our Native Language. We have enough in *England* to supply our necessity; but if we will have things of Magnificence and Splendour, we must get them by Commerce. Poetry requires Ornament, and that is not to be had from our Old *Teuton* Monosyllables; therefore if I find any Elegant Word in a Classick Author, I propose it to be Naturaliz'd, by using it my self; and if the Publick approves of it, the Bill passes.[19]

Given his respect for plain living sustained by cultures of subsistence, Wordsworth would likely have favored neither the substance nor the wit of this fantasy of commercial one-upmanship, increasing the national wealth (and diminishing its debt) without spending any real money. Good English coin has Latin behind it as its guarantor of value, and the desire for splendor can be satisfied without any loss to the treasury: this is a "luxury" economy that enhances rather than diminishing our well-being. Dryden's vocabulary is brilliantly confusing here. He wants to argue that it is necessity and not luxury that is being appeased; we import not just what we desire but what we need. But it is magnificence and splendor, not mere subsistence, that is gained, so that subsistence bizarrely comes to include magnificence. In this way, in the realm of the language (and there only?), the desire for distinction

19. John Dryden, *The Works of Virgil in English*, ed. Alan Roper and Vinton A. Dearing (Berkeley: University of California Press, 1987), 336.

and display can coexist with the integrity of the core investment in "the *English* Idiom." This is naturalization, not foreignization. The strangeness of the stranger is softened by public approval and above all by the universality of the money form which makes everything translatable into everything else.

Later in the century, after Dryden and Pope had made their money out of the market for a measure of magnificence, the popularity of a middling diction begins to show up in the claims made by various translators of Greek and Latin, who now looked to the classics as models of the kind of plain speaking that English needed and could attain. Here, the foreign is adduced as a means of keeping English to its own straight and narrow path. Philip Francis found a "natural Simplicity" in Horace that could, in the hands of a good translator like himself, easily accord with the capacities of English. Martin Madan found in Juvenal a "plainness" derived from the "honesty and integrity of his own mind."[20] Suddenly, Horace and Juvenal sound like Wordsworth: there is no foreignization here. The Langhornes' translation of Plutarch proposed to keep their English "unmixed with Greek," because their author was usually read by young people "who ought to read their own language in its native purity, unmixed and untainted with the idioms of different tongues."[21] In the light of such vigorously nationalistic sentiments (often taking the form of a celebration of Anglo-Saxon and sometimes of its liberties), Wordsworth's own commitment to ordinary language seems almost modest.

Shelley, Keats, Coleridge, and Byron, other major figures in the traditional poetry-based canon that has endured until quite recently, were more overtly cosmopolitan in both politics and literature. The exotic tales of Byron and Shelley and Keats's (albeit pastiche) classicism bespeak an internationalism much more apparent than anything in Wordsworth's writings; they are part of a turn away from the northern Gothic vocabulary that had by then become, as Marilyn Butler has shown, the signature of a political alliance not only against Napoleon but also against enlightenment and reform in general.[22] The Gothic predilection had indeed never been hegemonic: Moore and Southey in Wordsworth's own generation, as well as Hemans and Landon in the next, were much more engaged with the classical and

20. Philip Francis, *A Poetical Translation of the Works of Horace*, 2nd ed. (London: A. Millar, 1747), 1:xi; Martin Madan, *A New and Literal Translation of the Works of Juvenal and Persius*, new ed. (Oxford: N. Bliss etc, 1807), 1:iv.

21. John and William Langhorne, *Plutarch's Lives* (Dublin: T. Ewing, 1771), 1: preface (n.p.).

22. Marilyn Butler, *Romantics, Rebels and Reactionaries: English Literature and its Background, 1760–1830* (Oxford: Oxford University Press, 1982), 113–38.

exotic-foreign than their better-known fellow authors, and this came with a commitment to translation. But the shift of emphasis over the hundred years or so between Dryden and Wordsworth is undeniable. Dryden not only produced well-received and widely circulated (and therefore profitable) translations of Ovid, Juvenal, Persius, Horace, Lucretius, and Virgil, among others, but freely acknowledged his immersion in and respect for the classics as the core of the modern British writer's identity. When not translating he was trying his hand at the *imitatio* that had by 1800 almost disappeared from sight. Much of the story of how this came to be is well-enough known: the cult of originality expressed in the native tongue contributed to the emergence of a national canon during a century of massive proto-imperial expansion and domestic nation-state consolidation. What is not so well known is the survival and transformation of both the letter and spirit of literary translation in the period called romanticism.

This oversight is partly the result of the inevitable distortion of quantitative literary history effected by an evaluative canonizing tradition that took high poetry as its benchmark. We know a lot about the publication of books like *Lyrical Ballads*, and in an extreme case like that of William Blake we can account for almost every single copy of every single book he produced (they are all singular). With the more popular and ephemeral publications it has been harder to assemble an adequate history. Those who have worked closely with the bibliographical data have remarked on the difficulties of proposing any precise accounting of the numbers and kinds of translations into English: the phenomena of secondary translation (e.g., into English from the German via the French) and of fake or unacknowledged translation, along with the fact that physical copies of many published books have not been recovered, makes it very hard to make claims for exact statistics. But broad trends can and have been identified. English versions of the Greek and Latin classics continued to appear throughout the eighteenth century, often in multiple editions, while translations of contemporary philosophical and literary works were predominantly from the French. Only in four of the years before 1800 were there more novels translated from German than from French, all in the 1790s (1794–96, 1798).[23] Even with the new fashion

23. Peter Garside, James Raven, Rainer Schöwerling, eds., *The English Novel 1770–1829: A Bibliographical Survey of Prose Fiction Published in the British Isles* (Oxford: Oxford University Press, 2000), 1:58. For a more general survey, see Stuart Gillespie and David Hopkins, eds., *The Oxford History of Literary Translation in English: Volume 3, 1660–1790* (Oxford: Oxford University Press, 2005), 123–46. William St Clair, *The Reading Nation in the Romantic Period* (Cambridge: Cambridge University Press, 2004), 130n, suggests that the demand for novels was such that only translation could meet the needs of the market.

for northern Gothic affiliations, French novels held their own well into the next century. Indeed, the 1803 Peace of Amiens saw a dramatic increase in translated French novels, as if to appease a readership painfully deprived by the wartime restraints on importation.[24] The peaks and troughs of the statistics we have, at least for the novel, do not suggest that the literary marketplace reflects any simple correlation between a slowly consolidating national canon and the number of translated books. 1799 was a banner year for foreign novels—twenty-five or more of ninety-nine published works were translations, all but two from French or German—while the years before and after (with the exception, already noted, of 1803–1804) show a much smaller proportion: nine out of seventy-two in 1800, and eight out of seventy-five in 1798, the year of *Lyrical Ballads*. Translation was going on, but it did not often feature in the high-cultural understanding of the best that could be known and thought in the world of English. Walter Scott got his start in life by translating Goethe's *Götz von Berlichingen* in 1799, and Coleridge's versions of Schiller's dramas were pitched at a marketplace keen to experience German ballads and drama, at least in the years before it became tainted by revolutionary associations. Shelley made no effort to publish any of his translation projects as independent or self-sufficient volumes, but Byron's second book, *Hours of Idleness* (1807), was subtitled *A Series of Poems Original and Translated*; his fourth was quite straightforwardly advertized as *Imitations and Translations* (1809). Byron knew that he could still create a whiff of scandal by invoking the foreign: translations of Rousseau's *Julie* and Goethe's *Werther* had become both best sellers and indices of visibly un-British behavior.

A BEAKER FULL OF THE WARM SOUTH

Before Byron, there was his friend Thomas Moore, who attained fame and some fortune with his *Odes of Anacreon* (1800). The book has gone almost undiscussed by latter-day critics and scholars, although it was in its tenth edition by 1820—not as popular as his Oriental epic poem *Lalla Rookh*, which saw six editions in its first year (1817) but still a significant success and the cornerstone of his early literary reputation. The Anacreontic poems, mostly about the pains and pleasures of love and drinking (together and separately), had been widely translated throughout the eighteenth century as offering what Penelope Wilson describes as "a miniaturized and ap-

24. Garside et al., *The English Novel 1770–1829*, 2:41.

parently classical alternative to the rigour, scholasticism, and authority of high classicism—in a word, a less formal version of classical taste."[25] Marshall Brown, in a comprehensive survey of the genre, has argued for Anacreontic poetry as a repressed but critical eighteenth-century precursor of what would become the romantic love lyric; he places it in an evolutionary process whose full articulation it represses, as if to foreclose the very tide of literary history that helps to make it what it is.[26] Brown proposes that the very genre of the Anacreontic creates an expectation of "trifles," and if one reads Moore's short lyrics one at a time in English, they do indeed have this effect. Read cumulatively, however, they take on more substance as pagan celebrations of pleasures that, in a world without other positive values or assurances of a life beyond, become both all-absorbing and melancholically impermanent. Some lyrics are rendered as antiwar poems, while others critique the martial and mercenary values of commercial culture.[27] Firmly in the tradition of Lucretian and Epicurean philosophical materialism, they can be read as hard-headed alternatives to (or versions of) an evolving culture of sentiment that made more ambitious claims for a language of feeling as capable of supporting civil society itself, claims to which the authors of *Lyrical Ballads* were not insensitive.

What most forcefully strikes the reader who is used to the bare typographic economy of that famous volume, however, is not the content of Moore's poems but their form and format. Moore gives his table of contents first in Greek, and in English only at the back of the second volume. The first printed poem is in Greek, but written by the translator himself.[28] There follows a thirty-page introduction in which Moore, like a latter-day Richard Bentley, spends a good deal of time upbraiding the inadequacies of previous translations. When we get to the poems, we find the translations sitting on top of extensive footnotes which themselves contain, among other things, other passages or entire poems in Greek, Latin, Italian, and English, sometimes translated and sometimes not. If these poems are trifles, they come embedded in a prodigious display of learning and invite a seemingly indefinite exploration of sources and analogs, whether addressing the

25. "Lyric, Pastoral and Elegy," in Gillespie and Hopkins, *The Oxford History of Literary Translation*, 181.

26. Marshall Brown, "Passion and Love: Anacreontic Song and the Roots of Romantic Lyric," *English Literary History* 66 (1999): 386.

27. See, for example, Thomas Moore, *Odes of Anacreon*, 2nd ed. (London: J. and T. Carpenter, 1802), 1:41–42, 60–62, 138–42.

28. Ibid., 1:xiii–xv.

physiognomy of erotic arousal or the associations of grasshoppers in Plato and Homer (1:38–39, 156–59). The lesson would seem to be that the anatomy of trifles is not a trifling matter. Like Southey and Shelley, Moore shows a disposition for untranslated footnotes, whether to keep dangerous knowledge from the mere Anglophone reader or simply to impress and involve the learned. He stands in a long tradition of eighteenth-century translations of the classics wherein a scholarly apparatus is attached to a translated text, sometimes with the original on the facing page (as with Philip Francis's popular *Works of Horace*), sometimes standing alone (like Pope's *Homer*). Dryden's English-only *Virgil* was, in comparison, only minimally annotated, and the notes were at the back. In this matter of annotation, Moore has, like so many of his predecessors, outdone (or overdone) Dryden, whether to flaunt his own credentials or to place his translations in an appropriately dense historical context of the sort that might recommend him as if by acclaim to distinguished membership of the "moderns."

I know of nothing else in the period quite like Moore's *Anacreon*; perhaps what is most significant about it is its anomalous status. Moore himself would return to the learned footnote (as we have seen in the previous chapter) in publishing *Lalla Rookh*, which has a distinct aura of cosmopolitanism but is not a translation: it is an Oriental verse tale in the manner of other such inventions, based on a certain amount of "fact"—travel narratives and translations of translations—but not primarily concerned with issues of semantic or metaphysical accuracy. Neither are the various translations of novels and plays from French, German and occasional other languages normally concerned with the complex issues of turning one language into another. Moore's volume does not present anything of the challenges of the truly strange stranger that Berman has found in the work of Hölderlin; Greek is Greek and English is English, and there is never any doubt where one begins and the other ends.

How much is there in British romanticism that is truly foreignizing? What is there that seeks to register the strangeness of the stranger? Keats, who did not have an elite classical education, managed to disturb his polite critics by perceived incompetence and cacaphony ("Not to the sensual ear, but, more endeared"; "O Attic shape! Fair attitude!"). And one could speculate that the language of his brilliant pastiche ballad "La Belle Dame Sans Merci" is not quite English. The French title is left untranslated and repeated as such in the body of a poem, which derives from a medieval original by Alain Chartier (written in 1424), read by Keats in a 1782 English translation, and is cleverly antiqued with bits of Chaucer, Spenser, Shakespeare, Burton's *Anatomy*, Dante (in Cary's translation), and probably more.[29] The belle dame herself speaks a "language strange" (l. 27), as does the poem in which she appears, which in one version resurrects a medieval Scots contraction—"gloam" (l. 41)—and spells "merci" as "mercy" in the text published in Leigh Hunt's *Indicator* (758). The range of possible meanings for merci/mercy, straddling English, French and Latin (thanks, compassion, pleasure, will, discretion, reward, market), which we have already seen at work in *The Merchant of Venice*, is left for conjecture. The poem poses a series of profitable puzzles, and yet its incursions into foreignizing are always contained within a dominant English-ballad diction. This is a poet whose uncouth coinages and comic-clunky classicizing—Dusketha and Breama feature in another poem of April 1819 (506)—seem to want to remain identifiably English: nothing of dignity or deliberate exteriority is brought into the language by these means, nothing profoundly strange is entertained. But the quality of *mercy/merci* remains a stubborn outlier of irreducible, multilingual compaction, demanding a basic decision even about how to pronounce it. A French word that wanders over into English, it pulls the center of gravity toward Keats's native tongue (as *mercy*) where it is also familiar enough in its foreign form (as *merci*, thanks) to be known to even a poorly schooled poet or reader. Yet French it must remain, leaving us to speculate about how much of its appearance is to be attributed to an affected, familiar, overreaching literariness ("Much have I travelled in the realms of gold") and how much to a purposive insistence on confronting an alien language. In a poem so deeply concerned with the uncanny, we should not judge Keats too readily.

Those more flagrantly cosmopolitan precursors of the 1780s and early 1790s from whom his critics often felt Keats had taken far too much—the Della Cruscans—were arguably even less invested in any purposeful task of foreignizing the English language, although they certainly challenged English taste. Robert Merry, the movement's chief figure, was a political liberal from the start: a pacificist and opponent of slavery, and thereafter a defender of the French Revolution.[30] Although they wrote from Florence and in the declared spirit of Mediterranean culture (they included Anacreontic verses in their anthologies), and although their volumes included poems written in

29. See the excellent annotations by editor Miriam Allott in *Keats: The Complete Poems* (London: Longman, 1970), 500–6.

30. See W. N. Hargreaves-Maudsley, *The English Della Cruscans and their Time, 1783–1828* (The Hague: M. Nijhoff, 1967); and M. Ray Adams, "Robert Merry, Political Romanticist," *Studies in Romanticism* 2 (1962): 23–37. For an account of the poetics (but not the politics) of the Della Cruscans, see Jerome McGann, *The Poetics of Sensibility: A Revolution in Literary Style* (Oxford: Clarendon, 1996), 74–93.

Italian and occasionally in French, usually with a translation immediately following, there is little if any crossing of languages in the warp and woof of the poetry itself. The Montgolfiers' hot air balloon is comically celebrated and mocked in Robert Merry's first volume, cowritten with Allan Ramsay, and at one point it is produced as evidence for demystifying the curse of Babel:

> Behold he mounts, and deems it fable,
> By gloomy Jews contriv'd of old,
> That those who rais'd the tow'r of Babel
> Were by th' Almighty's hand controul'd.[31]

But any prospect of reinventing a universal language is undercut when the next poem reverts to ballooning as a conventional instance of "high-towering pride" (12). Proto-Byronic rhymes like "Ferdinandos/any man does" and "brag on/Dragon" (16–17), along with mock translations "from the original Babelonian" and "from the Celtic" (25, 29), do produce much play on language but nothing much in the way of interlingual formations. The critical hostility to the Merry circle, most famously set out in Gifford's *Baviad* (1791) and *Maeviad* (1795), sees in them a threat to sexual propriety and purity of diction, but the source of the corruption is not any foreignizing tendency: the poetry is deemed just plain bad and bad in its use of English words in English senses. Hester Lynch Piozzi published a *British Synonymy* in 1794, whose avowed purpose was to assist foreign speakers who want to refine their study of English literature; some of her explanations are so complex that in order to follow them her reader would have to have had a sophisticated command of the language already in place. But there is no reciprocal invitation for native speakers to take anything of the foreign into English, much as they might be encouraged to appreciate the food, the wine and the climate of the sunny south.

Among the best-known romantic writers, it may well be Shelley who most fully commits himself to an engagement with the foreign, and here too it is most often by way of a Mediterranean turn. It was Shelley, we may recall, who wrote of language as vitally metaphoric, and thereby analogous to and even generative of an ethics of love, a medium within which the stranger might be welcomed. Poetry, its highest expression, reproduces a "common Universe" and "participates in the eternal, the infinite, and the

31. [Robert Merry and Allan Ramsay], *The Arno Miscellany; Being a Collection of Fugitive Pieces Written by the Members of a Society called the Oziosi at Florence* (Florence, 1784), 11.

one"; each true poet contributes to "that great poem" built up through time as if through "the co-operating thoughts of one great mind."[32] The essence of poetry here, one supposes, can be translated well enough between languages, just as distinctions of time, place and person are "convertible with respect to the highest poetry without injuring it as poetry" (279). And yet Shelley's most famous statement about translation is a negative one: "It were as wise to cast a violet into a crucible that you might discover the formal principle of its color and odor, as to seek to transfuse from one language into another the creations of a poet" (280). This statement comes in the context of a discussion of the power of sounds, which are indeed specific to the languages in which they are spoken: think, for instance, of the intractable difficulties of sensing or fully understanding classical quantitative meter in English. But something can be carried over, and Shelley has to have this argument both ways if he is to propose high poetry as the core of a worldwide dissemination of vital knowledge open in principle to all who are not hopelessly mired in delusions of atomic selfhood. Poetry must ultimately reflect "the similitudes of things" and not the differences between them (277).

How does his own work attempt to meet these requirements? If not by translation, then how? Compared to Southey or Swinburne, Shelley is not a compulsive imitator of non-English meters, although his command of *terza rima* shows real virtuosity. His predilection for Greek titles (*Epipsychidion*, *Alastor*, and the Greek-Hebrew *Adonais* among them) does seem to commit to gestures of foreignization at the level of the word. But like most other poets of the time, he chooses to use the familiar Latin forms of gods and goddesses when translating from Greek to English, thereby making only a minimum challenge to his readers: Jove, Juno, Mercury, Venus and Minerva are part of the standard poetic diction. Translation is nevertheless a significant part of his oeuvre, principally from Greek, Italian, Spanish, and German, with a little Latin and French. It appears that his way of welcoming strange literature reflects the position set forth in the "Defence of Poetry": he is more concerned with the sound and spirit rather than the letter of his source literature, assuming perhaps that "the great poem" building up through time is best served by giving access to what he deems universal and therefore translatable without too much focus on the techniques of translation itself. Kelvin Everest has argued that "Adonais," for example, displays a comprehensive absorption of Greek and Latin sources arrayed together with allusions to Keats's own poetry, with the effect of dignifying the dead

32. *Shelley's Prose*, 295, 279, 287.

(and famously unlearned) English poet by placing him in the company of the classical immortals.[33] This is more than just a standard homage to his unjustly treated fellow countryman; it enacts the major argument of the "Defence" for a common transcultural and transhistorical society of those embodying high poetic genius in spite of the constraints of place and time and those petty limitations of local moralities and customs which bind us to "the accident of surrounding impressions."[34]

TRANSLATING INTO PHILOSOPHY

Derrida has consistently maintained that translation is at the heart of philosophy, that the problem of one is the problem of the other, indeed, that the very concept of philosophy is premised on a notion of absolute translatability—and untranslatability. In the "violent difficulty" accompanying "the transference of a nonphilosopheme into a philosopheme," the philosopher purports to limit the play of meanings that a word can have: so *pharmakon* must become, say, *remedy*, and only that.[35] Once the clear definition is assumed, as it must be for philosophy to thrive and without which we will not be able to claim that we know what we are talking about, it becomes untranslatable within its own language and absolutely translatable, without remainder, into others. It means what it means, always and everywhere, as if taking on the authority and charisma of the proper name. But the translation has already occurred—and occurred *within* the language—at the moment when one sense out of many is given to the term in order to charge it with philosophical precision and gravity. The passage of a foreign philosophical term into English thus generates an ideal of consistency as coterminous with meaning that mimics what has already happened in the original language wherein the term has been rendered philosophic in the

33. Kelvin Everest, "Shelley's *Adonais* and John Keats," *Essays in Criticism* 57. 3 (2007): 237–64. See also John Knapp, "The Spirit of Classical Hymn in Shelley's 'Hymn to Intellectual Beauty,'" *Style* 33.1 (1999): 43–66. The fullest studies of Shelley's idea of translation are Timothy Webb, *The Violet in the Crucible: Shelley and Translation* (Oxford: Clarendon, 1976); and Jennifer Wallace, *Shelley and Greece: Rethinking Romantic Hellenism* (London: Macmillan, 1997). The case for the continued importance of Rome within the Romantic popularization of Hellenism is made by Jonathan Sachs, "Greece or Rome? The Uses of Antiquity in Late Eighteenth-Century and Early Nineteenth-Century British Literature," *Literature Compass* 6.2 (2009): 314–31. Webb finds "Epipsychidion" to be "bilingual in conception" (304) in that it reflects Shelley's deep immersion in Dante (among others) and daily use of Italian.

34. *Shelley's Prose*, 295.

35. Derrida, *Dissemination*, 72.

first place. In both cases, the choices are disguised and manifold other options repressed.

In the 1790s, the most challenging instance of translation came in the form of German philosophy. Nonphilosophical literature was being translated into English and (in the case of drama) adapted for performance on the London stage with remarkable speed and energy, but there is little evidence of the English language being modified in the process; here, to recall Schleiermacher's terms, the authors were very definitely being brought wholesale toward the readers. Philosophy presented a different challenge, because it made for rebarbatively difficult reading and because it was often thought to be reinventing the discipline by specifying a wholly new vocabulary for wholly new ideas. Surely here, in the play of *Vorstellung* and *Darstellung*, *Vernunft* and *Verstand*, *Begriff*, *Geist*, and other such obvious untranslatables, one might expect to see English stretched to the point of inevitable openness to the language of the stranger. The case of Kant is perhaps preeminent: no full translation into English of *The Critique of Practical Reason* appeared until 1838; *The Critique of Pure Reason* followed (by a different hand) two years later, and *The Critique of Judgment* only in 1882. But from at least the mid-1790s, those in the know knew of Kant as someone they ought to know better.[36] F. A. Nitsch's *General and Introductory View of Professor Kant's Principles* (1796) was a summary (based on Reinhold) rather than a translation—and not a very accurate one. It offered itself only as a prelude to translations yet to come. But Beck's *Principles of Critical Philosophy* (1797) does expound the arguments of the three great critiques and makes a careful effort at explaining Kant's key terms and principles in English. His translator (probably John Richardson) makes the fateful decision to translate *Begriff* as notion (rather than concept), thus setting a confusing precedent that would recur in a later, influential English translation of Hegel.[37] He also confesses the difficulty of translating a language that is "better adapted to philosophising than probably any other, whether ancient or modern, our own multiform tongue not excepted" (xvi), though he takes

36. On Kant's transmission into English, see René Wellek, *Immanuel Kant in England, 1793–1838* (Princeton, NJ: Princeton University Press, 1931), an account significantly updated by Giuseppe Micheli, "The Early Reception of Kant's Thought in England, 1785–1805," in *Kant and his Influence*, ed. George MacDonald Ross and Tony McWalter (London: Continuum, 2005), 202–314.

37. James Sigismund Beck, *The Principles of Critical Philosophy, Selected from the Works of Emmanuel Kant, Expounded by James Sigismund Beck . . . Translated by an Auditor* (London, 1797), xxvii.

courage from the relation of English and German as "sister-dialects of the Teutonic" (xvii).

Richardson went on to publish his own two-volume edition of Kant's works, in which he makes the case for a necessary measure of foreignizing. Writing of himself in the third person, he points out that some license with the "idiom of the English language" occurred because "he was under the unavoidable necessity of introducing several alien scientific terms, which he hopes, however, will be deemed, by major critics, not unworthy of naturalization."[38] In the same year, Willich's *Elements of the Critical Philosophy* (1798) printed summaries and digests of Kant's philosophy made by others, rather than offering translations of the primary works. There is an extensive glossary which seeks to explain the key terms, albeit often without giving the German word being translated into English.[39] But Willich is skeptical of the philosopher's aspiration to absolute terminological precision of the sort described by Derrida as involving a "violent difficulty in the transference of a nonphilosopheme into a philosopheme"[40] The violence, which enacts translation to make translation redundant, lies in the production of seemingly clear definitions cutting out the play of polysemous meanings. But no one can maintain this standard, Willich says. Even the best—Bacon, Newton, Kant—"not rarely deviate from the original, or primary, definitions of terms" because of the "unsettled state of language in general" (35). They cannot fully compensate for the nominalistic economy of ordinary language, whereby one word must do duty for different meanings. Willich's glossary represents a comprehensive effort to address those meanings. But he seems to resist the impulse to foreignize when he criticizes those who are prone to "adopting new idioms in one language which are borrowed from another" (36). The struggle to get over Kant's meanings to Anglophone readers must, we assume, be carried out in conventional English.

Among the well-known romantics, it is probably Coleridge who makes the biggest and most visible effort to incorporate the findings of the new German philosophy into English. Coleridge was famous as a coiner of new words—*esemplastic* being just the most famous among many—and one of the unintended good consequences of his notorious borrowings (or plagiarisms, as some contend) is that we can often see exactly how he translated

38. [John Richardson], *Essays and Treatises on Moral, Political, and Various Philosophical Subjects, by Emanuel Kant* (London, 1798–99), 1:vii.

39. Willich translates *Begriff* as "conception": A. F. M Willich, *Elements of the Critical Philosophy, containing a concise account of its origin and tendency; a view of all the works published by its founder, Professor Immanuel Kant* . . . (London, 1798), 149.

40. Derrida, *Dissemination*, 72.

between the two languages. While he took a good deal from Kant, Fichte, and Jacobi, among a multitude of others, it is Schelling whose work is most thoroughly stitched into the text of *Biographia Literaria*. Thanks to the editing skills of James Engell and Walter Jackson Bate, it is now easy to mount an unpolemical word-for-word comparison of some of the key passages with their German originals. Chapter 12 of Coleridge's book, which is where the use of Schelling is at its most dense, is a good place to track some key terms as they migrate from German into English. Coleridge justifies neologism on many occasions, and here, in the case of "potence" (from *Potenz*), it is as usual the aspiration to precision which justifies the inevitable inconvenience of forming new words.[41] A similar dream of exactitude governs his hopes for a new Greek lexicon that would present together all the English, French, German, and Latin synonyms.[42] Coleridge endorsed a model of language whereby the vocabulary of the schools would gradually percolate down to influence the language of the marketplace, a top-down theory intended to guarantee the intelligentsia's control over the common tongue. One of the means by which he saw this occurring was by way of "a certain collective, unconscious good sense working progressively to desynonymize those words originally of the same meaning, which the conflux of dialects had supplied to the more homogeneous languages, as the Greek and German; and which the same cause, joined with accidents of translation from original works of different countries, occasion in mixt languages like our own."[43] Incremental specification develops through historical time thanks to the efforts of genius (in desynonymizing) both creating and reflecting a more and more precise human experience. In English, this happens in part through foreignization, or "accidents of translation," in much the same way Cicero felt that Latin could learn from Greek. But what is lost in this process is the multivalence of primary terms. *Pharmakon*, recalling Derrida's platonic example, might be desynonymized into its range of "meanings" (poison, cure, drug, recipe, and so on) so that one and one only is fixed in

41. Coleridge, *Biographia Literaria*, 1:287. The literature on Coleridge's use of both new words and German sources is substantial. The editors offer a very convenient overview (1:xiv–xxvi). See also Thomas McFarland, *Coleridge and the Pantheist Tradition* (Oxford: Clarendon, 1969), esp. 1–52. Fred Shapiro has compiled a useful list of the neologisms in the notebooks, which includes such now-familiar words as *idealize, psychologize, subconsciousness*, and *psycho-analytic*: see "Neologisms in Coleridge's Notebooks," *Notes and Queries* 32.3 (1985): 346–47.

42. Coleridge, *Biographia Literaria*, 1:239. Adelung's unfinished *Mithridates* (the lack of access to which De Quincey claimed to regret when the Malay traveler knocked at his door) attempted something like this in setting out to compare around five hundred languages through parallel translations of the Lord's Prayer.

43. Ibid., 1:82–83.

place according to context; what comes with this is the fantasy (and only the fantasy) of translatability. The more we decompose and disambiguate, the more scientific language becomes, and the more it is possible to imagine a comparable exactitude evolving in another language. Everything, at least at the level of the word, becomes translatable.[44] The goal of philosophy is the absence of remainders.[45]

How then does Coleridge himself go about translating Schelling in the *Biographia?* Some of his decisions at the level of the word are intriguingly inconsistent. *Begriff* becomes either *notion* or *conception;*[46] here there may or may not be an effort to decide whether and when Schelling himself intends a "precise" reference to the Kantian term of art (for which *concept* has become the accepted English equivalent). *Naturwissenschaft* becomes both *natural philosophy* and *the science of nature* but also simply *natural science*, which causes a bit of trouble when Coleridge has to translate *Natur-Philosophie*, which also becomes *natural philosophy* (1:255–57). Complete precision, in other words, is not possible, as Coleridge more or less admits in deciding to expand the Kantian *Anschauung* to include the intellectual intuitions that Kant himself precluded (1:289). The foreignizing of English, whereby, for example, *Natur-Philosophie* (a term we do not have) must be registered as different from "natural science" (which we do have), is seemingly not manageable without ambiguity. The clarity of a term in the source language runs into the generality of the chosen translation in the target language, and as a result the new knowledge does not come across. *Begriff* and *Anschauung* pose similar problems.

De Quincey, also an able Germanist and a translator of Kant, was unkind to Coleridge, whom he accused of retarding the British acceptance of Kant not only by occasional misunderstandings but also by "expounding the oracle in words of more Delphic obscurity than the German original could have presented to the immaturest student."[47] Kant, he thought, was committed to restoring the original meanings of Greek and Latin terms, and when he did create new terms it was because of their relation to new ideas

44. For a fine discussion of Coleridge an desynonymization, see James McKusick, *Coleridge's Philosophy of Language* (New Haven, CT: Yale University Press, 1986), 91–100.

45. See Jacques Derrida, *The Ear of the Other: Otobiography, Transference, Translation*, ed. Christie McDonald, trans. Peggy Kamuf (Lincoln: University of Nebraska Press, 1988), 120: "The origin of philosophy is the thesis of translatability . . . Philosophical discourse cannot master a word meaning two things at the same time and which therefore cannot be translated without an essential loss."

46. Coleridge, *Biographia Literaria*, 1:243, 255, 262–63.

47. Thomas De Quincey, *The Collected Writings of Thomas De Quincey*, ed. David Masson (Edinburgh: Adam and Charles Black, 1889–90), 10:77.

(10:72, 74–75).[48] Any obscurity this might cause is hardly to be considered a fault. But the Kantian sentence is another matter: "He has sentences which have been measured by a carpenter, and some of them run two feet eight by six inches" (10:259). The German disposition runs toward packing sentences with as many words as possible, and because there is no established public language culture, nothing has modified this disposition (10:122–23). Left to himself, Kant "might naturally enough have written a book from beginning to end in one vast hyperbolical sentence" (10:161).

English, for De Quincey, occupies a middle ground between the long-windedness of German and the extreme concision of French. At this point any impulse toward foreignization is displaced by a point-scoring comparison of the national languages, which itself nests all too readily within the comparative estimation of the various national cultures popular during the eighteenth century and given a sharper edge in times of war. Here the proclivity of the British for a middle ground was already notorious, and in linguistic terms this means a little bit of borrowing but not too much. While French had already been deemed an aristocratic deviation, German took on revolutionary associations in the 1790s, partly through the content of the plays of Schiller and Kotzebue and partly thanks to the readiness of some of Kant's interpreters to associate the progress of the critical philosophy with the efforts of the founder of the Illuminati, Adam "Spartacus" Weisshaupt. This is turn would fade into a mentalist-metaphysical alternative of the sort preferred by De Quincey, Carlyle, and the later Coleridge during the period of the German states' contributions to the northern alliance against France.

GLOSSING SCOTLAND, ESTRANGING AMERICA

In the preceding chapter I used the term *impacted reading* to describe the effect of heavily annotated texts, suggesting that the experience is particularly striking when it occurs in poetry, where the expectation of aesthetic pleasure may be at its highest. A related effect can be ascribed to the glossary, the appended word list at the back of the book to which we must turn for the elucidation of difficult or unfamiliar words. Shelley, we recall, claimed

48. The list of words that came into English by way of the first four translations of the first *Critique* between 1838 and 1929 is impressive, and includes many now-commonplace terms, among them *all-embracing, coexistently, naturalistic, ontologically, regressively, subsumed, unilaterally,* and *view-point*. Many of these are in the first translation (1838) by Haywood. See Roland Hall, "Kant's *Critique of Pure Reason*: New Words and Antedatings for the Translations," *Notes and Queries* 32.3 (1985), 347–55.

that poetry, in the expanded sense in which he used the word (where language is but its supreme instance), could lead us beyond the curse of Babel and essentially beyond the predicaments of translation among languages, because the acts of mind (and heart) involved in this experience are those of inexhaustible love and sympathy and hence a recognition of infinite relationality. Insofar as this entails the shedding of "inharmonious barbarisms" by the "music" of measured sound, which is what Shelley describes Dante doing to Italian,[49] it suggests an intolerance for abrasive, eccentric, and difficult locutions that disturb the measure: the sorts of words, perhaps, that call for a gloss. These are the words that Schleiermacher's foreignizing strategy imagined might be received as alien and ungainly, words that represent differences rather than reflecting identities. Such words, however, can convey thought-provoking knowledge of the kind that Bakhtin finds in dialects and class-diversified dictions and that he proposes as the core of a truly democratic language, a language that is other to itself and in itself. For Bakhtin, this could be found only in the novel and never in a poetry compelled to squeeze out discordant words in the service of mellifluous form. Wordsworth was indeed famously engaged in a purification of poetic language, which he wanted to be based on the speech of ordinary people but which, he felt, had to be shorn of all sorts of local encumbrances: obscenities, dialect forms, professional dictions, and other idiosyncrasies. This has come down to us as perhaps the primary legacy of British romanticism.

But the theoretical justification for *Lyrical Ballads* was itself a reaction against a widespread reading and publishing culture that was used to reading English poetry accompanied by a glossary. This recognition of the need for intralingual translation, to use Roman Jakobson's term, suggests that the stranger is already within and that the process of foreignization is by no means restricted to sources outside the British Isles. What is one's own language, after all? Does it include regional dialect? Old or Middle English? Can it, for a London speaker, stretch to Robert Burns's version of Lallans? At what point exactly does English cease to be itself and become some other language? Are all languages, strictly construed, made up of what Deleuze and Guattari call "minor" literatures, assemblages rather than coherent entities, politicized rather than merely conventional, deterritorialized rather than at home?[50] Glossaries are commonplace in eighteenth-century poetry. Allan Ramsay's *Poems* (1720) prints not only a list of Scots words "rarely

49. *Shelley's Prose*, 291.

50. See Gilles Deleuze and Félix Guattari, *Kafka: Toward a Minor Literature*, trans. Dana Polan (Minneapolis: University of Minnesota Press, 1986), 16–27.

or never found" in modern English but also a table showing how many northern and southern words are "originally the same."[51] The first edition of Percy's *Reliques*, one of the best-selling volumes of its time, prints an extensive glossary of "obsolete and Scottish words" for each of its three volumes while also occasionally marking analogs in or derivations from French, Latin, Anglo-Saxon, and "Islandic."[52] Others followed: Robert Fergusson's *Poems* (1773) has a glossary of Scots words, while Chatterton's editor sensed the market for exoticism and listed "uncommon words" with a note of caution, "a considerable number of them being (as far as the Editor can judge) unsupported by authority or analogy."[53] Joseph Ritson glosses both Scots and English dialects in his various collections. Most famously of all, Robert Burns's poetry first took printed form with a glossary and was published thereafter with even longer ones. The 1786 Kilmarnock edition has a five-page glossary with a headnote on Scots participle endings, while the Edinburgh edition of 1787 (reprinted in London and then elsewhere) is accompanied by a closely printed twenty-three-page glossary and a headnote on the pronunciation of Scots words. There are, in other words, significant strangers within the language. When John's Clare's first book of poems appears in 1821 with a glossary, it is harking back to a lively earlier tradition only apparently deflected by the plain text of *Lyrical Ballads* and some of the other major romantic editions.

But how truly strange are these strangers? The publication of glossaries suggests that an occasional word-for-word conversion is enough to get us to an understanding of the text. The implication is that grammar and syntax are close enough to the familiar forms that full-fledged translation is not called for: we can just look up the strange words and insert them in a one-to-one substitution. When this does not work, it is mostly because the poet or editor has forgotten or declined to list the word (which often seems to be the case with Burns's first volume). The glossed word is indeed the image of the foreigner or stranger within, but there is a sense that the stranger can be managed, accommodated easily enough by being transposed (if not quite translated) into the textual household. The published notes and prefaces to Burns's poems do not, for example, raise the question of whether Lallans might lay claim to its own grammar. Early reviewers noticed an obscurity attending the use of the Scots dialect but also remarked Burns's tendency to

51. Allan Ramsay, *Poems* (Edinburgh, 1720), 365.

52. [Thomas Percy], *Reliques of Ancient English Poetry* (London, 1755), 1:330.

53. [Thomas Chatterton], *Poems, Supposed to have been written at Bristol, by Thomas Rowley and others, in the Fifteenth Century* (London: T. Payne, 1777), 289.

turn to English at critical moments. In the words of James Currie, the influential editor of the 1800 edition, "Where he rises into elevation of thought, he assumes a purer English style."[54] Currie proposes a single-language model for Scots-English that was regrettably broken up when the Scots poets turned to Latin and the Scots king went to England in 1603, bifurcating the two cultures and turning against his native tongue (14–19). With the union of 1707, some of this lost commonality can be readmitted, and dialect poetry is one means to it. Burns, in this context, can be marketed as a patriot, his poems being "peculiarly calculated to increase those ties which bind generous hearts to their native soil, and to the domestic circle of their infancy" (48). Such strangeness as there is in Burns's poems functions, in other words, to make us feel at home, and to appreciate the value of having a homeland.[55] Thus, Burns's dialect can be at once the shared native speech of the Scots and a prototype of what a reunited Anglo-Scottish kingdom might entertain within its current national language.

As perhaps it was from the start. Nigel Leask finds a well-developed eighteenth-century tradition of Scots-language writing in the pastoral genre to which he assimilates Burns. Because pastoral is the low item in the Augustan hierarchy, the recourse to a Scots "Doric" is acceptable and eventually establishes Scots as "the dominant nonstandard literary language of the Anglophone world." Perhaps this is one of the conditions for Burns's popularity, suggesting that his readers might be briefly befuddled but never deeply threatened.[56] The appearance of word-for-word correspondence between normative and dialect or archaic forms registers the existence of

54. John D. Ross, ed., *Early Critical Reviews on Robert Burns* (1900; repr. New York: AMS Press, 1973), 49.

55. Currie is also perhaps the first to note the power of Burns's poetry over the Scottish diaspora, those "estranged from their native soil and spread over foreign lands" (50). For an account of Currie's influence on early readers of Burns, see Nigel Leask, *Robert Burns and Pastoral: Poetry and Improvement in Late Eighteenth-Century Scotland* (Oxford: Oxford University Press, 2010), 276–92.

56. Leask, *Robert Burns and Pastoral*, 57, 59. Burns's language and the larger topic of Scots Englishes have been widely discussed and debated. Leask gives a good account and interpretation of the current state of the discussion (43–80). The glossary of the Kilmarnock edition was, he suggests, largely aimed at Edinburgh readers; the much larger Edinburgh edition glossary is pitched at a wider readership (75). See also, among many, Nigel Leask, "Burns, Wordsworth, and the Politics of Vernacular Poetry," in *Land, Nation and Culture: Thinking the Republic of Taste, 1740–1840*, ed. Peter de Bolla, Nigel Leask, and David Simpson (London: Palgrave-Macmillan, 2005), 202–22; Sorensen, *The Grammar of Empire*; Leith Davis, *Acts of Union: Scotland and the Literary Negotiation of the British Nation, 1707–1830* (Stanford, CA: Stanford University Press, 1999); and various books and essays by Robert Crawford, beginning with *Devolving English Literature* (Oxford: Clarendon, 1992).

different speakers and subcultures within the nation-state but implicitly gathers them together within the parameters of a common grammar; the provision of the glossary is the means of apprehending that grammar. The more seriously challenging languages—Irish, Scots Gaelic, and Welsh—cannot be thus finessed by glossaries.

By the turn of the nineteenth century, another variant of English was coming to notice, this one written and spoken by foreigners who at first glance might have seemed much closer to the metropolitan norm than the poets of Edinburgh or Ayrshire: American English. Some Americans were of the opinion, after 1776, that the new republic should adopt another tongue (for example, German) in order to signal a clean break from old affiliations. But despite the fact that Americans then, as now, spoke many different languages, English was the obvious winner, so that the argument soon turned to whether there should be—and how there could be—an authentic American English. Noah Webster's 1806 dictionary made a trenchant case for adherence to the Anglo-Saxon paradigms as best fitted for the speech of the new nation, and many American critics and authors took positions for and against distancing American English from its old-world associations. Meanwhile, for British writers, the issue was how to represent America and American English to British readers. How much if any translation is required? Or, better put, what ends are served by the *claim* to be translating from a strange or foreign culture into familiar English?

Thomas Campbell's "Gertrude of Wyoming" (1809) was written by a man who had never crossed the Atlantic, but it pretends to be doing a certain amount of translation. It tells the story of a massacre that happened in Wyoming, Pennsylvania, in 1778, when Indians allied with the British destroyed a frontier settlement inhabited by new Americans. The poem's historical fabric is vague and obfuscatory. The loyalist Major John Butler was in charge of the attack, and some among the loyalist troops were disguised as Indians, fighting alongside the "real" Indians. In the poem, the British presence is barely acknowledged, even though it was widely discussed in the press at the time and then again by Coleridge in the 1790s. So too the French contribution to an earlier massacre in the war of 1756–63, also described in the poem, is minimized. In each case the Indians are presented as the prime movers, with American citizens (and the British before them) the victims. The global-political determination of the violence between Britain and France and the American colonies is sidelined in order to depict events as driven by the rivalries of different Indian tribes, rendering the conflict a racial one marked by the customs of a savage people.

Campbell's Wyoming is a cosmopolitan settlement gathering together all the exiles of a war-torn and socially divided old Europe. Germans, Spaniards, Scots, and Englishmen all live together in an economy founded in shepherding and pastoral leisure (there must have been some farming but that goes unmentioned):

For here the exile met from every clime,
And spoke in friendship every distant tongue:
Men from the blood of warring Europe sprung
Were but divided by the running brook.[57]

There is no formal sovereignty and no legal bureaucracy: "one venerable man beloved of all" (the heroine's father) is enough to decide such conflicts as arise, and they arise rarely (47). Special notice is taken of the Scots exiles, who earn an informative footnote on the legend of the Corybrechtan whirlpool: Tim Fulford reasonably sees in this earthly paradise a romantic relocation of "Scottish clan values" to rural Pennsylvania.[58] But Gertrude is a true "rose of England,"[59] the daughter of an English republican exile. It is Shakespeare she reads in her leisure hours. What is destroyed here is thus the best of both England and Scotland, the independent Highlander and the liberty-loving Englander. Britain, in other words, destroys its own best elements in the Wyoming massacre.

But that is not quite how Campbell puts it. As I have said, he does not play up the British role in the affair beyond an introductory mention of the "junction of European with Indian arms."[60] The first edition's misattribution of blame for the slaughter to the Mohawk Joseph Brant (in later editions the subject of a long footnote explaining the mistake) completely omits mention of the complex history of diplomatic cooptation and betrayal governing Britain's relations with the Indian nations, as Fulford has shown.[61] America is thus imaged as a separate place, one not yet implacably embedded in the politics of global conflict set going by the rivalries of the European empires. The rhetoric of separateness—indeed, of foreignness—is enhanced by references to the distinctive ethnographic and zoological fea-

57. *The Complete Poetical Works of Thomas Campbell*, ed. J. Logie Robertson (New York: Haskell House, 1968), 46.

58. Tim Fulford, *Romantic Indians: Native Americans, British Literature, and Transatlantic Culture, 1756–1830* (Oxford: Oxford University Press, 2006), 9.

59. *The Complete Poetical Works of Thomas Campbell*, 48, 58.

60. Ibid., 44.

61. See Fulford, *Romantic Indians*, esp. 211–23.

tures of a faraway continent. Campbell (who, remember, had never been to America), appears to have been lazy in his researches, for he gets a lot of things wrong. Flamingos, buffalo, crocodiles (i.e., alligators), and condors, not to be found in Pennsylvania, are all mentioned in the poem and sometimes further explained in footnotes. Indians are also treated to a separatist ethnography, playing up the exceptionalities of native life and culture: wampum, moccasins, and manitou are all glossed, along with native navigational and survival skills and physical stoicism. Whites and good Indians alike share a primitive republican ideal long since satirized in Smollett's *Humphry Clinker* but remaining serviceable well into the nineteenth and twentieth centuries. Campbell makes America more separate and distinctive than it historically was in order to sustain this ideal. Exotic flora and fauna add emphasis and color to the impression of a real world elsewhere. As part of the effect, the poet puts himself in the position of interpreter and translator; he creates the *effect* of translation as if to repress the evidence of contact and common history.

And what is the language of that world? English, it goes without saying. But Campbell told us that these happy exiles "spoke in friendship every distant tongue." Had they done only this, they could not have understood one another. The *lingua franca* was presumably English. The image of people speaking "every distant tongue" but communicating as successfully as if there were only one tongue conflates life before Babel with life after it, but in either case the language spoken is some form of English. While they *can* speak every distant tongue, they are learning not to. The gestures of or claims to translation implicit in, for example, the detailed footnote making the mockingbird intelligible to those who have never seen it[62]—as if bearing new and strange knowledge back across the Atlantic—covers over the degree to which everything has already been circulated and recirculated, like the books upon which Campbell is drawing for his zoological and ethnographic information. The proclaimed strangeness of Indian customs (projected as requiring explanation) is already familiar to the point of cliché in the transatlantic political-economic theory of the time; it colludes with the implied exotic savagery of the Wyoming massacre as the outcome of a politics driven not by the transatlantic superpowers but by the implacable mutual hatred of the indigenous tribes. The assumption that interpretation is needed, that translational acts must intervene to explain mockingbirds, moccasins, and manitous to the British reader, serves as a screen to obscure the degree to which everything is already part of a single world system.

62. *The Complete Poetical Works of Thomas Campbell*, 77.

Native America is being destroyed by French and British alike, as well as by the new Americans themselves, but it is figured here as of equal or superior standing, inhabiting an intact ecological space full of solid objects and life-ways so secure that they are capable of destroying those who interfere with it. At the same time, the game is somewhat given away by the relegation of these items to the small print of footnotes (or endnotes) that smack inevitably of antiquarianism. Insofar as they are the ornamental supplements to narrative, they stand aside from the course of a history that will suppose that everyone already speaks English, however distant the climes of their respective origins.

Native American languages, however, were notoriously strange and not easily translatable into English orthography or familiar phonemes. As such, they offered promising material either for parody or for diligent (albeit mostly romantic) foreignizing. Southey's *Madoc* is a tour de force of strange names, combining as it does a Welsh and a Native American storyline. The one gives us such figures as Aelgyvarch, Celynin, and Gwynodyl; the other elicits Erillyab, Coanacotzin, and Yuhidthiton, among others. These names, as proper names, are imaged as untranslatable in their failure to accord with easily manageable English sounds (though, of course, transliteration has already occurred). Most readers will find the rhythm of the affected lines at first hopelessly impacted and even sense the onset of cacaphony before repetition breeds recognition. Here we might recall Jan Assmann's argument for the original translatability of divine names before the onset of competitive monotheisms insisted that there be no principle of conversion between different deities.[63] Southey's Aztecs are determined separatists very much in the business of imposing their own gods upon others. Their gods, too, must be untranslatable. The nominal intransigence of their proper names reflects a resistance to conversion of all kinds. But Welsh presents just as many phonetic and orthographic problems as Nahuatl. Translation occurs constantly in any contact zone where one language is taking over from another, whether or not it is accompanied by religious conversion. In James Fenimore Cooper's *The Pioneers*, Chingachgook's name is too hard for the white settlers, so he becomes Indian John. As Derrida puts it, "The battle of proper names follows the arrival of the foreigner."[64] Southey's decision to front the exotic and orthographically estranged North American names (as well as the Welsh ones) may be judged as little more than romantic rac-

63. Assmann, *The Price of Monotheism*, 19; Assmann, *Moses the Egyptian*, 3.
64. Derrida, *Of Grammatology*, 113.

ism, but it interrupts the flow of familiarity just as surely as it interrupts the flow of the poetic line. It suggests a poet not entirely comfortable with speaking only English, a poet making some effort to foreignize.[65]

Felicia Hemans's "The Forest Sanctuary" (1825) presents a quite different example of the "translation" of America, one that seems almost entirely to avoid any staging of translation at all. The poem is structured around displacement. It is displaced in time, set as it is in the sixteenth century; it is culturally displaced, being imagined as the dramatic monologue of a Spanish Protestant fleeing persecution; and it is displaced in space, set in the heart of a remote North American forest. As soon as we enter the narrator's mind, we are displaced again. He speaks from North America, but his imagination is fully embedded in his European past, which comes back to life as if happening in a compulsively repeating present. The first half of the poem is given over to a traumatic reliving of the spectacle of his best friend and that friend's sisters being burned alive as heretics back in Spain; only in the very last stanza of part 1 does the narrative return briefly to the poem's present, and by the third stanza of part 2 we are back in the past again. This time the narrator remembers his wife's burial at sea; once again the location in an American present is specified only briefly before the poem ends. The power of memory makes it impossible for the exiled narrator to register his immediate environment in any absorptive detail. The poem is thus almost completely empty of any words or phrases that denote its exotic location. There are a few indicators of names and places that belong to Spain or to the Americas: *llanos* is briefly glossed in a footnote, as is the "popular Spanish romance" *Rio Verde*.[66] There is the decorative smattering of a Latin prayer (308), along with a few indicators in the verse that these memories are occurring in America rather than in another place. But in general the text is remarkably bare of geographical markers. No wild creatures or birds are registered, and only one plant, sugarcane (270), earns an explanation.[67] The footnotes are only minimally informative and tend simply to refer us to the standard accounts: Humboldt and Grant are Hemans's main sources (although Campbell's "Gertude" figures once). Notwithstanding the claim

65. Or it might suggest a poet who is keen to discourage being read aloud. Andrew Elfenbein, *Romanticism and The Rise of English* (Stanford, CA: Stanford University Press, 2009), 141–43, discusses the resistance to "percussive Romanticism" developing at the time.

66. *Felicia Hemans: Selected Poems, Letters, Reception Materials,* ed. Susan J. Wolfson (Princeton, NJ: Princeton University Press, 2000), 311, 315.

67. Ironically enough, these "feathery canes" were first cultivated in the eastern Mediterranean before moving west to the Americas by way of the islands off West Africa.

that this is a poem about a sixteenth-century Spaniard in sixteenth-century North America, *almost nothing here is marked as requiring translation.* Hemans seems not at all interested in communicating anything but the most minimal impression of foreignness. Or, we might say, the power of traumatic memory is such as to prevent the narrator from being open to the novelties that surround him. There is no need for translation, because in his mind he never left home.

This strikingly transparent English accords with the language of the rest of Hemans's poetry, where a heavy use of monosyllables and a reliance upon the most familiar words and phrases (one almost never needs a dictionary)—a much freer and more casual diction than the King James Bible–inspired gravity of Wordsworth's poetry—produces what it is tempting to call a global poetic English, readable by anyone anywhere who has the basics of the language, and seemingly applicable to almost any location in the world. If we take it as a truism that all languages are to some important degree foreign to themselves—that every "national" language is seeded with cosmopolitan and multilingual ingredients—then Hemans's verse perhaps goes further than any other in repressing or displacing that multiplicity. Bakhtin thought that poetry in general does exactly this. Her *settings* are cosmopolitan—she must surely be the most geographically comprehensive of all nineteenth-century storytellers, and to read through the table of contents of her complete works is to take a virtual trip around the world—but the language in which she describes them is the most basic of basic English. She herself was a talented linguist, and she is given to footnotes and untranslated citations of foreign sources. She was an assiduous translator. But the language of the verse itself is notably unforeignized.

How might we assess this? Is it the signature of a blandly imperialistic imagination that reduces all times and places to the easeful cadences of the middle register of the English language? Or the unembarrassed admission of how a global language must tend to function as soon as it goes truly global? Campbell makes gestures at foreignization but finally ends up not so far from the Hemans model, despite his moccasins and manitous. Both write versions of a global English and register the incidence of a global political system even if (in Campbell's case) they choose not to mention it. Hemans, in making only the most minimal efforts at staging the otherness of the other, could be seen as expressing the coming into being of a *lingua franca* whose later incarnations might include, for example, the *Cambridge International Dictionary of English*, which represents an Anglophone consensus based principally in British *and* American English. The global scene of translation today is marked by many more translations *from* English than into it. In 1998, only 2 percent to 4 percent of publications in English were translated texts; comparable figures are 6 percent for Japan, 10 percent for France, and 15 percent for Germany, with the vast majority being translations from English.[68] In 1987, the worldwide figure for translated books was approximately 65,000, of which 32,000 were from English and (for example) 479 from Arabic (p. 160). These days, few, if any, British feathers are ruffled at visibly American books, while a common mid-Atlantic diction is becoming more and more the norm. No one inside the Anglophone consensus much bothers explicitly with questions of translation.

Hemans, in this sense, has proved eerily prophetic. The language of her poems might well have been suited to an imperial pedagogy, teaching foreigners how to speak English, and to a domestic discipline seeking to avoid the markers of class distinction. But their content is more challenging. Andrew Elfenbein suggests that Hemans was significant in demonstrating an identification of poetry with expressive vocalization and with the rehearsal of strong emotion.[69] That itself is disruptive enough. And the emotions themselves are often tragical; it would not be going too far to suggest that cosmopolitanism in Hemans takes the form of death by travel. England's dead are all over the world: drowned, blown to pieces, unburied, or buried in unmarked or untended graves. *This* is the new homeland, the terrifying consequence of an imperial ambition built on war and violence (often felt most cruelly by women and children) and on the global movement of persons who can never go home because home itself has been emptied of domestic peace.[70] Hemans may write an unchallenging, global English diction that tends toward eradicating foreignization, but what she writes about is overwhelmingly deathly or death-directed. Campbell too transcribes shared suffering and the violent destruction of a community. If there is less and less perceived need to engage with the complex problems of translation, then what remains as the dominant universal—beyond and before Babel—is a residuum of pain. Globalization brings not peace but the sword. The untroubled sequence of familiar words tells a terrible story of how violence

68. Lawrence Venuti, *The Scandals of Translation: Towards an Ethics of Difference* (London: Routledge, 1998), 88.

69. Elfenbein, *Romanticism and the Rise of English*, 105–07.

70. On the ambivalence of Hemans's poetry of empire, see Tricia Lootens, "Hemans and Home: Victorianism, Feminine 'Internal Enemies,' and the Domestication of National Identity," *Publications of the Modern Language Association* 109 (1994): 238–53. Lootens finds Hemans to be "self-subversive," holding an "erratic course among and through contradictions" (241).

against strangers is also, eventually, violence against the homeland. There is no more telling (and testing) instance of this paradox than the economy of plantation slavery, another variant on the romantic stranger syndrome's interrogation of the conventions of translation and hospitality, and one addressed in the next chapter.

CHAPTER SIX

Hands across the Ocean: Slavery and Sociability

TEATIME ON THE BEACH

On August 9, 1783, the East India Company ship *Antelope*, under the command of Captain Henry Wilson, was driven upon the rocks and wrecked just offshore from one of the Pelew Islands, Ulong, now part of the Republic of Palau in the western Caroline Islands. The sailors made it to shore in the ship's boats, where they were met by some of the natives. Wilson had left Macau in June, presumably on his way back to India. There is no mention of a cargo beyond the livestock and stores needed for the voyage, though the ship, which was on its one and only voyage under company registration, is listed in the records as a "packet," which usually describes a mail and passenger service running regularly between two ports.[1] She did carry a swivel gun, which proved a useful political ally in the Pelews, but there is no mention of a heavier armament of the sort that the larger Indiamen usually carried to protect their crews and cargoes from privateers and pirates. At this time, those cargoes were dominantly raw cotton and opium, imported from Bengal into China in an effort to redress the balance of payments deficit occasioned by the British appetite for tea. We do know that the crew included sixteen Chinamen taken on in Macau, along with one Thomas Rose, a "Linguist, a native of BENGAL, calling himself a *Portuguese*."[2]

1. Jean Sutton, *Lords of the East: The East India Company and its Ships* (London: Conway Maritime Press, 1981), 166.

2. George Keate, *An Account of the Pelew Islands, situated in the western part of the Pacific Ocean* (Dublin, 1788), 3.

What Keate's account of the voyage calls the "singular accident"[3] of Rose's enlistment was a happy one for the Europeans, because Rose spoke Malay, and by a "still more singular circumstance" (26) there just happened to be a Malay speaker, another shipwrecked sailor, who had been among the natives long enough to learn some Pelew (he also knew a little Dutch and English). By such means an "easy intercourse" was established where there would otherwise have been a "thousand misconceptions" (26). Potential hostility is displaced by hospitality as the two parties sit down to tea and biscuits (rescued from the ship's stores) on the beach. Strong bonds of affection develop between the Pelew king Abba Thule and the shipwrecked sailors, and by the time the ship is repaired and ready for sea again, the king has decided to send his son along with Captain Wilson in order that he might learn to be an Englishman and return to his people ready to share all the benefits of his education. At the same time, as if to complete the symmetry of the host-guest exchange, one of the English sailors decides to go native and stay on the island. The ship, now renamed the *Oroolong* after the island where it had fetched up, made it back to Macau where it was sold off, and the crew made their way back to England on several different company ships. Meanwhile, the strangers became friends.

The Pelew prince, Lee Boo, never made it home to the Pelews; he died of smallpox in London in December 1784 after a brief period as a much-loved resident of Wilson's house. He is buried in the churchyard of St. Mary's, Rotherhithe. The story of Lee Boo, excerpted from Keate's account, was published in 1789 as a tale of piety and adventure aimed at young readers, and by 1819 it had reached its fifteenth edition. The fortunate beginnings of the prince's European encounter in an efficient act of translation had developed into a narrative of generous hospitality first given and then returned. But the symmetry of mutual affection is not matched by a comparable evaluation of the two ways of life: we hear no more of the Englishman who stayed in the Pacific. Keate's book, although based on Wilson's journals, offered itself as an ethnography and even included an extensive vocabulary of the Pelew language.[4] It advertized itself as an instance of that thirst for new knowledge that was associated with Cook's voyages, which were seen as motivated not by "ambition or avarice" (v) but by sheer curiosity. The redaction that became *The History of Prince Lee Boo* contained none of this beyond the minimum necessary to make sense of the basic narrative of a native impressed with and improved (though tragically cut off) by contact

3. Ibid., 25.
4. Ibid., 364–78.

with England and the English. At no point in the story is Lee Boo described as experiencing anything like homesickness, even though homesickness was widely discussed and theorized at the time as endemic to the dynamics of global travel.[5] And here too the encounter between strangers, though sustained by the dynamics of global trade and the profits of the East India Company, is eerily silent on what went where in the holds of ships like the *Antelope*. Moving opium, which Nigel Leask has called "the biggest narcotics trade in history," is never mentioned.[6]

The story we would most like to hear is perhaps that of Thomas Rose, the translator, probably one of the Lascars, who made up much of the crews working the cotton and opium trades between Calcutta and Canton. The year 1783 was a peak one for East India Company profits from selling Indian goods to China, not equaled until "well into the next century."[7] Much of this came from opium, which had fallen under British control after the capture of Bengal. In 1773, the company took over the monopoly of all opium sales and in 1797 they did the same for production, cutting out the independent middlemen. Conditions approaching monopoly may have been in place as early as 1761.[8] Importing opium was officially forbidden by the Chinese, and the company tried to keep its hands clean in the shipping of the drug, which was conventionally carried by private contractors (in ships with British officers and largely Lascar crews) who bought the crop at the Calcutta auction. Its unofficial status actually contributed to the success of the opium trade in moving company funds around via bills of exchange, since it could not appear as a commodity, per se.[9] Burke's speeches and reports against Warren Hastings are eloquent regarding the ill effects of the company's imposition of an opium monoculture and even more censorious of the use of company resources for private speculation.[10] Bengal produced three thousand chests of opium in 1775 and five times as much in 1840;

5. See Kevis Goodman, "'Uncertain Disease': Nostalgia, Pathologies of Motion, Practices of Reading," *Studies in Romanticism* 49 (2010): 197–227.

6. Leask, *British Romantic Writers and the East*, 218.

7. Michael Greenberg, *British Trade and the Opening of China, 1800–42* (1951; repr., Cambridge: Cambridge University Press, 1969), 11.

8. David Edward Owen, *British Opium Policy in China and India* (1934; repr., Hamden, CT: Archon Books, 1968), 20.

9. Greenberg, *British Trade and the Opening of China*, 105–6. There was one famous exception to company policy, when, in response to a shortage of ships in 1781, Warren Hastings authorized two company ships to carry opium directly to China. This was not a success: one was lost and the other had to sell its cargo at a loss. See Owen, *British Opium Policy*, 53–59.

10. See, e.g., *The Works of the Rt. Hon. Edmund Burke* (Boston: Little, Brown & Co., 1866), 8:116–41, 9:63–70.

almost all of it went to China.[11] It is hard to be sure of the source of the piece of opium in Thomas De Quincey's pocket since there was a worldwide market, including Malwa opium from western India (which only came under company control much later) as well as Turkish opium (largely carried by American traders). Even if the *Antelope* was not employed in carrying the drug, much of its mail and passenger trade would have had to do with the buying and selling of opium.

Keate infers that Wilson and his crew were the first Europeans to set foot in the Pelews, but Lee Boo was not the first Pacific Islander to set foot in London. That honor goes to Omai (or Mai), who arrived in October 1774, when James Cook returned from his second voyage; he and Cook sailed back to Tahiti on the third voyage in 1776. Painted by Reynolds and introduced to King George, Samuel Johnson, Fanny Burney, and Hester Thrale, among others, he was very much the celebrity.[12] But he was not a prince, and Cook did not think much of him either as an interpreter or as a human being; Omai had not taken the opportunity of much improving himself by contact with European civilization, and what he had acquired partook more of vice than virtue.[13] Despite Reynolds's somewhat dashing portrait, his physical appearance was not always admired—certainly not by Cook nor indeed by Forster, whose estimate of the "depravation" of the Patagonians is measured by the fact that "even OMAI became the object of concupiscence of some females of rank."[14] His return to the Pacific was marked by a farcical pastiche of the contact narrative, whereby he arrived burdened with guns, swords, fireworks, drums, and toys and wearing a suit of pseudo-medieval armor presented to him by Lord Sandwich.[15] A few years after his departure his visit provided Philippe Jacques de Loutherbourg and three collaborators with the material for a very successful pantomime, *Omai or a Trip Round the World*, first staged in December 1785 (when it ran for over fifty nights) and revived several times thereafter. Greg Dening's account of the

11. Tan Chung, "The Britain-China-India Trade Triangle, 1770–1840," *Indian Economic and Social History Review* 11.4 (1974): 417. A Bengal chest weighed 149 pounds.

12. For Omai in the news, see Goodman, *Georgic Modernity*, 93–98.

13. See Harriet Guest, *Empire, Barbarism, and Civilization: Captain Cook, William Hodges, and the Return to the Pacific* (Cambridge: Cambridge University Press, 2007), 93. Chapters 3 and 6 are devoted to an analysis of the popular British interest in Omai. The fullest account is E. H. McCormick, *Omai: Pacific Envoy* (Auckland: Auckland University Press and Oxford University Press, 1977).

14. Johann Reinhold Forster, *Observations Made During a Voyage Round the World*, ed. Nicholas Thomas, Harriet Guest, and Michael Dettelbach (Honolulu: University of Hawaii Press, 1996), 167.

15. See McCormick, *Omai*, 224–60; and Leask, *Curiosity and the Aesthetics of Travel Writing*, 62.

performance reports another scene of "translation": John O'Keefe's lyrics included some Tahitian words (translated in the footnotes to the program) mixed in among "extempore nonsense patter."[16] The services of a Thomas Rose were not apparently required. One might wonder whether the details of Omai's actual return to his home islands, mounted and in armor, could possibly have been upstaged in the theater.

Omai functioned for some as an agent of cosmopolitan sociability, for others as an ethnographic curiosity, and perhaps both at once. His career also dramatizes language as a key component in the encounter with the stranger. On the way back to Tahiti, Omai seems to have taken up the role of interpreter-translator, though there is disagreement among the records as to how much he really knew of the Maori language. Fanny Burney, who was fond of him, reports that he picked up only a little English during his time in England, though many things were attributed to him which he could not possibly have uttered: complex comparisons between Pacific and European civil societies, for example. The time he spent with George Colman's son apparently included some mutual language learning (the boy acquired a few words of Tahitian), but in general it seems that Omai was no prodigy. The efforts, however, were mutual. A few of the English speakers had acquired some Polynesian, including Banks and Solander, who were on the first voyage, and Fanny Burney was very proud of her brother Jem's abilities in this respect.[17] As the result of Cook's voyages, modest foreignization impacted English, *tattoo* (from 1769) and *taboo* (from 1777) being perhaps the most visible and familiar words.

For all the obvious paradoxes, condescensions, and complications latent or explicit in the life stories of Lee Boo and Omai as they came to English eyes and ears, and notwithstanding all the symptoms of the imperialist imagination they reveal, there is a fundamental reciprocity embodied in the stories of their relations with the British. They are able to come and go, as Omai did and Lee Boo might have done had he lived. They first met the British when in a position of security and even superiority, from whence they could choose to dispense hospitality. Omai did not convince everyone that he was a noble savage (although the pantomime did remake him as a prince after all), but Lee Boo did better in being packaged as a figure of human virtue and natural sensitivity, an emblem of the universality of

16. Greg Dening, *Mr. Bligh's Bad Language: Passion, Power and Theatre on the Bounty* (Cambridge: Cambridge University Press, 1992), 271; see also 269–76, 292–93. Further information on the pantomime can be found in *Cook & Omai: The Cult of the South Seas*, exhibition catalog (Canberra: Australian National University, 2001); and McCormick, *Omai*, 313–18.

17. McCormick, *Omai*, 94–95,155, 202, 334–35.

sociable sentiment. Their interactions with the English language required the services of translators, but because those interactions were not obviously or exclusively prompted by racist or imperialist designs or unsavory gender politics, the translators and their masters have escaped the bad press sometimes bestowed on La Malinche and Sacajawea and their patrons. Lee Boo and Omai were guests rather than hostages, free to come and go, and were treated accordingly. The South Sea experience was a wildly popular topic in the late eighteenth century—Hawkesworth's lavish compilation of the voyages was a best seller—not least because it could be presented as exotic ethnography. The awkward ingredient of commerce—and particularly the opium trade—was written out of the Lee Boo story to clear the stage for larger than life human emotions. How much freedom of movement existed for those working the ships of the East India Company is hard to know, but if conditions were anything like those governing Atlantic merchant shipping at the time, one assumes not very much.[18] What was the status of those Chinamen who shipped in the *Antelope*? When India became a theater of war for the European powers (as it was in 1756–63), merchant seamen were liable to impressment not only on the Atlantic segment of their run but on those occasions when they met navy ships in the Far East.[19] Where exactly is the boundary between hospitality and indentured labor? Between sociability and slavery, empire and equity?

HOSPITALITY BETRAYED: THE STRANGER PROTESTS

That question, as is very well known, was much more clearly answered in the Atlantic theater both in the historical record and in the literary representations of the triangular trade that governed the transport of slaves from Africa to the Caribbean and the Americas. In September 1781, two years before the *Antelope* was wrecked in the Pelew Islands, an infamous event occurred on the Atlantic crossing. Luke Collingwood, the master of the slave ship *Zong*, en route from West Africa to Jamaica, threw overboard 122 living slaves over the course of three days. Collingwood feared—or claimed to fear for—the safety of the ship and the shortage of drinking water; 7 of

18. Marcus Rediker suggests that the pay and private rewards for crewmen were higher on the Indiamen than elsewhere, but also that discipline may have been even stricter than the already strict norm: see *Between the Devil and the Deep Blue Sea: Merchant Seamen, Pirates and the Anglo-American Maritime World, 1700–1750* (Cambridge: Cambridge University Press, 1989), 40–41, 213.

19. Sir Evan Cotton, *East Indiamen: The East India Company's Maritime Service* (London: Batchworth Press, 1949), 52–54.

the crew and some 60 slaves had already died of malnutrition or disease. We know the number of the dead because they were valued as insurable cargo at £30 a head; had they died a natural death (whatever that might have been in such conditions) in the course of a routine voyage or arrived in Jamaica at the point of death, they would have been worth nothing. But if they were killed during an insurrection or because of a state of emergency, the insurers were liable for the losses. The voyage of the *Zong* became a cause celèbre; the abolitionists took up and printed the story, and 60 years later Turner painted a famous picture of the event.[20] In 1783, the year of the *Antelope* shipwreck, the case came to trial, and the decision favored the owners. A retrial in the same year was presided over by no less a figure than Lord Chief Justice Mansfield, the "hero" of the Somersett case of 1772. At this trial, evidence was presented of the rainfall that made nonsense of the captain's claim of a water shortage, and Mansfield was able to invoke this fact as evidence of mismanagement, although he did uphold the principle that without the rains the insurers would have been obliged to pay up. A planned third trial never came about.[21]

The legal twists and turns of the *Zong* case had much to do with the marine insurance industry, but in the eyes of many observers there was no problem in sorting out right from wrong: they thought that the slaves were brutally murdered. The event was widely taken up as an instance of the spectacular inhumanity of the slave trade. No hospitality was described as betrayed, because none was offered; the slaves were instanced and imagined entirely as cargo conveyed for profit. No acts of translation were required in a world where human beings are accorded only the status of passive objects.

The story of the *Zong* might have come as a shock to those familiar only with the literary norms governing the representation of black slaves, which were much more invested in romantic and sentimental constructions of the interaction between masters and slaves. Aphra Behn's *Oroonoko* (1688) is foundational in this respect.[22] The hero is an African prince of exceptional humanity, dignity, courage, and grace who is twice betrayed by the

20. For a magisterial account of the incident and its emblematic force, see Ian Baucom, *Specters of the Atlantic: Finance Capital, Slavery, and the Philosophy of History* (Durham, NC: Duke University Press, 2005). Baucom gives the details of Granville Sharp's involvement in the court case (123–35). For a history of events, see James Walvin, *The Zong: A Massacre, the Law, and the End of Slavery* (New Haven, CT: Yale University Press, 2011).

21. Baucom, *Specters of the Atlantic*, 123–40, 195–207; and Jeremy Krikler, "The *Zong* and the Lord Chief Justice," *History Workshop Journal* 64 (2007): 29–47.

22. For an account of the Oroonoko cult, see Srinivas Aravamudan, *Tropicopolitans: Colonialism and Agency, 1688–1804* (Durham, NC: Duke University Press, 1999), 29–33.

honeyed language of British civility, the first time in a flagrant breach of the conventions of hospitality. He is a sophisticated cosmopolitan; indeed, it is his cosmopolitan credentials that get him into trouble in the first place. He speaks English and French, and this, together with his rank and reputation, opens him to developing a fatal affection for his English business partner, to whom he himself had been selling slaves. It is while pretending to return Oroonoko's generous hospitality that the British captain seizes him and transports him across the ocean. Oroonoko's natural superiority is noted by all who encounter him, inspiring either admiration or jealous hatred but never indifference. He is never just cargo or commodity. The display of civility and civility betrayed is used powerfully by Behn when the time comes to describe the hideous circumstances of his torture and death, when all the polite rituals are put aside. But he remains the noblest of noble savages to the end, true to himself and to his people.

Hospitality and affection (sometimes erotic) extended and betrayed are core components of the literature of slavery. From Inkle and Yarico to William Earle's three-fingered Jack, the natural human sympathies of native people move them to save the lives of the white traders who will then promptly enslave them.[23] Any forcible enslavement of another was open to dispute, although John Locke, among others, tried to deflect objections by claiming that one who is conquered in war voluntarily resigns his right to life over to his captor, who may then do with him as he wishes. The betrayal of hospitality and friendship is more unambiguously wrong, for this is a breach of a relationship among equals. Ottobah Cugoano, perhaps the most radical among the authors of eighteenth-century slave narratives, is clear about the obligation to strangers:

> there is but *one law and one manner* prescribed universally for all mankind, *for you, and for the stranger that sojourneth with you*, and wheresoever they may be scattered throughout the face of the whole earth, the difference of superiority and inferiority which are found subsisting amongst them is no way incompatible with the universal law of love, honor, righteousness, and equity.[24]

23. The Inkle and Yarico story was hugely popular in the eighteenth century; see Peter Hulme, *Colonial Encounters: Europe and the Native Caribbean, 1497–1797* (London: Methuen, 1986), 225–63.

24. Quobna Ottobah Cugoano, *Thoughts and Sentiments on the Evil of Slavery*, ed. Vincent Carretta (London: Penguin, 1999), 50–51 (original emphasis).

If hospitality is a mark of civilization, then the European exploitation of guest status for pursuing monetary gain through the slave trade becomes true barbarism. Kant's *Perpetual Peace* made specific mention of this outrage: the right of visitation permits only an invitation to commerce and nothing more. The abuse of hospitality appears over and over again in the literature, leading the pro-slavery Edward Long to counter it as precisely as he can in his 1774 *History of Jamaica*, where he seeks to undercut the dignity of African politeness:

> Their hospitality is the result of self-love; they entertain strangers only in hopes of extracting some service or profit from them; and in regard to others, the hospitality is reciprocal; by receiving them into their huts, they acquire a right of being received into theirs in turn. This in fact is a species of generosity which gives no decisive evidence of goodness of heart, or rectitude of manners, except in those countries where no advantage is expected to be made by the host.[25]

Even Long cannot deny the *appearance* of hospitality. Indeed, it hardly supports his case for the primitive bestiality of African life to suggest, as he does, that the natives might have such a sophisticated understanding of the culture of reciprocity as an insurance against future need and the prospect of violence on the part of the stranger—a thought which was not discredited by philosophers from Plato to Kant. He also inadvertently draws attention to the numerous instances where native hospitality is clearly *not* shown as having any ulterior motive—as if it were likely, indeed, that everyone assisting a shipwrecked sailor or starving traveler would be looking for a future dinner date in a London club. Above all, he lays upon the African host the sins of the European guest, and leaves the guest's behavior unremarked.

The primitivization of Africa might have seemed a necessary move in justifying the historical expansion of plantation slavery in the eighteenth century. Even Hegel, whose formative exposition of the master-slave relation in the *Phenomenology* has been attributed to his sympathetic response to the Haitian Revolution, suggests that it is only through the struggle unto death that occurs in the slave economy that the African can emerge into evolutionary history; without contact with the European, in other words,

25. Cited in Peter J. Kitson and Debbie Lee, eds., *Slavery, Abolition and Emancipation: Writings in the British Romantic Period* (London: Pickering and Chatto, 1999), 8:22.

he remains benighted in a world without time.[26] Walter Scott represented slavery as internal to European society, but only in its premodern phases. In *Ivanhoe*, Gurth the swineherd bears a brass ring around his neck as the sign of his serfdom, but in the course of the novel he receives his freedom as the reward for extraordinary loyalty to his master, a moment which also encapsulates the forward movement of history itself. In *The Talisman*, both Crusaders and Saracens keep slaves, and Kenneth of Scotland himself experiences servitude in his disguise as a Nubian slave sent to King Richard by Saladin. His loyalty preexists his disguise: it is part of his feudal-aristocratic culture. But his disguise also undoes the fixity of the master-slave relation and exemplifies the logic of a progressive history. The disguised Kenneth is wounded in defending the life of the king, and when no one else will assist in the treatment of a "black chattel," King Richard himself sucks the poison from the wound, thus dissolving social difference in the most dramatic way possible.[27] Gurth too risked being tortured in his master's place; both he and Kenneth stand in for their masters with their own suffering bodies, and in so doing are admitted to a new equality. Europe, it seems, is on the way to its modernity; the struggle unto death projected by Hegel is displaced by a suffering on behalf of the master, which absorbs all violence into the body of the slave and relies for its historical resolution on the awakened conscience of the one who escapes violence altogether. Scott's model of progress is based not on struggle but on sacrifice.

Cugoano's case against slavery turns to the Bible, which he presumes not to be dependent upon a Eurocentric evolutionary paradigm with only a grudging place for Africans or slaves. He spends much of his narrative in distinguishing the nature of biblical slavery from that practiced by the modern slave trade; biblical slavery, indeed, becomes almost a form of hospitality in that the slave is taken into the household and "employed in an honourable service."[28] It is this distinction above all (open to dispute as it was) that allows Cugoano to defend the right of resistance (and revolt) of modern slave populations, an argument that likely earned him a much smaller readership than was enjoyed by his more famous contemporary, Olaudah Equiano. Cugoano mediates his own status as a stranger through the common lan-

26. For Hegel and Toussaint, see David Brion Davis, *The Problem of Slavery in the Age of Revolution, 1770–1823* (Oxford: Oxford University Press, 1999), 557–64; and Susan Buck-Morss, *Hegel, Haiti, and Universal History* (Pittsburgh, PA: University of Pittsburgh Press, 2009).

27. Scott, *Tales of the Crusaders*, 4:161. It should also be noted that Richard is trusting his scientific knowledge that "the venom is harmless on the lips, though fatal when it mingles with the blood" (160).

28. Cugoano, *Thoughts and Sentiments on the Evil of Slavery*, 37.

guage of the English Bible, but at the same time estranges both himself and the Bible through his rigorous and extended analysis of the anthropology of slavery among the Jews and early Christians. Biblical doctrine can thus assist the yet unconverted slaves not only with the promise of a better life after death but with a call to resistance in the life they now have.[29]

A key part of Cugoano's analysis of the biblical account of slavery depends upon his understanding of figurative language—the very language that was, as we have seen, frequently identified or associated with the incursion of the stranger. Those who use the Israelite enslavement of the Canaanites as "precedents and pretences to encourage and embolden themselves to commit cruelty and slavery on their fellow creatures" are failing to understand that these and similar parts of the sacred texts are a "parallel allusion to other things signified thereby."[30] Following Augustine and Aquinas, Cugoano holds that much of the Bible is composed of "figures, types and emblems" (39) for the better instruction of its readers. Thus the immanence of black skin or spots on the leopard alludes not to race or species but to the state of sin in us all that cannot be wished away; and mention of an established state of slavery refers not to a civil institution but to "spiritual subjection and bondage to sin" (41). Exodus from Egypt indicates escape not from a physical place but from sin itself, and the "laws respecting bond-servants" are intended to remind us of the need to discipline not our fellow beings but our bodily lusts (42). Anything in the Bible that seems not to endorse equity and justice is to be taken as "spiritual uses and similitudes, for giving instruction to the wise" (43). The Canaanites not only continue to exist among us; they exist within us as the strangers we must recognize and confront. Cugoano reads the enslavers' Bible against slavery itself.

In a similar spirit, he seeks consistently to make his English readers strangers to themselves. When he first sees the *browsow*, the "white faced people," he thinks they are going to eat him, thus inverting the myth of cannibalism familiarly deployed by Europeans against Africans.[31] The British participants in the slave trade teach only an upside-down version of Christian doctrine, the "oaths and blasphemies" that come from their own

29. Tadmor, *The Social Universe of the English Bible*, 82–118, shows in great detail how the early English translations finessed the matter of slavery in the Bible by substituting for it the language of contractual service, most often using the word "servant" and thereby producing "a Bible for freeborn Englishmen" (105). The King James Bible has only one instance of the word "slave"; the New English Bible (1970) restored 253 uses of the word to the Old Testament (99–100). On the other hand, the same early English Bibles played up the monarchy by conflating no fewer than fourteen Hebrew words into the English "prince" (125).

30. Cugoano, *Thoughts and Sentiments on the Evil of Slavery*, 46–47.

31. Ibid., 14.

status as "wicked and apostate" (23). If there were any historical Canaanites, then they might well have been the literal progenitors of "that wicked generation still subsisting among the slave-holders in the West-Indies" (33). The slave-dependent plantation economy in the Caribbean produces slavery in the homeland, for all "stock-jobbing, lotteries and useless business" that displace actual work have "a tendency to slavery and oppression" (69): here Cugoano taps into a standard anticommercial rhetoric and also comes close to the argument of Hegel's *Phenomenology*, where the slave is ontologically more powerful than his master precisely because of an experience of physical work which the master can only contemplate. Slavery in this way makes the master a slave to his own slave. Those who mistreat "the African strangers" are at risk of becoming strangers to themselves and to their own homeland, becoming "unjust barbarians" and inviting "impending danger and ruin to their country" (79–80).

Equiano's *Interesting Narrative* also introduces its author as a "stranger" and in turn proceeds to estrange British readers from their likely assumptions. He too recalls assuming that he was going to be eaten by his captors, points out that his culture did not have the habit of swearing, and makes clear that the treatment of slaves among his own people was far more humane than what he has experienced on the Caribbean plantations.[32] But he also uses the familiar icons of the global textile trade to imply a common humanity depicted in a shared fashion sense for the same "calico" and "muslin" (34) that is worn on the backs of Jane Austen's heroines and whose price is discussed by Henry Tilney and the Bath society ladies in *Northanger Abbey*. Equiano's story is much more reader friendly than Cugoano's, having about it a generous element of ethnography (perhaps derivative rather than firsthand, some now think) and of the captivity and providence narrative, as well as of the seafaring yarn, but the effect of collecting all of these genres and marketing them as the product of an "unlettered African" (7) is arguably to place the English reader at a critical distance from the forms and conventions more usually encountered in the writings of fellow English authors. The effect is one of mimicry, of "almost the same but not quite," as Homi Bhabha puts it.[33]

Even more is this the case with Ignatius Sancho's *Letters*, described by Thomas Jefferson as written in a language

32. Olaudah Equiano, *"The Interesting Narrative" and Other Writings*, ed. Vincent Carretta (London: Penguin, 1995), 31, 34, 41, 55.

33. Homi K. Bhabha, *The Location of Culture* (London: Routledge, 1994), 86.

> easy and familiar, except when he offers a Shandean fabrication of words. But his imagination is wild and extravagant, escapes incessantly from every restraint of reason and taste, and, in the course of its vagaries, leaves a tract of thought as incoherent and eccentric, as is the course of a meteor through the sky.[34]

Jefferson's judgment comes in the middle of a critical diatribe against the talents of black writers as "incapable of a thought above the level of plain narration"; religion, he says, "indeed has produced a Phyllis Whately [*sic*]; but it could not produce a poet." But Sancho seems to stand convicted of the opposite error: he does not have enough plain narration, but is "always substituting sentiment for demonstration" (141). Jefferson resorts to a traditional association of excessive imagination with the barbarians (or with poets unable to control their appetite for metaphor and figure), deflecting entirely any threat that might come to him from the estranging functions of Sancho's mimicking the bizarre style of Sterne's narrators—almost the same but not quite. While Omai was held to account for failing to adopt English manner and manners, the problem with Sancho seems to be that he took on a bit too much of the Irish, which he could project as both a mastery of one of the most visible literary styles of the time and at the same time as the "warm ebullitions of African sensibility."[35] At one moment, he cast himself with distinctly mock-modesty as "only a poor, thick-lipped son of Afric" (216); and three weeks later, in the face of the "worse than Negro barbarity of the populace" during the Gordon Riots, he wrote, "I am not sorry that I was born in Afric" (217, 219). He was capable of waspish directness in describing the high-born admirers of Wheatley's poems as approving of "Genius in bondage" and then passing by with "not one good Samaritan among them" (122), and of equally astringent sarcasm in introducing himself to Sterne as "one of those people whom the illiberal and vulgar call a Nee-gur" (331). His readers may find him identifying with the tragic Othello, with the true-blooded patriot Englishman, and with the most abject slave, all in the space of a few pages. What a rich measure of irony there is (or could be, for it is an incalculable measure) in requesting Sterne to "give half an hours attention to slavery" (331): is it that half an hour from such a talented man is more than enough for the task, or that Sterne is deemed too quixotic to

34. Thomas Jefferson, *Notes on the State of Virginia*, ed. William Peden (New York: Norton, 1972), 140; cited in Ignatius Sancho, *Letters of the Late Ignatius Sancho*, ed. Vincent Carretta (London: Penguin, 1998), xx.

35. Sancho, *Letters*, 170. Carretta makes a good case for the self-consciousness with which Sancho places himself in the genre of letters for publication (xxi–xxxii).

dwell upon it seriously and at length? Sterne himself perfectly catches the irony and the question in promising to make a pilgrimage to Mecca that exceeds Sancho's own willingness to walk ten miles to shake hands with Uncle Toby (332). Sancho's ability to hold his own here with the master of inscrutable but passionate indirection was too much or too threatening for Jefferson; it is a mark of both his integration and of his alienation, a "Nee-gur" who could write of himself as just that. Something having to do with translation is going on, but we are not quite sure what. The measure of sameness in difference that Derrida specified as governing the *devoir-traduire* in Schelling confronts Jefferson with a risk he chooses not to take.

Comparable, if less dramatic, manifestations of double (or multiple) identity are built into the Cugoano and Equiano narratives, which can also be said to place English readers at a distance from themselves as they replicate (but not quite) the familiar genres, making them eerily unfamiliar and compacting the *heimlich* with the *unheimlich*. Cugoano is baptized as John Stewart and goes by either name or both; Equiano describes his African name in fulsome detail as signifying "vicissitude, or fortunate also; one favoured, and having a loud voice and well spoken"; he is subsequently called Jacob, then Michael, and eventually Gustavus Vasa.[36] Vincent Carretta has discovered ship's registers also listing him as Gustavus Worcester and Gustavus Weston and/or Feston.[37] The multiplicity of imposed identities speaks to the subjection of the black subject, but its literary effect is precisely that it *does* so speak, and that it stages the subject as something of a trickster, a figure who goes by many names, perhaps a Dionysus in the making. The controversy over whether Equiano really was born in Africa rather than in South Carolina or the Caribbean—as evidence for or against we might look closely at the somewhat formulaic ethnography of the recounted early memories, but it is not decisive—in a way reenacts this play of identities and faces the reader with questions about who is and is not properly entitled to speak on behalf of whom. These are very modern questions although they came up as early as 1792 in an effort to discredit Equiano's narrative as a whole.[38] Put another way: exactly how much strangeness makes one a true stranger able to speak on behalf of strangers so as to be believed? Believed by whom?

36. Equiano, *"The Interesting Narrative,"* 41, 63, 64. Caretta's introduction gives a good account of the manipulation of identities.

37. Vincent Carretta, *Equiano, the African: Biography of a Self-Made Man* (New York: Penguin Group, 2006), 147–48.

38. Equiano, *"The Interesting Narrative,"* 5ff. On the place of birth question, see Carretta, *Equiano, the African*, 319–23, 350–53.

The Esu-figure at the heart of Henry Louis Gates's foundational study of the black aesthetic offers a way to describe the multiple effects of reading Equiano, Sancho, and Cugoano: the guardian of the crossroads, the mediator, the trickster, the parodist, the disrupter (also the hypersexual copulator, not an identity sought or invoked by these slave narrators).[39] But the defamiliarization they achieve in writing English, whatever analogs or origins it might have in their native cultures, comes from the reader's awareness that they are writing as strangers. Reading Sterne is not like reading Sancho, because we know that Sancho is a black writer and because we know that he is mimicking Sterne. The power of Cugoano's interpretation and deployment of the Christian Bible comes partly from our knowing that this is not for him a native tradition: he has come to it from the outside, and in this he differs from British readers while also reminding them that anyone can become a stranger to the truth. He is not the foundational stranger as lawgiver, but he is the stranger who administers a stern reminder of the content of the laws that is being ignored and traduced. The effect is to move us away not just from a center that can somehow be later reoccupied but from any faith in the idea of a center at all. The agent of this is language: language worked up into rhetorically complex arrangements and affiliations so as to remind us that no one, finally, can lay claim to ownership of a mother tongue.

Carretta ponders the possibility that the Gustavus Vassa who signed letters to the *Morning Post* in 1778 might have been Equiano rhetorically positioning himself as "the stranger in a strange land."[40] As with Sancho's control of a rhetorical range that would seem at first glance to be other than a birthright, and indeed with Cugoano's relentlessly forensic intensity in smoking out the misuse of the scriptures for defending the institution of slavery, questions of authenticity are generated and sustained by the mere printing of the name of the stranger as the author. Did he write it? Could he have written it? Should he be writing it? And what do any or all of these questions mean to us who think of ourselves as at home in our homeland? Caretta speculates that Clarkson's need for a completely and visibly authentic African voice might have had something to do with the story of Equiano's early years among the Igbo in West Africa, and that his claim to high social rank—one of the rare moments of linguistic foreignizing in the book comes when he translates the term *Embrenché* as "importing the highest distinction, and signifying in our language a mark of grandeur" (32)—serves

39. Henry Louis Gates Jr., *The Signifying Monkey: A Theory of African-American Literary Criticism* (New York: Oxford University Press, 1989), 6.

40. Carretta, *Equiano, the African*, 195.

similarly to attract attention by placing the hero in the company of Oroonoko and other princely slaves.[41] A primitivization of expressivity is also apparent in the narrator's observation that "we are almost a nation of dancers, musicians, and poets" (32), giving the lie to Jefferson on the matter of poetry while firmly inscribing the ethnographic cliché about the energy and imagination of premodern societies.

The debate about Equiano's birth suggests that the categories of authenticity that govern the publishing culture of the twenty-first century were already very much in place in the eighteenth century. And indeed, the production of biographies and autobiographies, slice-of-life narratives like anecdotes and conversations, and recollections of the famous (and sometimes rich) was a dominant feature of the eighteenth-century literary marketplace.[42] As Carretta has observed, the more one doubts the truth of Equiano's early-life narrative, the more one has to admire his skill as a compiler and creative writer. Certainly the author's protestation that his work is "wholly devoid of literary merit."[43] is belied by the book's success as well as by the multiplicity of marketable genres it incorporates: spiritual autobiography, conversion narrative, captivity narrative, ethnography, voyage narrative, and perhaps others.[44] The English propensity for betraying hospitality and trust is recorded as a critical countervoice to the gratitude expressed at being introduced to the Christian religion; like Behn, Equiano appeals to sentiment to disprove the bonding power of sympathy or of the language of rights when they are in competition with economic self-interest. The narrator's legal status as a free man and a man of feeling is thus much less important than the fact that he can be passed off and sold as a slave.

The life stories published by Equiano, Sancho, and Cugoano collectively work to estrange British readers from themselves by staging the literary genres familiar in the homeland as not quite in place because of an unexpected or unpredictable voice. Mastery looks like mimicry, while mimicry appears masterful. The narrative voice of the slave turned free man and of the African turned proto-Englishman (Sancho actually voted in an election) explores a range of attitudes and experiences that vary from mastery to slav-

41. Ibid., 320–21. The term appears as "Brutchie" in Cynric Williams's 1827 novel *Hamel, the Obeah Man*, ed. Candace Ward and Tim Watson (Peterborough, ON: Broadview, 2010), 116.

42. See David Simpson, *The Academic Postmodern and the Rule of Literature: A Report on Half-Knowledge* (Chicago: University of Chicago Press, 1995), 41–71.

43. Carretta, *Equiano, the African*, 7.

44. For a good account of the book's distinctly literary merits, see Carretta, *Equiano, the African*, 303–29.

ery and bring up for inspection some radical questions about friendship and enmity, hostility and hospitality, dwelling and displacement. They are narratives written by strangers that often starkly expose the strangeness of the Europeans to themselves and to their own preferred self-images. They are not much given to foreignizing by way of language; indeed, the heaviest use of this technique probably occurs in those parts of Equiano's narrative whose originality has been most disputed. Instead, the form taken by the foreign is dialectical and pervasive, exposing and exploring schisms within the homeland itself about questions of human property, abolition, and emancipation and about the propriety and proper tenancy of literary genres within and between which there occur all sorts of ungovernable translations.

In this context, it is worth recalling the origins of the word *vernacular*, which began its life in English as referring to English itself—the language of ordinary people who did not know Latin—and subsequently came to describe the common, familiar, or vulgar tongue, or the local dialect form that is somehow common but not quite officially approved. In the first instance it is that into which things can be translated but which, as the language of a majority, itself needs no translation. In the second instance, where the word is associated with purely local currencies, the assumption of ready and easy recognition is weaker. But the origin of the word is in the Latin *verna* (adjectival form, *vernaculus*), meaning house-born (or sometimes family) slave, the person who is in and of the home but not fully a member or possessor of the household. In Larry Scanlon's words:

> The Roman slave was by birth or ancestry a foreign element introduced into the household and necessary to its constitution: he or she embodied a household's imbrication with Rome's imperial might. The *verna*, the Roman-born slave, embodies at once a local household's imperial power of appropriation and its continuing dependence on the foreign.[45]

He goes on to cite Mulcaster, one of the early defenders of the English vernacular, who casts Latin as the master and English as the slave whose "thraldom and bondage" should be shaken off in the cause of "our libertie and fredom" (227). By the late eighteenth century, things had changed: English had been firmly established and Latin had become an elite special diction. The slaves were now real and working the Caribbean plantations. They too

45. Larry Scanlon, "Poets Laureate and the Language of Slaves: Petrarch, Chaucer and Langston Hughes," in *The Vulgar Tongue: Medieval and Post-Medieval Vernacularity*, ed. Fiona Somerset and Nicholas Watson (University Park: Pennsylvania State University Press, 2003), 226.

were embodiments of the power of appropriation and the dependence upon the foreign—in this case, Britain's dependence. They too had a language which was and was not that of the household and the homeland. It figures not only in the form of glossed words denoting their foreignness, where it is obvious enough, but also in the performance of mimicry, mastery, or pastiche (who can tell exactly which is which?) in narratives like those of Sancho and Equiano. Here the house-slave has taken over the master's language and thrown it back in his face, outperforming his education even as he testifies to its efficiency and asking awkward questions about the relation of language to imagined categories of identity and authority. He is asking whether he has been or can be translated, carried across the threshold.

The same phenomenon is visible in Phyllis Wheatley's most famous poem, "On Being Brought from Africa to America," where it is almost impossible to decide between sardonic irony and conventionally pious gratitude as the speaker attributes her translation across the ocean to Christian "mercy," and poses another question about her literary knowingness in suggesting a comparison between the refinement of savages and the processing of sugarcane from dark to white.[46] A similar instability of tone characterizes Blake's "Little Black Boy." The famous hymn "Amazing Grace" also proved fully amphibolous, originally written by John Newton as a record of his own salvation from a state of sin but later tenanted by slave voices as an expression of equal rights to both worldly and otherworldly deliverance. A more critical and formally contrived instance of the mirroring and cohabitation of rhetorical styles and strategies is staged in William Earle's *Obi* (1800), where the plantation-class narrator mimics the brutalized slave's agonies in his own scriptorial body, so that writing down the story becomes "an insufferable burden" and his pen is "worn down to the stump" in an echo of the protagonist's loss of two fingers.[47] But the novel queries this identification as a fantasy of equivalent suffering; when the narrator tells his correspondent how often his "tears floated on the page" (95), we are to be fully aware that this is an easier grief than that experienced by the slave he writes about. Scott showed the slave suffering as the proxy of the master and thereby being inscribed into a liberating historical pattern; Earle stages

46. Reprinted in James G. Basker, ed., *Amazing Grace: An Anthology of Poems About Slavery, 1660–1810* (New Haven, CT: Yale University Press, 2002), 177–78. On Wheatley, see Helen Thomas, *Romanticism and Slave Narratives: Transatlantic Testimonies* (Cambridge: Cambridge University Press, 2000), 201–25.

47. William Earle, *Obi; or the History of Three-Fingered Jack*, ed. Srinavas Aravamudan (Peterborough, ON: Broadview, 2005), 69, 82.

the inefficacy of the master class's attempt to participate in the suffering of the slave, and the resulting historical inertia. Earle's narrator may be haunted by his subject as by a "spell" (70), but the *obeah* that figures in the book is always shown as acting upon and within the slave community rather than on their masters. The most fully developed man of feeling in the book, Captain Harrop, is a total hypocrite able to fetch up a tear whenever it suits his ruthless plans. By showing the tragic results of slave participation and belief in the British culture of sentimentality—so often a bonding agent in abolitionist writings—Earle demonstrates the danger of accepting a shared rhetoric: better not to want or claim to be a man and a brother on such terms. Here the mutual inhabiting of a common language works against the slaves' cause and inhibits the efficiency of revolt. It is the dark side of Equiano's and Sancho's mastery of the master tongue that is here displayed. Jack (somewhat against the historical record of the 1790 rebellion upon which the book is based) dies alone as a tragically isolated defender of the rights of man, while the narrator continues to shed sympathetic tears so uncontrollable that they almost prevent him from writing. Earle's message seems uncompromising: Africans must refuse hospitality and conversion, while slaves must keep their secrets and show no mercy. Strangers had best remain strangers, and at a distance. Polite British readers, meanwhile, should perhaps think of something more significant to do than cry their eyes out over moving accidents.

The brutal cycle of violence described in *Obi* starts with the villain's invitation to the African stranger to join him in his own forms of worship and behavior: Christianity and torture come together. Harrop makes no effort to occupy the place of the stranger, to acknowledge the obligations of hospitality, or to negotiate a common contractual or emotional space between self and other. The writer of the letters can only do so through the protectively mediated experience of writing itself. Can one occupy the place of the other or do so in a way that is not compromised by condescension or self-deception or by the kinds of necessary fictions upon which, for example, Adam Smith's theory of moral sentiments depended? And if this is possible at all, can it ever be so in situations marked by massive inequalities of power and influence? Can acts of sympathetic imagination overcome facts about who possesses the power of death? Thomas Clarkson tries out the tactic of putting himself in the place of the other:

> I shall suppose myself on a particular part of the continent of Africa, and relate a scene, which, from its agreement with unquestionable facts,

> might not unreasonably be presumed to have been presented to my view, had I been actually there.[48]

Clarkson's hope is that this will afford him "the clearest, and most conspicuous point of view." And yet the position he puts himself in is not that of a native sufferer but of a curious Englishman speaking on site to an "intelligent African" (148), who reports, in decorously polite English, on the demise of those being loaded on to slave ships. There is perhaps no formal solution to the problem of how one speaks effectively on behalf of the other. Anything in writing (or, indeed, in lived social behavior) can be queried as somehow inauthentic or inadequate, whether it be first or third person, testimony or documentary. This is especially the case where the stakes are highest and where the questions raised are most demanding (our contemporary parallel might be Holocaust literature). During the abolition and emancipation debates they were very high indeed, so it is no surprise that Equiano was suspected of misrepresenting his birth (as indeed he might well have been) and Sancho of overdoing the fine writing. Clarkson's first edition (1786) had been critiqued for its credibility and competence, leading him to deploy for the second edition (1788) a series of strategies aiming at the effect of the real: interviewing seamen, visiting ships and inspecting records, giving exact numbers and measurements (see p. 55). Along with this, he offers a learned disquisition on the history of slavery in Greece and Rome and in the Bible (his book was originally written in Latin as a Cambridge prize essay), and an engagement with the political theory of submission and dependence. The book employs a miscellany of styles and discourses; the effort to speak in the voice of the other occurs only once in the narrative. It is as if Clarkson wishes to explore as many kinds of rhetoric as possible in order to make his point, as if the variety itself might work against any critical dismissal of his work as limited to a single and perhaps falsifiable point of view.[49]

STRANGE WRITINGS

Clarkson would not have been unreasonable in worrying over his possible reception. Skepticism and outright disbelief directed at testimonies and reports of foreign places and persons seems to have been at least as common

48. *Thomas Clarkson and Ottobah Cuguano: Essays on the Slavery and Commerce of the Human Species*, ed. Mary-Antoinette Smith (Peterborough, ON: Broadview Press, 2010), 147.

49. For a reading of Clarkson's style, see Baucom, *Specters of the Atlantic*, 265–76.

as fascination and good faith. Nor was it only the non-British narrators who were suspect. Nigel Leask has described the suspicious reception afforded to James Bruce on his return to London in 1774, where he was one of the first to meet Omai, his major rival as a source of exoticism.[50] The returning explorer was widely suspected to be a teller of tall tales, such as those about Africans eating live animals and enjoying sex in public; the long gap between the oral circulation of such stories and their appearance in 1790 in the five volume *Travels to Discover the Source of the Nile* seems only to have added to the skepticism generated by Bruce's original reportage. Hawkesworth too was criticized for his overcreative compilation of the four major Pacific voyages. But both books were instant (and expensive) best sellers, suggesting that controversy about the boundaries between fact and fiction was a good marketing tool. More public trust seems to have been placed in Mungo Park's *Travels* (1799), which was published at a time when both northern and southern Africa had become sites for the global conflict between England and France and when popular interest in the slavery question was high.[51] Park announces himself as driven by a lust for knowledge and an eagerness to cultivate "new sources of wealth, and new channels of commerce."[52] Mary Louise Pratt has further characterized the book as embodying the "mystique of reciprocity," whereby the vulnerable narrator places himself on a par with the natives and performs a series of gift exchanges with the locals that serves to heighten his own vulnerability and to gloss over the imminence of the more fully capitalist-imperialist relations that would follow in his wake—hence the book's popularity.[53] This is true enough. Indeed, Park does displace a scientific by a sentimental narrative, as Pratt suggests, but this allows him a complex report on the relation between hostility and hospitality. His hosts are all or mostly "Mahometans" among whom he stimulates a range of responses. Some—the majority—take him into their houses as an honored guest or as a curiosity, or at least as a tolerated transient with a right to the sort of temporary residence that Kant had written about, one premised on our mutual impermanence and necessary sharing of space. Park's receipt of hospitality is the means of his very

50. Leask, *Curiosity and the Aesthetics of Travel Writing*, 54–101.

51. Debbie Lee, *Slavery and the Romantic Imagination* (Philadelphia: University of Pennsylvania Press, 2002) 23, suggests that Bryan Edwards (and behind him Joseph Banks) had a significant hand in the writing of Park's book. See pp. 142–64 for an account of British interest in Africa.

52. Mungo Park, *Travels in the Interior Districts of Africa*, ed. Kate Ferguson Marsters (Durham, NC: Duke University Press, 2000), 68.

53. Mary Louise Pratt, *Imperial Eyes: Travel Writing and Transculturation* (London: Routledge, 1992), 69–85.

survival. But among the "Moors" he also encounters a sort of antihospitality, one founded in suspicion and hostility, minimal yet adequate to keep him alive. As a *"stranger"* and an unprotected Christian he is especially vulnerable here and is subject to "rudeness" from the men and sexual voyeurism from the women. As the "king's stranger," his life seems to be safe, although he frequently feels that it is not.[54] For a long period in the narrative he lives the life of a slave or prisoner and sees the world through the eyes of a person denied his liberty. His account of African slavery is thus at the same time autobiographical and ethnographic. Slaves born in the house are better treated than those bought for money, who are "considered as strangers and foreigners, who have no right to the protection of the law, and may be treated with severity, or sold to a stranger, according to the pleasure of the owners." The value of a slave, he reports, increases in proportion to the distance from the slave's homeland, since those furthest from home are the least likely to try to escape, given the seemingly "universal wish of mankind, to spend the evening of their days where they passed their infancy." But Park is no abolitionist, and downplays the likely positive effects of doing away with the Atlantic slave trade. So his own declared experience as "a stranger in a strange land" allows him to disclaim the rights of others to any relief from the same condition. It is Providence "who has condescended to call himself the stranger's friend" and presumably those who are not its beneficiaries do not survive.[55]

Park's inscription of himself as the "stranger in a strange land" echoes the hospitality offered to Moses in the house of Reuel in Exodus, chapter 2 and thus asserts his providentially driven superiority in the very expression of his insecurity; as such, it may also be a seriocomic allusion to the problematic and violent scene of circumcision (Exodus, chapter 4), which results from this hospitality (wherein Moses is given the mother of his firstborn son), since the Moorish ladies are also curious about the state of Park's own private parts in this respect.[56] What is notoriously complex and difficult to interpret in the Bible (Moses being also described at 4:10 as "of a slow tongue") is handled with erotic flirtatiousness in the *Travels*: the moment passes as a joke, and even as a occasion for bonding between the two cultures here at issue. Such bonding is indeed a subtle undercurrent running throughout the narrative, from the first moment when Park cites Othello in claiming to be publishing a "plain unvarnished tale" (45) to the last few

54. Park, *Travels in the Interior Districts of Africa*, 149, 152–54, 203, 202.

55. Ibid., 257, 259, 263, 227.

56. Ibid., 154.

pages where he accounts for not being recognized by an old acquaintance because "my dress and figure were now so different from the usual appearance of an European, that she was very excusable in mistaking me for a Moor" (302). It might also have been part of the cultural memory that Mungo, although a good Scots name, was also the name of the negro servant in Isaac Bickerstaffe's popular comic opera of 1768, *The Padlock*. This was light entertainment indeed, but it is hard not to notice the allusions to plantation slavery as the put-upon Mungo laments and resents the abuses he suffers from a master in whose erotic downfall he assists.

Running the gamut of various roles between master and slave, Park indeed lived as a Moor—and as a prisoner to the Moor—and here the scene of language is significant. At various moments in the early part of the narrative Park listed the numbers 1 through 10 in the various African languages he had encountered.[57] This contributes to the sense of the story as an ethnography while at the same time being visibly convenient for anyone interested in pursuing future commercial transactions: unlike Adelung, who gave us the Lord's Prayer in five hundred or so languages, Park offers a multilingual calculator. There is a list of commonly occurring African words at the front of the volume (56–57), and a longer vocabulary of the Mandingo language at the end (307–13). At one point he sets out to learn Mandingo, because it is the most common language of the region (71). And close to the end of his travels he is able to console some of the slaves traveling with him by speaking to them "in their native language" (305)—though it is not clear whether this is Arabic or Mandingo.

But it is the matter of writing rather than speaking that mediates Park's role most tellingly among those he visits or otherwise encounters. Writing is taken by most of the natives, Moslems or not, as "bordering on magic; and it is not in the doctrines of the Prophet, but in the arts of the magician, that their confidence is placed."[58] Later on a Moslem believer asks him for a Christian written charm, which he provides on a board: "and my landlord, to be certain of having the whole force of the charm, washed the writing from the board into a calabash with a little water, and having said a few prayers over it, drank this powerful draught; after which, lest a single word should escape, he licked the board until it was quite dry" (222). De Quincey expresses his astonishment at the ability of his Malay guest to ingest a large lump of opium; Park must have been no less surprised at this display of faith in the power of well-digested written words, the gift of which earns him a

57. Ibid., e.g., 70, 77, 106, 109.
58. Ibid., 92.

generous measure of hospitality. It is during his captivity among the Moors that the art of writing proves most valuable to him. He resolves to while away the time "by learning to write Arabic" (158). This turns out to be an astute political decision. His jailers and visitors are so taken with his efforts that they help him with the characters, and thereby "were not so troublesome as otherwise they would have been; indeed when I observed any person whose countenance I thought bore malice towards me, I made it a rule to ask him, either to write in the sand himself, or to decipher what I had already written; and the pride of shewing his superior attainments, generally induced him to comply with my request" (158–59). Performing the effort to learn the written language of the other here eases the terms of Park's captivity and initiates a nonviolent relation between prisoner and guard. Nothing is said to imply that this has anything at all to do with Park's eventually being set free, but one supposes that it cannot have done him any harm. He is acquainted with Richardson's *Arabic Grammar* (166) and seems to have at least minimal word recognition of the language (274). In fact he carries Richardson along with him, and produces it to the astonishment of those who cannot believe that "any European should understand, and write, the sacred language of their religion" (275). This too has potential cash and survival value when he is offered "an ass, and sixteen bars of goods" (275) for the book. The stranger responds positively to the sight of others who have made an effort to make him more familiar. Language-learning is not just a convenience for the carrying on of commerce (though it is certainly that) but also, as the Whig political economists would have affirmed, an engine of sociability and peaceful interaction.

The scene of language and language learning is in many contact narratives an interesting parallel and sometimes alternative to the scene of religious conversion. Oroonoko, who spoke French and English, never converts to Christianity, but he can certainly converse; Sancho, Cugoano, and Equiano are converts whose conversibility stretches the expectations and threatens the comfort of their readers by its display of hypercompetence. The encounter with the book is a trope which appears in other slave narratives. Gronniosaw's life story, first published in 1772, recalls seeing a ship's captain read prayers to his crew: "When I first saw him read, I was never so surprized [*sic*] in my life, as when I saw the book talk to my master, as I observed him to look upon it, and move his lips."[59] He picks up the book himself, puts his ear to the cover, and is hugely disappointed to hear noth-

59. *A Narrative of the most remarkable particulars in the Life of James Albert Gronniosaw, an African Prince, as related by himself*, 2nd ed. (Glasgow, 1785), 15–16.

ing. This he takes as a rejection of his blackness and a further incentive to pursue what has already been introduced as an instinctive, providential disposition toward the Christian religion. Almost exactly the same experience is recounted by Equiano, and it occurs in at least two other cases.[60] But Cugoano's version of the encounter with the book is rather different. He goes back to the meeting of the "base treacherous bastard Pizarra" with the Inca emperor Atahualpa, who asks the priest where he had learned the religion to which he was being asked to convert. The priest points to the book, which Atahualpa takes from him: "The Inca opened it eagerly, and turning over the leaves, lifted it to his ear: This, says he, is silent; it tells me nothing; and threw it with disdain to the ground."[61] Thereafter began the conquest of Peru.

Cugoano had become a Christian, but he is able to use his anti-Catholicism as an acceptable vehicle for expressing the dignity of a flourishing oral culture able to refuse the offer of the written book, with the emperor perhaps knowing full well that subjection was coming his way whatever he said, read, hid, or did. These dead letters do not come to life in a grateful conversion to Christianity but stand as emblems of an unresolved conflict that Cugoano preserves as such. There is no meeting or mixing of languages and certainly no acceptance of the magic of writing. In fact the book does not speak in *any* of these cases; it is just that Gronniosaw and Equiano are willing to accept the silence as the mark of their own nonelect status and to strive to amend it by embracing Christian metaphysics, while Atahualpa is not. This is the framework within which Lévi-Strauss reads the Nambikwara chief in the famous encounter reported in *Tristes Tropiques* (though there are other ways to read it): the chief wants access, Lévi-Strauss thinks, to the power and privilege that writing provides.

So too does the Bambarran host who dissolves and swallows Mungo Park's writing and licks the board clean in case he missed anything. But this is a different transaction. Here there is no sense of writing as having a significant content beyond its own material form; its power is purely accessible to and fully absorbable in the physical body of the recipient, who quite literally (and only literally) takes it to heart and eats his words. It is a potion,

60. Equiano, *The Interesting Narrative*, 68. Carretta's note (254–55) lists the other cases. Gates, *The Signifying Monkey*, 127–69, gives a detailed account of the trope of the talking book, in which he discovers an artful play between the European wealth of words and the African wealth of gold, each turning into the other in the hands of trickster writers.

61. Cugoano, *Thoughts and Sentiments*, 62, 64. William Robertson, the likely source for this story, adds in the influence of an "unskillful interpreter" (*The Works of the Late William Robertson, D.D.* [London, 1826], 6:57).

just like opium. The power of writing is not displayed but ingested in a homeopathic fantasy that is also not divisive but socially bonding: Park shares access with his host, and the power imparted displaces the need for the host to eat the body of his visitor to achieve the same effect. Eating words, that is, takes the place of cannibalism and comically defuses one of the most popular myths about black Africans and their kind. Park also avoids feeding his readers' appetites for another such myth, that of the erotic uninhibitedness of native peoples, which could take the form of idealized or titillating innocence (as it sometimes did in the reports about Pacific Islanders) or of outright depravity (as with the public sex and sexual forwardness that Bruce reported with, for some of his readers, far too little disapproval[62]). Park's major account of contact with native women is one of contact avoided in a shared enjoyment of the "jest" that resolves the Moorish women's desire for "ocular demonstration"[63] of whether he is circumcised or not. The sly allusion to Othello's call for "ocular proof"—recall that Park has introduced himself by citing Othello—thereby finesses the potentially tragical or uncontrollable threat embodied in sex between black and white partners. A similar decorum is observed in *Oroonoko*, where the white planter has a strong fancy for Imoinda but resigns his claim on becoming aware that she belongs to Oroonoko himself. In both cases, the play of power and pornography that underpins so much "plantation gothic" is avoided. But so too is any positive outcome of the desire for the stranger that might take form as transracial marriage or romance.

Prurient interest in the body of the conquered black stranger is well known as a feature of the literature of slavery and does not need extended comment here.[64] But the primary sexual transgression that had come to be associated with black persons was not just empirical; it was an offense against the law of the father and a breach of the veil preserving his control of the phallic imaginary. Cugoano takes up the episode of the curse of Ham early on in his *Thoughts and Sentiments*, recognizing it as a kingpin in the arguments of the defenders of slavery. The story occurs in Genesis, chapter 9. Noah discovers viticulture and gets drunk on his own wine, falling asleep naked. Ham sees him in this state and tells his two brothers, who modestly replace the veil (pointedly without looking). Noah wakes and curses both

62. See Leask, *Curiosity and the Aesthetics of Travel Writing*, 83–91.

63. Park, *Travels in the Interior Districts of Africa*, 154.

64. See, among others, Pratt, *Imperial Eyes*, 86–107. Stedman's narrative seems to have been a gathering point for this tradition at the end of the century: see Lee, *Slavery and the Romantic Imagination*, 66–119; and Thomas, *Romanticism and Slave Narratives*, 125–46. See also chapter 7.

Ham and his son Canaan, but most emphatically Canaan, who is consigned to be a servant to his cousins. Genesis says nothing about Canaan's participation in the scene, making his punishment either arbitrary or an indirect punishment of Ham by cursing his line.[65] Cugoano, as if sensing a problem here, writes in a scene wherein Ham allows Canaan to "meddle with, or uncover" his grandfather.[66] Ham fails to chastise his son and also expresses "ridicule" for his father. Cugoano is at pains to point out that it is *only* Canaan and his descendants, and not those of the other sons of Ham, who are implicated here; this is presumably why he devises a role in the primary transgression for Canaan himself. The other children of Ham—Cush, Mizraim and Phut—were not punished. It was the Cushites who were conventionally deemed the ancestors of black Africans. In other words the curse of Ham should not be used to justify the conventions of plantation slavery.[67]

The biblical story is, however, a striking example of what it is that the master culture most fears about those it subjugates: revolt against the "law" that the figure of the father embodies, and a revelation of the imaginary underpinnings of that law in the figure of the phallus that, when reduced to a sighting of a mere penis, cannot be further sustained. Perhaps it is a variant or inversion of this same phobia that has popularly imagined black persons as hypersexual.[68] Here the master's concern is not with any fact about black male bodies or any evidence of what they have wrought, but a fear of losing control over the laws preserving difference through a revelation of the fictive status of the laws' foundation. It is not or not just the fact of interracial sex but the fear of undermining the phantasm that maintains the authority of *all* lawgiving that is at stake here. Power over the sexual body is also the

65. On this crux, see David M. Goldenberg, *The Curse of Ham: Race and Slavery in Early Judaism, Christianity, and Islam* (Princeton, NJ: Princeton University Press, 2005), 157–67.

66. Cugoano, *Thoughts and Sentiments*, 31, 32.

67. According to Cugoano's editor, the identification of Ham's children with blackness was a twelfth-century invention; see Cugoano, *Thoughts and Sentiments*, 158n46. Goldenberg, *The Curse of Ham*, 141–56, offers a more detailed history whereby Ham came to signify not only blackness but also heat, darkness and evil, *none* of which he finds to be convincing interpretations, and all of which were in place by the fourth century CE. See also pages 101–6 for other early associations of Ham with forbidden sexual acts, including having sex with his wife on the ark in despite of Noah's orders; and the discussion of blackness and beauty on pages 79–92, where Goldenberg shows how the Song of Songs can support (at least) two different translations: "black but beautiful" and "black and beautiful." Robert Alter, *The Five Books of Moses: A Translation with Commentary* (New York: Norton, 2008), 52, reports that "no one has ever figured out exactly what it is that Ham does to Noah"; homosexual rape is one among various possibilities.

68. Here it might be noted that the depiction of the macrosexual (usually male) black body images both the master's fear and his own displaced potency; it is that which he controls but of which he fears to lose control, according as he can or cannot redirect sexual energy into work.

power to inflict cruelty and torture and to be continually able to threaten to do so. Torture and sexual humiliation are justified on the premise that the bestiality of the black race is primary and must be disciplined in a reciprocal fashion.[69]

There is some evidence that the paranoid sexualization of the black body becomes more common as the debates about abolition and emancipation become more public and unavoidable toward the end of the eighteenth century. Roxann Wheeler has argued that the popularity of intermarriage novels shows that "even at midcentury, it was still possible for Britons to subordinate a discomfort with dark skin to the profession of Christianity and high rank in relation to some populations."[70] But among these novels, the incidence of marriage between Britons and black Africans is uncommon; the "Moor" figures as a flexible type tending toward whiteness, and high-born converts are preferred to ordinary persons as fictional partners. The historically most common marriages between working-class British women and African men living in England do not usually come in for novelization (the first edition of Edgeworth's *Belinda* is an exception); nor does the matter of sex between West Indies planters and female slaves. The benign representation of skin color as finally irrelevant is then a message made possible largely by leaving out any mention of the most common situations affecting actual persons. Thomas Day and John Bicknell's "The Dying Negro" (1773) does draw upon "fact" in telling of the embittered suicide of a black servant sold into slavery just as he is about to marry a white fellow-servant.[71] This is a tale of hospitality betrayed and conversion and true love set aside by greed, culminating in a wishful vision of Africa's triumphant revenge that instances, like Rushton's *Eclogues* and sections of Cugoano's *Thoughts and Sentiments*, the abolitionists' invocation of a justified violence. Still in the realm of fact, Equiano's *Interesting Narrative* almost offhandedly mentions the author's 1792 marriage to an Englishwoman, Susanna Cullen, in all editions published after the event.[72] Cugoano, who according to Adam Hoch-

69. See, for example, the remarks made in Edward Long's *History of Jamaica*, reprinted in Kitson and Lee, *Slavery, Abolition and Emancipation*, 8:3, 11. Edward Rushton's *West-Indian Eclogues* (1787) argues that the sequence goes the other way, with slave violence erupting in response to rape and torture by the masters and overseers; see ibid., 4: 31–62.

70. Roxann Wheeler, *The Complexion of Race: Categories of Difference in Eighteenth-Century British Culture* (Philadelphia: University of Pennsylvania Press, 2000), 46. In what follows I draw upon Wheeler's discussion on pages 137–75. See also Nussbaum, *The Limits of the Human*, 1–20, 151–212.

71. The poem is reprinted in Kitson and Lee, *Slavery, Abolition and Emancipation*, 4:10–24.

72. Equiano, *The Interesting Narrative*, 235. Carretta, *Equiano, the African*, 366, takes this to be a consciously crafted signal of the possibilities for commercial union between Africa and

schild "was said to have married an Englishwoman," makes no mention of this (or of much else of a purely autobiographical nature) in his book, and no record has been discovered.[73]

It is perhaps surprising, given the importance of sentimentalism in abolitionist print culture ("Am I not a man and a brother?"), that more is not made of the ordinarily intense and decent affections possible between man and wife. Gronniosaw is the most aggressively Christian of the slave narrators, which may be why he feels able to express the spirit of a companionate attraction and marriage more fully than others. Even though the toxic views of Edward Long about black hypersexuality seem to have been very much a minority opinion, it may be that interracial erotic lives were best left undescribed, even when the slave laid claim to royal birth and savage nobility. Or perhaps the power of the trope whereby the planter class was, ever since the *Spectator*'s publication of the story of Inkle and Yarico, identified with the cynical extinction of the erotic life in the pursuit of wealth, was too persuasive a tool to give up lightly. Whatever the reason, what seems not to be open to the slave narrators is any artful exploitation or representation of a perceived or reputed desire for the stranger, of the sort that had hovered around the figures of Omai and Lee Boo, whose cultures represented an innocent sexuality that could be envied as easily as it was despised.

Mirza Abu Talib, who spent two years in England (1800–1802) and whose narrative was translated into English in 1810, felt no such restrictions. As Daniel O'Quinn puts it, "Abu Talib's willingness to play out a scene that exists primarily in European fantasies of Eastern sexuality allows him to isolate and ridicule the mediating role played by Orientalist desire within European subjectivity."[74] O'Quinn makes a convincing case for the author's crafted and self-conscious performance of the role of the figuratively inclined Oriental sensualist, thereby inviting his "Persian" readers to participate in his exercise of power as a guest, and his English readers to choose between confirming their own prejudices and seeing themselves gently mocked for having them. Equally deft is his ability to describe the relative conditions of England and Ireland as analogs and prototypes of what might be happening or about to happen in India. Abu Talib is, of course, no slave, and is

Europe. More striking perhaps is the complete absence of any expression of erotic or emotional closeness of the sort depicted in "The Dying Negro." Gronniosaw is considerably more fulsome in expressing his love for his English wife. Sancho married a fellow black.

73. Adam Hochschild, *Bury the Chains: Prophets and Rebels in the Fight to Free an Empire's Slaves* (Boston: Houghton Mifflin, 2006), 135.

74. *The Travels of Mirza Abu Taleb Khan*, ed. Daniel O'Quinn (Peterborough, ON: Broadview, 2009), 19.

received throughout (to his no small amusement) as an important person of high social rank and a distinguished guest. He is also the emissary of and conduit to important political interlocutors in the subcontinent. So he is certainly not a conquered or subaltern stranger, but he is astute enough to imagine being one and has perhaps experienced at first hand the personality of the British as an imperialist power (an estimated ten million people died in the Bengal famine of 1769–73). Above all he is (or was) visibly real, and as such a fitting alternative and response to the series of fake Orientals who had been invented by European writers like Montesquieu and Goldsmith as vehicles for commenting on the virtues and vices of their own societies.[75] Like Cugoano, Equiano, and Gronniosaw, Mirza is a stranger who writes his own book. Unlike them, he also controls the representation of his own exoticized sexuality. This was a rare privilege. His ability to play the role of a modern Dionysus is class-based; although he has no power of vengeance, he is warmly received and allowed to depart when he wishes. The conjurers who have the power to come and go unpredictably and to perform magical acts of shape-shifting on the West Indian plantations—the obi men like Earle's Three-Fingered Jack and Williams's Hamel—are more threatening to their English neighbors and therefore finally disempowered, at least in the consolatory realm of fiction, even as they are feared and even admired. In this the exotic stranger, slave or prince or both, runs parallel to the final figure in the romantic stranger syndrome that has been the topic of this book: woman, the ultimate stranger who is always closest to home.

75. The most recent of these, Elizabeth Hamilton's 1796 *Translations of the Letters of a Hindoo Rajah*, was an overt attack on Muslim India and a passionate defense of Warren Hastings, but one that also registered the variety of the Indian subcontinent's contributions to foreignizing the English language.

CHAPTER SEVEN

Strange Women

THE VULNERABLE BODY

Back in 1972, at a time when feminism was again freshly impacting popular consciousness (as it had been regularly doing since at least the 1790s), Leslie Fiedler identified woman as "an unassimilated, perhaps forever unassimilable, stranger, the first other of which the makers of our myths, male as far back as reliable memory runs, ever became aware."[1] So indeed it may seem. That "forever unassimilable" sounds a depressing note or perhaps presents an intractable challenge. Medea, Medusa, the two Helens, Dido, Cleopatra, Morgan La Fay, and many other mythic precursors of the (perhaps equally mythic) Freudian castration anxiety do indeed populate literary history, inviting an ungovernable variety of masculinized emotions ranging from loathing to liking, contempt to compassion. Touching on all of these there is desire, of or for woman, blamed for destroying the topless towers of Ilium, the rise and fall of the Roman Empire, and the demise of the sacred fellowship of Camelot, as well as the collapse of endless numbers of supposedly stable bourgeois marriages. For Fiedler, woman is "the original stranger" (47), and it is not hard to agree that there is ample evidence to support his case. When the woman is also foreign or uncanny by birth or origin, the strangeness is yet further enhanced. Although such anxieties are not uniquely attached to women—for both men and women can and do respond to strangers of both sexes—the dreary history of male efforts to preserve power over females and thereby over their own maleness produces countless examples of how easy it has been to associate women with the threatening and potentially revisionary category of the stranger.

1. Fiedler, *The Stranger in Shakespeare*, 45.

Indeed, with the stranger in the home, it is the principle of *Unheimlichkeit* that is, as Freud insisted, at the heart of the *heimlich*. The familiar figure of the angel in the house that famously typifies so much nineteenth-century literature is just one variant of the response to a more unstable and threatening figure, described for example by Adriana Craciun as the "fatal woman" who disturbs the "natural boundaries of bodies" and the borderline between the living and the dead, and who exercises power instead of displaying passivity; or by Terry Castle as the presiding figure of an alternative eighteenth century preoccupied with paranoia, repression, manic masquerade, and the blurring of identities.[2] Theory too has sought to protect its thresholds, as Derrida has been vigilant in pointing out, whether it be in the long-standing culture of *fraternité* and friendship that runs from Plato to Hegel, figuring along the way in the heroic discourse of the Revolution and consistently excluding women, or in Levinas's quieter but still palpable construction of woman as at once preethical and foundational to the primary welcome of an uncomplicated, primitive hospitality.[3] Throne, home, and altar have not managed, however, to wall themselves off from the incursions of the stranger-woman—which perhaps helps explain the occasionally extravagant violence of their historical-empirical responses. This violence is particularly apparent in the literature of plantation slavery, the economy of which provided an all-too-empirical situation within which the sexual fantasies and phobias of the "civilized" group could be embodied in and upon the persons over whom they had near-absolute control (although claims to documentary reporting of the sexual components of the master-slave relation have, quite predictably, been disputed from the beginning). A good example is the debate around the famous print titled *The Abolition of the Slave Trade*, published in 1792 and attributed to Isaac Cruikshank. Captain John Kimber of the *Recovery*, heading to Grenada with a cargo of slaves in 1791, was accused of killing a young female slave by hanging her up by an ankle and whipping her to death. The ship's surgeon told the story to Wilberforce, who had the details published. At the ensuing trial, members of

2. Adriana Craciun, *Fatal Women of Romanticism* (Cambridge: Cambridge University Press, 2003), 11; Terry Castle, *The Female Thermometer: Eighteenth-Century Culture and the Invention of the Uncanny* (Oxford: Oxford University Press, 1995). See also Charlotte Sussman, *Consuming Anxieties: Consumer Protest, Gender and British Slavery, 1713–1833* (Stanford, CA: Stanford University Press, 2000), 110–29, for the association of the vulnerable female body with the appetite for sugar.

3. Derrida, *Politics of Friendship*, trans. George Collins (London: Verso, 1997), e.g., 180, 238, 265, 277–78; Derrida, *Adieu to Emmanuel Levinas*, 37–45.

the ship's crew gave conflicting testimony, and Kimber was acquitted of the charges against him. One account says that the girl refused to eat, another that she refused to dance on deck. Cruikshank captions his print by specifying that she was made to suffer for "her virgin modesty," that is, she had resisted the captain's sexual advances. The print shows the girl upside down and naked except for a loincloth that no longer conceals anything, while Kimber's face is contorted by what we take to be sado-sexual excitement as he wields the whip. Meanwhile the sailor holding the rope expresses his discomfort with the proceedings and others voice their disapproval.

Thus, an ambiguous historical record is made into a dramatically sexualized encounter driven by brutal masculine desires.[4] It would be correct to say that this imagining goes beyond the evidence in this one case, strictly construed, but incorrect to say that it is therefore essentially wrong. The recent past and present in Africa, the Balkans, Iraq, and Afghanistan (to mention only the best-known instances) offer ample evidence of the behavior of persons holding absolute power over those deemed enemies or threats, or those merely unable to resist: rape, torture, and recurrent sexual humiliation of both men and women. Back in the romantic period, John Gabriel Stedman's narrative of his time in Suriname (also the location of Behn's *Oroonoko*) explicitly conveys the sexual dynamics of the imbalances of power that govern plantation life. The book is now most famous because it contains sixteen engravings by William Blake, but its contemporary reputation had more to do with the account of Stedman's relationship to the mulatto slave Joanna, who lived with him as a wife in South America and bore him a much-loved son who was given his father's name. The published version of the narrative presents a loving romantic relationship of a conventionally honorable kind, only thwarted by Joanna's refusal to move with her *de facto* husband to a land—his English homeland—where she feels that she will never be treated as an equal. She dies in Suriname, apparently a victim of poisoning. Stedman grieves appropriately but later finds himself an English wife.

We now know that the published version of the narrative was a heavily edited rewrite of an original transcript completed in 1790, one which itself reworks passages from Stedman's diaries; there are, in other words, three texts to reckon with. Stedman's editors suppose that Stedman himself was not able to supervise the work of his ghostwriter, William Thomson, who

4. See Nussbaum, *Torrid Zones*, 30–41, 76–94, on the tradition of sexualized exotic women, especially black women, in the eighteenth century.

turned the text into something of a proslavery argument and tidied up the sexual material beyond what Stedman himself had already done in making the transition from diary to transcript.[5] The diaries are explicit about Stedman's routine indulgence in the commonly available sex between white masters and female slaves (Oroonoko claims that he killed his wife, Imoinda, to spare her this fate). In the 1790 transcript this information is still available, albeit more politely described. In the 1796 published text there is yet more decorum; while there is mention of the practice of concubinage, Stedman is presented as heroically fighting off the attentions of a negress "of masculine appearance" by hiding in his room, while in the transcript he coyly declines to give details of "the rest of this adventure" and draws a "sable curtain" over the outcome.[6] Other explicit details are omitted in the 1796 version. We may infer how and where the red hot poker enters the body of a tortured young woman whose story he recounts, but we are not directly told, as we are in 1790; and the 1796 text omits Stedman's claim that negro "genitals are conspicuously larger."[7] But the essential features of the 1790 account of the sexual mores of plantation life are clearly preserved in essence and outline. Particularly noticeable in both versions is Stedman's emphasis on the sexual frustrations of European women, whose husbands abandon them for a life of debauchery with their female slaves and consequently die an early death. This produces in white women a hunger for newly arrived European men, as well as excessive cruelty toward their servants motivated by jealousy and enforced sexual abstinence. For, while sex between white men and black women is accepted, white women taking black partners results in the death of the male slave and thus is a measurable economic loss. These women are also cynical enough to pimp their female slaves to the highest bidders, and they demonstrate their power and status by making their young house servants perform their duties in a state of nakedness (for the women) or near-nakedness (for the men). Imprisoned Dionysus figures with no divine power stride the halls of not-so-

5. See *Stedman's Surinam: Life in an Eighteenth-Century Slave Society*, ed. Richard Price and Sally Price (Baltimore, MD: Johns Hopkins University Press, 1992), xlv–lxviii; see also xxvii–xxxiv. This edition is an abridged version of the same editors' complete text of the 1790 transcript published by the same press in 1988.

6. John Gabriel Stedman, *Narrative; of a five years' expedition; against the revolted negroes of Surinam, in Guiana, on the wild coast of South America; from the year 1772, to 1777 . . .* (London, J. Johnson and J. Edwards, 1796), 1:20–21; *Stedman's Surinam*, 19. On language and sex as coevolutionary in generating concerns about miscegenation, see Robert J. C. Young, *Colonial Desire: Hybridity in Theory, Culture and Race* (New York: Routledge, 1995), e.g., 5–6. 20–21, 64ff., 150–58.

7. Stedman, *Narrative*, 1: 126, 2: 252; *Stedman's Surinam*, 56, 258.

stately homes in which the culture of hospitality is founded on the rituals of incarceration and the imagery of the brothel.

Even the tidied, published version of Stedman's narrative is clear about the moral degeneration that affects all Europeans, men and women, when given absolute power over the lives of others. Sadism and sexuality combine to produce a culture of obscene cruelty and torture. The strangeness of the other—and in the 1796 text this is enhanced by a good deal of ethnographic, botanical, and zoological detail about the New World—produces an estrangement of the self, or perhaps the eruption of a self that we would rather not acknowledge as our own. At no point in any of Stedman's texts is there a persisting sense that the slaves themselves are at fault here; they do not incite the behavior of their masters but merely suffer the consequences, often with great dignity and fortitude. He reports the shocking loss of life among the slaves, but it is the moral and physical decline of the Europeans and its effect *on* the slaves that occupies most of his attention. In 1796 Joanna is introduced as a somewhat sanitized image of "female virtue in distress" which, "especially when accompanied with youth and beauty, must ever claim protection."[8] Even the more eroticized relationship described in 1790 projects a clear emotional propriety and reciprocity that speaks to the human equivalence of master and slave. This is reflected (or staged) in the shared use of polite (and even ornate) diction by both whites and negroes—not just Joanna but also the medically literate old man who advises on the benefits of regular bathing.[9] Whether or not we fully accede to the claim to "real history" and to a "plain and MANLY TRUTH" that comes from writing "ON THE SPOT,"[10] it is hard not to suppose that Stedman's story catches something about the dynamics of slave society, something perhaps publishable (and marketable) only because its worst excesses can be attributed principally to the Dutch and the Jews.

The editor of the 1831 first edition of *The History of Mary Prince*, Thomas Pringle, also makes much of the inevitable barbarity that ensues wherever slavery is established. The Brazilians, for example, are "naturally a people of a humane and good-natured disposition," but such disposition cannot survive the experience of mastery over a slave population: "the natural tendency to cruelty and oppression in the human heart, is continually evolved by the impunity and uncontrolled licence in which they are exercised."[11]

8. Ibid., 1:iv.

9. *Stedman's Surinam*, 48–49, 62–63.

10. Stedman, *Narrative*, 1:iv, vi, v.

11. *The History of Mary Prince, a West Indian Slave, Related by Herself*, ed. Moira Ferguson (London: Pandora, 1987), 112.

Prince's story is also made up of one brutal event after another, although she (or her editor) seems to have felt the need to disguise the sexual exploitation she experienced in order to meet the perceived standards of her abolitionist patrons. At the same time, as Moira Ferguson notes, she manages to encode her sexual abuse "through accounts of angry jealous mistresses and a master who forced her to wash him naked" (4). She also has frequent recourse to the rhetoric of the stranger and of the host-guest dynamic. Mary first enters a "strange house" and lives among "strange people" at twelve years old when she is removed from her first family and sent to another five miles distant (48). Turk's Island becomes another "strange land" (60), and she is subsequently a "stranger" in London (79, 86). The reiterated biblical designation of the slave girl as yet another "stranger in a strange land" (Ex 2:22) familiarizes her into the Judeo-Christian exilic tradition even as it purports to register her social alienation. The stranger, in this instance, is rendered strange and not so strange at the same time.

Stedman's lack of investment in the rhetoric of Christian piety produces a much starker and less familiarized narrative. Burke's speeches against Warren Hastings's administration of the East India Company similarly describe habits of torture and rape, including the forcing of women's nipples "between the sharp and elastic sides of cleft bamboos" and the application of "lighted torches and slow fire" to the genitals of Indian women, "planting death in the source of life."[12] Burke and Stedman are only the most explicit transcribers of a rape-torture constellation that can be glimpsed in the shadows of even the most decorous slave narratives; it makes normative an excess of human brutality that does not distinguish between Dutch, Brazilian, or British masters. The body of the woman is not its only object, but it is the most easily available and perhaps the most affecting, since it tends not to reproduce the stoical, masculinizing self-control that Oroonoko demonstrated by smoking his pipe throughout the worst of his agonies. (Imoinda, however, bravely welcomes death.) Stedman, like Behn, shows violence directed at both men and women by both men and women, offering a comprehensive account of the breaking down of even the most familiar gender distinctions and habits when the conditions afford uncontingent power over others.

West Indian plantation culture is in this sense an extreme example of what happens when all power is concentrated in the hands of a master class that is effectively immune from serious oversight. The incidents it generates are analogous to the numerous torture scenes in *Ivanhoe* and to those

12. *The Works of the Rt. Hon. Edmund Burke*, 10:88.

found in the most violent gothic novels, with the difference that these were real. As such they perhaps help to explain the popularity of the Gothic during the period when the abolition movement was gaining maximum publicity. Violence transposed into the Catholic Middle Ages and other culturally remote locations might well have relieved the pressure on those reluctant to confront their own complicity in the contemporary slave economy. Such things, as Henry Tilney smugly remarks in *Northanger Abbey*, are not to be looked for in the middle counties of England. On the other hand, when the gothic novel transcribes extreme violence against women, as it often does, the alert reader may be expected to sense some common ground between medieval maidens and contemporary chattel slaves, especially at a time when Wollstonecraft and others were emphasizing the condition of women as tantamount to slavery. Plantation slavery may not have been visible in the middle counties of England, but the unfree labor, economic dependence, and coerced thought of women have hardly been eradicated, a fact of which even the "polite" novels of Jane Austen offer ample testimony. Nor have they yet; so it might seem appropriate that Bonnie Honig offers the genre of female (not horror) gothic, where complex disturbances (rather than terror) impact the romantic settlements as a medium through which to imagine an adequately critical address to contemporary democratic life in the United States.[13]

THE *PHARMAKON* OF LOVE

Two novels by Sydney Owenson (Lady Morgan) and one by Germaine de Staël explore the possibilities and limits of fully accepting and integrating strange women, and thereby bring up questions about the rights and limitations of all visitors and guests in the dwelling of the other. The hero of *The Wild Irish Girl* (1806) is a sophisticated, cosmopolitan traveler open to having his unfavorable view of the Irish corrected by firsthand experience even before he has set foot on shore. The Irish were the most familiar of strangers, romantically primitivized in their own land as the instinctual vehicles for music and poetry, and feared and abjected in England the more they came to be needed as a mobile laboring class for the building of canals and, thereafter, roads and railways. Their own land was not their own, of course, since they subsisted under the rule of a plantation settler culture not wholly unlike that governing the West Indian economy, albeit without formally sanctioned slavery. Owenson's attribution of "the transmigrated

13. See Honig, *Democracy and the Foreigner*, 108–22.

soul of some *West Indian* planter" to the cruel overseer of the hero's family estates instances a comparison that was often made.[14] The Irish also had their own rebellion in 1798, which the dating of the events of the novel suggests may be still to come. Burke's sensitivity to the misdemeanors of the East India Company has been attributed to his awareness of the sufferings of the Irish peasantry; famine (and the prospect of famine) was not restricted to Bengal.[15] And Abu Talib's passage through Ireland is recounted in a way that suggests that he sees there an example of what may happen (or is already happening) to India under British rule.[16] As Britain's oldest colony, Ireland's forms of strangeness had become familiar both in themselves and as prospective analogs of encounters deriving from a continually expanding global empire.

Owenson's novel comes with an extensively devolved ethnographic apparatus, and includes (often lengthy) footnotes explaining (and justifying) the more arcane elements of Irish culture: it is another instance of the popularity of small print. Ironies abound. The Irish impulse to find an Irish origin for everything of value, and their assertion of the superiority of everything Irish, is mocked; so too is the verbose cosmopolitanism of the English visitor who is constantly seeking to position his hosts within some or other grand high-cultural context or large overview of Western civilization. Much is made of the hospitality of a people who "find in the name of stranger, an irresistible lure to every kind attention"[17]; my informal count produced no fewer than nine other passages in which the extent and quality of Irish hospitality is experienced and discussed, and it is pointedly *not* discovered among the Ulster Protestants (198–99). On at least one occasion Horatio claims to find this attention wearying (35), but the emphasis is clearly positive. In all cases but one this is pure hospitality, unmarked by disruptive forms of host-guest desire and innocent of any expectation of a return.[18]

14. Sydney Owenson, Lady Morgan, *The Wild Irish Girl*, ed. Kathryn Kirkpatrick (Oxford: Oxford University Press, 1999), 34.

15. See, for example, Luke Gibbons, *Edmund Burke and Ireland: Aesthetics, Politics and the Colonial Sublime* (Cambridge: Cambridge University Press, 2003), 113. But see also Sara Suleri, *The Rhetoric of English India* (Chicago: University of Chicago Press, 1992), 24–74, who sees in Burke's speeches a more comprehensive anxiety about the struggle between merchants and the state, as well as a recourse to the aesthetics of the public theater.

16. The point is made by Daniel O'Quinn, ed., *The Travels of Mirza Abu Taleb Khan*, 35.

17. Owenson, *The Wild Irish Girl*, 16.

18. Whereas in Williams's *Hamel*, a constantly mentioned "hospitality" is barely if ever enough to hold together the components of a West Indian plantation society constantly on the point of radical violence.

The one exception is at the heart of the plot: the family of the Prince of Inismore and above all the Irish girl herself, Princess Glorvina, in whom Horatio dreams of encountering the head of the Gorgon (60) but who turns out to be everything good and beautiful. Glorvina is wild and mysterious but highly educated in several languages, an embodiment of primitive innocence and energy who yet reads the latest London papers, and more than a match for the narrator in her understanding of his presuppositions about subaltern society.

It is intermarriage, albeit after a troubling detour through the political romance fantasy entertained by Horatio's father (who had planned to marry Glorvina himself), that settles the relation between the two countries and renders their rivalry as wishfully "forever buried."[19] The son's taking the place of the father is staged as the erotic resolution of what was first claimed as a pure gesture of redress, giving back to the Irish something of what they had lost. But Horatio's own erotic disposition hardly ever (if ever) escapes the comic mode. He protests that he is too passionately carried away to keep up his ethnographic narrative, telling his correspondent that he will transcribe no more Irish history (161), but after a few pages the footnotes come back as fast and thick as ever. The romance plot is very much a game played by equal parties; Glorvina's economic dependency is more than offset by her intellectual and emotional dignity and freedom from self-deception. The fantasy is that a humanized Protestant ascendancy will make amends for the sins of the past, because the essential Ireland is imaged *as* a thing of the past, although there are subtle signals—those newspapers, for example—that modernization has impinged on rural Ireland in despite of its antiquarian appearances and protestations. Glorvina's father, the prince of Inismore, has himself been something of an "agricultural speculator" (168), and the debts in which he finds himself enmeshed are very much of the modern commercial world. But the marriage settlement does not suggest that Horatio is "going native" except in the most enjoyable and manageable ways. The strange woman is welcomed, because the male self is finally not estranged from itself. The encounter between strangers is enabling for both parties.

Other romantic novels are less confident about the availability of such happy solutions of male encounters with strange women. Things are more troubling in a much more famous novel published the year after *The Wild Irish Girl*, and the two have enough in common that one has to wonder

19. Owenson, *The Wild Irish Girl*, 250.

whether either author could have read the other: Germaine de Staël's *Corinne*. The novel was translated twice into English in its year of publication (1807), although its cult status as the "nineteenth century's master narrative on the conflicted role of women in the public sphere" seems to have developed later, in the 1820s, mostly among women poets.[20] The currency of *Corinne* contributed to an association between women and cosmopolitanism, and between cosmopolitanism and suffering. For the romantic relation between the main characters is overpowered by the dogged demands of the English national character, which Oswald is unable to transcend and which Corinne herself (who is half-English) internalizes. Corinne, a transnational figure whose true identity is kept secret for much of the novel, is embraced by the Italians as well as by foreign visitors as the spirit and image of Italy. She is the stranger who functions as the lawgiver, though here entirely in the realm of the aesthetic. Oswald, the dour Scotsman, is dazzled by her beauty and her talents. He falls in love with her, and she with him. But Oswald cannot shake off the lure of his native land, which, indeed, has conditioned his very emotions. Albeit that "home" is associated with pain (the father's death) and compulsion (the father's command), home is where his heart is: "It is in vain that an Englishman momentarily likes foreign ways; his heart always returns to the first impressions of his life."[21] In a tragic playing out of the familiar north-south dyad of reason and passion, repression and expression, Corinne, who elects the Italian way of life as her own, cannot break through the carapace of the English (actually Scottish) national character nor fully remain in her own, and the romance becomes disabling for both. Oswald can neither disentangle nor tolerate the two sides of the *pharmakon* that love presents him with, telling her: "You are a sorceress who alternately makes people anxious and reassures them, who appears sublime and suddenly disappears from the sphere where you are alone to mingle with the crowd. Corinne, Corinne, I cannot but fear you as I love you!" (97–98). He ends up with the English wife his father has chosen for him, and Corinne dies of a broken heart.[22]

20. Patrick H. Vincent, *The Romantic Poetess: European Culture, Politics and Gender, 1820–1840* (Hanover, NH: University Press of New England, 2004), 13. See especially the discussion on 97–221.

21. Madame de Staël, *Corinne, or Italy*, trans. Sylvia Raphael (New York: Oxford University Press, 1998), 195.

22. See Kari Lokke, "Sibylline Leaves: Mary Shelley's *Valperga* and the Legacy of *Corinne*," in *Cultural Interactions in the Romantic Age: Critical Essays in Comparative Literature*, ed. Gregory Maertz (Albany: State University of New York Press, 1998), 157–73: "*Corinne* derives its psychological power from an unrelenting depiction of its heroine's self-destructive internalization of the patriarchal values and modes of thinking and feeling represented by Oswald and

In Staël's novel the very qualities projected by Edmund Burke—patriotism, domesticity, habit, nostalgia for the homeland—as important to the legitimation of the war effort against France are rendered interpersonally tragic. Whatever might be positive about them turns punitive and repressive. Corinne is no "belle dame sans merci." The onset of love disempowers her and renders her ultimately unthreatening. The suffering is uneven and falls more upon the woman than the man: the stranger is abjected and defeated. Oswald is not unmoved, but Corinne is shattered beyond repair. The Englishman's encounter with the stranger-woman leaves him alive, but it destroys her. The British culture whose identity is fundamentally exclusionary wins out over the Italian culture whose impetus is more open and tolerant. There is finally no place for "foreign ways." Similar tensions and comparably tragic outcomes govern the events of Sydney Owenson's 1811 novel *The Missionary*. The story is set in the 1630s and tells of a missionary expedition to India undertaken by Hilarion, a Portuguese Franciscan monk. Here he encounters a Hindu priestess, portentously (but unsuitably) named Luxima. Both start out secure in their commitments to their own religions, but both are estranged from them—and from themselves—by the experience of falling in love. When they first meet, it is as perfect exempla of their respective cultures, "the noblest specimens of the human species, as it appears in the most opposite regions of the earth; she, like the East, lovely and luxuriant; he, like the West, lofty and commanding."[23] Two possible resolutions—a happy interracial marriage or the total destruction of one personality by the other—are avoided. What we get instead is a complex dynamic in which the security of each is undermined by the desire for the other. Extremes do not meet in the middle but destroy each other as extremes, consigning both characters to a tragic middle ground where stable personalities have collapsed and where no lasting happiness can be forthcoming. The novel analyzes the breaking down of rigidly doctrinaire orthodoxies without suggesting that any compensatory position is available, partly because no one else will tolerate it. Hilarion learns that pleasure and sin need not be "inseparably connected" and that there are some earthly pleasures that it is "more culpable to neglect than to embrace" (141). He passes into "a world of newly connected and newly modified ideas" which he cannot resist yet cannot fully embrace (145); he is caught in the middle. The same thing

the deceased father who haunts his conscience: obsession with duty, propriety, and violence to feelings and desires" (167).

23. Sydney Owenson, Lady Morgan, *The Missionary*, ed. Julia M. Wright (Peterborough, ON: Broadview, 2002), 109.

happens to Luxima, who trembles at the point of converting to Christianity and is actually at one point baptized, but who dies in the faith of her fathers as well as in the love of her Christian companion. Neither can fully articulate or feel comfortable with the purely natural religion that would break down the barriers between them, though that is what the missionary senses as innate in Luxima's "sublime and contemplative mind" (129). The Hindu comes closer to it than the Christian, partly because she is a woman and holds to the holiness of the heart's affections, but also because her religion does not "shut the gates of Heaven against all who sought it by a different path" (178). The to and fro between conversion, unconversion, and reconversion that dominates Luxima's life in the middle of the novel is resolved only in a *Liebestod* scene in which, seeking death as a sati, she runs into a Christian dagger intended for Hilarion and dies in his arms.

Far more passionately than *The Wild Irish Girl*, this novel preaches the power and value of love as the thing that should and perhaps—without the interference of repressive, orthodox outsiders—actually could overpower the impediments of cultures and religions that are strangers or enemies to each other. Love does not here conquer all, partly because the prejudices and presuppositions of the two religions have been so deeply internalized by the lovers, but also, and more importantly, because of the inflexible dogmatisms of their fellow believers who afford them no space for independent choice. On those occasions when a meeting of minds and hearts is about to occur, others step in to thwart any happy outcome. Among these forces, the cruelest is the Spanish Jesuit Inquisition. The end of the story reveals that after the death of Luxima, Hilarion went back to the place in Kashmir where he first met her and lived on as a "stranger," a recluse in the forest, where he "prayed at the confluence of rivers" and "at the rising and the setting of the sun"[24] in a pantheistic acknowledgement of what was or should have been common to them both. Emphatically, he has *not* become the public, interdenominational preacher of the "spirit of peace" (257) that Luxima herself recommended for him after her death. He is too broken a man for that, and there is too little evidence of his likely success in a world as divided as this one continues to be. On his own death he is discovered to have been praying to "the deity of his secret worship" (261), but who exactly that might be remains a secret. Luxima's ashes rest beside his body, along with a Christian cross and a Brahmin "dsandum" (261).

The word "dsandum," coming a few lines before the end of the book, is a challenge, unless we recall that it appeared and was explained on page 92

24. Ibid., 260.

and again on page 241 as the three threads that Brahmins wear around the neck as the mark of their caste: this too is one of the things Luxima gave up in following a Christian. Owenson's book contains a number of foreignizing moments, not only in its vocabulary but also in its heavy use of footnotes: as Julia Wright points out, eleven of the novel's seventeen sources are from texts not written in English and direct the reader "to an overtly cosmopolitan body of scholarship in which firsthand accounts from a variety of national perspectives, rather than British scholarship, are given priority."[25] British India is only indirectly at issue in the story, but the Portuguese and Spaniards represent a set of European attitudes that cannot simply be explained away as the misperceptions of benighted seventeenth-century Catholics. In particular, Owenson is responding to a popular debate about the pros and cons of missionary activity and the conversion experience in early-nineteenth-century Britain. As we have seen, Scott's *Ivanhoe* and Edgeworth's *Harrington* explore this in their treatment of the figure of the Jew. Scott's Rebecca refuses the temptation to convert into a Christian marriage and denies the romance plot by choosing exile from a doggedly anti-Semitic medieval England. Edgeworth's novel ends with a marriage only because the heroine, Berenice, in a fairy-tale revelation that does little to disturb the otherwise intransigent decision against conversion, turns out to have been a Protestant all along. *The Missionary* also weighs in against the credibility or desirability of conversion in favor of a tolerance of others and a respect for the general or natural common components of all faiths and a disavowal of divisive doctrines. Toward the end of the novel the Pundit of Lahore, whose well-meant ideals have to some extent set going the whole tragedy, rescues Luxima from captivity and gives her into "the care of a Jewess, who lived with him, and who, though outwardly professing Christianity from fear and policy, hated equally the Christians and the Pagans; love, however, secured her fealty to her protector, to whom she was ardently devoted; and pity secured her fidelity to the trust he had committed to her care" (244). In this world, a certain degree of shrewd disguise is required for the effective exercise of the virtues of love and pity, but they remain virtues nonetheless. Personal affections can and should overcome the barriers raised by established religions. Hilarion loses faith not only in some of the doctrines he grew up with but also in the usefulness of aggressive missionary activity, especially when combined with a visible appetite for material profit (226).[26]

25. Ibid., 51 (editor's introduction).

26. Owenson revised and retitled her novel for publication in 1859 (see 5–56; see also Viswanathan, *Outside the Fold*, 27–31).

The Missionary thus subverts what Katie Trumpener has plausibly identified as the besetting convention of the earlier national tale, wherein the story ends "with the traveler's marriage to his or her native guide."[27] Here there is no happy ending of the sort that, as in *The Wild Irish Girl*, conjures away the discrepancies between England and Ireland. What does survive is a depiction of a universal human heart that struggles unsuccessfully to flourish in a hostile world. Luxima is indeed exoticized as the image of Oriental sensuality, but Hilarion is also staged as the hyper-masculinized, uptight Christian. Both begin to learn that there are better ways to live. The strange woman is first introduced by way of her stereotype, but that stereotype gradually falls away; her struggles with the loss of her religion and her cultural bearings reveal the brutality of the conversion experience. Luxima, despite the lurid promise of her very name, is not an object of racialized, pornographic fascination but subsists as flesh and blood, and in her responsiveness to the visit of the stranger she undergoes a painful dismantling of that large part of human identity that comes from culture and habit. But here, unlike in *Corinne*, man and woman suffer equally, although the death of the woman still comes first. The book's message is a bleak one: even if exemplary individuals can, after great difficulty, struggle through to the point of accepting strangeness as ordinary, as the property of a shared human heart, then no one around them is likely to tolerate their achievement. Among the defenders of the faiths, the pagan stranger can only be distrusted and despised.

Contact and conversion are again the major themes of Southey's *A Tale of Paraguay* (1825), where the strange women at the heart of the story are fully de-eroticized and made as unsusceptible as possible to any aspiringly prurient male gaze. Southey's position on conversion is less explicit and more conservative than Owenson's. There is indeed enough evidence in his considerable body of writings to accuse him of a "militant imperialism,"[28] and on the matter of missionary work he seems to have generally held that a nonviolent broad church Protestantism would be a good thing for most parts of the world. In *The Curse of Kehama*, he is less respectful of Hinduism than Owenson seems to be. But he is consistently suspicious of the excesses of priestcraft and state-supported violence, and in *A Tale of Paraguay* this complex of concerns produces a highly nuanced narrative of

27. Katie Trumpener, *Bardic Nationalism: The Romantic Novel and the British Empire* (Princeton, NJ: Princeton University Press, 1997), 141.

28. David M. Craig, *Robert Southey and Romantic Apostasy: Political Argument in Britain, 1780–1840* (Woodbridge, UK: Royal Historical Society and Boydell Press, 2007), 142.

the inadvertent destruction of indigenous people by a mix of both good and bad intentions. Unlike Owenson's Jesuits, those who inhabit the remoter regions of Paraguay in Southey's poem are both well-intentioned and on the whole good. But they are compromised by operating as both rearguard and vanguard for a ruthless plundering of South American wealth by the Spanish armies and for breaking the resistance of the native peoples "with the Cross alone, when arms had fail'd."[29] In other words, they are agents of conquest even as they are preaching peace. Whenever the Spanish fear "an Indian enemy" they call upon "Loyola's sons" to take up the cross and gather the Indians into towns (3:13).

The tale begins in the forest dwelling of a mother and her two children, the last survivors of a tribe wiped out in a smallpox epidemic. They have never seen white people, but they have suffered the effects of their presence through the invisible agency of disease. They enjoy a life that is not primally innocent but that has reverted to innocence, because they are no longer required to observe the habits and beliefs of their own vanished culture: they have been renatured. But they have dim memories of tribal legends concerning a race of peaceful visitors who worship a female deity as the embodiment of love. Southey makes very clear that the benefits of Jesuit Mariolatry are by no means this simple, not least because they operate alongside a rapacious *matte*-harvesting industry that despoils the forest and practices a de facto slavery. But the seed of a desire for wider society has been planted, so that when the three survivors are finally discovered they embrace the opportunity to join the wider world. Their first night in the settlement is, however, imaged as a fall:

> The peace wherewith till now they have been blessed
> Hath taken its departure. In the breast
> Fast following thoughts and busy fancies throng;
> Their sleep itself is feverish, and possest
> With dreams that to the wakeful mind belong.[30]

Cross-cultural contact, as it does for Luxima and Hilarion, produces not harmony but confusion. Here the disturbance is not erotic but still psychologically profound: a whole lifeworld is being transformed, and the new

29. Robert Southey, *A Tale of Paraguay* (London: Longman, Hurst, Rees etc., 1825), 83 (Canto 3:12).

30. Ibid., 3:50 (102).

does not comfortably replace the old. An entire structure of "habits" is displaced:

> such mutation is too rude
> For man's fine frame unshaken to remain.
> And these poor children of the solitude
> Began ere long to pay the bitter pain
> That their new way of life brought with it in its train.
> (4:28; 119)

The mother, Monemma, succumbs to a "strong malady" (4:29) that seems to be both psychological and physiological. She dies with "Christian rites" (4:29; 119), but it is not clear whether she had been formally baptized, not least because we have been told of the Jesuit policy of waiting until firm proof of faith has been demonstrated. Mooma dies next, in very much the same manner, and then Yeruti, her brother, for whom a special dispensation provided an early baptism. For all his willingness to believe that the Jesuits are governed by the best intentions, Southey still makes clear that the rigid policy of probation before baptism can only add to the anxieties and psychological insecurities of persons already suffering the effects of a radical cultural displacement. The Jesuits are unintentionally cruel, but cruel nonetheless.

It seems significant that Southey invents a contact-drama of psychological suffering that is not in his source, Martin Dobrizhoffer's Latin history of the Abipones, and that reduces both men and women to a condition of abjection.[31] In so doing he radically questions the logic and effect of all missionary activity, not just that carried out by early modern Catholics in South America. Monemma and Mooma lose a world and may or may not believe that they gain Christian salvation in an afterlife. Southey does not beat the Protestant drum in suggesting that a life of theological risk, even if it brings death with it, is to be preferred to a life of happiness. True, the original happiness itself was only relative, premised on the destruction of the tribe and troubled by deceptive rumors of a beneficial white civilization lying just out of reach. But as a renatured happiness, one made out of adverse circumstances, it was better than what they found in the Christian settlement. The strangers in the forest, two of them women, are not eroticized

31. For an extended account of this poem and its relation to the sources, along with a review of other work on the poem, see my "Romantic Indians: Robert Southey's Distinctions," *Wordsworth Circle* 38 (2007): 20–25.

or primitivized; they are not classic "noble savages" because they have had to create the world they are able to enjoy and because there is no moment of precontact independence ever given to them to inhabit. But they have evolved into a caring and compassionate family group that does no damage and deserved something better than what it received from contact with Christian culture. These are figures who would have been happier had they remained untranslated, but in whom the impulse toward self-translation had been implanted by a contact that is historically unavoidable even as it is psychologically destructive. It seems unlikely that Southey intends an indictment of Christianity at large, rather than a more limited critique of the militarized sectarian dogma disseminated in its name; but he does undoubtedly explore the negative dynamics of that Christ-figure who comes "not to send peace on earth . . . but a sword," and who demands of his followers that they estrange themselves from fathers and mothers in order to be worthy of him (Mt 10:34–37). What is not clear in Southey's poem is any sure conviction that "he that loseth his life for my sake shall find it" (Mt 10:39).

The Missionary allows for erotic desire for the stranger, which produces not a ravenous and destructive sexual appetite but a normalizing of relations between Hilarion and Luxima, who learn to love one another both physically and spiritually precisely because they do not succumb to instant, exoticized sexual gratification. It is the punishing and denaturing cruelty of institutional religion that impedes what promises to become a relationship of true physical and mental reciprocity. Coleridge transcribes the suffering endured by women who are made the objects of legalized masculine fantasy-phobias in his history of the life and death of Maria Eleonora Schöning.[32] This was very much Wordsworth's project in poems like "The Thorn" or "The Mad Mother': to show the real-life circumstances through which vulnerable women could find themselves reclassified as witches or fairies at the dictates of popular superstition. Even in "Lamia," which explores the melodramatic conjunction of strange woman and serpent with apparently full commitment, Keats manages to summon up a strong enough measure of sympathy for the demon woman (or antipathy toward her persecutor) as a suffering pseudo-mortal to render the poem, famously, an exercise in dialectical thinking. Shelley's "Witch of Atlas" notably casts his supernatural woman as the apostle of love and enlightenment reason. Radcliffe's *Sicilian Romance* works toward revealing the quasi-supernatural ghost figure of the haunted tower as a mistreated wife and suffering mother; like a number of

32. Samuel Taylor Coleridge, *The Friend*, ed. Barbara E. Rooke, 2 vols. (Princeton, NJ: Princeton University Press, 1969), 1:341–55.

other gothic novels it replaces fantastic figures with earthly forms. And in *Records of Woman*, Hemans shows time after time that the extraordinary strength and courage of women under duress is not the result of demonic inspiration but of the intensity of human love and faith "enduring to the last."[33] The instances of female courage here adduced are on a global scale—in England, France, Germany, India, Greece, Switzerland, Italy, and North America—and they are often exercised in the cause of political as well as emotional freedom.

Perhaps the depiction of so many ordinary women proving themselves capable of extraordinary things when going among or receiving visits from often hostile strangers is an index of the demographics of an expanding empire, when many men and women bred up in Jane Austen's England really were crossing the oceans often never to return. Certainly the relentless transcription of lonely or unmourned deaths in far-off places constitutes in Felicia Hemans's work a sort of negative cosmopolitanism, wherein (as for Southey's native Paraguayans) the brave new world turns out to come down to a lonely grave.[34] The single human heart that Southey finds in South America and Owenson in India does indicate, however, a utopian alternative, if only *in potentia*, to the divisive and destructive effects of a rigid reliance upon country, class, and creed. And in each case that heart is most obviously housed in the body of a woman. Both men and women suffer from the failure of the cosmopolitan ethic and the impact of national prejudice and convention upon the creative possibilities of desire. But women suffer more. The human heart that is depicted in the experiences of global womanhood is mostly a suffering one, so that what is generalized is not only a shared human nature but a predicament of often violent inequality. When the strange woman is normalized and made familiar in emotional terms, then she brings along with her a critique of the similarly normative powers and dispositions that keep her in a vulnerable state.

"MYSELF A MISERABLE SLAVE"

Burke's *Reflections* made memorable the conjunction between wildly sexualized lower-class women and the violence of the French Revolution when it embodied, in 1790, the "Theban and Thracian Orgies" and the "furies of

33. Felicia Hemans, *Records of Woman with other Poems*, ed. Paula R. Feldman (Lexington: University Press of Kentucky, 1999), 40.

34. For a strong reading of the self-divided image of patriotism in Hemans, see Lootens, "Hemans and Home."

hell" in the women who marched on Versailles.[35] The dangerous appeal of Dionysus lives on, though now he wields not the thyrsus but the rights of man, which were at least briefly also those of women. Political and sexual freedoms were polemically conflated in the British conservative press and print market, producing a composite figure of what it most feared. It would not have helped that in the same year Helen Maria Williams attested to the power of women in bringing about the great events in Paris: "we often act in human affairs like those secret springs in mechanisms, by which, though invisible, great movements are regulated."[36] Secret and invisible, wild women become instances of the unknown unknowns. Burke also invoked or invented the revolutionaries' characterization or self-characterization as "a gang of Maroon slaves broke loose from the house of bondage" (36) and therefore to be forgiven (they claimed) for the occasional abuse of liberty. Slaves, like women, were indeed freed for a time, and in Haiti they freed themselves. The by-then well-established discursive equation of women and slaves is not one that Burke could afford to make explicit; his admiration of the French queen was a keystone of the defense of chivalry mounted in the *Reflections* and goes to the heart of the class identification upon which his social theory depends. His lower class women are imaged as freed slaves, given to wild abandon, but the comparison is not pursued. Not so among the radicals. Wollstonecraft compared women to slaves in their being denied access to the "sharp invigorating air of freedom," although their de facto slavery is disguised by their being treated as despots, empty figures worshiped by adoring males.[37]

The slave status of women was a commonplace in the feminist novels of the 1790s. Charlotte Smith is able to draw upon both Wollstonecraft and (parodically) Burke when Geraldine Verney, about to leave for France, describes herself as a slave going among freed slaves:

> If I get among the wildest collection of those people whose ferocity arises not from their present liberty, but their recent bondage, is it possible to suppose they will injure *me*, who am myself a miserable slave, returning with trembling and reluctant steps, to put on the most dreadful of all fetters?—Fetters that would even destroy the freedom of my mind.[38]

35. Burke, *Reflections on the Revolution in France*, 72.

36. Williams, *Letters Written in France*, 79.

37. *The Works of Mary Wollstonecraft*, 5: 105, 123–24.

38. Charlotte Smith, *Desmond*, ed. Antjie Blank and Janet Todd (Peterborough, ON: Broadview, 2001), 303–4.

She is the prisoner of a loveless and despotic marriage to a man who is prepared to pimp her to another and who thus treats her as a piece of "property" (333). The buying and selling of female flesh is not restricted to the West Indian plantations. Leonora Sansay's *Secret History*, published in Philadelphia in 1808, depicts not only the racialized violence between whites and blacks and men and women (including white women on black women) that was a standard component of novels set in slave societies, but also the sexual brutality deployed by white men over their white wives. Clara says of her husband, M. St. Louis, "often . . . he has treated me with the most brutal violence,—this you never knew, nor many things which passed in the loneliness of my chamber, where, wholly in his power, I could only oppose to his brutality my tears and my sighs."[39] St. Louis's absolute power over his wife (as over his slaves) adds spice to a sexual appetite locked into sadistic-erotic compulsion (139). The more superficially mainstream novels of Fanny Burney, from *Evelina* onward, also offer withering analyses of male violence that constantly threatens to—and often does—get out of control. The exemplary behaviors of her heroes and heroines are not typical of a native English culture that she otherwise presents as rooted in violent behavior. Only the most providential of narratives allows the novels to project their happy endings. Women like Madame Duval and the neurotic Lydia Larpent (in *Evelina*) adapt to this culture and inadvertently support it by developing explicitly masochistic personalities. Unlike Jane Austen, Burney plays up the physical and sexual violence that governs relations between men and women in the supposedly civilized drawing room, showing that the lineaments of the gothic novel are after all to be discovered in the middle counties of England. Sensibility here does not work as a force for sociability and bonding, as it does in the ideal "man of feeling" narrative, but as a symptom tending toward the explosive loss of self-control: the temper tantrum, the violent self-laceration, the blows delivered or intended. Burney's men are often dangerous, both to others and to themselves. No unprotected woman is safe from their attentions, and keeping them in line is constantly difficult and sometimes impossible.

Women and slaves have in common a social position that tempts men in power to abuse and exploit them, and in this way they ask a radical question of those who believe in the existence of a single human heart: is that heart more disposed to kindness or cruelty? Joanna Baillie, who set out to write

39. Leonora Sansay, *Secret History; or, the Horrors of St. Domingo*, ed. Michael J. Drexler (Peterborough, ON: Broadview, 2008), 137.

plays about the elemental passions, resolves this firmly in a positive direction: "the dark and malevolent passions are not the predominant inmates of the human breast," which "hath produced more deeds—O many more! of kindness than of cruelty."[40] The torture practiced by native American tribes upon their captured enemies is accordingly explained not as an eruption of primary cruelty but as an anthropological rite intended to honor the strength of human courage under duress (1:6–7). Life in the slave economy, on the other hand, suggests that kindness and cruelty can coexist with very little mediation of extremes, and no enduring middle ground of the sort that allows us to think of ourselves as civilized. So too, not uncommonly, does the male response to women. At least since the extraordinary popularity of Richardson's *Pamela* and the controversy that surrounded it, the figure of the female as one capable of educating men (and especially upper class men) out of their instinct for violence had been a leitmotif of British fiction, although there are limits on what can be hoped for, not least because that same female figure can also *incite* violence, as it did in *Pamela* before Squire B.'s conversion to polite and conversable behavior. Fanny Burney's novels represent a powerful male culture of hunting, dueling, fighting, and womanizing that has not been at all softened by the culture of civility whose emergence (from Shaftesbury on) makes up only one version of the eighteenth-century social narrative. Perhaps these fictional constructions tell us that we should not conceive of kindness and cruelty as utterly distinct inclinations, but rather as belonging together, making the human "heart" yet another among the class of *pharmakon* terms whose complexity we simplify at our peril.

Burney's last novel, *The Wanderer* (1814), incarnates the foreign woman as the compound stranger who tests out the integrity of the homeland, a motif that first took seriocomic life in *Evelina* thirty-six years earlier, and is here again produced as the core of the narrative. The story is still wrapped around with the elements of providential fairy tale, where the persecuted woman turns out to be a princess-equivalent after all and appropriate rewards and punishments are administered, leaving no loose ends. Yet in its finer and darker details it fully explores the paradigm of women as "boundary subjects," in Kristeva's words, whose function can be judged in terms of their "ability to modify the nation in the face of foreigners" and "to orient foreigners confronting the nation toward a still unforeseeable conception

40. Joanna Baillie, *A Series of Plays: in which it is attempted to delineate The Stronger Passions of the Mind*, 5th ed. (London: Longman, Hurst, Rees and Orme, 1806), 1:12.

of a polyvalent community."[41] It explores, in other words, the limits of hospitality and of the plausibility of a cosmopolitan culture of welcome. Some of Burney's women fail spectacularly in this task: the venomous cruelty and hostility of the middle-aged society ladies—Mrs. Ireton, Mrs. Howel, and Mrs. Maple—toward the strange and vulnerable woman whose name and rank are unknown is not only imaged as the revenge of fading sexual allure upon the young and the beautiful but also as the punitive energy of the defenders of class and nation: what Kristeva describes as the "regressive sado-masochistic leanings" (34) that can arise when women demonstrate their secondary status by an overidentification with orthodoxy. That orthodoxy is never purely national or patriotic, Burney shows, but at all times thoroughly imbued with and mobilized by class affiliation: the desire to maintain one's own status by denying it to others.

The story begins with a party of émigrés leaving France in a hurry, in a ship whose passenger list constitutes a picaresque cast of persons who will encounter one another again and again over the next nine hundred pages. A disguised young woman is taken on board at the last moment, after a lengthy debate (the first of many) on the topics of hospitality, charity, and one's obligations to strangers. The "Incognita" is at first completely inscrutable; she is in blackface, but as the disguise fades she turns into a white person. She is variously deemed to be a nun, a housemaid, a prostitute, a beggar, and a spy. She is an incarnation of woman's capacity for metamorphosis and as such she stimulates a whole range of prejudices and fantasies among her shipmates. Mrs. Ireton speaks the truth, albeit with uncharitable motives: "You have been bruised and beaten; and dirty and clean; and ragged and whole; and wounded and healed; and a European and a Creole, in less than a week."[42] Later she is compared to the Wandering Jew (465). In being suspected of coming from Africa or the West Indies, she is imaged as a slave: "Can such a skin . . . be worth so much breath?" (29), says Mrs. Ireton, prefiguring both her own callous treatment of her "favourite young negro" (481) and the heroine's status as a "bond-woman" shackled to a dreadful marriage (848). Juliet, the woman who is the object of these attentions, wonders whether it will ever be possible to break the cycle of mastery and slavery that pertains both between the classes and between genders, "between oppression on one side, and servility on the other?" (489).

41. Julia Kristeva, *Nations without Nationalism*, trans. Leon S. Roudiez (New York: Columbia University Press, 1993), 35.

42. Frances Burney, *The Wanderer; or Female Difficulties*, ed. Margaret Anne Doody, Robert L. Mack, Peter Sabor (Oxford and New York: Oxford University Press, 2001), 46.

Juliet herself, as an inadvertent trickster, traverses the entire spectrum of social and occupational roles, even as it is clear to Burney's reader that she is of noble stock: there is no ultimate contradiction between nature and nurture here. Like Dionysus, she is adept at disguise and is of higher status than she seems. Unlike Dionysus, she has no power. She discovers the pain and indignity of female labor in an economy where it is all too seldom rewarded; as a seamstress she finds that payment for her work is constantly deferred by those who commission it; as a lady's companion she is treated as a punching bag for her employer's cruel and whimsical disposition; and as music teacher she is frequently humiliated by being made to perform in public as a kind of showpiece. As "the wanderer" she travels up and down the social scale from the castle to the cottage and experiences both the city and the country, finding that kindness and generosity are rare everywhere. She loses her purse not once but twice, allowing her to function as a yardstick for the charitable instincts of others, instincts often nonexistent. Burney manages to inform her reader that it is not only foreign or unknown persons who can be thought of as strangers; it is also the domestic working class, among whom "undivided attention to manual toil"[43] and the "uninteresting monotony" (454) of divided labor inhibits the cultivation of polite habits and civilized pleasures. It takes an exiled Frenchwoman (who is in fact English) to point out to patriots and political theorists on both sides of the Channel that "freedom" is "but a name, for those who have not an hour at command from the subjection of fearful penury and distress" (473–74).

Above all Juliet functions as a litmus test of the national standard for hospitality, which turns out to be spectacularly low: "I feel myself, though in my native country, like a helpless foreigner; unknown, unprotected, and depending solely on the benevolence of those by whom, accidentally, I am seen, for kindness,—or even for support!"[44] She is both native and foreign, the foreigner within, and never more so than when she is classed as outside the social elite. By withholding the secret of her name she prevents her potential hosts and hostesses from resorting to mere class solidarity as a way of masking their lack of human kindness; as an indigent noblewoman she would be welcomed by most of her peers, but as a needy stranger of unknown origins she is held to be unworthy of attention. As Mrs. Maple says, "I have a great right to know the name of a person that comes, in this manner, into my parlour" (57). For Mrs. Howel, any hospitality shown to one who is not "a lady of fashion" is sheer "indignity" (132).

43. Ibid., 395.
44. Ibid., 214.

Juliet is a partial rewrite of Corinne, who also conceals her name and who also turns out to be (half) English. Like Corinne, she suffers for her anonymity. To know a name is to be able to make a decision about hospitality, for or against. This is a crucial component of Derrida's distinction between "absolute or unconditional" and "conditional" hospitality. The second, offered to the foreigner who has a name, brings hospitality within the law; the first is extended to the "absolute, unknown, anonymous other" and is outside the law, including the law of returns.[45] The urge to know the name that obsesses Juliet's English hosts or would-be hosts is a request to be excused the offer of absolute hospitality and the risks it brings with it. Derrida supposes that absolute hospitality will involve silence, a giving up on language, above all a "holding back on the temptation to ask the other who he is" (135). The *arrivant* could be anyone or anything: human, animal or god, dead or alive (77). The unknown human, because unknown, can turn into any of these other unknowns. Even in the possession of a proper name, Derrida says, the new arrival is always untranslatable—no name being open to translation into another language (137). If we tend to forget this in our daily encounters in which the name is regarded as a known thing, the guarantor of conditional hospitality, then Burney reminds us of the cunning of the name in having her heroine go by several, in sequence: L.S., Ellis, Juliet. Only the last is acceptable to the law; the others are signs of namelessness.

It is hard to imagine any society meeting the standards of an absolute hospitality (as Derrida admits), and in fact, Juliet's physical and emotional demeanor argue from the start against her representing any risk of the radically unknown. In this sense she is no Dionysus. When Oedipus comes to die outside Thebes, even he is a known figure whose alliance with divine forces can be shrewdly surmised by a prudent ruler, as it is by Theseus. Juliet models from the first an ideal of true feeling and respectful sympathy whose ultimate association with noble birth can be guessed at from the very beginning of the book, but only by its readers. The sentimental bonds of true feeling are otherwise generated and sustained only by a few exemplary figures in the book, and they are ineffective against the social consensus until the secret is out and Juliet is revealed as one of the right sort and a close relative, the strange stranger familiar after all. Along the way, the matter of Juliet's foreignness is far less of an impediment to compassionate treatment than her dubious class status, as is made clear when her benefactor the Bishop finally makes his way to England to a warm welcome from the English elite. In Burney's first novel, *Evelina*, the rough treatment of

45. Derrida, *Of Hospitality*, 25.

Madame Duval occurs not only because she is French (though, once again, also English) but because she is vulgar, a former tavern girl who has not learned any fine manners. In the case of Juliet, the manners are impeccable but they are not enough to earn her the respect of the uppers; or, to put it more exactly, they are not enough to discourage some of the uppers from exhibiting their constitutional cruelty and violence. Old English hospitality is not much to be found; the roast beef has turned cold, and few indeed are to be welcomed to the table.[46]

Many of the women in this novel are strangers—to each other and sometimes to themselves. A small community of sympathetic souls—Juliet, Gabriella, Lady Aurora, Lady Barbara, Mrs. Fairfield—does remain intact, but it is estranged from the middle-aged consensus that runs "society." So too is Elinor Joddrel's wildly unpredictable and often destructive effort to live out the new model of female liberation, which renders her open to the ridicule or censure of the more composed personalities and adds an arguably sour note to Burney's otherwise sympathetic portrayal of female aspirations: it is hard to be sure whether Elinor exemplifies the misconceptions of 1790s feminism, or their imperfect application by one who does not understand them, or both. Elinor's privileging of passion clearly goes against Wollstonecraft's argument that passion must be controlled because it is readily exploited as a tool for woman's oppression; in this respect she is her own worst enemy. Her behavior is much more clearly aligned with Rousseau's emotionally unstable St. Preux, to use the only name he is given by the characters in *Julie*, the novel whose wide circulation in English translation sustained the connection between sexual and emotional abandon and the alien cultures of continental Europe. Elinor's mimicry of St. Preux shows that the Gothic personality can indeed take up residence in the middle counties of England, but her self-deceptions are presented as the symptoms of a real disorder and not just of a lifestyle derived from novels. The domestic reality of the Gothic experience is further exemplified in what happens to Juliet when the thin veneer provided by a culture of civility breaks down or is not observed. As an unprotected female stranger she is constantly subjected to "terrour,"[47] is quite literally threatened with confinement in a castle, and suffers serious mental and physical torture both in the drawing room and on the highways where she is vulnerable to a whole gallery of sexual predators.

46. See Maria Jerenic, "Challenging Englishness: Frances Burney's *The Wanderer*," in *Rebellious Hearts: British Women Writers and the French Revolution*, ed. Adriana Craciun and Kari Lokke (Albany: State University of New York Press, 2001), 63–84, who notes that Burney's critique of the national culture was not popular in 1814 (66).

47. Burney, *The Wanderer*, e.g., 564, 565, 576.

The similarities between *Evelina* (1778) and *The Wanderer* suggest that the French Revolution, while an obligatory reference point even for a novel that seeks to diminish rather than to appeal to "national animosity" (4), has not radically altered Burney's analysis of the improbability of finding any profound cosmopolitanism or deep commitment to hospitality in the English heartland. The figure of the strange woman in both cases presents a challenge to an image of national self-esteem that was radically tested both by foreigners without and within—women of indecipherable social class. Evelina too was taken for a prostitute, survived several attempted rapes, learned what it was like to live on a limited and unpredictable income, and descended the social ladder into the merchant-artisan class. In this light, one of the most noticeable features of the plot of *The Wanderer*, supposedly set during the time of Robespierre's rule in France, is how easy it seems to be for revolutionary Frenchmen who are in power to cross the Channel in search of truant women. One could read this as a lapse in historical credibility or as testimony to the power of a transnational culture of male enforcement that survives and transcends the fluctuations of political alliances. The pursuit of Juliet across rural England and her constantly meeting with the very persons she is trying to avoid, signifies Burney's adaptation of the picaresque norms of such eighteenth-century novels as *Joseph Adams* and *Humphry Clinker* to the new realities of a surveillance society whose use of spies was justified by a declared national emergency, a synthesis also at work in, for example, Godwin's *Caleb Williams* and, I have suggested, in the shadows of Coleridge's "Frost at Midnight." Burney gives us a world where men pursue women, bringing to the homeland one of the stereotypic plots of the gothic novel but one there confined largely to continental Europe and/or to times long past. Burney's portrayal of a present-day homeland society suggests that the middle counties of England may not be such comforting places after all.

A LEGACY OF ABJECTION

In Burney's novel, the laws of conditional hospitality turn out to be of little use in controlling the violence against women that was, after all, one of the besetting conditions not only of ordinary life but of an aristocratic culture that took for granted the availability of any unprotected female for casual sexual use: no second thoughts here about how to treat strange women. The name that Juliet might have revealed would have saved her from this only by virtue of her social rank among the elite; no other name would have afforded her the effective protection of the law. In Aeschylus's *Suppliant*

Women, the stranger women announce themselves at once as Greeks and follow through on all the appropriate rituals of arrival and request; to deny them is a risk while accepting them is made easy by their lineage, by their observance of the proprieties and by the improper behavior of the Egyptian herald who does not know how to be a stranger. Violence, whether of forced marriage or suicide, is headed off: hospitality preempts violence and refreshes the local gene pool. In Genesis, chapter 19, the outcome is less comforting. Lot's commitment to the host-guest contract in refusing to give up his guests for the sexual gratification of the Sodomites is expressed only in his willingness to hand over his virgin daughters instead. It doesn't happen; it is just a ploy in god's plot to destroy the cities of the plain. But Lot seems willing enough to have women suffer in the place of male guests.[48] Guests here are placed before family, but also men before women: would Lot have sent out his sons just as readily? Women here are also being deployed to assert the priority of heteronormative over homosexual sex: Lot says no to the rape of men by proposing the rape of women, who happen to be his daughters. He is also averting the risk that the strange men might be gods, and indeed they do turn at least out to be angels, god's emissaries who have some of his powers. Nothing, his behavior implies, is worth the risk of offending a god. Lot is already a foreigner to Sodom, making him a stranger harboring strangers, but he is also a man protecting other men. Women are scapegoats, *pharmakoi*.

Then there is Abraham, a foundational figure for three world religions, who is made a stranger by his god in Genesis, chapter 12—"Get thee out of thy country, and from thy kindred" (12:1)—in another of the many Old Testament dispersal narratives, and saves his own skin by making his comely wife pretend that she is his sister in order not to arouse the competitive anger of the pharaoh. Pharaoh does indeed take Sarai into his "house" (12:15), and Abraham profits accordingly with a generous supply of livestock and slaves. Such pimping is not punished but rewarded by god sending plagues upon the pharaoh, who asks Abraham why he did not tell him that Sarai was really his wife, and sends them away with "all that he had" (12:20). Abraham gets to have his cake and eat it; his life is saved, his wife is restored, and he departs a richer man. Sarai's views are not reported. Does the story show us god's reward for Abraham's cleverness, or god's determination to preserve Abraham at all costs? Why does the pharaoh, who is punished (like Oedipus) for something he does not know he has done, seem

48. A point oddly finessed in *Paradise Lost*, where Milton tells how "the hospitable door / Exposed a matron to avoid worse rape" (1: 504–5).

to have more respect for the marriage contract than the patriarch himself? (What truly rapacious tyrant would, after all, let a mere formality stand in his way?). Is the pharaoh's "what *is* this *that* thou hast done unto me?" (12:18) an acknowledgment of the power of Abraham's god and of his special ability to call it forth? Abraham has already been promised Canaan, fulfilling the curse on the Canaanites in Genesis, chapter 9, to which the previous chapter adverted. But however ingeniously one reads, it is hard to ignore the figure of the speechless woman as a scapegoat, even if a willing one. Is the founding of a nation built upon the silent and obedient self-sacrifice of a woman? Is the woman a modern wife or a disposable good, a biblical concubine? Naomi Tadmor tells us that biblical unions were ordinarily polygamous, and that "biblical Hebrew spelled no categorical difference between "woman" and "wife" . . . indeed, the designation of *'ishah* was so broad that it could even be applied to female animals."[49]

Things are murkier still in Judges, chapter 19, where another traveler, the Levite of Ephraim, is housed by another foreigner, this time one who lives in Gibeah, and another homosexual rape of a guest is avoided by the host's offering to send out his own daughter and the guest his "concubine" (the preferred King James translation).[50] Somehow, the daughter is let off the hook (there is no clear explanation), but the concubine is gang raped and left lying at the door of the house. In the morning her master/husband finds her, whether dead or alive is not completely clear (though some versions do insist that she is dead). He later chops her body into twelve pieces which are sent to "all the coasts of Israel" (19:29). Thus begins a war of extermination against the Benjaminites. According to the King James Bible, the concubine/wife had previously "played the whore" (19:2) and left her master/husband for her father's house, from which she was being returned only with reluctance. So there is a revenge motif here. Nonetheless it is a high price that she pays. Moreover, the reference to adultery is contested and does not appear in earlier sources: the Hebrew is ambiguous and may be a metaphor intending simply a strong condemnation of her leaving her husband's house in the first place. Derrida pointedly asks, "Are we the heirs to this tradition of hospitality?"[51] What is the world in which Lot's daughters are spared their part in preserving the male guests from rape only by divine happenstance while the Levite's concubine is sacrificed to save her

49. Tadmor, *The Social Universe of the English Bible*, 53, 58.

50. Ibid., 61–64. Tadmor explains that the word here used, *pilagesh*, has a less negative force than that implied in the English translation.

51. Derrida, *Of Hospitality*, 155.

man, repeatedly raped and then dismembered? Is class once again a factor? Concubine marriage was allowed under the law (*Vulgate* calls this woman both *uxor* and *concubina*, and makes no mention at all of her whoredom). Burney might have understood that: once again, the woman has no name.

Was the concubine, legal as she was under Mosaic law, and the subject of what seems to be an extended gesture of reconciliation between her husband and her father, here sacrificed as the slave of her husband, imagined as a piece of property he could discard when his interests demanded? Is the whole dreadful story just an instance intended to show the impossible nature of a world without kings? ("And it came to pass in those days, when there was no king in Israel" [Jgs 19.1].) The Levite of Ephraim, as it happens, was the subject of a short work by Rousseau, published posthumously in 1781 but written, he tells us, over three days in June 1762, during the "cruellest moments" of his life when he was fleeing Paris and the prospect of arrest, and himself in need of help and hospitality.[52] Rousseau takes considerable liberties with all versions of the Bible story. Anarchy rules the land; the crime is laid at the door of Benjamin himself, in the manner of Greek family destiny; the relationship of the Levite and his partner is outside the law and begins in a state of paradisal happiness with which the girl gets bored and goes back to her father's household. After the Levite comes to reclaim her, it is the old man's fondness that delays their departure until late enough in the day that an overnight stop becomes necessary. Rousseau paraphrases and plays up Judges 19:12, where the Levite passes by Jebus because it is "the city of a stranger," whereas Gibeah, further along the road, is the home of one of the tribes of Israel. There is no mention of anything but love on the part of the Levite for his lady, with whom he is indeed still besotted, and nothing is said about her being a "whore." It is the sight of the host (again, a fellow man of Ephraim living among the Benjaminites) being prepared to offer his own daughter in defense of "sacred hospitality"[53] that compels him to send out his own "beloved companion" to her fate (358). In the morning he finds her dead on the doorstep, and the rest follows: as in the scriptures, there is war upon the Benjaminites and the eventual reintegration of the tribes by way of punishing another (Jabesh-gilead) to provide virgin wives for the surviving Benjaminites.

52. Jean-Jacques Rousseau, *Essay on the Origin of Languages etc.*, 351. Thomas M. Kavanagh, *Writing the Truth: Authority and Desire in Rousseau* (Berkeley: University of California Press, 1987), 103ff., gives a good argument for Rousseau's psychic investment in the story, seeing it as an imaginary avenging of Rousseau's own persecution. For another reading of Rousseau's complex motives, see Melville, *Romantic Hospitality*, 25–33.

53. Rousseau, *Essay on the Origin of Languages etc.*, 357.

But Rousseau (notorious for giving up his own children) adds another episode that makes the final political reconciliation between the tribes a function of a father's will and thereby a second abjection of the woman. The virgins do not want to marry the Benjaminites, since they are already betrothed to their own young men. A representative daughter, called Axa, is persuaded by her father to renounce her former lover in the cause of national unity. She does so, and her young man declares that he will become henceforth a priest of the lord, implicitly a celibate, unlike the Levite, whose love of woman started the whole cycle of violence. Or did it? Neither the scriptural nor the Rousseauvian stories are easy to interpret. They are both riven with paradoxes about strangers and intimates. Jebus is a city of strangers but it is the Benjaminites, supposedly coreligionists, who reveal themselves to be enemies. The stranger among the Benjaminites who alone offers hospitality is a fellow man from Ephraim, so it is a case of like assisting like: conditional hospitality, indeed. If this is the lord's work, then the lord once again believes in testing his faithful, since the Israelites are massacred on the first two days of the campaign and lose forty thousand men (i.e., in the scriptural convention, a lot). Only on the third day does the lord allow them the victory, and he says nothing about political unity or kingship. By the end of this train of events, the dead concubine seems to have been forgotten both by Rousseau and by the author(s) of the Book of Judges. Neither comments on the sacrifice as worthwhile or otherwise. Neither turns the narrative back to notice that the path to the reintegration of the Benjaminites has been tracked by way of the raped and dismembered body of a woman. Wife or slave? Wife *as* slave? The conjunction that Mary Wollstonecraft found to be constitutive of the life of women in late-eighteenth-century England and that was so emphatically registered as reality in the lives of actual slaves goes back to the foundational documents of Judeo-Christian culture.

The conclusion of the narrative generated by the Levi of Ephraim concludes Judges. What follows in the King James Bible is the Book of Ruth. This is another story of a strange woman, in this case a Moabite who converts, makes herself familiar in ways that are either devious or obedient but fully within the law, and reinvigorates the bloodline by marrying Boaz, giving birth to a son from whom will descend no less a founding father than King David himself. This is most plausibly a story about reconciliation rather than conflict, about loyalty between women as the key event in welcoming the stranger, and again about the coming kingship of Israel, here explained as the outcome of the arrival and integration of a foreigner. There seems to be no disruption caused by desire of the sort that governs Rousseau's version of the Levite narrative and perhaps underpins the scriptural one also, allowing it to be read from a masculinist point of view in which the Levite is punished for his devotion to a woman. But of course he does not suffer; she suffers in his place, which is what happens in an unequal society where the woman can be deployed for the self-interest of the man. Nothing of this radical violence occurs in the Book of Ruth, but it is possible to ruffle the smooth surface of the story, as Bonnie Honig does in her brilliant reading of the episode.[54] Honig sees Ruth as a reborn Moses figure, the foreign lawgiver who returns to Israel from Moab (where Moses dies) and who retains an element of the threat that the stranger always represents. Ruth allows Israel to "reperform the social contract of Sinai," not through the violence of the Mosaic encounter but in "the wondrous experience of awe before the law" (46). The foreign founder has become an immigrant joining up with an already formed legal-cultural entity. But Honig finds something just a little disquieting in the scene where Ruth goes to Boaz's bed. Boaz, she surmises, reacts to her as a lillith/Lillith figure (category and proper name), which, indeed, she is. Moabite women were apparently seen as seductresses (52), and lilliths were threats to male control, capable of causing nocturnal emissions and impotence. They are counterimages to woman as carer and progenitor; they cannot procreate or enter into marriage (149n52) so their role is that of the spoiler and the taker. They were also, interestingly enough, feared for their refusal to adopt the submissive posture during sex.[55] This component of the figure of Ruth is tamed in the story: she does marry and procreate. But it is retained, Honig suggests, in this moment of Boaz's awakening to the strange woman by his bedside. Prejudicial associations of Moab with human sacrifice and perverted sex are still latent, allowing Ruth to remind Israel of the enemy even as she is incorporated as a friend. Reading the story in this way, we can see a harking back to the Levite of Ephraim, who sacrifices the woman of his desire in order to spare himself becoming the object of a perverted sexuality, the preference of an enemy who is, as a Benjaminite, also within the constellation of Israel. Both stories, then, blur the boundaries between the strange and the familiar, the legal and the illicit. Both suggest a world where the unifying authority of the single state or the powerful king is sorely needed.

The exemplary romantic descendant of Lillith is of course Keats's Lamia, who is also stopped short at the marriage ceremony, who is also unable

54. Bonnie Honig, *Democracy and the Foreigner*, 41–72.

55. See eds. Kristin E. Kvam, Linda S. Schearing, Valerie H. Ziegler, *Eve and Adam: Jewish, Christian, and Muslim Readings on Genesis and Gender* (Bloomington and Indianapolis: Indiana University Press, 1999), 162–63.

to procreate, and whose intervention into civil society causes the death of her mortal lover. Lamia is not absorbed into the world of human culture, and her encounter with the law destroys her. She, like Burney's Juliet, is without a name; the lamia is a category, which Keats embodies as a proper name, as had those who conjured with Lillith. Lycius asks for the name as a part of his plan for a public marriage, but he does not get it.[56] If Honig is right that the figure of the foreign founder embodies the sense that the law is always alien, always to be explained as the production of a stranger, then Keats refigures the pattern by showing the strange woman-animal (she is also a snake) as excluded by the law whose maintenance may involve repressing desire as well as destroying its own devotees. (We will see this syndrome again in Hegel's Antigone.) In Burton's *Anatomy of Melancholy*, one of Keats's major sources for the poem, Lamia introduces herself to Lycius as a Phoenician, a foreigner, and the source of foreign pleasures. But it was Corinth itself that, according to its Greek reputation, was the foremost site of sybaritic life and sexual pleasure, and a place to which strangers were attracted for that reason, as Keats could also have read in Burton. Lycius wants more of what he has already, and the stern Apollonius, also a bit of a magician, is engaged in a struggle against his own city, with its "populous streets and temples lewd" (1:352), a place decadent enough that Lamia's virtual pleasure palace does not seem wholly out of place, while Lycius himself is motivated by a less-than-spiritual desire to display his trophy wife among a population all too well-attuned to admire conspicuous consumption. Keats's poem is famously constructed as an antinomy, with Lycius's "mad pompousness" (2:114) and Apollonius's harsh and eventually serpentine philosophy no less culpable than Lamia's desire for a life of uninterrupted secret sex. There is an equivalence of suffering (for it is not clear whether Lamia lives on or dies) among the young; only the old man survives as the figure of the law, an educator with no pupil left to educate.

The figure of philosophy does not fare well in Keats's poem; besides clipping angels' wings and decomposing rainbows, it destroys the strange woman whose evident threat is at least balanced and perhaps even overbalanced by her appeal. Life without Lamia is death, and the fate of Lycius reveals the logic of the law as an agent of punishment rather than preservation. The foreign alternative that is rejected is in fact already within. Corinth is still Corinth even without Lamia. What is preserved by Apollonius's behavior is the city's exclusive control of the relation between sex and commerce: Corinth is a hub of prostitution as well as a financial center,

56. *Keats: Complete Poems*, 638 (2: 85–92).

and each supports the other. Lamia's desire for total—and private—sex disturbs both the circulation of wealth and the community's ability to see it, control it and profit from it.[57] Immersed in such a life, no money is made by anyone, and there is no surplus income to maintain a philosopher-class. Simmel's identification of the stranger with money again comes to mind, here routed through the body of the woman. The temple prostitutes for whom the city is famous have in common with Lamia their embodiment of sex, but she does not share *in* the culture of money even if she represents its formal operations. The alternative law that Apollonius fears is a law of a pure pleasure that cannot be bought and sold. The philosopher, not for the first or last time, is in the service of a state whose values he apparently disdains but implicitly supports.

Lamia's identity as a serpent-human solidifies an implication in the tradition of abjection that we have been following, whereby woman as scapegoat really is treated as a goat, as an animal, something less than human. The sacrifice of the woman—of Yarico, of the Levite's wife/concubine, perhaps of Sarai and incipiently of Lot's daughters—enables the establishment of maintenance of a community among men, even as it precludes the onset of homosexual sex. The prospect of unconditional hospitality, which includes the possibility of the arrival of the animal as stranger, is displaced by a punitive and highly conditional hospitality, a chosen welcome premised on a chosen violence. The scapegoat woman is and is not human, is and is not animal. She is the monster, the uncontainable shape and indeterminate being, the figure that Hemans indeed invoked in naming as an "altogether foreign monster" none other than the poetess.[58] Monstrosity, from Mary Shelley and Marx to Helène Cixous and Donna Haraway, has been a familiar figure of crisis in the Western and often male imagination. The monster is another familiar stranger, or strange familiar. And the monster-woman's fate is not so far from that of other abjected women: Luxima, the women of Paraguay, Joanna, Corinne, the Levite's wife/mistress. One could of course load the argument in the other direction, highlighting the eventually positive fates of Juliet, Glorvina, and the biblical Ruth, and looking to the happy

57. See Marjorie Levinson, *Keats's Life of Allegory: The Origins of a Style* (Oxford: Blackwell, 1990), 251–99. Levinson argues that Lamia is in fact the embodiment of the money form, as of metamorphosis and illusion: she is "the fabulous face of the exchange system" (288). I would add that as the emblem of the money *form*, she cannot herself be cashed in.

58. Cited in Vincent, *The Romantic Poetess*, 74. Denise Gigante, *Life: Organic Form and Romanticism* (New Haven, CT: Yale University Press, 2009), 208–46, sees monstrosity in Lamia as defined by her possession of a self-propagating power, which might also place her outside the money system.

romantic outcomes of many other novels. The fact is that both happy and unhappy resolutions are to be found, that they belong together as different emanations of the stranger syndrome, and that when there is a happy ending it is often because the stranger turns out to be comfortably familiar after all: a cousin, a distant relative, or someone from one's own class. Here what is remarkable is how narrowly the world must often be walled in if sociability and romance are to flourish: this is a world where Mr. Darcy's marrying Elizabeth Bennet causes a social tremor.

And so to Antigone, or rather, to what Hegel made of her. Women, strange or otherwise, are few and far between in the plot of the encyclopedic project, so that what does appear has attracted a lot of attention. What appears is the story of Antigone, or part of it. Hegel does not focus on the Antigone who preoccupies Derrida: she who leads by the hand her blind father who is also her half-brother, who is denied the right to mourn in the place of his burial, who becomes the voice lamenting the unmarked gravesite and the impossibility of proper mourning.[59] Hegel chooses the event leading to her death: the burial of Polynices, her brother and the enemy of her other brother, both of them cursed (as she is) directly or indirectly by belonging to the house of Labdacus, as also is Thebes itself, condemned to further self-estranging in the very moment that it thinks it has freed itself from the alien threat embodied in the Sphinx. Hegel concentrates on the quality of the brother-sister relation as free of desire and debt; neither seeks the other as a sexual partner, neither looks to the other as the author of his or her being, as they would to a parent. Here the blood they share has "reached a state of rest and equilibrium."[60] Each sees the self in the other without the mediation of desire. Hegel is emphatic about this: that we have the blood (*Blut*) of consanguinity without the stirrings of the blood that come from physical or psychological excitation. The recognition is "pure and unmixed" (*rein und unvermischt*) with desire (275). But it is hard to imagine anything in the house of Labdacus as pure and unmixed, peaceful and at rest.[61] Perhaps the superior duty to the brother that Hegel discovers in Antigone is to be read as the effort at the emergence of precisely a relationship free of desire, as of in-

59. Derrida, *Of Hospitality*, 85–87, 111–13. On Hegel and Antigone, see, among others, Judith Butler, *Antigone's Claim: Kinship Between Life and Death* (New York: Columbia University Press, 2000).

60. *Hegel's Phenomenology of Spirit*, trans. A. V. Miller (Oxford: Clarendon P, 1979), 274.

61. Luce Irigaray calls this effort at sidelining the struggle between the sexes the "Hegelian dream" which itself emanates from the patriarchal commitment to reason: see *Speculum de l'autre femme* (Paris: Minuit, 1974), 269. See also Clark, "Kant's Aliens," 266–72, on Kant's anxieties about women both as strangers and as too curious about strange kinds of knowledge.

cest, fate and secrecy. It is the exit point from the life of the family, a life of conflict and dependence, toward a "consciousness of universality" (258), an exit from the natural, chthonic world governed by and embodied in woman to the upper world of light and reason which is the province of men.

But the path to reason is incomplete, unrestful, and impure. It is partly so because, in the strange synthesis of ontogyny and phylogeny that characterizes the *Phenomenology*, everything that seems to be left behind with the progress of historical time toward absolute spirit is prone to recur in the life of every individual living at any point in the grand teleological scheme: each of us is liable at some point in our lives to replay, in other words, the drama of the house of Labdacus. Put simply, at whatever point in time we are living, whether close to the origin or the end of the progress of *Geist* through history, we are still going to be embodied as men and women living in families, and we are going to experience variously intense versions of the family dynamic. But there is another reason for the immanence of unrest. It has to do with the nonsubsumable nature of woman: woman's strangeness. As the agents of birth and the monitors of death and mourning, women, like Dionysus, remind the state and its rational citizens of the presence of the dark underworld in the world we have. Antigone performs a funeral that the state has forbidden because she recognizes the superior rights of the chthonic powers that govern the family, but she also fulfils upon herself the terms of an inherited curse and educates the imperfect state (whose incarnation in Creon is clearly inadequate) into a too-late awareness of its own need for equity in matters of burial. These reminders will not cease to occur as long as the state or the community (at this early stage it is what Hegel calls *das Gemeinwesen*) continues to establish itself precisely upon conflict with the family, by selecting out family members (mostly men) for citizenship and rational judgment.

Hegel knows this, and suggests that the communal life will always operate like this.[62] That is why he describes woman as the "everlasting (*ewige*) irony" of/in the community.[63] Not just irony, which in its historical appearance as romanticism did not much appeal to Hegel, but *everlasting* irony.

62. See Kelly Oliver, "Antigone's Ghost: Undoing Hegel's *Phenomenology of Spirit*," *Hypatia* 11, no. 1 (1996): 67–90. Oliver finds that the discussion of the family and of woman's place in it "undermines" Hegel's project, noting that after this moment woman is "never resuscitated or preserved" (70). Woman as the unconscious has no opposite (the unconscious being a formless manifold) and cannot progress through the dialectic (72). This is half of the situation; the other half is that woman is always there. See also the special issue of *The Owl of Minerva: Journal of the Hegel Society of America* 33, no. 2 (2002), which is devoted to Antigone.

63. *Hegel's Phenomenology of Spirit*, 288.

The tension is immanent. It appears also in another of the tactics whereby the community seeks to lift the family out of the sphere of its natural immediacy and into participation in the life of *Allgemeinheit*, generality tending to universality: the recourse to war. War may be the work of *Geist* in its effort to lift humanity out of its purely local, physical attachments and impel it toward the ethical (*sittliche*) order (273), but *Geist* requires government (*Regierung*) as its executive power here, and government is exercised by and through other human beings. In this way the state/community sets itself against the historical and temperamental inertia of woman, both as the mother who does not want to lose her sons in battle and as the lover or wife who is faced with the death of her sexual partner. Hegel writes tellingly of "the brave youth in whom woman finds her pleasure" as having his "worth" acknowledged in battle (289). But this depends on nothing more than physical strength and "luck," not on some transcendent quality of mind or spirit. There is nothing visibly irrevocable or inevitable in who lives and who dies, and so there is no way that the surviving women can be fully persuaded that the sacrifice of their men has been absolutely necessary.

Perhaps we are not so far as we first seemed to be from the dark matter apparent in the story of the Levite of Ephraim and, in domesticated form, in the story of Ruth. The world beyond the family, be it tribe, commune or nation-state, is, according to this reading of Hegel, *inevitably* in the business of attacking women—as voices from the underworld, as defenders of the family, and as agents of the sexual body, both in itself and in its role as seducer-tempter of the merely natural man. (The Levite was this, even if he was a priest). Creon is explicit that his priority is not only to deploy a certain concept of justice but to avoid being ruled by women (*Antigone* l. 649, 678–79). And there is at least one chthonic power that the community will not allow woman to possess or repossess: the power of death, of putting to death. The declaration of war represents the state's assumption of the power of life and death—which individuals die may be a matter of chance, but death there will be, and lots of it. So too does the right of execution (and the reciprocal forbidding of suicide). The state demands control of who dies and how they die, and in so demanding it creates woman as its enduring enemy, the enemy within (*innern Feind*).[64] It is the man, destined to be

64. *Hegel's Phenomenology of Spirit*, 288. Thus, Jacques Derrida, *Glas*, trans. John P. Leavey and Richard Rand (Lincoln: University of Nebraska Press, 1990): "So, in its head, the government must become the enemy of just what it governs" (146); and again, "murder no longer proceeds from a voluntary decision; it is inscribed in the fatality of the operation's structure" (171). Derrida's reading of Hegel's Antigone is, as ever, indispensable.

absorbed into the state, who enacts the "danger and trial of death" (278) in the upper world, while the woman speaks for the passage of *all* life toward death. Death is everywhere, not to be avoided; the struggle is over who will dispense it. The coming together of the deaths demanded by the curse (the chthonic powers) and those demanded by the state undercuts the entire claim to difference (and reason) the state makes in its own defense. Its most imperative performative moments thus come to look predetermined and derivative. The origin is elsewhere, and its earthly voice is female.

No wonder, then, that Hegel looks to Antigone and to the brother-sister relation as his best attempt to produce the family-state dialectic as something amenable to progress rather than repetition. The woman who can enter into this progressive repression of woman has already repressed (or rather not encountered) her desire. But the house of Labdacus is full of incest, or misdirected desire. The brother is the son of the brother who is the father. Antigone's tragic dignity may lie for Hegel in her effort to sustain the utopian moment of the passage beyond or around desire, but she is caught in a system whereby the very embodiment of desire-free public reason, the city state of Thebes, is both itself enmeshed in the curse and imperfect in its distribution of justice.[65] Antigone is rendered sexless by circumstance: she has spent her life leading around her disabled, toxic father and she will go to her death for burying the brother who must not be the object of her desire. Meanwhile, the lover waiting in the wings will kill himself on witnessing her suicide. If we decide in favor of the reactionary Hegel, we will see here a condescending judgment on woman as a historical anachronism, best studied far from the modern world among the ancient Greeks. Reading differently and I think more dutifully, we can perceive a point in the system where ontogeny overpowers phylogeny and progress itself seems something of a wishful fiction. Woman has reduced Hegelian*ism* to an aporetic impasse, and Hegel has written it that way.[66] The topic and tone are quite different, but here he is the proper contemporary of the poet who wrote "Lamia," and of the many and various writers who took up the subject and often the cause of strange women.

65. She does, after all, make a claim herself for the exceptionality of the relation to the brother as beyond substitution, irreplaceable, and therefore due *more* than what would be due to a dead child or husband (*Antigone* 902–12). According to a Hegelian reading, this would be the cunning of reason at work, making a statement that comes otherwise as very odd in one who has already (in a play yet to be written by Sophocles) found such grief in being denied a sight of the father-brother's grave.

66. For Heidegger's use of Antigone as embodying the uncanniness of Being and of an at-homeness that is inevitably lost and dispersed, wayless, see Gasché, *Europe, or the Infinite Task*, 181–207.

The task of philosophy may be to produce rational order out of disorderly life; the task of reading philosophy requires not just attending to that order but also to the bits and pieces it scatters along its way to reason, and the roads it chooses not to take. Hegel provides much evidence of the resistance to reason in the body and in the social world and suggests that *Geist*'s (spirit's) passage is attended with a pile of dead and damaged bodies. Here too he keeps company with the poets, the Southey of "Hohenlinden," the Byron who took Childe Harold to the field of Waterloo, and above all, perhaps, the "altogether foreign monster" Felicia Hemans, whose "The Graves of a Household" chronicles the destruction of the family in the service of the state, with the result that its children are buried—or left unburied—all over the earth.[67] The trope of young men proving their worth by dying in battle, embedded by Hegel in the plot whereby the state seeks to control women and sexuality, is produced by another of Hermans's poems, "England's Dead," as now operating across the entire world:

> The warlike of the isles,
> The men of field and wave!
> Are not the rocks their funeral piles,
> The seas and shores their grave?
>
> Go, stranger! Track the deep,
> Free, free the white sail spread!
> Wave may not foam, nor wild wind sweep,
> Where rest not England's dead.
>
> (266–67)

According to its modern editor, this poem was "widely approved and admired" (267). What were they admiring? The global reach of the British Empire? The pantheistic integration of English body parts (and of many Scots, Welsh, and Irish) into microscopic dust? Why is it a *stranger* who is bidden to set sail and track the deep, and how can he seek what cannot be located, since the graves are commonly unmarked or nonexistent? Rocks, seas, and shores are not gravestones. English Antigones cannot bury their brothers: there are too many of them and they are too far away. The world has been made empty of human life, except for the voyaging stranger whose quest is fulfilled everywhere and nowhere, wherever there are rocks and shores

67. *Felicia Hemans*, 422. The pertinence of Hegel's Antigone to Hemans's work is discussed by Lootens, "Hemans and Home," 242–43.

and seas. Fewer and fewer living strangers can be anticipated in the thin blue flames that flicker on the grate. England's wanderings across the world have made a desert that seems like peace, but it is a troubling peace. There are no strangers left to worry about, because there is no life at all. Known unknowns and unknown unknowns are finally all the same in the eyes of the last man, who is more than ever a stranger.

Or is it woman who reads the poem? The ten years after 9/11 have been dominated by masculine power doing the state's business at the often fatal expense of strange men, women, and children. Even if one accepts the impossibility of an absolute, unconditional hospitality, it seems clear that the pendulum has swung very far in the other direction, with juridical and informal restrictions widely and radically applied in the name of homeland security. The risk involved in hospitality is imaged as both undesirable and avoidable, and extraordinary methods have been deployed to seal off our protected space. Romanticism as I have described it is not a pure fountain of right thinking on the treatment of strangers, because there is no completed right thinking, no point of rest or achievement, no way to foreclose or prefigure the nature and challenge of the stranger who is always yet to come. The promise of the unthreatened life cannot be kept and should not be made. The stranger to come is anyway already here. Romanticism articulates and analyzes an inexhaustible dialectic of desire and abjection that we have still not come to understand. It does not project security, but a recognition (hardly an obligation, since there is no choice) of the immanent insecurity that is and must be at the heart of discovery and development, and of the individual and social imagination at its best. In its attentions to all kinds of strangers, it often shows the limits of hospitality, sometimes in the form of outright violence and rejection, sometimes through selective domestication by way of class or creed. It also shows, in its appetite for the disseminating energies of small print and the uncontainable presence of translation, ways beyond accepting a life within the given boundaries policed by others on our behalf. In chapter 2 we left Coleridge by his midnight fire pondering the nature and possibility of risk, of a stranger actually arriving. In some ways my whole effort here has been an extended meditation on the prospect he floated for his infant son: the prospect of living by other laws, "far other laws" than those we have.

BIBLIOGRAPHY

Aarsleff, Hans. *The Study of Language in England, 1780–1860.* Minneapolis: University of Minnesota Press, 1983.

Adams, M. Ray. "Robert Merry, Political Romanticist." *Studies in Romanticism* 2 (1962): 23–37.

Alexander, J. H., and David Hewitt, eds. *Scott in Carnival.* Aberdeen: Association for Scottish Literary Studies, 1993.

Alter, Robert. *The Five Books of Moses: A Translation with Commentary.* New York: Norton, 2008.

Anidjar, Gil. *The Jew, the Arab: A History of the Enemy.* Stanford, CA: Stanford University Press, 2003.

Aravamudan, Srinivas. *Tropicopolitans: Colonialism and Agency, 1688–1804.* Durham, NC: Duke University Press, 1999.

Aristotle. *The "Art" of Rhetoric.* Translated by J. H. Freese. Cambridge, MA: Harvard University Press; London: W. Heinemann, 1982.

———. *The Poetics.* Translated by W. Hamilton Fyfe. Cambridge, MA: Harvard University Press; London: W. Heinemann, 1973.

Assmann, Jan. *Moses the Egyptian: The Memory of Egypt in Western Monotheism.* Cambridge, MA: Harvard University Press, 1997.

———. *The Price of Monotheism.* Translated by Robert Savage. Stanford, CA: Stanford University Press, 2010.

Augustine. *On Christian Doctrine.* Translated by D. W. Robertson. Indianapolis: Bobbs-Merrill, 1958.

Austen, Jane. *Northanger Abbey.* Edited by Susan Fraiman. New York: Norton, 2004.

———. *Northanger Abbey.* Edited by Marilyn Gaull. New York: Pearson-Longman, 2005.

———. *Sense and Sensibility.* Edited by Ros Ballaster. London: Penguin, 2003.

Bachelard, Gaston. *The Psychoanalysis of Fire.* Translated by Alan C. M. Ross. Boston: Beacon, 1998.

Baillie, Joanna. *A Series of Plays: in which it is attempted to delineate the Stronger Passions of the Mind.* 5th ed. 2 vols. London: Longman, Hurst, Rees and Orme, 1806.

Balibar, Renée, and Dominique Laporte. *Le français national: politique et practique de la langue nationale sous la Révolution*. Paris: Hachette, 1974.

Barrell, John. *Imagining the King's Death: Figurative Treason, Fantasies of Regicide, 1793–1796*. Oxford: Oxford University Press, 2000.

———. *The Infection of Thomas De Quincey: The Psychopathology of Imperialism*. New Haven, CT: Yale University Press, 1991.

Basker, James G. *Amazing Grace: An Anthology of Poems about Slavery, 1660–1810*. New Haven, CT: Yale University Press, 2002.

Baslez, Marie-France. *L'étranger dans la Grèce antique*. Paris: Société d'Édition les Belles Lettres, 1984.

Baucom, Ian. *Specters of the Atlantic: Finance Capital, Slavery, and the Philosophy of History*. Durham, NC: Duke University Press, 2005.

Bayle, Pierre. *An Historical and Critical Dictionary by Monsieur Bayle*. 4 vols. London, 1710.

Beck, James Sigismund. *The Principles of Critical Philosophy, Selected from the Works of Emmanuel Kant, Expounded by James Sigismund Beck . . . Translated by an Auditor*. London, 1797.

Beckford, William. An *Arabian Tale, from an Unpublished Manuscript, with Notes Critical and Explanatory*. London: J. Johnson, 1786.

———. *Vathek, with the Episodes of Vathek*. Edited by Kenneth W. Graham. Peterborough, ON: Broadview, 2001.

Benedict, Barbara M. *Curiosity: A History of Early Modern Inquiry*. Chicago: University of Chicago Press, 2001.

Benhabib, Seyla. *Another Cosmopolitanism*. Oxford: Oxford University Press, 2006.

Benstock, Shari. "At the Margin of Discourse: Footnotes in the Fictional Text." *Publications of the Modern Language Association* 98 (1983): 204–25.

Benveniste, Émile. *Le vocabulaire des institutions indo-européennes*. 2 vols. Paris: Minuit, 1969.

Berman, Antoine. *The Experience of the Foreign: Culture and Translation in Romantic Germany*. Translated by S. Heyvaert. Albany: State University of New York Press, 1992.

Bewell, Alan. *Romanticism and Colonial Disease*. Baltimore, MD: Johns Hopkins University Press, 1999.

———. "Erasmus Darwin's Cosmopolitan Nature." *English Literary History* 76 (2009): 19–48.

Bhabha, Homi K. *The Location of Culture*. London: Routledge, 1994.

Blake, William. *The Complete Poetry and Prose of William Blake*. Edited by David V. Erdman. Berkeley: University of California Press, 1982.

Bolton, Carol. *Writing the Empire: Robert Southey and Romantic Colonialism*. London: Pickering and Chatto, 2007.

Bowersock, G. W. "The Art of the Footnote." *American Scholar* 53 (1983–84): 54–62.

Brown, Marshall. "Passion and Love: Anacreontic Song and the Roots of Romantic Lyric." *English Literary History* 66 (1999): 373–404.

———. *The Gothic Text*. Stanford, CA: Stanford University Press, 2005.

Brown, Wendy. *Walled States, Waning Sovereignty*. Brooklyn, NY: Zone Books, 2010.

Buck-Morss, Susan. *Hegel, Haiti, and Universal History.* Pittsburgh, PA: University of Pittsburgh Press, 2009.

Burke, Edmund. *Reflections on the Revolution in France.* Edited by L. G. Mitchell. Oxford: Oxford University Press, 1999.

———*The Works of the Rt. Hon. Edmund Burke.* 12 vols. Boston: Little, Brown & Co., 1886.

Burney, Frances. *The Wanderer; or Female Difficulties.* Edited by Margaret Anne Doody, Robert L. Mack, and Peter Sabor. Oxford: Oxford University Press, 2001.

Butler, Judith. *Antigone's Claim: Kinship between Life and Death.* New York: Columbia University Press, 2000.

———. *Frames of War: When is Life Grievable?* London: Verso, 2010.

Butler, Marilyn. "Orientalism." In *The Romantic Period,* edited by David Pirie, 395–447. London: Penguin, 1994.

———. *Romantics, Rebels and Reactionaries: English Literature and its Background, 1760–1830.* Oxford: Oxford University Press, 1982.

Campbell, Thomas. *The Complete Poetical Works of Thomas Campbell.* Edited by J. Logie Robertson. New York: Haskell House, 1968.

Carretta, Vincent. *Equiano, the African: Biography of a Self-Made Man.* New York: Penguin, 2006.

Cassin, Barbara, ed. *Vocabulaire européen des philosophies: dictionnaire des intraduisables.* Paris: Seuil, 2004.

Castle, Terry. *The Female Thermometer: Eighteenth-Century Culture and the Invention of the Uncanny.* Oxford: Oxford University Press, 1995.

Castro, Americo. "The Presence of the Sultan Saladin in the Romance Literatures." In *An Idea of History: Selected Essays of Americo Castro,* translated by Stephen Gilman and Edmund L. King, 241–69. Columbus: Ohio University Press, 1954.

[Chatterton, Thomas]. *Poems, Supposed to have been written at Bristol, by Thomas Rowley and others, in the Fifteenth Century.* London: T. Payne, 1777.

Christensen, Jerome. *Coleridge's Blessed Machine of Language.* Ithaca, NY: Cornell University Press, 1981.

Chung, Tan. "The Britain-China-India Trade Triangle, 1770–1840." *Indian Economic and Social History Review* 11.4 (1974): 411–31.

Cicero, Marcus Tullius. *De Oratore,* bks. 1 and 2. Translated by E. W. Sutton, H. Rackham. Cambridge, MA: Harvard University Press, 2001.

———. *De Oratore,* bk. 3. Translated by H. Rackham. Cambridge, MA: Harvard University Press; London: W. Heinemann, 1977.

Clark, David L. "Bereft: Derrida's Memory and the Spirit of Friendship." *South Atlantic Quarterly* 106.2 (2007): 291–324.

———. "Kant's Aliens: The *Anthropology* and Its Others." *New Centennial Review* 1.2 (2001): 201–89.

———. "Lost and Found in Translation: The Legacies of Jacques Derrida." *Studies in Romanticism* 46 (2007): 161–82.

———. "'Waving not Drowning': On the Lives of Theory." *Studies in Romanticism* 44 (2005): 261–70.

Clarkson, Thomas. *Thomas Clarkson and Ottobah Cuguano: Essays on the Slavery and*

Commerce of the Human Species. Edited by Mary-Antoinette Smith. Peterborough, ON: Broadview, 2010.

Clery, E. J. *The Rise of Supernatural Fiction, 1762–1800*. Cambridge: Cambridge University Press, 1995.

Cohen, Murray. *Sensible Words: Linguistic Practice in England, 1640–1785*. Baltimore, MD: Johns Hopkins University Press, 1977.

Coleridge, Samuel Taylor. *Biographia Literaria*. Edited by James Engell and W. J. Bate. 2 vols. Princeton, NJ: Princeton University Press, 1983.

———. *The Collected Letters of Samuel Taylor Coleridge*. Edited by Earl Leslie Griggs. 6 vols. Oxford: Clarendon, 1956–71.

———. *The Friend*. Edited by Barbara E. Rooke. 2 vols. Princeton, NJ: Princeton University Press, 1969.

———. *Poems by S. T. Coleridge; Second Edition, to which are now added Poems by Charles Lamb and Charles Lloyd*. Bristol, UK: J. Cottle and Messrs. Robinsons, 1797.

———. *Poetical Works, Part 1*. Edited by J. C. C. Mays. 2 vols. Princeton, NJ: Princeton University Press, 2001.

Cook & Omai: The Cult of the South Seas. Canberra: Australian National University, 2001. Exhibition catalog.

Cotton, Sir Evan. *East Indiamen: The East India Company's Maritime Service*. London: Batchworth, 1949.

Cowper, William. *The Poems of William Cowper*. Edited by John D. Baird and Charles Ryskamp. 3 vols. Oxford: Clarendon, 1995.

Craciun, Adriana. *Fatal Women of Romanticism*. Cambridge: Cambridge University Press, 2003.

Craig, David M. *Robert Southey and Romantic Apostasy: Political Argument in Britain, 1780–1840*. Woodbridge, UK: Royal Historical Society and Boydell Press, 2007.

Crawford, Robert. *Devolving English Literature*. Oxford: Clarendon, 1992.

Cuguano, Quobna Ottobah. *Thoughts and Sentiments on the Evil of Slavery*. Edited by Vincent Carretta. London: Penguin, 1999.

Curran, Stuart. *Poetic Form and British Romanticism*. Oxford: Oxford University Press, 1986.

Darwin, Erasmus. *The Botanic Garden*. 2nd ed. London: J. Johnson, 1791.

Davis, David Brion, ed. *The Fear of Conspiracy: Images of Un-American Subversion from the Revolution to the Present*. Ithaca, NY: Cornell University Press, 1979.

———. *The Problem of Slavery in the Age of Revolution, 1770–1823*. Oxford: Oxford University Press, 1999.

Davis, Leith. *Acts of Union: Scotland and the Literary Negotiation of the British Nation, 1707–1830*. Stanford, CA: Stanford University Press, 1999.

Davis, Leith, Ian Duncan, and Janet Sorensen, eds. *Scotland and the Borders of Romanticism*. Cambridge: Cambridge University Press, 2004.

Defoe, Daniel. *Robinson Crusoe*. Edited by Michael Shinagel. New York: Norton, 1975.

Deleuze, Gilles, and Félix Guattari. *Kafka: Toward a Minor Literature*. Translated by Dana Polan. Minneapolis: University of Minnesota Press, 1986.

De Man, Paul. *Allegories of Reading: Figural Language in Rousseau, Nietzsche, Rilke and Proust*. New Haven, CT: Yale University Press, 1979.

Dening, Greg. *Mr. Bligh's Bad Language: Passion, Power and Theatre on the Bounty.* Cambridge: Cambridge University Press, 1992.

De Quincey, Thomas. *Confessions of an English Opium Eater.* Edited by Alethea Hayter. Harmondsworth, UK: Penguin, 1975.

———. *The Collected Writings of Thomas De Quincey.* Edited by David Masson. 14 vols. Edinburgh: Adam and Charles Black, 1889–90.

Derrida, Jacques. *Acts of Religion.* Edited by Gil Anidjar. New York: Routledge, 2002.

———. *Adieu to Emmanuel Levinas.* Translated by Pascale-Anne Brault and Michael Naas. Stanford, CA: Stanford University Press, 1999.

———. *Archive Fever: A Freudian Impression.* Translated by Eric Prenowitz. Chicago: University of Chicago Press, 1996.

———. *Dissemination.* Translated by Barbara Johnson. Chicago: University of Chicago Press, 1981.

———. *The Ear of the Other: Otobiography, Transference, Translation.* Edited by Christie McDonald. Translated by Peggy Kamuf. Lincoln: University of Nebraska Press, 1988.

———. *Eyes of the University: Right to Philosophy 2.* Translated by Jan Plug et al. Stanford, CA: Stanford University Press, 2004.

———. *Glas.* Translated by John P. Leavey and Richard Rand. Lincoln: University of Nebraska Press, 1990.

———. *Margins of Philosophy.* Translated by Alan Bass. Chicago: University of Chicago Press, 1982.

———. *Negotiations: Interventions and Interviews, 1971–2001.*Edited and translated by Elizabeth Rottenberg. Stanford, CA: Stanford University Press, 2002.

———. *Of Grammatology.* Translated by Gayatri Chakravorty Spivak. Corr. ed. Baltimore, MD: Johns Hopkins University Press, 1997.

———. *Of Hospitality: Anne Dufourmontelle Invites Jacques Derrida to Respond.* Translated by Rachel Bowlby. Stanford, CA: Stanford University Press, 2000.

———. *Politics of Friendship.* Translated by George Collins. London: Verso, 1997.

———. *Specters of Marx: The State of the Debt, the Work of Mourning, and the New International.* Translated by Peggy Kamuf. New York: Routledge, 1994.

———. "What is a 'Relevant' Translation?" Translated by Lawrence Venuti. *Critical Inquiry* 27 (2001): 174–200.

Drew, John. *India and the Romantic Imagination.* Delhi: Oxford University Press, 1987.

Dryden, John. *The Works of Virgil in English.* Edited by Alan Roper and Vinton A. Dearing. Berkeley: University of California Press, 1987.

Dummett, Michael. *On Immigration and Refugees.* London: Routledge, 2001.

Duncan, Ian. "Primitive Inventions: *Rob Roy,* Nation, and World System." *Eighteenth-Century Fiction* 15, no. 1 (2002): 81–102.

———. "Scott's Romance of the Empire: The *Tales of the Crusaders.*" In *Scott in Carnival,* edited by J. H. Alexander and David Hewitt, 370–79. Aberdeen: Association for Scottish Literary Studies, 1993.

Earle, William. *Obi; or the History of Three-Fingered Jack.* Edited by Srinivas Aravamudan. Peterborough, ON: Broadview, 2005.

Edgeworth, Maria. *Tales and Novels by Maria Edgeworth.* 18 vols. London: Baldwin and Cradock, 1833.

Elfenbein, Andrew. *Romanticism and the Rise of English.* Stanford, CA: Stanford University Press, 2009.

Eliot, T. S. *The Complete Poems and Plays of T.S. Eliot.* London: Faber and Faber, 1969.

Ellis, Markman, ed. *Tea and the Tea-Table in Eighteenth-Century England.* 4 vols. London: Pickering and Chatto, 2010.

Ellison, Julie. "News, Blues, and Cowper's Busy World." *Modern Language Quarterly* 62.3 (2001): 219–37.

Endelman, Todd M. *The Jews of Georgian England, 1714–1830: Tradition and Change in a Liberal Society.* Philadelphia: Jewish Publication Society of America, 1979.

Equiano, Olaudah. *"The Interesting Narrative" and Other Writings.* Edited by Vincent Carretta. London: Penguin, 1995.

Euripides. *The Bacchae.* Translated by Arthur S. Way. Cambridge, MA: Harvard University Press; London: W. Heinemann, 1962.

Everest, Kelvin. "Shelley's *Adonais* and John Keats." *Essays in Criticism* 57.3 (2007): 237–64.

Favret, Mary. *War at a Distance: Romanticism and the Making of Modern Wartime.* Princeton, NJ: Princeton University Press, 2010.

Ferguson, Margaret W. "Augustine's Region of Unlikeness: The Crossing of Exile and Language." In *Innovations of Antiquity,* edited by Ralph Hexter and Daniel Selden, 69–94. London: Routledge, 1992.

Fiedler, Leslie. *The Stranger in Shakespeare.* New York: Stein and Day, 1972.

Forster, John Reinhold. *Observations Made During a Voyage Round the World.* Edited by Nicholas Thomas, Harriet Guest, and Michael Dettelbach. Honolulu: University of Hawaii Press, 1996.

Fraistat, Neil. "The Material Shelley: Who Gets the Finger in *Queen Mab*?." *Wordsworth Circle* 33 (2002): 33–36.

Francis, Philip. *A Poetical Translation of the Works of Horace.* 2nd ed. 4 vols. London: A Millar, 1747.

Freud, Sigmund. *Mass Psychology and Other Writings.* Translated by J. A. Underwood. Introduction by Jacqueline Rose. London: Penguin, 2004.

Friedländer, Paul. *Plato: The Dialogues.* Translated by Hans Meyerhoff. 3 vols. Princeton, NJ: Princeton University Press, 1969.

Frye, Northrop. *Anatomy of Criticism: Four Essays.* New York: Atheneum, 1967.

Fulford, Tim. Introduction to *Robert Southey: Poetical Works,* edited by Lynda Pratt, 3: vii–xxxvi. London: Pickering and Chatto, 2004.

———. *Romantic Indians: Native Americans, British Literature, and Transatlantic Culture, 1756–1830.* Oxford: Oxford University Press, 2006.

Garside, Peter, James Raven, and Rainer Schöwerling, eds. *The English Novel, 1770–1829: A Bibliographical Survey of Prose Fiction Published in the British Isles.* 2 vols. Oxford: Oxford University Press, 2000.

Gasché, Rodolphe. *Europe, or the Infinite Task: A Study of a Philosophical Concept.* Stanford, CA: Stanford University Press, 2009.

Gates, Henry Louis Jr. *The Signifying Monkey: A Theory of African-American Literary Criticism.* New York: Oxford University Press, 1989.

Genette, Gérard. *Paratexts: Thresholds of Interpretation.* Translated by Jane E. Lewin. Cambridge: Cambridge University Press, 1997.

Gibbons, Luke. *Edmund Burke and Ireland: Aesthetics, Politics and the Colonial Sublime.* Cambridge: Cambridge University Press, 2003.

Gigante, Denise. *Life: Organic Form and Romanticism.* New Haven, CT: Yale University Press, 2009.

Gillespie, Stuart, and David Hopkins, eds. *The Oxford History of Literary Translation in English.* Vol. 3, *1660–1790.* Oxford: Oxford University Press, 2005.

Goldenberg, David M. *The Curse of Ham: Race and Slavery in Early Judaism, Christianity and Islam.* Princeton, NJ: Princeton University Press, 2005.

Goodman, Kevis. *Georgic Modernity and British Romanticism: Poetry and the Mediation of History.* Cambridge: Cambridge University Press, 2004.

———. "'Uncertain Disease': Nostalgia, Pathologies of Motion, Practices of Reading." *Studies in Romanticism* 49 (2010): 197–227.

Goodwin, Albert. *The Friends of Liberty: The English Democratic Movement in the Age of the French Revolution.* London: Hutchinson, 1979.

Gossman, Lionel. "History as Decipherment: Romantic Historiography and the Discovery of the Other." *New Literary History* 18 (1986): 23–57.

Grafton, Anthony. *The Footnote: A Curious History.* Cambridge, MA: Harvard University Press, 1997.

Greenberg, Michael. *British Trade and the Opening of China, 1800–42.* 1951. Reprint, Cambridge: Cambridge University Press, 1969.

Greenslade, S. L., ed. *The Cambridge History of the Bible: The West from the Reformation to the Present Day.* Cambridge: Cambridge University Press, 1987.

Gronniosaw, James. *A Narrative of the most remarkable Particulars in the Life of James Albert Gronniosaw, an African Prince, as Related by Himself.* 2nd ed. Glasgow, 1785.

Grose, Francis. *A Provincial Glossary, with a Collection of Local Proverbs and Popular Superstitions.* London, 1787.

Guest, Harriet. *Empire, Barbarism, and Civilization: Captain Cook, William Hodges, and the Return to the Pacific.* Cambridge: Cambridge University Press, 2007.

———. *Small Change: Women, Learning, Patriotism, 1750–1810.* Chicago: University of Chicago Press, 2000.

Habermas, Jürgen. *The Divided West.* Edited and translated by Ciaran Cronin. Cambridge, MA: Polity, 2007.

Hall, Edith. *Inventing the Barbarian: Greek Self-Definition through Tragedy.* Oxford: Clarendon, 1989.

Hall, Roland. "Kant's *Critique of Pure Reason*: New Words and Antedatings for the Translations." *Notes and Queries* 32.3 (1985): 347–55.

Hargreaves-Maudsley, W. N. *The English Della Cruscans and Their Time, 1783–1828.* The Hague: M. Nijhoff, 1967.

Hazlitt, William. *The Complete Works of William Hazlitt.* Edited by P. P. Howe. 21 vols. New York: AMS Press, 1967.

Hegel, G. W. F. von. *Hegel's Phenomenology of Spirit.* Translated by A. V. Miller. Oxford: Clarendon, 1979.

Heidegger, Martin. *Off the Beaten Track.* Translated by Julian Young and Kenneth Haynes. Cambridge: Cambridge University Press, 2002.

Hemans, Felicia. *Felicia Hemans: Selected Poems, Letters, Reception Materials.* Edited by Susan J. Wolfson. Princeton, NJ: Princeton University Press, 2000.

———. *Records of Woman with other Poems.* Edited by Paula R. Feldman. Lexington: University Press of Kentucky, 1999.

Herder, Johan Gottfried von. *Reflections on the Philosophy of the History of Mankind.* Translated by T. O. Churchill (1800). Edited by Frank E. Manuel. Chicago: University of Chicago Press, 1968.

Hochschild, Adam. *Bury the Chains: Prophets and Rebels in the Fight to Free an Empire's Slaves.* Boston: Houghton Mifflin, 2006.

Homer. *The Odyssey.* Translated by A. T. Murray. 2 vols. Cambridge, MA: Harvard University Press; London: W. Heinemann, 1976.

Honig, Bonnie. *Democracy and the Foreigner.* Princeton, NJ: Princeton University Press, 2001.

Howard, Jean E. *Theater of a City: The Places of London Comedy, 1598–1642.* Philadelphia: University of Pennsylvania Press, 2007.

Howland, Jacob. *The Paradox of Political Philosophy: Socrates' Philosophic Trial.* Lanham, MD: Rowman and Littlefield, 1998.

Hulme, Peter. *Colonial Encounters: Europe and the Native Caribbean, 1497–1797.* London: Methuen, 1986.

Hume, David. *The History of England.* 8 vols. London: T. Cadell, 1789.

Hunt, Leigh. *A Day by the Fire; and Other Papers, hitherto Uncollected.* Boston: Roberts Brothers, 1870.

Hunter, G.K. "The Social Function of Annotation." In *In Arden: Editing Shakespeare,* edited by Ann Thompson and Gordon McMullan, 177–93. London: Thomson, 2003.

Irigaray, Luce. *Speculum de l'autre femme.* Paris: Minuit, 1974.

Iwanisziw, Susan B., ed. *Troping "Oroonoko" from Behn to Bandele.* Aldershot, UK: Ashgate, 2004.

Jacobs, Margaret C. *Strangers Nowhere in the World: The Rise of Cosmopolitanism in Early Modern Europe.* Philadelphia: University of Pennsylvania Press, 2006.

Jameson, Fredric. *Marxism and Form: Twentieth-Century Dialectical Theories of Literature.* Princeton, NJ: Princeton University Press, 1974.

Jefferson, Thomas. *Notes on the State of Virginia.* Edited by William Peden. New York: Norton, 1972.

Jerenic, Maria. "Challenging Englishness: Frances Burney's *The Wanderer.*" In *Rebellious Hearts: British Women Writers and the French Revolution*, edited by Adriana Craciun and Kari Lokke, 63–84. Albany: State University of New York Press, 2001.

Johns, Adrian. *The Nature of the Book: Print and Knowledge in the Making.* Chicago: University of Chicago Press, 1998.

Johnson, Samuel. *The Works of Samuel Johnson.* Edited by Arthur Murphy. 12 vols. London, 1824.

Johnston, Kenneth R. *The Hidden Wordsworth: Poet, Lover, Rebel, Spy.* New York: Norton, 1998.

Judt, Tony. *Postwar: A History of Europe Since 1945.* New York: Penguin, 2005.

Kant, Immanuel. *Anthropology, History and Education.* Edited by Günter Zöller and Robert B. Loudon. Cambridge: Cambridge University Press, 2007.

———. *Practical Philosophy.* Edited and translated by Mary J. Gregor. Cambridge: Cambridge University Press, 1996.

Katz, David S. *The Jews in the History of England, 1485–1850.* Oxford: Clarendon, 1996.

Kavanagh, Thomas M. *Writing the Truth: Authority and Desire in Rousseau.* Berkeley: University of California Press, 1987.

Kearney, Richard. *Strangers, Gods and Monsters: Interpreting Otherness.* London: Routledge, 2003.

Keate, George. *An Account of the Pelew Islands, situated in the Western Part of the Pacific Ocean.* Dublin, 1788.

Keats, John. *Keats: The Complete Poems.* Edited by Miriam Allott. London: Longman, 1974.

Kierkegaard, Søren. *Repetition: An Essay in Experimental Psychology.* Translated by Walter Lowrie. New York: Harper and Row, 1964.

Kitson, Peter J., and Debbie Lee, eds. *Slavery, Abolition, and Emancipation: Writings in the British Romantic Period.* 8 vols. London: Pickering and Chatto, 1999.

Knapp, John. "The Spirit of Classical Hymn in Shelley's 'Hymn to Intellectual Beauty.'" *Style* 33.1 (1999): 43–66.

Krikler, Jeremy. "The *Zong* and the Lord Chief Justice." *History Workshop Journal* 64 (2007): 29–47.

Krishnan, Sanjay. *Reading the Global: Troubling Perspectives on Britain's Empire in Asia.* New York: Columbia University Press, 2007.

Kristeva, Julia. *Nations without Nationalism.* Translated by Leon S. Roudiez. New York: Columbia University Press, 1993.

———. *Strangers to Ourselves.* Translated by Leon S. Roudiez. New York: Columbia University Press, 1991.

Kroll, Richard. "Mise-en-Page, Biblical Criticism, and Inference During the Restoration." *Studies in Eighteenth-Century Culture* 16 (1986): 3–40.

Kvam, Kristen E., Linda S. Schearing, and Valarie H. Ziegler, eds. *Eve & Adam: Jewish, Christian and Muslim Readings on Genesis and Gender.* Bloomington: Indiana University Press, 1999.

Land, Stephen K. *From Signs to Propositions: The Concept of Form in Eighteenth-Century Semantic Theory.* London: Longman, 1974.

Langhorne, John, and William Langhorne. *Plutarch's Lives.* 5 vols. Dublin: T. Ewing, 1771.

Leask, Nigel. *British Romantic Writers and the East: Anxieties of Empire.* Cambridge: Cambridge University Press, 1992.

———. "Burns, Wordsworth, and the Politics of Vernacular Poetry." In *Land, Nation and Culture: Thinking the Republic of Taste, 1740–1840,* edited by Peter de Bolla, Nigel Leask, and David Simpson, 201–22. London: Palgrave-Macmillan, 2005.

———. *Curiosity and the Aesthetics of Travel Writing, 1740–1840: "From an Antique Land."* Oxford: Oxford University Press, 2002.

———. "Mythology." In *An Oxford Companion to the Romantic Age: British Culture, 1776–1832,* edited by Iain McCalman, 338–45. Oxford: Oxford University Press, 1999.

———. *Robert Burns and Pastoral: Poetry and Improvement in Late Eighteenth-Century Scotland.* Oxford: Oxford University Press, 2010.

———. "'Wandering Through Eblis': Absorption and Containment in Romantic Exoticism." In *Romanticism and Colonialism: Writing and Empire, 1780–1830,* edited by Tim Fulford and Peter J. Kitson, 165–88 Cambridge: Cambridge University Press, 1998.

Lee, Debbie. *Slavery and the Romantic Imagination.* Philadelphia: University of Pennsylvania Press, 2002.

Lemire, Beverely. *Fashion's Favourite: The Cotton Trade and the Consumer in Britain, 1660–1800.* Oxford: Oxford University Press, 1991.

Levine, Joseph M. *The Battle of the Books: History and Literature in the Augustan Age.* Ithaca, NY: Cornell University Press, 1991.

Levinson, Marjorie. *Keats's Life of Allegory: The Origins of a Style.* Oxford: Blackwell, 1990.

Lipking, Lawrence. "The Marginal Gloss." *Critical Inquiry* 3 (1977): 609–55.

Lokke, Kari. "Sibylline Leaves: Mary Shelley's *Valperga* and the Legacy of *Corinne.*" In *Cultural Interactions in the Romantic Age: Critical Essays in Comparative Literature,* edited by Gregory Maertz, 157–73. Albany: State University of New York Press, 1998.

Lootens, Tricia. "Hemans and Home: Victorianism, Feminine 'Internal Enemies,' and the Domestication of National Identity." *Publications of the Modern Language Association* 109 (1994): 238–53.

Lupton, Julia Reinhard. "*Othello* Circumcised: Shakespeare and the Pauline Discourse of Nations." *Representations* 57 (1997): 73–89.

McCormick, E. H. *Omai: Pacific Envoy.* Auckland: Auckland University Press and Oxford University Press, 1977.

McCracken-Flesher, Caroline. *Possible Scotlands: Walter Scott and the Story of Tomorrow.* Oxford: Oxford University Press, 2005.

McFarland, Thomas. *Coleridge and the Pantheist Tradition.* Oxford: Clarendon, 1969.

McGann, Jerome J. *The Beauty of Inflections: Literary Investigations in Historical Method and Theory.* Oxford: Clarendon, 1988.

———. *The Poetics of Sensibility: A Revolution in Literary Style.* Oxford: Clarendon, 1996.

McKusick, James. *Coleridge's Philosophy of Language.* New Haven, CT: Yale University Press, 1986.

Madan, Martin. *A New and Literal Translation of the Works of Juvenal and Persius.* New ed. 2 vols. Oxford: N. Bliss etc., 1807.

Majeed, Javed. *Ungoverned Imaginings: James Mill's "The History of British India" and Orientalism.* Oxford: Clarendon, 1992.

Mathiez, Albert. *La révolution et les étrangers: cosmopolitisme et défense nationale.* Paris: La Renaissance du Livre, 1918.

Melville, Peter. *Romantic Hospitality and the Resistance to Accommodation.* Waterloo, ON: Wilfrid Laurier University Press, 2007.

Mergenthal, Sylvia. "The Shadow of Shylock: Scott's *Ivanhoe* and Edgeworth's *Harrington.*" In *Scott in Carnival,* edited by J. H. Alexander and David Hewitt, 320–31. Aberdeen: Association for Scottish Literary Studies, 1993.

[Merry, Robert, and Allan Ramsay]. *The Arno Miscellany: Being a Collection of Fugitive Pieces Written by the Members of a Society called the Oziosi at Florence.* Florence, 1784.

Micheli, Giuseppi. "The Early reception of Kant's Thought in England, 1785–1805." In *Kant and his Influence*, edited by George McDonald Ross and Tony McWalter, 202–315. London: Continuum, 2005.

Miller, J. Hillis. "The Critic as Host." In *Deconstruction and Criticism*, edited by Harold Bloom et al., 217–53. New York: Seabury, 1979.

Miller, John C. *Crisis in Freedom: The Alien and Sedition Acts.* Boston: Little Brown, 1951.

Millgate, Jane. *Scott's Last Edition: A Study in Publishing History.* Edinburgh: Edinburgh University Press, 1987.

Mintz, Sidney. *Sweetness and Power: The Place of Sugar in Modern History.* New York: Viking, 1985.

Mirza Abu Taleb. *The Travels of Mirza Abu Taleb Khan.* Edited by Daniel O'Quinn. Peterborough, ON: Broadview, 2009.

Moore, Thomas. *The Odes of Anacreon.* 2nd ed. 2 vols. London: J. and T. Carpenter, 1802.

Morton, Timothy. *The Ecological Thought.* Cambridge, MA: Harvard University Press, 2010.

———. "The Notes to *Queen Mab.*" In *The Unfamiliar Shelley*, edited by Timothy Webb and Alan Weinberg. Aldershot, UK: Ashgate, forthcoming.

———. *The Poetics of Spice: Romantic Consumerism and the Exotic.* Cambridge: Cambridge University Press, 2000.

Nussbaum, Felicity A. *The Limits of the Human: Fictions of Anomaly, Race and Gender in the Long Eighteenth Century.* Cambridge: Cambridge University Press, 2003.

———. *Torrid Zones: Maternity, Sexuality and Empire in Eighteenth-Century English Narratives.* Baltimore, MD: Johns Hopkins University Press, 1995.

Oliver, Kelly. "Antigone's Ghost: Undoing Hegel's *Phenomenology of Spirit.*" *Hypatia* 11.1 (1996): 67–90.

Orgel, Stephen. "Shylocks in Shakespeare's England." In *The Merchant of Venice*, by William Shakespeare, edited by Leah S. Marcus, 239–43. New York: Norton, 2006.

Owen, David Edward. *British Opium Policy in China and India.* New Haven, CT: Yale Historical Studies, 1934. Reprint, Hamden, CT: Archon Books, 1968.

Owenson, Sydney, Lady Morgan. *The Missionary.* Edited by Julia M. Wright. Peterborough, ON: Broadview, 2002.

———. *The Wild Irish Girl.* Edited by Kathryn Kirkpatrick. Oxford: Oxford University Press, 1999.

Page, Judith W. *Imperfect Sympathies: Jews and Judaism in British Romantic Literature and Culture.* New York: Palgrave-Macmillan, 2004.

Park, Mungo. *Travels in the Interior Districts of Africa.* Edited by Kate Ferguson Marsters. Durham, NC: Duke University Press, 2000.

Percy, Thomas. *Reliques of Ancient English Poetry.* 3 vols. London, 1755.

Plato. *Laws.* Translated by R. G. Bury. Cambridge, MA: Harvard University Press; London: W. Heinemann, 2001.

———. *The Republic.* Translated by Paul Shorey. Cambridge, MA: Harvard University Press, 2003.

———. *Statesman, Philebus, Ion.* Translated by Harold North Fowler and W. R. M. Lamb. Cambridge, MA: Harvard University Press, 2001.

———. *Theatetus, Sophist.* Translated by Harold North Fowler. Cambridge, MA: Harvard University Press, 2006.

Plug, Jan. "The Rhetoric of Secrecy: Figures of the Self in 'Frost at Midnight.'" In *Coleridge's Visionary Languages: Essays in Honour of J.B. Beer*, edited by Tim Fulford and Morton D. Paley, 27–39. Cambridge: D. S. Brewer, 1993.

Pope, Alexander. *The Iliad of Homer.* Edited by Gilbert Wakefield. 5 vols. London: J. Johnson etc., 1806.

Porter, Dahlia. "Formal Relocations: The Method of Southey's *Thalaba the Destroyer* (1801)." *European Romantic Review* 20 (2009): 671–79.

Pratt, Mary Louise. *Imperial Eyes: Travel Writing and Transculturation.* London: Routledge, 1992.

Prince, Mary. *The History of Mary Prince, a West Indian Slave, Related by Herself.* Edited by Moira Ferguson. London: Pandora, 1987.

Quintilian, Marcus Fabius. *The Orator's Education.* Translated by Donald A. Russell. 5 vols. Cambridge, MA: Harvard University Press, 2001.

Rabin, Dana. "The Jew Bill of 1753: Masculinity, Virility and the Nation." *Eighteenth-Century Studies* 39 (2006): 157–71.

Ragussis, Michael. *Figures of Conversion: "The Jewish Question" and English National Identity*. Durham, NC: Duke University Press, 1995.

Rajan, Balanchandra. "Monstrous Mythologies: Southey and *The Curse of Kehama.*" *European Romantic Review* 9 (1998): 201–16.

Ramsay, Allan. *Poems.* Edinburgh, 1720.

Rediker, Marcus. *Between the Devil and the Deep Blue Sea: Merchant Seamen, Pirates, and the Anglo-American Maritime World, 1700–1750.* Cambridge: Cambridge University Press, 1989.

Regier, Alexander. *Fracture and Fragmentation in British Romanticism.* Cambridge: Cambridge University Press, 2010.

[Richardson, John]. *Essays and Treatises on Moral, Political and Various Philosophical Subjects, by Emanuel Kant.* 2 vols. London, 1798–99.

Ricoeur, Paul. *On Translation.* Translated by Eileen Brennan. New York: Routledge, 2004.

———. *Oneself as Another.* Translated by Kathleen Blamey. Chicago: University of Chicago Press, 1992.

Robertson, William. *The Works of the Late William Robertson, D.D.* 6 vols. London, 1826.

Robespierre, Maximilien. *Virtue and Terror.* Translated by John Howe. London: Verso, 2007.

Robison, John. *Proofs of a Conspiracy Against all the Religions and Governments of Europe, carried on in the Secret Meetings of Free Masons, Illuminati and Reading Societies.* Edinburgh, 1797.

Ross, John D., ed. *Early Critical Reviews on Robert Burns.* Glasgow: W. Hodge, 1900. Reprint, New York: AMS Press, 1973.

Rousseau, Jean-Jacques. *Discourse on the Origins of Inequality.* Translated by Judith Bush et al. Hanover: University Press of New England, 1992.

———. *Essay on the Origins of Language and Writings Related to Music.* Translated by John T. Scott. Hanover, NH: University Press of New England, 1998.

———. *The Social Contract etc.* Edited by Roger D. Masters and Christopher Kelly. Hanover, NH: University Press of New England, 1994.

Russett, Margaret. *De Quincey's Romanticism: Canonical Minority and the Forms of Transmission.* Cambridge: Cambridge University Press, 1997.

———. *Fictions and Fakes: Forging Romantic Authenticity, 1760–1845.* Cambridge: Cambridge University Press, 2006.

Sacks, Jonathan. "Greece or Rome? The Uses of Antiquity in Late Eighteenth-Century and Early Nineteenth-Century British Literature." *Literature Compass* 6.2 (2009), 314–31.

Said, Edward. *Culture and Imperialism.* New York: Knopf, 1993.

———. *Freud and the Non-European.* London: Verso, 2004.

Sale, George. *The Koran; commonly called the Alcoran of Mohanmmed.* London, 1734.

Sancho, Ignatius. *Letters of the Late Ignatius Sancho.* Edited by Vincent Carretta. London: Penguin, 1998.

Sansay, Leonora. *Secret History; or, the Horrors of St. Domingo.* Edited by Michael J. Drexler. Peterborough, ON: Broadview, 2008.

Scanlon, Larry. "Poets Laureate and the Language of Slaves: Petrarch, Chaucer and Langston Hughes." In *The Vulgar Tongue: Medieval and Post-Medieval Vernacularity,* edited by Fiona Somerset and Nicholas Watson, 220–56. University Park: Pennsylvania State University Press, 2003.

Schleiermacher, Friedrich. "On the Different Methods of Translation." Translated by Susan Bernofsky. In *The Translation Studies Reader,* edited by Lawrence Venuti, 43–63. 2nd ed. New York: Routledge, 2004.

Schmitt, Cannon. *Alien Nation: Nineteenth-Century Gothic Fictions and English Nationality.* Philadelphia: University of Pennsylvania Press, 1997.

Scodel, Harvey Ronald. *Diaeresis and Myth in Plato's Statesman.* Göttingen: Vandenhoek and Ruprecht, 1987.

Scott, Walter. *Ivanhoe.* Edited by Graham Tulloch. Edinburgh: Edinburgh University Press, 1998.

———. *Tales of the Crusaders.* 4 vols. Edinburgh: Constable, 1825.

———. *The Talisman.* Edinburgh: Robert Cadell, 1832.

Shaffer, E. S. *"Kubla Khan" and* The Fall of Jerusalem*: The Mythological School in Biblical Criticism and Secular Literature, 1770–1880.* Cambridge: Cambridge University Press, 1975.

Shaftesbury, 3rd Earl of, Anthony Ashley Cooper. *Characteristics of Men, Manners, Opinions, Times.* Edited by Lawrence E. Klein. Cambridge: Cambridge University Press, 2001.

Shakespeare, William. *The Merchant of Venice.* Edited by Leah S. Marcus. New York: Norton, 2006.

———. *Othello.* Edited by E. A. J. Honigman. London: Arden, 2001.

Shapiro, Fred. "Neologisms in Coleridge's Notebooks." *Notes and Queries* 32.3 (1985): 346–7.

Shapiro, James. *Shakespeare and the Jews.* New York: Columbia University Press, 1996.

Sharafuddin, Mohammed. *Islam and Romantic Orientalism: Literary Encounters with the Orient*. London: Tauris, 1994.

Shaw, Harry E. *Narrating Reality: Austen, Scott, Eliot.* Ithaca, NY: Cornell University Press, 1999.

Shelley, Percy Bysshe. *The Letters of Percy Bysshe Shelley.* Edited by Frederick L. Jones. 2 vols. Oxford: Clarendon, 1964.

———. *Shelley's Prose.* Edited by David Lee Clark. New York: New Amsterdam Books, 1988.

Simmel, Georg. *On Individuality and Social Forms.* Edited by Donald N. Levine. Chicago: University of Chicago Press, 1971.

———. *The Philosophy of Money.* Translated by Tom Bottomore and David Frisby. Boston: Routledge and Kegan Paul, 1978.

Simmons, Claire. "'Useful and Wasteful Both': Southey's *Thalaba the Destroyer* and the Function of Annotation in the Romantic Oriental Poem." *Genre* 27 (1994): 83–104.

Simpson, David. *The Academic Postmodern and the Rule of Literature: A Report on Half-Knowledge*. Chicago: University of Chicago Press, 1995.

———. "Romantic Indians: Robert Southey's Distinctions." *Wordsworth Circle* 38 (2007): 20–25.

———. *Romanticism, Nationalism, and the Revolt against Theory*. Chicago: University of Chicago Press, 1993.

Smith, Charlotte. *Desmond.* Edited by Antjie Blank and Janet Todd. Peterborough, ON: Broadview Press, 2001.

Smith, Chloe Wigston. "'Callico Madams': Servants, Consumption, and the Calico Crisis." *Eighteenth-Century Life* 31.2 (2007): 29–55.

Sorensen, Janet. *The Grammar of Empire in Eighteenth-Century British Writing.* Cambridge: Cambridge University Press, 2000.

Southey, Robert. *Robert Southey: The Critical Heritage.* Edited by Lionel Madden. London: Routledge and Kegan Paul, 1972.

———. *Robert Southey: Poetical Works, 1793–1810.* Edited by Lynda Pratt. 5 vols. London: Pickering and Chatto, 2004.

———. *Roderick, the Last of the Goths.* London: Longman, Hurst, Rees, Orme and Brown, 1814.

———. *A Tale of Paraguay.* London: Longman, Hurst, Rees etc., 1825.

———. *Thalaba the Destroyer*. 2 vols. London: Longman and Rees, 1801.

———. *Thalaba the Destroyer.* Facsimile of the first edition. Edited by Jonathan Wordsworth. Oxford: Woodstock Books, 1991.

Spivak, Gayatri Chakravorty. *A Critique of Postcolonial Reason: Toward a History of the Vanishing Present.* Cambridge, MA: Harvard University Press, 1999.

Staël, Germaine de. *Corinne, or Italy.* Translated by Sylvia Raphael. New York: Oxford University Press, 1998.

Stam, James H. *Inquiries into the Origin of Languages: The Fate of a Question*. New York: Harper and Row, 1976.

St. Clair, William. *The Reading Nation in the Romantic Period.* Cambridge: Cambridge University Press, 2004.

Stedman, John Gabriel. *Narrative; of a five years' Expedition; against the Revolted Negroes of Surinam, in Guiana, on the Wild Coast of South America; from the Year 1772 to 1777.* London: J. Johnson and J. Edwards, 1796.

———. *Stedman's Surinam: Life in an Eighteenth-Century Slave Society.* Edited by Richard Price and Sally Price. Baltimore, MD: Johns Hopkins University Press, 1992.

Stevenson, Jill Heydt. *Austen's Unbecoming Conjunctions: Subversive Laughter, Embodied History.* New York: Palgrave-Macmillan, 2005.

Suleri, Sara. *The Rhetoric of English India.* Chicago: University of Chicago Press, 1992.

Sussman, Charlotte. *Consuming Anxieties: Consumer Protest, Gender, and British Slavery, 1713–1833.* Stanford, CA: Stanford University Press, 2000.

Sutton, Jean. *Lords of the East: The East India Company and Its Ships.* London: Conway Maritime, 1981.

Sweet, Rosemary. *Antiquaries: The Discovery of the Past in Eighteenth-Century Britain.* Hambledon, UK: Palgrave-Macmillan, 2004.

Swift, Jonathan. *A Tale of a Tub.* Edited by A. C. Guthkelch and D. Nichol Smith. Oxford: Clarendon, 1958.

Tadmor, Naomi. *The Social Universe of the English Bible: Scripture, Society, and Culture in Early Modern England.* Cambridge: Cambridge University Press, 2010.

Temple, Sir William. *Sir William Temple's Essays on Ancient and Modern Learning and on Poetry.* Edited by J. E. Spingarn. Oxford: Clarendon, 1909.

Thelwall, John. *Poems Chiefly Written in Retirement.* Hereford, UK, 1801.

Thomas, Helen. *Romanticism and Slave Narratives: Transatlantic Testimonies.* Cambridge: Cambridge University Press, 2000.

Thomas, Keith. *Man and the Natural World: Changing Attitudes in England, 1500–1800.* London: Allen Lane, 1983.

Todorov, Tzvetan. *The Fear of Barbarians.* Translated by Andrew Brown. Chicago: University of Chicago Press, 2010.

———. *Nous et les autres: la réflexion française sur la diversité humaine.* Paris: Seuil, 1989.

Tredennick, Bianca. "'A Labor of Death and a Labor Against Death': Scott's Cenotaphic Paratexts." *European Romantic Review* 21 (2010): 49–64.

Trumpener, Katie. *Bardic Nationalism: The Romantic Novel and the British Empire.* Princeton, NJ: Princeton University Press, 1997.

Tudeau-Clayton, Margaret. "'This Is the Strangers' Case': The Utopic Dissonance of Shakespeare's Contribution to *Sir Thomas More.*" *Shakespeare Survey.* Forthcoming.

[Tytler, Alexander Fraser]. *Essay on the Principles of Translation.* 2nd ed. London, 1797.

Venuti, Lawrence. *The Scandals of Translation: Towards an Ethics of Difference.* New York: Routledge, 1998.

———. *The Translator's Invisibility: A History of Translation.* 2nd ed. London: Routledge, 2008.

Vincent, Patrick. *The Romantic Poetess: European Culture, Politics and Gender, 1820–1840.* Hanover, NH: University Press of New England, 2004.

Viswanathan, Gauri. *Outside the Fold: Conversion, Modernity, and Belief.* Princeton, NJ: Princeton University Press, 1998.

Volney, Constantin. *Volney's Ruins; or Meditations on the Revolutions of Empires*. New York: Dickens and Sickels, 1828.

Young, Edward. "Conjectures on Original Composition." In *The Norton Anthology of Theory and Criticism*, edited by Vincent B. Leitch, 426–37. New York: Norton, 2001.

Young, Robert J. C. *Colonial Desire: Hybridity in Theory, Culture and Race*. New York: Routledge, 1995.

Wahnich, Sophie. *L'impossible citoyen: l'étranger dans le discours de la révolution française*. Paris: Albin Michel, 1997.

Wallace, Jennifer. *Shelley and Greece: Rethinking Romantic Hellenism*. London: Macmillan, 1997.

Wallace, Tara Ghoshal. "Competing Discourses in *Ivanhoe*." In *Scott in Carnival*, edited by J. H. Alexander and David Hewitt, 294–308. Aberdeen: Association for Scottish Literary Studies, 1993.

Walvin, James. *Fruits of Empire: Exotic Produce and British Trade, 1660–1800*. London: Macmillan, 1997.

———. *The Zong: A Massacre, the Law, and the End of Slavery*. New Haven, CT: Yale University Press, 2011.

Watt, James. "Scott, the Scottish Enlightenment, and Romantic Orientalism." In *Scotland and the Borders of Romanticism*, edited by Leith Davis, Ian Duncan, and Janet Sorensen, 94–112. Cambridge: Cambridge University Press, 2004.

Webb, Timothy. *The Violet in the Crucible: Shelley and Translation*. Oxford: Clarendon, 1976.

Weinbrot, Howard D. *Menippean Satire Reconsidered: From Antiquity to the Eighteenth Century*. Baltimore, MD: Johns Hopkins University Press, 2005.

Wellek, René. *Immanuel Kant in England, 1793–1838*. Princeton, NJ: Princeton University Press, 1931.

Wheeler, Roxann. *The Complexion of Race: Categories of Difference in Eighteenth-Century British Culture*. Philadelphia: University of Pennsylvania Press, 2000.

Williams, Anne. *Art of Darkness: A Poetics of Gothic*. Chicago: University of Chicago Press, 1995.

Williams, Cynric. *Hamel, the Obeah Man*. Edited by Candace Ward and Tim Watson. Peterborough, ON: Broadview, 2010.

Williams, Helen Maria. *Letters Written in France*. Edited by Neil Fraistat and Susan S. Lanser. Peterborough, ON: Broadview, 2001.

Willich, A. F. M. *Elements of the Critical Philosophy, containing a Concise Account of its Origins and Tendency; a View of all the Works published by its Founder, Professor Immanuel Kant*. London, 1798.

Wilson, Penelope. "Lyric, Pastoral and Elegy." In *The Oxford History of Literary Translation in English*. Vol. 3, *1660–1790*, edited by Stuart Gillespie and David Hopkins, 173–90. Oxford: Oxford University Press, 2005.

Wilt, Judith. *Secret Leaves: The Novels of Walter Scott*. Chicago: University of Chicago Press, 1985.

Wollstonecraft, Mary. *The Works of Mary Wollstonecraft*. Edited by Janet Todd and Marilyn Butler. 7 vols. New York: New York University Press, 1989.

Wordsworth, William. *The Prelude: 1799, 1805, 1850*. Edited by Jonathan Wordsworth, M. H. Abrams, and Stephen Gill. New York: Norton, 1979.

———. *The Prose Works of William Wordsworth*. Edited by W. J. B. Owen and Jane Worthington Smyser. 3 vols. Oxford: Clarendon, 1974.

Žižek, Slavoj, Eric L. Santner, and Kenneth Reinhard. *The Neighbor: Three Inquiries in Political Theology*. Chicago: University of Chicago Press, 2005.

Zuckert, Catherine. *Plato's Philosophers: The Coherence of the Dialogues*. Chicago: University of Chicago Press, 2009.

INDEX

Aarsleff, Hans, 50
Adams, M. Ray, 159
Adelung, J. C., 76, 165, 201
Aeschylus, 234–35
Alien Act, 22
Alien and Sedition Acts, 20–21, 23
Allott, Miriam, 159
Alter, Robert, 34, 205
Anidjar, Gil, 85, 87
Antigone, 242–46
Aravamudan, Srinavas, 185
Aristotle, 40–41
Assmann, Jan, 36, 40, 174
Augustine, 46–49
Austen, Jane, 12, 76–81, 190, 215, 226

Bacchae, 23–24, 33, 53, 106
Bachelard, Gaston, 58
Baillie, Joanna, 228
Bakhtin, M. M., 168
Barbauld, Anna L., 136
Barrell, John, 22, 64, 72
Barruel, Abbé, 22
Baslez, Marie-France, 27
Baucom, Ian, 185, 198
Bayle, Pierre, 116, 133
Beck, James Sigismund, 163
Beckford, William, 122–23
Benedict, Barbara M., 142
Benhabib, Seyla, 6, 39
Benstock, Shari, 112
Bentley, Richard, 128–29, 132, 157
Benveniste, Emile, 5, 28, 73
Berman, Antoine, 148, 158
Bewell, Alan, 11, 57
Bhabha, Homi, 190
Blake, William, 4, 31, 58, 154, 196, 211
Bolton, Carol, 133
Boo, Lee, 14, 179–84
Bowersock, Glen, 133
Brown, Marshall, 60, 157
Brown, Wendy, 7
Bruce, James, 143, 204
Buck-Morss, Susan, 188
Burke, Edmund, 2, 3, 21, 28, 181, 214, 216, 226–27
Burney, Frances (Fanny), 183, 228–34
Burns, Robert, 169–71
Butler, Judith, 242
Butler, Marilyn, 133, 154
Byron, Lord, 86, 126, 154, 156, 246

Campbell, Thomas, 125, 171–74
Carretta, Vincent, 191–94, 206
Cary, Henry Francis, 152
Cassin, Barbara, 145
Castle, Terry, 210
Castro, Americo, 94
Chatterton, Thomas, 169
Christensen, Jerome, 140
Chung, Tan, 182
Cicero, 43–44, 46
Clare, John, 169
Clark, David L., 9, 72, 150, 242
Clarkson, Thomas, 193, 197–8
Clery, E. J., 60
Cohen, Murray, 50
Coleridge, Samuel Taylor, 119, 126, 152, 164–66, 225; "Frost at Midnight," 11–12, 54–69, 73, 109, 234, 247; "The Rime of the Ancient Mariner," 28, 119, 138–43

Cook, James, 180, 182–83
cotton, 78–81
Cotton, Sir Evan, 184
Cowper, William, 11, 56–61, 64–66, 68, 73–74, 77, 151–52
Craciun, Adriana, 210
Craig, David M., 222
Crawford, Robert, 170
Cruikshank, Isaac, 210–11
Cugoano, Quobna Ottobah, 186, 188–90, 192–93, 203–6
Curran, Stuart, 133–34, 137
Currie, James, 170
curse of Ham, 204–6

Darwin, Erasmus, 138
Davis, David Brion, 23, 188
Davis, Leith, 170
Day, Thomas, and John Bicknell, 206
Defoe, Daniel, 8
Deleuze, Gilles, and Felix Guattari, 168
Della Cruscans, 159–60
De Man, Paul, 51
Dening, Greg, 182–83
De Quincey, Thomas, 12, 69–76, 95, 166–67, 182, 201
Derrida, Jacques: 33, 38, 42, 46, 49, 51–52, 97, 106, 113, 127, 149–50, 192, 242, 244 (*see also* pharmakon); on hospitality, 2, 9, 28, 52, 55, 73, 108, 210, 232, 236; on philosophy, 5, 11, 149, 162, 164, 166; on proper names, 35–36, 174; on translation, 5, 35–36, 83–84, 144, 162, 164, 166.
Dionysus, 23–24, 26, 28, 31, 36, 49, 148; figures of, 37, 45, 81, 94, 106, 192, 208, 212, 227, 232
Drew, John, 124
Dryden, John, 151–54, 158
Dummett, Michael, 7
Duncan, Ian, 89, 105

Earle, William, 196–97
Edgeworth, Maria, 86, 90–91, 103, 125, 206, 221
Elfenbein, Andrew, 175, 177
Eliot, T. S., 109–10
Ellis, Markman, 75
Ellison, Julie, 56
Endelman, Todd M., 86, 102, 104
Equiano, Olaudah, 188, 190, 192–95, 203, 206
Everest, Kelvin, 161

Favret, Mary, 56
Fenimore Cooper, 174
Ferguson, Margaret W., 48
Ferguson, Moira, 214
Fergusson, Robert, 169
Fiedler, Leslie, 82–83, 87, 209
Forster, John Reinhold, 182
Fraistat, Neil, 138
Francis, Philip, 154, 158
Freud, Sigmund, 5, 32–36, 69, 210
Friedländer, Paul, 25
Frye, Northrop, 121
Fulford, Tim, 115, 118, 172

Gasché, Rodolph, 6, 245
Gates, Henry Louis, 193, 203
Gaull, Marilyn, 79
Gebir, 122, 125
Genette, Gérard, 112
Gertrude of Wyoming, 125, 171–74
Gibbon, Edward, 133
Gibbons, Luke, 216
Gifford, William, 160
Gigante, Denise, 241
Goldenberg, David M., 205
Goodman, Kevis, 56, 135, 181, 182
Goodwin, Albert, 22, 64
Gossman, Lionel, 134–35
Grafton, Anthony, 113, 133
Greenberg, Michael, 181
Grégoire, Abbé, 149
Gronniosaw, James Albert, 202–3, 207
Grose, Francis, 58
Guest, Harriet, 58, 182

Habermas, Jürgen, 6
Hall, Edith, 28
Hall, Roland, 167
Hamilton, Elizabeth, 208
Hanway, Jonas, 75
Hargreaves-Maudsley, W. N., 159
Hazlitt, William, 58–59, 64
Hegel, G. W. F., 187–88, 190, 240, 242–46
Heidegger, Martin, 144, 245
Hemans, Felicia, 14, 152, 154, 175–78, 226, 246–47
Herder, J. G., 89–90, 106
Heydt-Stevenson, Jill, 79
History of Mary Prince, The, 213–14
Hochschild, Adam, 207
Hölderlin, Friedrich, 148, 158

Homer, 24, 26, 127, 129–32
Honig, Bonnie, 17, 33, 215, 239–40
Horace, 154
Howard, Jean E, 55
Howland, Jacob, 27
Hulme, Peter, 186
Hume, David, 89–90, 94, 133
Hunt, Leigh, 59, 138
Hunter, G. K., 132
Husserl, Edmund, 5

Inkle and Yarico, 186, 207, 241
Irigaray, Luce, 242

Jacobs, Margaret, 8
Jameson, Fredric, 135
Jefferson, Thomas, 190–91
Jeffrey, Francis, 119, 134, 137
Jerenic, Maria, 233
Johns, Adrian, 113, 120, 139
Johnson, Samuel, 75
Johnston, Kenneth R., 64
Judt, Tony, 6
Juvenal, 154

Kant, Immanuel, 35–37, 39, 71–72, 163–67, 187, 199
Katz, David S., 86, 91
Kavanagh, Thomas M., 237
Kearney, Richard, 37
Keate, George, 179–80, 182
Keats, John, 154, 158–59, 225, 239–42
Kierkegaard, Søren, 67
King James Bible, 33–35, 139, 189, 200, 204–6, 235–39
Knapp, John, 162
Krikler, Jeremy, 185
Krishnan, Sanjay, 72–73
Kristeva, Julia, 2, 17, 229–30
Kroll, Richard, 113

Lamb, Charles, 58–60
Land, Stephen K., 50, 51
Landor, Walter Savage, 122, 125
Langhorne, John and William, 154
Leask, Nigel, 72, 120, 133, 143, 170, 181, 204
Lee, Debbie, 199, 204
Lemire, Beverly, 79–80
Levinas, Emanuel, 5
Levine, Joseph, 128, 131
Levinson, Marjorie, 241
Levite of Ephraim, 236–39, 244
Lipking, Lawrence, 113, 135, 140
Lloyd, Charles, 59–60
Lokke, Kari, 218
Long, Edward, 187, 206–7
Lootens, Tricia, 177, 226, 246
Lupton, Julia Reinhard, 87
Lyrical Ballads, 118–19, 126, 155, 168–69

Madan, Martin, 154
Majeed, Javed, 117, 137
Marx, Karl, 80
Mathiez, Albert, 2, 17, 19
Mays, J. C. C., 65
McCormick, E. H., 182–83
McCracken-Flesher, Caroline, 88
McFarland, Thomas, 165
McGann, Jerome, 138–39, 159
McKusick, James, 166
Melville, Peter, 2, 65, 72
Merchant of Venice, The, 82–87, 107
Mergenthal, Silvia, 90
Merry, Robert, 159–60
metaphor, 39–49, 144–45
Micheli, Giuseppe, 163
Miller, J. Hillis, 113
Miller, John C., 2, 21
Millgate, Jane, 95, 98
Mintz, Sidney, 75
monotheism, 35–37, 39, 48–49
Moore, Thomas, 58, 136–37, 154, 156–58
Morton, Timothy, 4, 7, 11, 75, 137
Moses, 32–36, 39, 200, 239

Nitsch, F. A., 163
Nussbaum, Felicity, 8, 87, 124, 206, 211

Oliver, Kelly, 243
Omai, 14, 182–84, 191
opium trade, 12–13, 69–76, 95–98, 179, 181–82
O'Quinn, Daniel, 207, 216
Orgel, Stephen, 83–85
Oroonoko, 185–86, 202, 204, 212, 214
Othello, 87, 92, 99, 191, 200, 204
Owen, David Edward, 181
Owenson, Sydney (Lady Morgan), 103, 125, 215–22, 225

Page, Judith W., 86
Paradise Lost, 64, 125, 235

Park, Mungo, 14, 199–204
Percy, Thomas, 169
pharmakon, 11, 18, 49, 70, 72–73, 92–93, 97–98, 106–7, 165
Piozzi, Hester Lynch, 160
Plato, 24–29, 40, 49, 62, 92, 106
Plug, Jan, 66
Pope, Alexander, 130–34, 154
Porter, Dahlia, 111
Pratt, Mary Louise, 199, 204
Prince, Mary. See *History of Mary Prince, The*

Quintilian, 41–43

Rabin, Dana, 86
Radcliffe, Ann, 225
Ragussis, Michael, 86, 104
Rajan, Balachandra, 124
Ramsay, Allan, 160, 168–69
Rediker, Marcus, 184
Regier, Alexander, 56
Reinhard, Kenneth, 34
Richardson, John, 163–64
Ricoeur, Paul, 5–6, 147
Ritson, Joseph, 169
Robespierre, Maximilien, 2, 17–18, 28, 31
Robison, John, 22–23
Rose, Jacqueline, 32
Rousseau, Jean-Jacques, 30–31, 51–52, 62, 233, 237–38
Rumsfeld, Donald, 3–4, 18
Rushton, Edward, 206
Russett, Margaret, 95, 143

Sachs, Jonathan, 162
Said, Edward, 33, 77, 113
Sale, George, 116
Sancho, Ignatius, 190–94, 197
Sansay, Leonora, 228
Santner, Eric, 34
Scanlon, Larry, 195
Schelling, F. W. J., 149–50, 165–66, 192
Schleiermacher, Friedrich, 145–49
Schmitt, Cannon, 61, 72
Schmitt, Carl, 5
Scodel, Harvey Ronald, 27
Scott, Walter, 13, 82–108, 125, 138, 143, 156; *The Betrothed*, 101–2; *Ivanhoe*, 91–108, 150–51, 188, 214–15, 221; *The Talisman*, 88–108, 109, 119, 188
Shaffer, E. S., 136, 138
Shaftesbury, Earl of, 8
Shapiro, Fred, 165
Shapiro, James, 83, 85
Sharafuddin, Mohammed, 116, 137
Shaw, Harry E., 103
Shelley, Percy Bysshe, 39–40, 44, 50, 126, 137–38, 152, 154, 160–62, 168, 225
Simmel, Georg, 29, 37, 40
Simmons, Claire, 133
Smith, Charlotte, 78, 125, 227
Sorensen, Janet, 79, 170
Southey, Robert, 13, 77, 103, 133, 152, 246; *The Curse of Kehama*, 123–25; *Madoc*, 103, 174–75; *Roderick the Goth*, 126, 132; *A Tale of Paraguay*, 103, 222–26; *Thalaba the Destroyer*, 110–23, 131–32, 134, 136, 141–43
Spivak, Gayatri Chakravorty, 72
Staël, Germaine de, 215, 218–19, 232
St. Clair, William, 155
St. Paul, 32,
Stam, James H., 50, 51
Stedman, John Gabriel, 204, 211–14
Sterne, Lawrence, 191–93
sugar, 75–76
Suleri, Sara, 216
Sussman, Charlotte, 210
Sutton, Jean, 179
Sweet, Rosemary, 133
Swift, Jonathan, 128–29, 131

Tadmor, Naomi, 34–35, 189, 236
Talib, Mirza Abu, 207–8, 216
tea drinking, 74–76
Temple, Sir William, 127–28
Thelwall, John, 65, 81
Thomas, Helen, 196
Thomas, Keith, 119
Todorov, Tzvetan, 2, 28
Tredennick, Bianca, 125
Trumpener, Katie, 222
Tudeau-Clayton, Margaret, 55
Tytler, Alexander, 151

Vathek, 122–23, 136, 142
Venuti, Lawrence, 13, 146, 177
Vincent, Patrick, 218, 241
Viswanathan, Gauri, 104, 221
Volney, Constantin, 115

Wahnich, Sophie, 17, 19

Waldron, Jeremy, 39
Wallace, Jennifer, 162
Wallace, Tara Ghoshal, 88
Walvin, James, 76, 185
Waste Land, The, 109–10
Watt, James, 89
Webb, Timothy, 162
Webster, Noah, 171
Weinbrot, Howard D., 121
Wellek, René, 163
Wheatley, Phyllis, 191, 196
Wheeler, Roxann, 206
Wigston Smith, Chloe, 79
Williams, Anne, 60
Williams, Cynric, 194, 216
Williams, Helen Maria, 20, 227
Willich, A. F. M., 164
Wilson, Penelope, 156–57
Wilt, Judith, 88, 93
Wollstonecraft, Mary, 58
Wordsworth, William, 7, 16–17, 61, 69, 80, 126, 151–52, 225, 227

Yerushalmi, Yusef, 36
Young, Edward, 44–46, 73
Young, Robert J. C., 212

Žižek, Slavoj, 34
Zong, The, 184–85
Zuckert, Catherine H., 27